THE OLD TESTAMENT

IN THE

JEWISH CHURCH

BY THE SAME AUTHOR.

THE RELIGION OF THE SEMITES:

THE FUNDAMENTAL INSTITUTIONS.

Second Edition.   Revised and enlarged by the Author.

Demy 8vo, cloth.   Price 15s. net.

THE PROPHETS OF ISRAEL.

New Edition, with Introduction and Notes by the
Rev. T. K. CHEYNE, D.D., Oriel Professor of the Interpretation
of Holy Scripture at Oxford.

Post 8vo, cloth.   Price 10s. 6d.

AGENTS IN AMERICA

THE MACMILLAN COMPANY

66 FIFTH AVENUE, NEW YORK

THE
OLD TESTAMENT

IN THE

JEWISH CHURCH

A COURSE OF LECTURES ON BIBLICAL CRITICISM

By W. ROBERTSON SMITH

SECOND EDITION REVISED AND MUCH ENLARGED

LONDON
ADAM AND CHARLES BLACK
1902

First Edition in Crown 8vo, published April 1881.
Reprinted in May and September 1881.
Second Edition, revised and enlarged, in Demy 8vo, published April 1892.
Reprinted in June 1895 *and April* 1902.

AMPLISSIMO · THEOLOGORVM · ARGENTINENSIVM · ORDINI

QVORVM · MVNERE

AD · GRADVM · DOCTORIS · THEOLOGIAE · PROVECTVS · EST

HVNC · LIBRVM · SACRVM · ESSE

VOLVIT · AVCTOR

PREFACE TO THE SECOND EDITION

IN republishing these Lectures, eleven years after their first appearance, I have had to consider what to emend, what to omit, and what to add. First, then, a careful revision of the whole volume has enabled me to correct a certain number of errors, and to make many statements more precise. In the second place, I have pruned away some redundancies more proper to oral delivery than to a printed book; and I have also removed from the "Notes and Illustrations" some things which seemed to be superfluous. As I was resolved to make no change on the general plan of the book, I at first hoped that these omissions would give me space for all necessary additions; for though much good work has been done within the last decade on special problems of Old Testament Criticism, there are not many points where these special researches affect the general arguments and broad results which I desired to set forth. But on mature consideration I came to see that in one direction the book might be profitably enlarged without a fundamental change of plan; it was desirable to give a fuller account of what the critics have to say about the narrative of the Old Testament Books. I have, therefore, made large additions to the part of Lecture V. that treats of the historical books, and, in consequence, have thrown the whole discussion of the Canon into Lecture VI. To the narrative

of the Hexateuch I have devoted a supplementary Lecture
(XIII.). Further, I have rewritten the greater part of the
Lecture on the Psalter (VII.), incorporating the main conclusions of my article on this subject in the ninth edition of
the *Encyclopædia Britannica.* I have also made considerable
changes on Lecture XI., and at several other places I have
introduced additional arguments and illustrations. Thus the
book has grown till, in spite of omissions, it contains about
one-third more matter than the first edition ; and so it now
appears with a larger page, and with most of the notes placed
under the text, instead of being relegated to the end of the
volume. Of the few "Additional Notes" which still stand
after the text, those marked B, C, and E, except the last
paragraph of B, are taken from the first edition ; the others
are new, and contain some observations which, I hope, may
be of interest to Hebrew scholars, as well as to the larger
class of readers for whom the book is mainly intended.

W. ROBERTSON SMITH.

CHRIST'S COLLEGE, CAMBRIDGE,
    31*st March* 1892

PREFACE TO THE FIRST EDITION

THE Twelve Lectures now laid before the public had their origin in a temporary victory of the opponents of progressive Biblical Science in Scotland, which has withdrawn me during the past winter from the ordinary work of my Chair in Aberdeen, and in the invitation of some six hundred prominent Free Churchmen in Edinburgh and Glasgow, who deemed it better that the Scottish public should have an opportunity of understanding the position of the newer Criticism than that they should condemn it unheard. The Lectures were delivered in Edinburgh and Glasgow during the first three months of the present year, and the average attendance on the course in the two cities was not less than eighteen hundred. The sustained interest with which this large audience followed the attempt to lay before them an outline of the problems, the methods, and the results of Old Testament Criticism is sufficient proof that they did not find modern Biblical Science the repulsive and unreal thing which it is often represented to be. The Lectures are printed mainly from shorthand reports taken in Glasgow, and as nearly as possible in the form in which they were delivered in Edinburgh after final revision. I have striven to make my exposition essentially popular in the legitimate sense of that word—that is, to present a continuous argument, resting

at every point on valid historical evidence, and so framed
that it can be followed by the ordinary English reader who
is familiar with the Bible and accustomed to consecutive
thought. There are some critical processes which cannot
be explained without constant use of the Hebrew Text; but
I have tried to make all the main parts of the discussion
independent of reference to these. Of course it is not
possible for any sound argument to adopt in every case
the renderings of the English Version. In important
passages I have indicated the necessary corrections; but in
general it is to be understood that, while I cite all texts by
the English chapters and verses, I argue from the Hebrew.

The appended notes are designed to complete and illustrate the details of the argument, and to make the book
more useful to students by supplying hints for further study.
I have made no attempt to give complete references to the
modern literature of the subject. Indeed, as the Lectures
have been written, delivered, and printed in three months,
it was impossible for me to reconsult all the books which
have influenced my views, and acknowledge my indebtedness
to each. My effort has been to give a lucid view of the
critical argument as it stands in my own mind, and to
support it in every part from the text of Scripture or
other original sources. It is of the first importance that
the reader should realise that Biblical Criticism is not the
invention of modern scholars, but the legitimate interpretation of historical facts. I have tried, therefore, to keep the
facts always in the foreground, and, when they are derived
from ancient books not in every one's hands, I have either
given full citations, or made careful reference to the original
authorities.

The great value of historical criticism is that it makes the Old Testament more real to us. Christianity can never separate itself from its historical basis on the Religion of Israel; the revelation of God in Christ cannot be divorced from the earlier revelation on which our Lord built. In all true religion the new rests upon the old. No one, then, to whom Christianity is a reality can safely acquiesce in an unreal conception of the Old Testament history; and in an age when all are interested in historical research, no apologetic can prevent thoughtful minds from drifting away from faith if the historical study of the Old Covenant is condemned by the Church and left in the hands of unbelievers.

The current treatment of the Old Testament has produced a widespread uneasy suspicion that this history cannot bear to be tested like other ancient histories. The old method of explaining difficulties and reconciling apparent contradictions would no longer be tolerated in dealing with other books, and men ask themselves whether our Christian faith, the most precious gift of truth which God has given us, can safely base its defence on arguments that bring no sense of reality to the mind. Yet the history of Israel, when rightly studied, is the most real and vivid of all histories, and the proofs of God's working among His people of old may still be made, what they were in time past, one of the strongest evidences of Christianity. It was no blind chance, and no mere human wisdom, that shaped the growth of Israel's religion, and finally stamped it in these forms, now so strange to us, which preserved the living seed of the Divine word till the fulness of the time when He was manifested who transformed the religion of Israel into a religion for all mankind.

The increasing influence of critical views among earnest students of the Bible is not to be explained on the Manichean theory that new views commend themselves to mankind in proportion as they ignore God.   The living God is as present in the critical construction of the history as in that to which tradition has wedded us.   Criticism is a reality and a force because it unfolds a living and consistent picture of the Old Dispensation ; it is itself a living thing, which plants its foot upon realities, and, like Dante among the shades, proves its life by moving what it touches.

"Così non soglion fare i piè de' morti."

W. ROBERTSON SMITH.

ABERDEEN, 4th April 1881.

CONTENTS

LECTURE I

PAGE

CRITICISM AND THE THEOLOGY OF THE REFORMATION . . 1

LECTURE II

CHRISTIAN INTERPRETATION AND JEWISH TRADITION . . 21

LECTURE III

THE SCRIBES 42

LECTURE IV

THE SEPTUAGINT 73

LECTURE V

THE SEPTUAGINT (continued)—THE COMPOSITION OF BIBLICAL
BOOKS 108

LECTURE VI

THE HISTORY OF THE CANON 149

LECTURE VII

THE PSALTER 188

LECTURE VIII

PAGE

THE TRADITIONAL THEORY OF THE OLD TESTAMENT HISTORY . 226

LECTURE IX

THE LAW AND THE HISTORY OF ISRAEL BEFORE THE EXILE . 254

LECTURE X

THE PROPHETS 278

LECTURE XI

THE PENTATEUCH : THE FIRST LEGISLATION . . . 309

LECTURE XII

THE DEUTERONOMIC CODE AND THE LEVITICAL LAW . . 346

LECTURE XIII

THE NARRATIVE OF THE HEXATEUCH 388

ADDITIONAL NOTES—

A. The Text of 1 Sam. xvii. 431
B. Hebrew Fragments preserved in the Septuagint . 433
C. Sources of Psalm lxxxvi. 435
D. Maccabee Psalms in Books I.-III. of the Psalter . 437
E. The Fifty-first Psalm 440
F. The Development of the Ritual System between Ezekiel
and Ezra 442

INDEX OF PASSAGES DISCUSSED 451
GENERAL INDEX 453

LECTURE I

CRITICISM AND THE THEOLOGY OF THE REFORMATION

I HAVE undertaken to deliver a course of lectures to you, not with a polemical purpose, but in answer to a request for information. I am not here to defend my private opinion on any disputed question, but to expound as well as I can the elements of a well-established department of historical study. Biblical criticism is a branch of historical science ; and I hope to convince you as we proceed that it is a legitimate and necessary science, which must continue to draw the attention of all who go deep into the Bible and the religion of the Bible, if there is any Biblical science at all.

It would be affectation to ignore the fact that in saying so much I at once enter upon ground of controversy. The science of Biblical Criticism has not escaped the fate of every science which takes topics of general human interest for its subject matter, and advances theories destructive of current views upon things with which every one is familiar and in which every one has some practical concern. It would argue indifference rather than enlightenment, if the great mass of Bible-readers, to whom scientific points of view for the study of Scripture are wholly unfamiliar, could adjust themselves to a new line of investigation into the history of the Bible without passing through a crisis of anxious thought not far removed from distress and alarm.

The deepest practical convictions of our lives are seldom formulated with precision. They have been learned by experience rather than by logic, and we are content if we can give them an expression accurate enough to meet our daily wants. And so when we have to bring these convictions to bear on some new question, the formula which has sufficed us hitherto is very apt to lead us astray. For in rough practical formulas, in the working rules, if I may so call them, of our daily spiritual life, the essential is constantly mixed up with what is unimportant or even incorrect. We store our treasures of conviction in earthen vessels, and the broken pipkin of an obsolete formula often acquires for us the value of the treasure which it enshrines.

The persuasion that in the Bible God Himself speaks words of love and life to the soul is the essence of the Christian's conviction as to the truth and authority of Scripture. This persuasion is not, and cannot be, derived from external testimony. No tradition as to the worth of Scripture, no assurance transmitted from our fathers, or from any who in past time heard God's revealing voice, can make the revelation to which they bear witness a personal voice of God to us. The element of personal conviction, which lifts faith out of the region of probable evidence into the sphere of divine certainty, is given only by the Holy Spirit still bearing witness in and with the Word. But then the Word to which this spiritual testimony applies is a written word, which has a history, which has to be read and explained like other ancient books. How we read and explain the Bible depends in great measure on human teaching. The Bible itself is God's book, but the Bible as read and understood by any man or school of men is God's book *plus* a very large element of human interpretation.

In our ordinary Bible-reading these two things, the divine
book and the human understanding of the book, are not kept
sharply apart. We are aware that some passages are obscure,
and we do not claim divine certitude for the interpretation
that we put on them. But we are apt to forget that the
influence of human and traditional interpretation goes much
further than a few obscure passages. Our general views of
the Bible history, our way of looking, not merely at passages,
but at whole books, are coloured by things which we have
learned from men, and which have no claim to rest on the
self-evidencing divine Word. This we forget, and so, taking
God's witness to His Word to be a witness to our whole conception of the Word, we claim divine authority for opinions
which lie within the sphere of ordinary reason, and which
can be proved or disproved by the ordinary laws of historical
evidence. We assume that, because our reading of Scripture
is sufficiently correct to allow us to find in it the God of
redemption speaking words of grace to our soul, those who
seek some other view of the historical aspects of Scripture
are trying to eliminate the God of grace from His own
book.

A large part of Bible-readers never come through the
mental discipline which is necessary to cure prejudices of
this kind, or, in other words, are never forced by the necessities of their intellectual and spiritual life to distinguish
between the accidental and the essential, the human conjectures and the divine truth, which are wrapped up together
in current interpretations of Scripture. But those who are
called in providence to systematic and scholarly study of the
Bible inevitably come face to face with facts which compel
them to draw distinctions that, to a practical reader, may
seem superfluous.

Consider what systematic and scholarly study involves in
contradistinction to the ordinary practical use of the Bible.

Ordinary Bible-reading is eclectic and devotional. A detached passage is taken up, and attention is concentrated on the immediate edification which can be derived from it. Very often the profit which the Bible-reader derives from his morning or evening portion lies mainly in a single word of divine love coming straight home to the heart. And in general the real fruit of such Bible-reading lies less in any addition to one's store of systematic knowledge than in the privilege of withdrawing for a moment from the thoughts and cares of the world, to enter into a pure and holy atmosphere, where the God of love and redemption reveals Himself to the heart, and where the simplest believer can place himself by the side of the psalmist, the prophet, or the apostle, in that inner sanctuary where no sound is heard but the gracious accents of divine promise and the sweet response of assured and humble faith. Far be it from me to undervalue such use of Scripture. It is by this power of touching the heart and lifting the soul into converse with heaven that the Bible approves itself the pure and perfect Word of God, a lamp unto the feet and a light unto the path of every Christian. But, on the other hand, a study which is exclusively practical and devotional is necessarily imperfect. There are many things in Scripture which do not lend themselves to an immediate practical purpose, and which in fact are as good as shut out from the circle of ordinary Bible-reading. I know that good people often try to hide this fact from themselves by hooking on some sort of lesson to passages which they do not understand, or which do not directly touch any spiritual chord. There is very respectable precedent for this course, which in fact is nothing else than the method of tropical exegesis that reigned supreme in the Old Catholic and Mediæval Church. The ancient fathers laid down the principle that everything in Scripture which, taken in its natural sense, appears unedifying must be made edifying by some

method of typical or figurative application.[1]   In principle
this is no longer admitted in the Protestant Churches (unless
perhaps for the Song of Solomon), but in practice we still get
over many difficulties by tacking on a lesson which is not
really taken out of the difficult passage, but read into it from
some other part of Scripture.   People satisfy themselves in
this way, but they do not solve the difficulty.   Let us be
frank with ourselves, and admit that there are many things
in Scripture in which unsystematic and merely devotional
reading finds no profit.   Such parts of the Bible as the
genealogies in Chronicles, the description of Solomon's temple,
a considerable portion of Ezekiel, and not a few of the details
of ritual in the Pentateuch, do not serve an immediate devotional purpose, and are really blank pages except to systematical and critical study.   And for a different reason the
same thing is true of many passages of the prophetical and
poetical books, where the language is so obscure, and the
train of thought so difficult to grasp, that even the best
scholars, with every help which philology can offer, will not
venture to affirm that they possess a certain interpretation.
Difficulties of this sort are not confined to a few corners of
the Bible.   They run through the whole volume, and force
themselves on the attention of every one who desires to
understand any book of the Bible as a whole.

And so we are brought to this issue.   We may, if we
please, confine our study of Scripture to what is immediately
edifying, skimming lightly over all pages which do not serve
a direct purpose of devotion, and ignoring every difficulty

---

[1] According to Origen, *Princip.* Bk. iv. p. 173, the literal sense of Scripture
is often impossible, absurd, or immoral,—and this designedly, lest, cleaving to
the letter alone, men should remain at a distance from the *dogmata*, and learn
nothing worthy of God.   Augustine in his hermeneutical treatise, *De Doctrina
Christiana* (Bk. iii. c. 10), teaches that "Whatever has no proper bearing on
the rule of life or the verity of faith must be recognised as figurative."   A good
example of the practical application of these principles will be found in the
preface to Jerome's Commentary on Hosea.

which does not yield to the faculty of practical insight, the power of spiritual sympathy with the mind of the Spirit, which the thoughtful Christian necessarily acquires in the habitual exercise of bringing Scripture to bear on the daily needs of his own life.   This use of Scripture is full of personal profit, and raises no intellectual difficulties.   But it does not do justice to the whole Word of God.   It is limited for every individual by the limitations of his own religious experience. Reading the Bible in this way, a man comes to a very personal appreciation of so much of God's truth as is in immediate contact with the range of his own life.   But he is sure to miss many truths which belong to another range of experience, and to read into the inspired page things from his own experience which involve human error.   No man's inner life is so large, so perfectly developed, in a word so normal, that it can be used as a measure of the fulness of the Bible.   The Church, therefore, which aims at an all-sided and catholic view, cannot be content with so much of truth as has practically approved itself to one man, or any number of men, all fallible and imperfect.   What she desires to obtain is the sum of all those views of divine truth which are embodied in the experience of the inspired writers.   She must try to get the whole meaning of every prophet, psalmist, or apostle,—not by the rough-and-ready method of culling from a chapter as many truths as at once commend themselves to a Christian heart, but by taking up each piece of Biblical authorship as a whole, realising the position of the writer, and following out the progress of his thought in its minutest details.   And in this process the Church, or the trained theologian labouring in the service of the Church, must not be discouraged by finding much that seems strange, foreign to current experience, or, at first sight, positively unedifying.   It will not do to make our notions the measure of God's dealings with His people of old.   The systematic

student must first, and above all, do justice to his text.
When he has done this, the practical use will follow of itself.

Up to the time of the Reformation the only kind of
theological study which was thought worthy of serious attention was the study of dogma. People's daily spiritual life
was supposed to be nourished, not by Scripture, but by the
Sacraments. The experimental use of Scripture, so dear to
Protestants, was not recognised as one of the main purposes
for which God has given us the Bible. The use of the Bible
was to furnish proof texts for the theologians of the Church,
and the doctrines of the Church as expressed in the Creeds
were the necessary and sufficient object of faith. The believer
had indeed need of Christ as well as of a creed, but Christ
was held forth to him, not in the Bible, but in the Mass.
The Bible was the source of theological knowledge as to the
mysterious doctrine of revelation, but the Sacraments were
the means of grace.

The Reformation changed all this, and brought the Bible
to the front as a living means of grace. How did it do so?
Not, as is sometimes superficially imagined, by placing the infallible Bible in room of the infallible Church, but by a change
in the whole conception of faith, of the plan and purpose
of revelation, and of the operation of the means of grace.

Saving faith, says Luther, is not an intellectual assent to
a system of doctrine superior to reason, but a personal trust
on God in Christ, the appropriation of God's personal word
and promise of redeeming love. God's grace is the manifestation of His redeeming love, and the means of grace are
the means which He adopts to bring His word of love to our
ears and to our hearts. All means of grace, all sacraments,
have value only in so far as they bring to us a personal
Word, that Word which is contained in the gospel and
incarnate in our Lord. The supreme value of the Bible does
not lie in the fact that it is the ultimate source of theology,

but in the fact that it contains the whole message of God's love, that it is the personal message of that love *to me*, not doctrine but promise, not the display of God's metaphysical essence, but of His redeeming purpose ; in a word, of Himself as my God. Filled with this new light as to the meaning of Scripture, Luther displays profound contempt for the grubbing theologians who treated the Bible as a mere storehouse of proof texts, dealing with it, as he says of Tetzel, "like a sow with a bag of oats." The Bible is a living thing. The Middle Ages had no eye for anything but doctrinal mysteries, and where these were lacking saw only, as Luther complained, bare dead histories "which had simply taken place and concerned men no more." Nay, say the Reformers. This history is the story of God's dealings with his people of old. The heart of love which He opened to them, is still a heart of love to us. The great pre-eminence of the Bible history is that in it God speaks—speaks not in the language of doctrine but of personal grace, which we have a right to take home to us now, just as it was taken by His ancient people.[1]

In a word, the Bible is a book of Experimental Religion, in which the converse of God with His people is depicted in all its stages up to the full and abiding manifestation of saving love in the person of Jesus Christ. God has no message to the believing soul which the Bible does not set forth, and set forth not in bare formulas but in living and experimental form, by giving the actual history of the need which the message supplies, and by showing how holy men of old received the message as a light to their own darkness, a comfort and a stay to their own souls. And so, to appro-

---

[1] See, in particular, the first part of the *Freiheit eines Christenmenschen*, and the preface to Luther's German Bible. On Tetzel see *Freiheit des Sermons vom Ablass* (*Werke*, ed. Irmischer, vol. xxvii. p. 13). Compare Calvin's *Institutio*, Bk. iii. chap. 2—"The Word itself, however it be conveyed to us, is like a mirror in which faith beholds God."

priate the divine message for our wants, we need no help of
ecclesiastical tradition, no authoritative Churchly exegesis.
All that we need is to put ourselves by the side of the
psalmist, the prophet, or the apostle, to enter by spiritual sympathy into his experience, to feel our sin and need as he felt
them, and to take home to us, as he took them, the gracious
words of divine love. This it is which makes the Bible perspicuous and precious to every one who is taught of the Spirit.

The history of the Reformation shows that these views
fell upon the Church with all the force of a new discovery.
It was nothing less than the resurrection of the living Word,
buried for so many ages under the dust of a false interpretation. Now we all acknowledge the debt which we owe to
the Reformers in this matter. We are agreed that to them
we owe our open Bible ; but we do not always understand
what this gift means. We are apt to think and speak as if
the Reformation had given us the Bible by removing artificial restrictions on its translation and circulation among the
laity. There is a measure of truth in this view. But, on the
other hand, there were translations in the vulgar tongues
long before Luther. The Bible was never wholly withdrawn
from the laity, and the preaching of the Word was the
characteristic office of the Friars, and the great source of
that popular influence which they strained to the uttermost
against the Reformation. The real importance of Luther's
work was not that he put the Bible into the hands of the
laity, but that he vindicated for the Word a new use and a
living interest which made it impossible that it should not
be read by them. We are not disciples of the Reformation
merely because we have the Bible in our hands, and appeal
to it as the supreme judge. Luther's opponents appealed to
the Bible as confidently as he did. But they did not understand the Bible as he did. To them it was a book revealing
abstract doctrines. To him it was the record of God's words

and deeds of love to the saints of old, and of the answer of their inmost heart to God. This conception changes the whole perspective of Biblical study, and, unless our studies are conformed to it, we are not the children of the Reformation.

The Bible, according to the Reformation view, is a history —the history of the work of redemption from the fall of man to the ascension of the risen Saviour and the mission of the Spirit by which the Church still lives. But the history is not a mere chronicle of supernatural deeds and revelations. It is the inner history of the converse of God with man that gives the Bible its peculiar worth. The story of God's grace is expounded to us by psalmists, prophets, and apostles, as they realised it in their own lives. For the progress of Revelation was not determined arbitrarily. No man can learn anything aright about God and His love, unless the new truth come home to his heart and grow into his life. What is still true of our appropriation of revealed truth was true also of its first communication. Inspired men were able to receive and set down new truths of revelation as a sure rule for our guidance, because these truths took hold of them with a personal grasp, and supplied heartfelt needs. Thus the record of revelation becomes, so to speak, the autobiography of the Church—the story of a converse with God, in which the saints of old actually lived.

Accordingly, the first business of the Reformation theologian is not to crystallise Bible truths into doctrines, but to follow, in all its phases, the manifold inner history of the religious life which the Bible unfolds. It is his business to study every word of Scripture, not merely by grammar and logic, but in its relation to the life of the writer, and the actual circumstances in which God's Word came to him. Only in this way can we hope to realise the whole rich personal meaning of the Word of grace. For God never spoke a word to any soul that was not exactly fitted to the occasion

and the man.   Separate it from this context, and it is no
longer the same perfect Word.

The great goodness of God to us, in His gift of the Bible,
appears very specially in the copious materials which He has
supplied for our assistance in this task of historical exegesis.
There are large passages in the Bible, especially in the Old
Testament, which, taken apart from the rest of the book, would
appear quite deficient in spiritual instruction.   Crude rationalism often proposes to throw these aside as mere lumber,
forming no integral part of the record of revelation.   And, on
the other hand, a narrowly timid faith sometimes insists that
such passages, even in their isolation, must be prized as highly
as the Psalms or the Sermon on the Mount.   Both these views
are wrong, and both err in the same way, by forgetting that
a Bible which shall enable us to follow the inner life of the
course of Revelation must contain, not only words of grace
and answers of faith, but as much of the ordinary history, the
everyday life, and the current thoughts of the people to whom
Revelation came, as will enable us to enter into their circumstances, and receive the Word as they received it.   From this
point of view we can recognise the hand of a wise Providence
in the circumstance that the Old Testament contains, in far
larger proportion than the New, matter of historical and
archæological interest, which does not serve a direct purpose
of edification.   For, in the study of the New Testament, we
are assisted in the work of historical interpretation by a large
contemporary literature of profane origin, whereas we have
almost no contemporary helps for the study of Hebrew
antiquity, beyond the books which were received into the
Jewish Canon.[1]

---

[1] The Old Testament writers possessed Hebrew sources now lost, such as
the Book of the Wars of Jehovah, the Book of Jashar, and the Annals of
the Kings of Israel and Judah.   (See below, Lectures V. and XI.) But
Josephus, and other profane historians, whose writings are still extant, had no

The kind of Bible study which I have indicated is followed more or less instinctively by every intelligent reader. Every Christian takes home words of promise, of comfort, or of warning, by putting himself in the place of the first hearers of the Word, and uses the Bible devotionally by borrowing the answer spoken by the faith of apostles or psalmists. And the diligent reader soon learns that the profit of these exercises is proportioned to the accuracy with which he can compare his situations and needs with those underlying the text which he appropriates. But the systematic study of Scripture must rise above the merely instinctive use of sound principles. To get from the Bible all the instruction which it is capable of yielding, we must apprehend the true method of study in its full range and scope, obtain a clear grasp of the principles involved, and apply them systematically with the best help that scholarship supplies. Let us consider how this is to be done.

In the Bible, God and man meet together, and hold such converse as is the abiding pattern and rule of all religious experience. In this simple fact lies the key to all those puzzles about the divine and human side of the Bible with which people are so much exercised. We hear many speak of the human side of the Bible as if there were something dangerous about it, as if it ought to be kept out of sight lest it tempt us to forget that the Bible is the Word of God. And there is a widespread feeling that, though the Bible no doubt

authentic Hebrew sources for the canonical history, except those preserved in the Bible.

It is only in quite recent times that the lack of contemporary books illustrative of the Old Testament period has been partly supplied by the discovery and decipherment of the monumental inscriptions of Palestine (the Moabite stone, the inscription of Siloam, the Phœnician inscriptions) and the cuneiform records of Babylonia, Assyria, and Persia. Valuable as these new sources are, they touch only individual parts of the Biblical record. The Egyptian monuments, again, from which so much was hoped, have hitherto given little help for Bible history.

has a human side, a safe and edifying exegesis must confine itself to the divine side. This point of view is a survival of the mediæval exegesis which buried the true sense of Scripture. Of course, as long as you hold that the whole worth of Revelation lies in abstract doctrines, supernaturally communicated to the intellect and not to the heart, the idea that there is a human life in the Bible is purely disturbing. But if the Bible sets forth the personal converse of God with man, it is absolutely essential to look at the human side. The prophets and psalmists were not mere impassive channels through whose lips or pens God poured forth an abstract doctrine. He spoke not only through them, but to them and in them. They had an intelligent share in the Divine converse with them; and we can no more understand the Divine Word without taking them into account than we can understand a human conversation without taking account of both interlocutors. To try to suppress the human side of the Bible, in the interests of the purity of the Divine Word, is as great a folly as to think that a father's talk with his child can be best reported by leaving out everything which the child said, thought, and felt.

The first condition of a sound understanding of Scripture is to give full recognition to the human side, to master the whole situation and character and feelings of each human interlocutor who has a part in the drama of Revelation. *Nay, the whole business of scholarly exegesis lies with this human side.* All that earthly study and research can do for the reader of Scripture is to put him in the position of the man to whose heart God first spoke. What is more than this lies beyond our wisdom. It is only the Spirit of God that can make the Word a living word to our hearts, as it was a living word to him who first received it. This is the truth which the Westminster Confession expresses when it teaches, in harmony with all the Reformed Symbols, that our full persuasion and assurance of the infallible truth and divine authority of Scripture is from the inward work of the Holy Spirit, bearing witness by and with the Word in our hearts.

And here, as we at once perceive, the argument reaches a practical issue. We not only see that the principles of the Reformation demand a systematic study of Scripture upon lines of research which were foreign to the Church before the Reformation; but we are able to fix the method by which such study must be carried on. It is our duty as Protestants to interpret Scripture historically. The Bible itself has a history. It was not written at one time, or by a single pen. It comprises a number of books and pieces given to the Church by many instrumentalities and at various times. It is our business to separate these elements from one another, to examine them one by one, and to comprehend each piece in the sense which it had for the first writer, and in its relation to the needs of God's people at the time when it was written. In proportion as we succeed in this task, the mind of the Revealer in each of His many communications with mankind will become clear to us. We shall be able to follow His gracious converse with His people of old from point to point. Instead of appropriating at random so much of the Word as is at once perspicuous, or guessing darkly at the sense of things obscure, we shall learn to understand God's teaching in its natural connection. By this means we shall be saved from arbitrariness in our interpretations. For of this we may be assured, that there was nothing arbitrary in God's plan of revelation. He spoke to the prophets of old, as the Epistle to the Hebrews tells us, "in many parts and in many ways." There was variety in the method of His revelation; and each individual oracle, taken by itself, was partial and incomplete. But none of these things was without its reason. The method of revelation was a method of education. God spake to Israel as one speaks to tender weanlings (Isa. xxviii.

9), giving precept after precept, line upon line, here a little and there a little. He followed this course that each precept, as He gave it, might be understood, and lay a moral responsibility on those who received it (ver. 13); and if our study follows close in the lines of the divine teaching, we too, receiving the Word like little children, shall be in the right way to understand it in all its progress, and in all the manifold richness of its meaning. But to do so, I again repeat, we must put ourselves alongside of the first hearers. What was clear and plain enough to the obedient heart then is not necessarily clear and plain to us now, if we receive it in a different attitude. God's word was delivered in the language of men, and is not exempt from the necessary laws and limitations of human speech. Now it is a law of all speech, and especially of all speech upon personal matters, that the speaker must express himself to the understanding of his hearer, presupposing in him a certain preparation, a certain mental attitude, a certain degree of familiarity with and interest in the subject. When a third person strikes into a conversation, he cannot follow it unless, as the familiar phrase has it, he knows where they are. So it is with the Bible. And here historical study comes in. The mind of God is unchangeable. His purpose of love is invariable from first to last. The manifold variety of Scripture, the changing aspects of Bible truth, depend on no change in Him, but wholly on the varying circumstances and needs of the men who received the Revelation. It is with their life and feelings that we must get into sympathy, in order to understand what God spoke to them. We must read the Bible as the record of the history of grace, and as itself a part of the history. And this we must do with all patience, not weary though our study does not at each moment yield an immediate fruit of practical edification, if only it conducts us on the sure road to edification by carrying us along the actual path trodden by God's people of old; if, opening to us their needs, their hopes, their trials, even their errors and sins, it enables our ears to receive the same voice which they heard behind them, saying, " This is the way; walk ye in it" (Isa. xxx. 21). It is the glory of the Bible that it invites and satisfies such study,—that its manifold contents, the vast variety of its topics, the extraordinary diversities of its structure and style, constitute an inexhaustible mine of the richest historical interest, in which generation after generation can labour, always bringing forth some new thing, and with each new discovery coming closer to a full understanding of the supreme wisdom and love of Him who speaks in all Scripture.

And now let us come to the point. In sketching the principles and aims of a truly Protestant study of Scripture I have not used the word criticism, but I have been describing the thing. Historical criticism may be defined without special reference to the Bible, for it is applicable, and is daily applied without dispute, to every ancient literature and every ancient history. The critical study of ancient documents means nothing else than the careful sifting of their origin and meaning in the light of history. The first principle of criticism is that every book bears the stamp of the time and circumstances in which it was produced. An ancient book is, so to speak, a fragment of ancient life; and to understand it aright we must treat it as a living thing, as a bit of the life of the author and his time, which we shall not fully understand without putting ourselves back into the age in which it was written. People talk much of destructive criticism, as if the critic's one delight were to prove that things which men have long believed are not true, and that books were not written by the authors whose names they bear. But the true critic has for his business, not to destroy, but to build up. The critic is an interpreter, but one who has a larger view of his task than the man of mere grammars and dictionaries,—one who is not content to reproduce the words of his author, but strives to enter into sympathy with his thoughts, and to understand the thoughts as part of the life of the thinker and of his time.   In this process the occasional destruction of some traditional opinion is a mere incident.

Ancient books coming down to us from a period many centuries before the invention of printing have necessarily undergone many vicissitudes.   Some of them are preserved only in imperfect copies made by an ignorant scribe of the dark ages.   Others have been disfigured by editors, who mixed up foreign matter with the original text.   Very often an important book fell altogether out of sight for a long time, and when it came to light again all knowledge of its origin was gone; for old books did not generally have title-pages and prefaces.   And, when such a nameless roll was again brought into notice, some half-informed reader or transcriber was not unlikely to give it a new title of his own devising, which was handed down thereafter as if it had been original. Or again, the true meaning and purpose of a book often became obscure in the lapse of centuries, and led to false interpretations.   Once more, antiquity has handed down to us many writings which are sheer forgeries, like some of the Apocryphal books, or the Sibylline oracles, or those famous Epistles of Phalaris which formed the subject of Bentley's great critical essay.   In all such cases the historical critic must destroy the received view, in order to establish the truth.   He must review doubtful titles, purge out interpolations, expose forgeries; but he does so only to manifest the truth, and exhibit the genuine remains of antiquity in their real character.   A book that is really old and really valuable has nothing to fear from the critic, whose labours can only put its worth in a clearer light, and establish its authority on a surer basis.

2

In a word, it is the business of the critic to trace back the steps by which any ancient book has been transmitted to us, to find where it came from and who wrote it, to examine the occasion of its composition, and search out every link that connects it with the history of the ancient world and with the personal life of the author.

This is exactly what Protestant principles direct us to do with the several parts of the Bible. We have to go back step by step, and retrace the history of the sacred volume up to the first origin of each separate writing which it contains. In doing this we must use every light that can be brought to bear on the subject. Every fact is welcome, whether it come from Jewish tradition, or from a comparison of old MSS. and versions, or from an examination of the several books with one another and of each book in its own inner structure. It is not needful in starting to lay down any fixed rules of procedure. The ordinary laws of evidence and good sense must be our guides. For the transmission of the Bible is not due to a continued miracle, but to a watchful Providence ruling the ordinary means by which all ancient books have been handed down. And finally, when we have worked our way back through the long centuries which separate us from the age of Revelation, we must, as we have already seen, study each writing and make it speak for itself on the common principles of sound exegesis. There is no discordance between the religious and the scholarly methods of study. They lead to the same goal; and the more closely our study fulfils the demands of historical scholarship, the more fully will it correspond with our religious needs.

I know what is said in answer to all this. We have no objection, say the opponents of Biblical criticism, to any amount of historical study, but it is not legitimate historical study that has produced the current results of Biblical

criticism. These results, say they, are based on the
rationalistic assumption that the supernatural is impossible,
and that everything in the Bible which asserts the existence
of a real personal communication of God with man is
necessarily untrue. My answer to this objection is very
simple. We have not got to results yet; I am only laying
down a method, and a method, as we have seen, which is in
full accordance with, and imperatively prescribed by, the
Reformation doctrine of the Word of God. We are agreed,
it appears, that the method is a true one. Let us go forward
and apply it; and if in the application you find me calling
in a rationalistic principle, if you can show at any step in my
argument that I assume the impossibility of the supernatural,
or reject plain facts in the interests of rationalistic theories,
I will frankly confess that I am in the wrong. But, on the
other hand, you must remember that all truth is one, that the
God who gave us the Bible has also given us faculties of
reason and gifts of scholarship with which to study the
Bible, and that the true meaning of Scripture is not to be
measured by preconceived notions, but determined as the
result of legitimate research. Only of this I am sure at the
outset, that the Bible does speak to the heart of man in words
that can only come from God—that no historical research
can deprive me of this conviction, or make less precious the
divine utterances that speak straight to the heart. For the
language of these words is so clear that no readjustment of
their historical setting can conceivably change the substance
of them. Historical study may throw a new light on the
circumstances in which they were first heard or written. In
that there can only be gain. But the plain, central, heartfelt
truths that speak for themselves and rest on their own inde-
feasible worth will assuredly remain to us. No amount of
change in the background of a picture can make white black
or black white, though by restoring the right background

where it has been destroyed the harmony and balance of the whole composition may be immeasurably improved.

So it is with the Bible. The supreme truths which speak to every believing heart, the way of salvation which is the same in all ages, the clear voice of God's love so tender and personal and simple that a child can understand it—these are things which must abide with us, and prove themselves mighty from age to age apart from all scientific study. But those who love the truth will not shrink from any toil that can help us to a fuller insight into all its details and all its setting ; and those whose faith is firmly fixed on the things that cannot be moved will not doubt that every new advance in Biblical study must in the end make God's great scheme of grace appear in fuller beauty and glory.

LECTURE II

CHRISTIAN INTERPRETATION AND JEWISH TRADITION

AT our last meeting, I endeavoured to convey to you a general conception of the methods and objects of Biblical criticism, and to show that the very same rules for the prosecution of this branch of Biblical study may be derived either from the general principles of historical science or from the theological principles of the Protestant Reformation. We ended by see-ing that it was the duty of criticism to start with the Bible as it has been delivered to us, and as it now is in our hands, and to endeavour to trace back the history of its transmission, and of the vicissitudes through which it has passed, up to the time of the original authors, so that we may be able to take an historical view of the origin of each individual writing of the Old Testament, and of the meaning which it had to those who first received it and to him who first wrote it.

For this purpose, in speaking to a general audience, it is necessary for me to begin with the English Bible. The Eng-lish Bible which we are accustomed to use gives us the Old Testament as it was understood by Protestant scholars at the beginning of the seventeenth century. It is not necessary for our present purpose that I should dwell upon the minor differences which separate the Version of 1611 from other versions made about the same period or a little earlier. Speaking broadly, it is sufficient to say that the Authorised

Version represents in a very admirable manner the understanding of the Old Testament which had been attained by
Protestant scholarship at the beginning of the seventeenth
century. We are now to look back and inquire what are
the links connecting our English Bible with the original
autographs of the sacred writers.

The Protestant versions, of which our Bible is one, were
products of the Reformation. To a certain extent they were
products of the controversy with the Church of Rome. In
other words, there were at that time two main views current
in Europe, and among the scholars of Europe, as to the proper
way of dealing with the Bible—as to the canon of Scripture,
the authentic text, and the method of interpretation. The
Pre-Reformation exegesis, with which the Protestants had to
contend, was the natural descendant of the exegesis of the
Old Catholic Church, as it was formed in opposition to the
heretics, as far back in part as the second century after
Christ. At the time of Luther, as we have already seen,
there was no dispute between Protestants and Catholics as to
the authority of Scripture; both parties admitted that authority to be supreme, but they were divided on the question of
the true meaning of Scripture. According to the Old Church,
on which the Catholic party rested, the Bible was not clear
and intelligible by its own light like an ordinary book. It
was taken for granted that the use of the Bible lies in those
doctrines higher than reason, those *noëtic truths*, as they were
called, of a divine philosophy, which it contains. But the
earliest fathers of the Catholic Church already saw quite
clearly that the supposed abstract and noëtic truths did not
lie on the surface of Scripture. To an ordinary reader the
Bible appears something quite different from a body of
supernatural mysteries and abstract philosophic doctrines.
This observation was made by the Catholic fathers, but it
did not lead them, nor did it lead the Gnostic heretics, with

whom they were engaged in controversy, to anticipate the
great discovery of the Reformation, and to see that the real
meaning of the Bible must be its natural meaning. On the
contrary, the orthodox and the Gnostics alike continued to
look in the Bible for mysteries concealed under the plain text
of Scripture—mysteries which could only be reached by some
form of allegorical interpretation. Of course, the allegorical
exegesis yielded to every party exactly those principles which
that party desired; and so the controversy between the
Gnostics and the Catholic Church could not be decided on
the ground of the Bible alone, which both sides interpreted
in an equally arbitrary manner. To tell the truth, it would
have been very difficult indeed for Christian theologians in
those days to reach a sound and satisfactory exegesis, conducted upon principles which we could now accept. Very
few theologians in the churches of the Gentiles possessed the
linguistic knowledge necessary to understand the original text
of the Old Testament. Hebrew scholars were few and far
between, and the Doctors of the Church were habitually
dependent upon the Alexandrian Greek translation, called
the Septuagint or Version of the Seventy. To this translation we shall have to advert at greater length by and by.
At present it is enough to say that it was a version composed
in Egypt and current among the Jews of Alexandria a considerable time before the Christian era, and that it spread
contemporaneously with the preaching of the Gospel through
all parts of Christendom where Greek was understood. In
many parts of the Old Testament this translation was very
obscure and really did not yield clear sense to any natural
method of exegesis. But indeed, apart from the disadvantage
of being thrown back upon the Septuagint, the Christians
could not have hoped to understand the Old Testament better
than their Jewish contemporaries. Even if they had set
themselves to study the original text, they would have

required to take their whole knowledge of the Hebrew Bible
from the Jews, who were the only masters that could then
have instructed them in the language ; and in fact, while the
Western churches were mainly dependent on the Septuagint,
and struck out an independent line of interpretation on the
basis of that version, the exegesis of the Oriental churches
continued to be largely guided by the teaching of the
Synagogue. In Syria and beyond the river Euphrates, the
Bible was interpreted by Christian scholars who spoke Syriac
—a language akin to Hebrew—upon the methods of the
Jewish schools ; but by this time the Jews themselves had
fallen into an abyss of artificial Rabbinical interpretation,
from which little true light could be derived for the understanding of Scripture.   The influence of the Jewish interpretation which ruled in the East can be traced, not only in the
old Syriac translation called the Peshito (or Pĕshîttâ), but in
the writings of later Syriac divines. In the Homilies of
Aphraates, for example, which belong to the first half of the
fourth century, we find clear evidence that the Biblical train-
ing and exegetical methods of the author, who, living in the
far East, was not a Greek scholar, were largely derived from
the Jewish doctors ; and the operation of the same influences
can be followed far down into the Middle Ages.[1]

Accordingly, in the absence of a satisfactory and scientific
interpretation, the conflict of opinions between the orthodox
and the heretics was decided on another principle. The
apostles, it was said, had received the mysteries of divine
truth from our Lord, and had committed them in plain and
living words to the apostolic churches. This is a point to
which the ancient fathers constantly recur. The written

[1] See, especially, the Arabic catena on Genesis published by Professor
Lagarde in his *Materialien zur Kritik und Geschichte des Pentateuchs* (Leipzig,
1867) from a Carshunic MS. of the sixteenth century. This compilation of a
Syriac scribe is full of Jewish traditions, and even in form, as the editor
observes, is quite of the character of a Jewish *Midrash*.

word, they say, is necessarily ambiguous and difficult, but the spoken word of the apostles was clear and transparent. In the apostolic churches, then, the sum of true doctrine has been handed down in an accurate form; and the consent of the apostolic churches as to the mysteries of faith forms the rule of sound exegesis. Any interpretation of Scripture, say the fathers, is necessarily false if it differs from the *ecclesiastical canon*—that is, from the received doctrinal testimony of the great apostolic churches, such as Corinth, Rome, and Alexandria, in which the teaching of the apostles still lived as it had been handed down by oral tradition.[1]

Such were the principles of exegesis to which the Catholic Church adhered up to the time of the Reformation. New elements were added from time to time to the body of ecclesiastical tradition, and in particular a very great change took place with regard to the received edition of the Old Testament. When the theory of the ecclesiastical canon was first formed, the churches of Europe read either the Greek translation of the Septuagint or a Latin text formed from the Septuagint; but about the year 400 A.D., Jerome, a man of unusual learning for that age, who had studied under Jewish teachers, made a new version direct from the Hebrew, which was greatly assailed at the time as a dangerous innovation, but by and by came to be accepted in the Latin churches as the authentic and received edition of the Bible. When I say that Jerome's version was received by the Western churches,

---

[1] On the *Regula Fidei*, and its connection with the ambiguity of the allegorical interpretation, so keenly felt in controversy with heretics, compare Diestel, *Geschichte des alten Testaments in der Christlichen Kirche*, p. 38 (Irenæus, Tertullian), p. 85 (Augustine). The principle is clearly laid down by Origen: "Many think that they have the mind of Christ, and not a few differ from the opinions of the earlier Christians; but the preaching of the Church, handed down in regular succession from the Apostles, still abides, and is present in the Church. Therefore, the only truth to be believed is that which in no point departs from ecclesiastical and apostolical tradition." (*Princip.*, *Praef.* § 2.)

it is proper to observe that it was not received in all its purity, and that the text of this *Vulgate* or received version (the word *vulgate* means "currently received"), as it actually existed in the Middle Ages and at the time of the Reformation, was considerably modified by things which had been carried over from the older Latin translations taken from the Greek. Still, the Western Church supposed itself to receive the version of Jerome as the authoritative and vulgate version, and this new Vulgate replaced the old Vulgate, the Greek Septuagint translation made by the Jews in Egypt before the time of Christ.

The Reformers, who were well read in church history, sometimes met their opponents by pointing out that the ecclesiastical tradition on which the Catholics relied as the proper norm or rule of interpretation had itself undergone change in the course of centuries, and they often appealed with success to the earliest fathers against those views of truth which were current in their own times. But Luther's fundamental conception of revelation made it impossible for the Protestants to submit their understanding of the Bible even to the earliest and purest form of the ecclesiastical canon. The ecclesiastical canon—the standard of doctrinal interpretation based on the supposed consent of the apostolic churches—had, as we have seen, been first invented in order to get over the ambiguities of the allegorical method of interpretation. When Luther taught the people that the Bible can be understood like any other book, that the true meaning of its words is the natural sense which appeals to ordinary Christian intelligence, it was plain that for him this whole method of ecclesiastical tradition as the rule of exegesis no longer had any meaning or value.

The Church of Rome, after the Reformation began, took up a definite and formal battle-ground against Protestantism in the Decrees of the Council of Trent. The positions laid

down by the Doctors of Trent in opposition to the movement
headed by Luther were these :—

I. The supreme rule of faith and life is contained in the
written books and the unwritten traditions of Christ and his
Apostles, dictated by the Holy Spirit and handed down by
continual succession in the Catholic Church.

II. The canonical books are those books in all their parts
which are read in the Catholic Church and contained in the
Latin Vulgate version, the authenticity of which is accepted
as sufficiently proved by its long use in the Catholic
Church.

III. The interpretation of Scripture must be conformed
to the tenets of Holy Mother Church and the unanimous
consent of the Fathers.

The Reformers traversed all these three positions ; for
they denied the validity of unwritten tradition ; they refused
to admit the authority of the Vulgate, and appealed to the
original text; and finally, they denied the existence and still
more the authority of the consent of the Fathers, and admitted no principle for the interpretation of the Bible that
would not be sound if applied to another book.   They affirmed
that the reader has a right to form his own private judgment
on the sense of Scripture ; by which, of course, they did not
mean that one man's judgment is as good as another's, but
only that the sense of a controverted passage must be decided
by argument and not by authority.   The one rule of exposition which they laid down as possessing authority for the
Church was that in a disputed point of doctrine the sense of
an obscure passage must be ruled by passages which are more
plain.   And this, as you will easily observe, is, strictly speaking, not a rule of interpretation but a principle of theology.
It rather tells us which passage we are to choose for the
proof or disproof of any doctrine than helps us to get the
exact sense of a disputed text.   All that it really means is

this—" Form your doctrines from plain texts, and do not be
led astray from the teaching of plain passages by a meaning
which some one may extort from an obscure one." So far as
the principle is exegetical, it simply means that an all-wise
Author—for to the Reformers God is the author of all Scripture—cannot contradict Himself.

I need not say more upon the first and third positions of
the Council of Trent; but the second position, as to the
claims of the standard Vulgate edition, is a point which
requires.more attention. In making the Vulgate the standard
edition, the Council of Trent implied two things :—(1) that
the Vulgate contains all the canonical books in their true
text; and (2) that the translation, if not perfect, is exempt
from errors affecting doctrine. The Roman Catholics, of
course, did not mean to assert that in every particular the
Vulgate edition represents the exact text and meaning of the
original writers. In justice to them, we must say that for
their contention that was not necessary, because all along
what they wished to get at was not the meaning of the
original writers, but the body of doctrine which had the seal
of the authority of the Church ; and therefore, from their
point of view, the authenticity of the text of the Vulgate was
sufficiently proved by the fact that the infallible Church had
long used that text without finding any ground of complaint
against it; and the authority of the translation, in like
manner, was sufficiently supported by the fact that theologians had always been able to deduce from it the received
doctrines of the Church. That, no doubt, was what they
meant. Nevertheless, the two theses which they laid down
were very curiously at variance with what Jerome, the
author of the Vulgate version, had once and again said about
the value of his own labours. They affirmed that the Vulgate
contained all the canonical books and none else, and that it
contained those books in the true text. Jerome, on the con-

trary, in that prologue to part of his translation which is generally called the *Prologus galeatus*, regards all books as apocryphal which he did not translate directly from the Hebrew ; and, following this rule, he excludes from the canon, that is, from the number of books that possess authority in matters of doctrine, the Book of Wisdom, Ecclesiasticus, Judith, Tobit, Baruch, and also the two books of the Maccabees, although he had seen the first of these in Hebrew. The Council of Trent accepts all these books as canonical, and also certain additions to Daniel and Esther which are not found in the Hebrew text.[1]

The second position of the Doctors of Trent also reads curiously in the light of Jerome's own remarks. According to the Council of Trent, the whole translation of Jerome is accurate for all purposes of doctrine, but Jerome in his prefaces makes a very different claim for himself. What he says is this : " If you observe my version to vary from the

---

[1] *Prologus galeatus.*—" This prologue may fit all the books which we have translated from the Hebrew. Books outside of these are apocryphal. Therefore the so-called Wisdom of Solomon, the book of Jesus son of Sirach, Judith, Tobit, and The Shepherd are not canonical. The first book of Maccabees I found in Hebrew, the second is Greek, as may be proved from its very idiom."

Praef. in Jeremiam.—" We have passed by the book of Baruch, Jeremiah's amanuensis, which the Hebrews neither read nor possess."

Praef. in Librum Esther.—" The Book of Esther has unquestionably been vitiated by various translators. I have translated it word for word as it stands in the Hebrew archives."

Praef. in Danielem.—" The story of Susanna, the Song of the Three Children, and the fables of Bel and the Dragon are not found in the Hebrew Daniel ; but as they are current throughout the world we have added them at the end, marking them with an obelus, lest the ignorant should fancy us to have excised a great part of the volume." Jerome adds an interesting account of arguments against the additions to Daniel, which he had heard from a Jewish doctor, leaving the decision to his readers.

Of the Apocryphal books contained in the English Authorised version of 1611, three are not accepted as canonical by the Church of Rome, viz. First and Second Esdras (otherwise called Third and Fourth Esdras), and the Prayer of Manasseh. The canonicity of the additions to Esther and Daniel is rightly held by Bellarmin to be implied in the decree of Trent which accepts the books of the Old Testament, "cum omnibus suis partibus, prout in ecclesia catholica legi consueverunt." (*Controv. I. De Verbo Dei*, Lib. i. capp. 7, 9.)

Greek or Latin copies in your hands, ask the most trust-
worthy Jew you can find, and see if he does not agree with
me."[1] Once and again Jerome claims this, and only this, for
his version, that it agrees with the best Jewish tradition; in
other words, Jerome sought to correct the current Bibles of
his day according to the Hebrew text, as the Jews of his
time received it, and to give an interpretation on a level
with the best Jewish scholarship. He did this partly by
the aid of earlier translations from the Hebrew into the
Greek (Aquila, Theodotion, but especially Symmachus) made
after the time of Christ, and more in accordance than the
Septuagint with the later Rabbinical scholarship;[2] and
partly by the help of learned Jews. On one occasion, he tells
us, he brought a famous Rabbi from Tiberias to instruct him.
At another time he brought a Jewish scholar from Lydda ;
and in particular he speaks of one called Bar Anina, a teacher
who came to him by night for fear of his co-religionists,
while the translator resided in Jerusalem and Bethlehem.[3]

[1] The quotation is from the *Prologus galeatus*. Compare the preface to
Chronicles addressed to Domnio and Rogatianus.

[2] The version of Aquila, a Jewish proselyte and disciple of the famous
Rabbi Akiba, was made expressly in the interests of Jewish exegesis, and
reproduced with scrupulous accuracy the received text of the second
Christian century. Symmachus and Theodotion followed later, but still in the
second century. The former, according to Eusebius and Jerome, was an
Ebionite, one of the sect of Jewish Christians who still held to the observance
of the law, like the opponents of Paul. It is uncertain whether Theodotion
was an Ebionite (Jerome), or a proselyte (Irenæus). Aquila, says Jerome,
sought to reproduce the Hebrew word for word ; Symmachus aimed at a clear
expression of the sense ; while Theodotion rather sought to give a revised
edition not very divergent from the Greek of the Septuagint. These versions
were arranged in parallel columns in the Hexapla of Origen, composed in the
first half of the third century. The fragments of them which remain in Greek
MSS. of the Septuagint, in the Patristic literature, or in the Syriac translation of the fifth column of the Hexapla made by Paul of Tella, in Alexandria,
617 A.D., are collected in Dr. Field's edition, *Origenis Hexaplorum quae
supersunt* (Oxford, 1867-75).

[3] *Praef. in Librum Job.*—"To understand this book I procured, at no
small cost, a doctor from Lydda, who was deemed to hold the first place
among the Hebrews."

In their earlier controversies with the Roman Catholics, the Protestants simply fell back upon these facts, quoting Jerome against the Council of Trent, as is done, for example, in the sixth of the Articles of the Church of England.[1] They quoted Jerome, and therefore adopted his definition that all books which were not extant in Hebrew and admitted to the canon of the Jews in the day of Jerome are apocryphal and not to be cited in proof of a disputed doctrine. Beyond that they did not care to press the question of the canon. There were differences among themselves as to the value of the Apocrypha on the one hand, and as to the canonicity of Esther and some other books of the old canon upon the other. But it was enough for the Protestants in controversy with Rome to be able to refuse a proof text drawn from the Apocryphal books, upon the plain ground that the authority of these books was challenged even by many of the fathers. Thus Calvin, in his *Antidote* to the Council of Trent, is willing to leave the question of the canon open, contenting himself with the observation that the intrinsic qualities of the Apocryphal books display a manifest inferiority to the canonical writings.[2]

Praef. in Chron. ad D. et R.—"When your letters reached me, asking a Latin version of Chronicles, I got a doctor of Tiberias, in high esteem among the Hebrews, and with him collated everything, as the proverb goes, from the crown of the head to the tip of the nails. Thus confirmed, I have ventured to comply with your request." Bar Anina is named in *Epist.* 84. Jerome never gained such a knowledge of Hebrew as gave him confidence to dispense with the aid of the Jews.

[1] The passage quoted in Art. VI. is from *Praef. in libros Salomonis.*—"As the Church reads Judith, Tobit, and the books of Maccabees, but does not receive them among the canonical Scriptures, so let her read these two books [Ecclesiasticus and the Wisdom of Solomon] for the edification of the laity, but not to confirm the authority of ecclesiastical doctrines."

[2] "On their promiscuous acceptance of all books into the Canon, I will say no more than that herein they depart from the consensus of the early Church. For it is known what Jerome reports as the common judgment of the ancients. . . . I am not aware, however, that the decree of Trent agrees with the third Œcumenical Council, which Augustine follows in his book *De Doctrina Christiana.* But as Augustine testifies that all were not agreed upon

On the question of the true interpretation of Scripture they had much more to say. The revival of letters in the fifteenth century had raised a keen interest in ancient languages, and scholars who had mastered Greek as well as Latin were ambitious to add to their knowledge a third learned tongue, viz. the Hebrew. At first this ambition met with many difficulties. The original text of the Old Testament was preserved only among the scholars of the Synagogue. It was impossible to learn Hebrew except from Jewish teachers; and orthodox Jews refused to teach men who were not of their own faith. Gradually, however, these obstacles were surmounted. Towards the close of the fifteenth century, Hebrew Bibles began to be printed, and some knowledge of the Hebrew tongue became disseminated to a considerable extent; and at length, in the year 1506, John Reuchlin, the great supporter of Hebrew studies north of the Alps, put forth in Latin his *Rudiments* of the Hebrew language. This Latin work, which was something of the nature of both grammar and dictionary, was almost entirely taken from the Hebrew manuals of the famous Jewish scholar and lexicographer, Rabbi David Kimhi, who flourished about the year 1200 A.D. As soon as Christians were furnished in this way with text-books, the new learning spread rapidly. It ran over Europe just at the time when the Reformation was spreading, and the Reformers, always keenly alive to the best and most modern learning of their time, read the Old Testament in the original Hebrew, and often found occasion to differ from Jerome's version. Observe, they agreed with Jerome in principle. They, like him, aimed only at rendering the text as the best Hebrew scholars would do, and to them, as to him, the standard of scholarship was that of the

the matter in his time, let this point be left open. But if arguments are to be drawn from the books themselves, there are many proofs, besides their idiom, that they ought to take a lower place than the fathers of Trent award to them," etc. Compare the statement, *Institut.* iv. 9, § 14.

most learned Jews. But when Jerome wrote, there was no such thing in existence as a Hebrew grammar and dictionary ; there were no written commentaries to which a Christian scholar had access. The Reformers had the text-book of Reuchlin, the grammar and lexicon of Kimhi, the commentaries of many Rabbins of the Middle Ages, with other helps denied to Jerome, and therefore they knew that their new learning put them in a position to criticise his work. Often, indeed, they undervalued Jerome's labours, and this ultimately led to controversies between Protestants and Catholics, which were fruitful of instruction to both sides. But, on the whole, the Reforming scholars did know Hebrew better than Jerome, and their versions, including our English Bible, approached much more nearly than his to the ideal common to both,—which was to give the sense of the Old Testament as it was understood by the best Jewish scholars. Of course, the Jewish authorities themselves sometimes differed from one another. In such cases, the Protestants leant sometimes on one authority, sometimes on another. Luther was much influenced (through Nicolaus de Lyra) by the commentaries of R. Solomon of Troyes, generally called Rashi, who died 1105 A.D. Our Bible is mainly guided by the grammar and lexicon of the later scholar, R. David Kimhi of Narbonne, who has already been mentioned as the author of the most current text-books of the Hebrew language. But the point which I wish you to observe is that the Reformers and their successors, up to the time when all our Protestant versions were fixed, were in the hands of the Rabbins in all matters of Hebrew scholarship. Their object in the sixteenth century, like Jerome's in the fourth, was simply to give to the vulgar the fruit of the best Jewish learning, applied to the translation of the Scriptures received among the Jews.

It may be asked why the Reformers stopped here. But

the answer is clear enough. They went as far as the scholarship of the age would carry them. All sound Hebrew
learning then resided with the Jewish doctors, and so the
Protestant scholars became their disciples.

But it would be absurd to suppose that the men who
refused to accept the authority of *Christian* tradition as to the
number of books in the canon, the best text of the Old Testament, or the principles upon which that text is to be translated, adopted it as a principle of faith that the *Jewish* tradition upon all these points is final. Luther again and again
showed that he submitted to no such authority; and if the
Reformers and their first successors practically accepted the
results of Jewish scholarship upon all these questions, they
did so merely because these results were in accordance with
the best lights then attainable. It was left for a later generation, which had lost the courage of the first Reformers
because it had lost much of their clear insight into divine
things, to substitute an authoritative Jewish tradition for the
authoritative tradition of the Catholic Church—to swear by
the Jewish canon and the Massoretic text as the Romanists
swore by the Tridentine canon and the Vulgate text. The
Reformers had too much reverence for God's Word to subject
it to the bondage of any tradition. They would gladly have
accepted any further light of learning, carrying them back
behind the time of Rabbinical Judaism to the first ages of
the Old Testament writings.

Scholarship moved onwards, and as research was carried
farther it gradually became plain that it was possible for
Biblical students, with the material still preserved to them,
to get behind the Jewish Rabbins, upon whom our translators
were still dependent, and to draw from the sacred stream at
a point nearer its source. I have now to explain how this
was seen to be the case.

From the time when the Old Testament was written,

down to the sixteenth century, there was no continuous
tradition of sound Hebrew learning except among the Jews.
The little that Christians knew about the Old Testament at
first hand had always come from the Rabbins. Among the
Jews, on the contrary, there was a continuous scholarly tradition. The knowledge of Hebrew and the most received ways
of explaining the Old Testament were handed down from
generation to generation along with the original text. I ask
you to understand precisely what this means. Before the
time of Christ, the Jews had already ceased to speak Hebrew.
In the New Testament, no doubt, we read once and again of
the Hebrew tongue as spoken and understood by the people
of Palestine ; but the vernacular of the Palestinian Jews in
the first century was a dialect as unlike to that of the
Bible as German is to English—a different language, although
a kindred one. This language is called Hebrew because it
was spoken by the Hebrews, just as the Spanish Jews in
Constantinople at the present day call their Spanish jargon
Hebrew. It was a form of Western Aramaic, which the
Jews had gradually substituted for the tongue of their ancestors, after their return from captivity, when they found themselves a small handful living in the midst of nations who
spoke Aramaic, and with whom they had constant dealings.
In those days Aramaic was the language of business and of
government in the countries between the Euphrates and the
Mediterranean, just as English is in the Highlands of Scotland, and so the Jews forgot their own tongue for it, as the
Scottish Celts are now forgetting Gaelic for English. This
process had already gone on to a great extent before the latest
books of the Old Testament were completed.[1] Such writers

---

[1] On the assumption that the Aramaic part of Daniel was written in
Chaldæa by Daniel himself, the Biblical Aramaic used to be called Chaldee,
and it was supposed that the Jews forgot their old tongue and learned that of
Chaldæa during the Captivity. It is now known that this opinion is altogether false. The Aramaic dialect of the Jews in Palestine, of which the

as the authors of Chronicles and Ecclesiastes still use the old
language of Israel for literary purposes, but in a way which
shows that their thoughts often ran not in Hebrew but in
Aramaic.   They use Aramaic words and idioms which would
have puzzled Moses and David, and in some of the later Old
Testament books, in Ezra and in Daniel, although not in
those parts of the former book which are autobiographical
and written by Ezra himself, there actually are inserted in
the Hebrew long Aramaic passages.   Before the time of
Christ, people who were not scholars had ceased to understand Hebrew altogether;[1] and in the synagogue, when the
Bible was read, a *Meturgeman*, as he was called, that is, a
"dragoman," or qualified translator, had to rise and give the
sense of the passage in the vulgar dialect.   The Pentateuch
was read verse by verse, or in lessons from the Prophets
three verses were read together, and then the Meturgeman
rose, and did not read, but give orally in Aramaic the sense
of the original.[2]   The old Hebrew, then, was by this time a

so-called Chaldee parts of Ezra and Daniel are the oldest monuments, is not
Babylonian, but Western in character, as appears unmistakably by comparison with the Aramaic monuments of other districts west of the Euphrates.
Peculiarities, for example, which used to be characterised as Hebraisms,
reappear on the Palmyrene and Nabatæan inscriptions.   The Jews, therefore,
lost their Hebrew, and learned Aramaic in Palestine after the return.   They
certainly still spoke Hebrew in the time of Nehemiah, whose indignation
against the contamination of the Jewish speech by the dialect of Ashdod
(Neh. xiii. 24) is quite unintelligible on any other supposition.   Compare for
the whole subject Nöldeke's article, SEMITIC LANGUAGES, in the ninth edition
of the *Encyclopædia Britannica*.

[1] See the evidence of this from the Rabbinical literature in Zunz's *Gottesdienstliche Vorträge der Juden*, p. 7 (Berlin, 1832).   Our Lord upon the cross
quoted Ps. xxii. in a Targum.

[2] Mishna, *Megilla*, iv. 4.—"He who reads in the Pentateuch must not
read to the Meturgeman more than one verse, and in the prophets three
verses.   If each verse is a paragraph, they are read one by one.   The reader
may skip in the prophets, but not in the law.   How long may he spend in
searching for another passage ?   So long as the Meturgeman goes on speaking."
The practice of oral translation into Aramaic led ultimately to the formation of
written Targums or Aramaic paraphrases ; but these were long discouraged by
the Scribes.

learned language, acquired not in common life but from a teacher. In order to learn it, the young Jew had to go to school, but he had no grammar or lexicon, or other written help, to assist him. Everything was done by oral instruction, and by dint of sheer memory, without any scientific principle. In the first place, the pupil had to learn to read. In our Hebrew Bibles now, the pronunciation of each word is exactly represented. This is done by a double notation. The letters proper are the consonants, and the vowels are indicated by small marks placed above or below the line of the consonants. These small marks are a late invention. They did not exist in the time of Christ, or even four hundred years after the Christian era, at the time of Jerome.[1] Before this invention the proper pronunciation of each difficult word had to be acquired from a master. When a pupil had learned to read a phrase correctly, he was taught the meaning of the words, and by such exercises, combined with the practice of constantly speaking Hebrew, which was kept up in the Jewish schools, as the practice of speaking Latin used to be kept up

---

[1] The structure of the Semitic languages makes it much easier to dispense with the vowels than an English reader might suppose. The chief difficulty lay with vowels, or still more with diphthongs, at the end of a word, and was met at a very early date by the use of weak consonants to indicate cognate vowel-sounds (e.g. W = au, u ; Y = ai, i). Such vowel-consonants are found even on the stone of Mesha, and have been adopted in various measure, not only in Hebrew, but in Syriac and Arabic. But in all these languages the plan of marking every vowel-sound by points above or below the line came in comparatively late, was developed slowly, and never extended to all books. The testimonies of the Talmudists and of Jerome are quite express to show that at their time the true vocalisation of ambiguous words was known only by oral teaching. Jerome, for example, says that in Hab. iii. 5 the Hebrew has only D, B, and R, without any vowel, which may be read either as *dabar*, "word," or *deber*, "plague." A supposed interest of orthodoxy long led good scholars like the Buxtorfs to fight for the antiquity and authority of the points. There is now no question on the subject ; for MSS. brought from Southern Russia and Arabia, containing a different notation for the vowels, prove that our present system is not only comparatively recent, but is the outcome of a gradual process, in which several methods were tried in different parts of the Jewish world. The rolls read in the synagogue are still un-pointed, a relic of the old condition of all MSS. Compare Lect. III. p. 58 *sq*.

in our grammar schools, the pupil gradually learned to understand the sacred texts and at the same time acquired a certain practical fluency in speaking or writing a degraded form of Hebrew, with many barbarous words and still more barbarous constructions, such as are certain to creep into any language which is dead in ordinary life and yet is daily used by teachers and learners, not as a mere philological exercise but as a vehicle of practical instruction in law, theology, and the like. The Jews themselves recognised the difference between this pedantic jargon and the language of their ancient books. The language of the Bible was called "the holy tongue," while the Hebrew spoken in the schools was called "the language of the wise." We have many volumes of the composition of these scholars, chiefly legal works, with some old *midrashim*, as they are called, or sermonising commentaries on Scripture. These books no doubt are Hebrew in a certain sense, but they are as unlike to the Biblical Hebrew as a lawyer's deed is to a page of Cicero. The men who wrote such a jargon could not have any delicate perception for the niceties of the old classical language, especially as it is written in the most ancient books ; and when they came to a difficult passage they could only guess at the sense, unless they possessed an interpretation of the hard text, and the hard words it contained, handed down to them from some older scholar.

Now let me ask you once more to realise precisely how these scribes, at and before the time of Christ, proceeded in dealing with the Bible. They had nothing before them but the bare consonantal text, so that the same words might often be read and interpreted in two different ways. A familiar example of this is given in Heb. xi. 21, where we read of Jacob leaning upon the top of his "staff ; " but when we turn to the Hebrew Bible, as it is now printed (Genesis xlvii. 31), we there find nothing about the "staff ; " we find the "bed."

Well, the Hebrew for "the bed" is "HaMmiTtaH," while the Hebrew for "the staff" is "HaMmaTteH." The consonants in these two words are the same; the vowels are different; but the consonants only were written, and doubled consonants were written only once, so that all that appeared in MSS. was HMTH. Thus it was quite possible for one person to read the word as "bed," as the translators of our English Bible did, following the reading of the Hebrew scribes, and for the author of the Epistle to the Hebrews, on the other hand, to understand it as a "staff," following the interpretation of the Greek Septuagint.

Beyond the bare text, which in this way was often ambiguous, the scribes had no guide but oral teaching. They had no rules of grammar to go by; the kind of Hebrew which they themselves wrote often admitted grammatical constructions which the old language forbade, and when they came to an obsolete word or idiom, they depended on their masters to give them the pronunciation and the sense. Now, beyond doubt, the Jewish scholars were most exact and retentive learners, and their teachers spared no pains to teach them all that they knew. We in the West have little idea of the precision with which an Eastern pupil even now can take up and remember the minutest details of a lesson, reproducing them years afterwards in the exact words of his master. But memory, even when cultivated as it is cultivated in the schools of the East, is at best fallible; and even if we could suppose that the whole of the Bible had been taught word by word in the schools, in unbroken succession from the day on which each book was first written, it would still have required a continued miracle to preserve all these lessons perfectly, and without writing, through long generations. But in point of fact the traditional teaching of the Jews was neither complete, nor continuous from the first, nor uniform.

It was not complete; that is, there never was an authoritative interpretation of the whole Bible. It was not continuous ; that is, many interpretations, which attained general currency and authority, had not been received by unbroken tradition from the time when the passage was first written, or even from the time when Hebrew became a dead language, but were mere figments of the Rabbins devised out of their own heads. And finally, the Rabbinical tradition was not uniform ; that is, the interpretation and even the reading of individual texts was often a subject of controversy in the schools of the Scribes, and at different times we find different interpretations in the ascendant. The proof of these propositions lies partly in the records of Jewish learning still preserved in the Rabbinical literature ; partly it lies in the translations and interpretations made at various times by Jewish scholars or under their guidance.

So long as the transmission and interpretation of the Bible were left to the unregulated labours of individual scholars or copyists, it is plain that individual theories and individual errors would have some influence on the work. The Bible had to be copied by the pen. Let us suppose then that the copyist, without any special instruction or guide, simply sat down to make a transcript, probably writing from dictation, of a roll which he had bought or borrowed. In the first place, he was almost certain to make some slips, either of the pen or of the ear ; but besides this, in all probability the volume before him would contain slips of the previous copyist. Was he to copy these mistakes exactly as they stood, and so perpetuate the error, or would he not in very many cases think himself able to detect and correct the slips of his predecessor ? If he took the latter course, it was very possible for him to overrate his own capacity and introduce a new mistake. And so bit by bit, if there were no control, if each scribe acted independently, and without the assistance of a regular school, errors were sure to be multiplied, and the text would be certain to present many variations. Thus we know that even in recent times the Gaelic version of the Old Testament contains certain alterations upon the original text made in order to remove seeming contradictions. Much more were such changes to be anticipated in ancient times, when there was a far less developed sense of responsibility with regard to the exact verbal transcription of old texts. A uniform and scrupulous tradition, watching over the reading and the meaning of the text in all parts of the Jewish world, could only be transmitted by a regular school of learned doctors, or, as the Jewish records call them, Scribes, in Hebrew *Sôpherîm* or men of the book—men who were professionally occupied with the book of the law.

We are all familiar with the Scribes, or professed Biblical scholars, as they appear in the New Testament. They were not merely, or primarily, verbal scholars, but, above all things, practical lawyers and theologians, who used their linguistic knowledge to support their own doctrines and principles. Their principles at that epoch, as we know, were those of the Pharisees ; in fact, the Pharisees were nothing else than the party of the Scribes, in opposition to the Sadducees or aristocratic party, whose heads were the higher priestly nobility. To the Pharisees, or party of the Scribes, belonged the great mass of Jewish scholars who were not closely associated with the higher ranks of the priesthood, together with many who, without being scholars, were eager to obey the law as the Scribes interpreted it. The Scribes were the men who had in their hands the transmission and interpretation of the Old Testament ; and our next task, in endeavouring to understand the steps by which the Old Testament has been handed down to us, must be to obtain a clear vision of their methods and objects, and of the work which they actually did upon the text of the Bible. This subject will occupy our attention in the next Lecture.

LECTURE III

THE SCRIBES [1]

THE subject with which we are to be occupied to-day is the part that was played by the Scribes in the preservation and transmission of the Old Testament. At the close of last Lecture we looked for a moment at the Scribes as they appear in the New Testament in association with the Pharisees. At that time, as one sees from the Gospels and the Acts, they constituted a party long established, and exercising a great and recognised influence in the Jewish state. In fact they can be traced back as far as the later times of the Old Testament. Their father is Ezra, "the Scribe," as he is called *par excellence*, who came from Babylon to Judæa with the law of God in his hand (Ezra vii. 14), and with a heart "prepared to study the law of the Lord, to do it, and to teach in Israel

---

[1] For the history of the period covered by this Lecture the best and most complete book is Schürer, *Gesch. des Jüdischen Volkes im Zeitalter Jesu Christi*, 2 vols., Leipzig, 1886, 1890 (also in an English translation), where a full account of the literature of the subject will be found. More popular and very useful is W. D. Morrison, *The Jews under Roman Rule*, in the "Story of the Nations" Series (2d ed., London, 1891). Wellhausen's monograph, *Die Pharisäer und die Sadducäer* (Greifswald, 1874), and the later chapters of Kuenen's *Religion of Israel* (Eng. trans., vol. iii., London, 1875), may also be specially recommended to the student; and among works by Jewish authors, J. Derenbourg, *Essai sur l'histoire . . . de la Palestine* (Paris, 1867). The oldest and most important traditions about the early Scribes are found in the Mishnic treatise *Aboth*, which has been edited, with an English version and notes, by Dr. C. Taylor (*Sayings of the Jewish Fathers*, Cambridge, 1877), and with German notes by Prof. H. Strack (Leipzig, 1882).

statutes and judgments" (Ezra vii. 10). Ezra accomplished
this task, not immediately, but with ultimate and complete
success. He did so with the support of the Persian king,
and with the active assistance of Nehemiah, who had been
sent by Artaxerxes as governor of Jerusalem. At a great
public meeting convened by Nehemiah, of which we read an
account in chapters viii. to x. of the book which bears his
name, the Law was openly read before the people at the
Feast of Tabernacles, and, with confession and penitence, the
Jews entered into a national covenant to make that law
henceforth the rule of their lives. Now I do not ask at present what were the relations of the people to the Law before
the time of Ezra. That question must come up afterwards;
but any one who reads with attention the narrative in the
book of Nehemiah must be satisfied that this work of Ezra,
and the covenant which the people took upon them to obey
the Law, were of epoch-making importance for the Jewish
community. It was not merely a covenant to amend certain
abuses in detailed points of legal observance; for the people
in their confession very distinctly state that the Law had not
been observed by their ancestors, their rulers, or their priests,
up to that time (Neh. ix. 34); and in particular it is mentioned that the Feast of Tabernacles had never been observed
with the ceremonial prescribed in the Law from the time that
the Israelites occupied Canaan under Joshua (Neh. viii. 17).
Accordingly this covenant must be regarded as a critical
epoch in the history of the community of Israel. From that
time forward, with the assistance and under the approval of
the Persian king, the Law—that is, the Pentateuch or Torah,
as we now have it, for there can be no doubt that the Law
which was in Ezra's hands was practically identical with our
present Hebrew Pentateuch—became the religious and municipal code of Israel. Now the Pentateuch, viewed as a code,
is such a book as imperatively calls for a class of trained

lawyers to be its interpreters. I do not ask at present whether, as most critics suppose, there are real contradictions between the laws given in different parts of the five books of Moses. At all events, it is a familiar fact that those who maintain that all the Pentateuchal laws can be reconciled, differ very much among themselves as to the precise method of reconciliation. In such an ambiguity of the Law it is manifest that the Scribes had an indispensable function as guides of the people to that interpretation which was in actual use in the practical administration of the code. Accordingly, by and by, in the time of the Chronicler (1 Chron. ii. 55), we find them organised in regular "families," or, as we should now say, "guilds," an institution quite in accordance with the whole spirit of the East, which forms a guild or trades-union of every class possessing special technical knowledge.

We see, then, that before the close of the Old Testament Canon the Scribes not only existed, continuing the work of Ezra, but that they existed in the form of guilds or regular societies. What were their objects? There can be no doubt that from the first the objects of the Scribes were not philological and literary, but practical. Ezra's object was so. He came to make the Law the practical rule of Israel's life, and so it was still in later ages. The wisdom of the Scribes consisted of two parts, which in Jewish terminology were respectively called "Halacha" and "Haggada." "Halacha" was legal teaching, systematised legal precept; while "Haggada" was doctrinal and practical admonition, mingled with parable and legend. But of these two parts the "Halacha," —that is, the system of rules applying the Pentateuchal law to every case of practice and every detail of life,—was always the chief thing. The difference between the learned theologian and the unlearned vulgar lay in knowledge of the Law. You remember what the Pharisees say in John vii. 49—"This people, which knoweth not the law, are cursed." The Law

was the ideal of the Scribes. Their theory of the history of
Israel was this :—In time past Israel had been chastised by
God's wrath ; the cause of this chastisement was that the
people had neglected the Law. Forgetting the Law, Israel
had passed and was still passing through many tribulations,
and was subjected to the yoke of a foreign power. What
was the duty of the Jews in this condition of things ? According to the Scribes, it was not to engage in any political
scheme whatever for throwing off the foreign yoke, but to
establish the Law in their own midst,—to apply themselves,
not only to obey the whole Torah, particularly in its ceremonial precepts, but so to develop these precepts that they
might embrace every minute detail of life. Then, when by
this means Israel had become a law-obeying nation in the
fullest sense of the word, Jehovah Himself, in His righteousness, would intervene, miraculously remove the scourge, and
establish the glory of His law-fulfilling people. These were
the principles of the Scribes and the Pharisees, the principles
spoken of by Paul in writing to the Romans, when he tells
us that Israel followed after a law of righteousness without
attaining to it ; that they, being ignorant of God's righteousness, and going about to establish their own, did not submit
themselves to the righteousness of God (Rom. ix. 31, x. 3).

All that the Scribes did for the transmission, preservation,
and interpretation of the Old Testament, was guided by their
legal aims. In the first instance, they were not scholars, not
preachers, but "lawyers" (νομικοί), as they are often called
in the New Testament. In their juridical decisions they were
guided partly by study of the Pentateuch, but partly also by
observation of the actual legal usages of their time, by those
views of the Law which were practically acknowledged, for
example, in the ceremonial of the temple and the priesthood.
There was thus, in the wisdom of the Scribes, an element of
use and wont,—an element of common law, which of course

existed in Jerusalem, as in every other living community, side by side with the codified written law ; and this element of common law, or use and wont, was the source of the theory of legal tradition familiar to all of us from allusions in the New Testament. According to this theory, Moses himself had delivered to Israel an oral law along with the written Torah. The oral law was as old as the Pentateuch, and had come down in authentic form through the prophets to Ezra. The conception of an oral law, as old and venerable as the written law, necessarily influenced the Scribes in all their interpretations of Scripture. It introduced into their handling of Scripture an element of uncertainty and falsity, upon which Jesus Himself, as you will remember, put His finger, with that unfailing insight of His into the unsound parts of the religious state of His time. Through their theory of the traditional law the Scribes were led into many a departure from the spirit, and even from the letter of the written Word (Matt. xii. 1-8, xv. 1-20, xxiii.).

To the Scribes, then, the whole law, written and oral, was of equal practical authority. What they really sought to preserve intact, and hand down as binding for Israel, was not so much the written text of the Pentateuch as their own rules, —partly derived from the Pentateuch, but partly, as we have seen, from other sources,—which they honestly believed to be equally an expression of the mind of the Revealer, even in cases where they had no basis in Scripture, or only the basis of some very strained interpretation. Now, you can readily conceive that the traditional interpretation of the law could not be stationary. In fact, we know that it was not so. The subject has been gone into with great care by Jewish scholars, who are more interested than we are in the traditional law ; and they have been able to prove, from their own books and written records of the legal traditions, that the law underwent, from century to century, not a few changes. This was no more than natural. So long as a nation has a national life, lives and develops new practical necessities, there must also from time to time be changes in the law and its application. In part, then, the growth of the traditional law was owing to changes and new necessities of the national life. It would doubtless, from this source alone, have grown and changed very much more, but for the fact that during the centuries between Ezra and Christ the Jews were almost continuously under foreign domination, so that they had not perfect freedom of civil or even religious development. At the same time, they always retained a certain amount of municipal independence; and so long as the municipal life remained active, the law necessarily underwent modifications from time to time.

But there was another reason for continual changes in the traditional law. The party headed by the Scribes, which finally developed into the sect of the Pharisees, were so carried away with the idea that God's blessing on Israel and the removal of all national calamity depended on a punctilious observance of the minutest legal ordinances, that they deemed it necessary to make, as they put it, "a hedge round the Law" —in other words, to fence in the life of the Israelite with new precepts of their own devising, at every point where the boundary line between the legal and the illegal appeared to be indistinctly marked. There was therefore a constant tendency to add new and more complicated precepts of conduct, and especially of ceremonial observance, to those already prescribed in the Pentateuch and in the oldest form of tradition, so that it might be impossible for a man, if he held by all traditional rules, to come even within sight of a possible breach of the Law.

The legal system thus developed had not at first the weight of an authoritative legislation; for the Scribes and Pharisees were not the governing class in Judæa. The rulers of the nation in its internal matters were the priestly aristo-

cracy, with the high priest at their head as a sort of hereditary
prince over Israel. And in the decay of the Greek power
in Syria, when the Jews were able for a time to assert their
political independence, the Hasmonean or Maccabee priest-
princes were the actual sovereigns of Judæa (142-37 B.C.)
Nevertheless the great Rabbins of the party of Scribes were
men whose legal ability gained for them a commanding
position and influence ; the mass of the Pharisees, by their
claim of special sanctity and special legality, also acquired
great weight with the common people ; and in consequence
of this the authority of the party ultimately became so great
that, as we learn from Josephus, the priestly aristocracy, who
were the civil as well as the religious heads of the Jews, and
who themselves were no more inclined than any other aristocracy to make changes that were not for their own personal
profit, yet found themselves compelled by the pressure of
public opinion to defer in almost every instance to the
doctrines of the Scribes.[1] The municipal and legal ad-

[1] Josephus, *Antiquities*, xiii. 10, § 6.—"The Sadducees had only the well-
to-do classes on their side. The populace would not follow them ; but the
Pharisees had the multitude as auxiliaries." *Ibid.* xviii. 1, § 4 : "The Sadducees are the men of highest rank, but they effect as good as nothing, for in
affairs of government they are compelled against their will to follow the dicta
of the Pharisees, as the masses would otherwise refuse to tolerate them."

The best account of the relative position of the Scribes and the governing
class at different periods is given in Wellhausen's monograph on the Pharisees
and Sadducees cited above. See also Ryle and James, *Psalms of the Pharisees,
commonly called the Psalms of Solomon* (Cambridge, 1891). On the position
of the two parties in the Sanhedrin, Kuenen's essay *Over de samenstelling van
het Sanhedrin*, in the Proceedings of the Royal Society of Amsterdam, 1866,
is conclusive. On this topic, and on the whole meaning of the antithesis of
the Pharisees and Sadducees, older scholars went astray by following too
closely the unhistorical views of later Jewish tradition. When Judaism had
ceased to have a national existence, and was merely a religious sect, the
schoolmen naturally became its heads ; and the tradition assumed that it had
always been so, and that the whole history of the nation was made up of such
theological and legal controversies as engrossed the attention of later times.
(See Taylor's *Sayings of the Fathers*, Excursus III.). This view bears its
condemnation on its face. Before the fall of the state the party of the Scribes
was opposed, not to another theological sect, but to the aristocracy, which

ministration took place by means of councils bearing the name of Synedria or Sanhedrin. There was a central council with judicial and administrative authority—the Great Sanhedrin in Jerusalem—and there were local councils in provincial towns. These councils were mainly occupied by Sadducees, or men of the aristocratic party; but ultimately the Scribes, as trained lawyers, gained a considerable proportion of seats in them; and during the latter time of the Maccabees under Queen Salome, and still more after the fall of the Hasmonean dynasty, when it was the policy of Herod the Great to crush the old nobility and play off the Pharisees against them, the influence of the Scribes in the national councils of justice came greatly to outweigh that of the aristocratic Sadducees. In this way, as you will observe, the interpreters of the law had a very important place in the practical life of Israel; and they continued active, developing and applying their legal system, until the overthrow of the city by Titus in A.D. 70. When the Temple was destroyed and the nationality crushed, a great part of the public ordinances decreed by the Scribes necessarily fell into desuetude; the private and personal observances of ceremonial righteous-

in the high priesthood, and pursued practical objects of political aggrandisement on very different lines from those of scholastic that the Sadducees are the party headed by the chief priests, as the party of the Scribes, is plain from the New Testament, Acts v. 17. The higher priesthood was in spirit a very secular interested in war and diplomacy than in the service of the theological tenets of the Sadducees, as they appear in the New Josephus, had a purely political basis. They detested the resurrection and the fatalism of the Pharisees, because these used by their adversaries to thwart their political aims. suffered a great loss of position by the subjection to a foreign which they had ruled in the early Hasmonean period, was a great prince. But the Pharisees discouraged all ness was only to seek after the righteousness of the the nation would follow in due time, without man's action would compensate those who had suffered in this reward made it superfluous for them to seek a

4

ness were still insisted upon, and in one sense the Scribes
became more influential than ever; for those parts of the law
which could still be put in force were the only remaining
expression of national spirit, and the doctors of the law were
accepted as the natural leaders of all loyal Jews. Now for
the first time Judaism and Pharisaism became identical; for
Pharisaism alone, with its strict code of ceremonial observance, made it possible for the Jew to remain a Jew when the
state had perished and the Temple lay in ruins. But at the
same time the legal system ceased to be subject to the play
of those living forces which during the ages of natio
municipal independence had continually modified i
Further development became impossible, or was
much narrower range; and after the last des
of the Jews for liberty under Hadrian, 13
Scribes, no longer able to find a practi
influence in the guidance of the state,
systematising and writing down the
stage which it had then reached.
shape in the collection which is c
completed by Rabbi Judah the

[1] The word *Mishna* means "instr
tion." From the same root in Ara
the name of *Tanná*, teacher (rep
collection and interpretation of
of scholars whose contribution
a vast and desultory comme
one Palestinian, the othe
recension of the Mishnic
be lost, but has recentl
bridge, 1883). The
Mishna and Gemar
was not complete
The whole M
G. Surenhusiu
translation
Jost (Berli
treatises,
Raphall

ministration took place by means of councils bearing the name of Synedria or Sanhedrin. There was a central cour with judicial and administrative authority—the Great Sanhe drin in Jerusalem—and there were local councils in provincial towns. These councils were mainly occupied by Sadducees, or men of the aristocratic party; but ultimately the Scribes, as trained lawyers, gained a considerable proportion of seats in them; and during the latter time of the Maccabees under Queen Salome, and still more after the fall of the Hasmonean dynasty, when it was the policy of Herod the Great to crush the old nobility and play off the Pharisees against them, the influence of the Scribes in the national councils of justice came greatly to outweigh that of the aristocratic Sadducees. In this way, as you will observe, the interpreters of the law gained a very important place in the practical life of Israel; and they continued active, developing and applying their peculiar system, until the overthrow of the city by Titus in the year A.D. 70. When the Temple was destroyed and the Jewish nationality crushed, a great part of the public ordinances decreed by the Scribes necessarily fell into desuetude; but private and personal observances of ceremonial righteous-

---

had its centre in the high priesthood, and pursued practical objects of political and social aggrandisement on very different lines from those of scholastic controversy. That the Sadducees are the party headed by the chief priests, and the Pharisees the party of the Scribes, is plain from the New Testament, especially from Acts v. 17. The higher priesthood was in spirit a very secular nobility, more interested in war and diplomacy than in the service of the Temple. The theological tenets of the Sadducees, as they appear in the New Testament and Josephus, had a purely political basis. They detested the doctrine of the Resurrection and the fatalism of the Pharisees, because these opinions were employed by their adversaries to thwart their political aims. The aristocracy suffered a great loss of position by the subjection to a foreign power of the nation which they had ruled in the early Hasmonean period, when the high priest was a great prince. But the Pharisees discouraged all rebellion. Israel's business was only to seek after the righteousness of the law. The redemption of the nation would follow in due time, without man's interference. The resurrection would compensate those who had suffered in this life, and the hope of this reward made it superfluous for them to seek a present deliverance.

4

ess were still insisted upon, and in one sense the Scribes
came more influential than ever; for those parts of the law
which could still be put in force were the only remaining
expression of national spirit, and the doctors of the law were
accepted as the natural leaders of all loyal Jews. Now for
the first time Judaism and Pharisaism became identical; for
Pharisaism alone, with its strict code of ceremonial observance, made it possible for the Jew to remain a Jew when the
state had perished and the Temple lay in ruins. But at the
same time the legal system ceased to be subject to the play
of those living forces which during the ages of national or
municipal independence had continually modified its details.
Further development became impossible, or was limited to a
much narrower range; and after the last desperate struggle
of the Jews for liberty under Hadrian, 132 to 135 A.D., the
Scribes, no longer able to find a practical outlet for their
influence in the guidance of the state, devoted themselves to
systematising and writing down the traditional law in the
stage which it had then reached. This systematisation took
shape in the collection which is called the Mishna, which was
completed by Rabbi Judah the Holy about 200 A.D.[1]

---

[1] The word *Mishna* means "instruction," literally "repetition," "inculca-
tion." From the same root in Aramaic form the doctors of the Mishna bear
the name of *Tanná*, teacher (repeater). After the close of the Mishna the
collection and interpretation of tradition was carried on by a new succession
of scholars whose contributions make up the *Gemara* ("decision," "doctrine"),
a vast and desultory commentary on the Mishna. There are two Gemaras,
one Palestinian, the other Babylonian, and each of these rests on a new
recension of the Mishnic text. The Palestinian Mishna was long supposed to
be lost, but has recently been printed by Lowe from a Cambridge MS. (Cambridge, 1883). The name for a doctor of the Gemara is *Amôra*, speaker.
Mishna and Gemara together make up the Talmud. The Babylonian Gemara
was not completed till the sixth century of our era.

The whole Mishna was published, with a Latin translation and notes, by
G. Surenhusius, in 6 vols. folio (Amsterdam, 1698-1703). There is a German
translation by Rabe (1760-1763), and another printed in Hebrew letters by
Jost (Berlin, 1832-1834). There is no complete English version, but eighteen
treatises, still important for the daily life of the Jews, were translated by
Raphall and De Sola (London, 1845). Another selection is given by Dr.

I have directed your attention to the history of the traditional law because its transmission is inseparably bound up with the transmission of the text of the Bible. As we have seen, the whole law, written and oral, was one in the estimation of the Scribes. The early versions and the early Jewish commentaries show us that the interpretation of the Pentateuch was guided by legal much rather than by philological principles. The Bible was understood by the help of the Halacha quite as much as the Halacha was based upon the Bible ; and so, as the traditional law underwent many changes, these reacted upon the interpretation and even to a certain extent upon the reading of the text of the Pentateuch. Let me take an example of this from what we find in the Bible itself. In Neh. x. 32 [33] we read that the people made a law for themselves, charging themselves with a yearly poll-tax of one-third of a shekel for the service of the Temple. In the time of Christ this tribute of one-third of a shekel had been increased to half a shekel (*didrachma* ; Matt. xvii. 24) ; and the impost which in the time of Nehemiah was a tax voluntarily taken upon themselves by the people without any written warrant, was in this later time supposed to be based upon Exodus xxx. 12-16. This view of the matter, indeed, is already taken by the Chronicler ; for he speaks of a yearly Mosaic impost for the maintenance of the Temple (2 Chron. xxiv. 5, 6), and therefore even in his time the law of Exodus must have been held to be the basis of the poll-tax. Yet that tax was a new tax ; it was first devised in the time of Nehemiah ; and it is only an afterthought of the Scribes to base it upon the Pentateuch.[1] This example illustrates one

Barclay, the late Bishop of Jerusalem, in his work, *The Talmud* (London, 1878). See further the article MISHNA, by Dr. Schiller-Szinessy, in the ninth edition of the *Encyclopædia Britannica*.

[1] For the purpose in hand it is not necessary to carry the argument further. But it may be observed that on the facts we must make a choice between two alternatives. Either Exod. xxx. is simply the historical record of an

way in which the conception of the law changed in the hands
of the Scribes. In other cases they actually took it upon
themselves to alter Pentateuchal laws. For example, the
tithes were transferred from the Levites to the priests, and
the use of the liturgy prescribed in Deuteronomy xxvi. 12-15
on occasion of the tithing, which was not suitable after that
change had been made, was abolished by John Hyrcanus,
the Hasmonean prince and high priest.[1] These are but single
examples out of many which might be adduced, but they are
enough to show that so long as the development of the oral
law was running its course, the written law was treated by
the Scribes with a certain measure of freedom.

Their real interest, I repeat, lay not in the sacred text
itself, but in the practical system based upon it. That comes
out very forcibly in repeated passages of the Rabbinical
writings, in which the study of Scripture is spoken of almost
contemptuously, as something far inferior to the study of the
traditional legislative system.

Now, people often think of the Jews as entirely absorbed,
from the very first, in the exact grammatical study and literal
preservation of the written Word. Had this been so, they
could never have devised so many expositions which are

---

impost once levied by Moses for a special purpose (and so it is taken in Exod.
xxxviii. 21-31), in which case we see that it was not made the ground of a
permanent ordinance till after the time of Nehemiah ; or, on the other hand,
Exod. xxx. 11 *sqq.* is meant as a general ordinance for future ages, in which
case the passage cannot have been written till after Nehemiah's time. In
support of the latter view see Kuenen, *Onderzoek*, 2d ed., I. i. § 15, note 30.
The point will be touched on again in Lecture XII.

[1] Mishna, *Maaser Sheni*, v. 15 (ed. Surenh., vol. i. p. 287), and *Sota*, ix.
10, with Wagenseil's note in Surenh., iii. 296. This is the earlier and undoubtedly the historical account, but the Gemara tries to establish the change
on a better footing by ascribing it to Ezra, who thus punished the Levites for
refusing to return from Babylon—an account which is in flat contradiction
with Nehem. x. 37 [38]. See Wellhausen, *Prolegomena*, p. 172 *sq.* On the
change in the law of redemption, introduced by Hillel, which is another
example in point, see Derenbourg, *Essai* (Paris, 1867), p. 188. Compare also
Zunz, *Gottesdienstliche Vorträge der Juden*, pp. 11, 45 (Berlin, 1832).

plainly against the idiom of the Hebrew language, but which
flowed naturally and easily from the legal positions then
current.   The early Scribes had neither the inclination nor
the philological qualifications for exact scholarly study, and
when they did lay weight upon some verbal nicety of the
sacred Text, they did so in the interest of their legal theories,
and upon principles to which we can assign no value.   No
doubt the Scribes and their successors in the Talmudic times
(200 to 600 A.D.) must themselves have been often aware that
the meanings which they forced upon texts, in order to carry
out their legal system, were not natural and idiomatic renderings.   But this did not greatly trouble them, for it was to
them an axiom that the oral and the written laws were one
system, and therefore they were bound to harmonise the two
at any sacrifice of the rules of language.   The objections to
such an arbitrary exegesis did not come to be strongly felt
till long after the Talmudic period, when a new school of
Jewish scholars arose, who had grammatical and scientific
knowledge, mainly derived from the learning of the Arabs.
When in the Middle Ages these Rabbins introduced a stricter
system of grammatical interpretation, it came to be felt that
the Talmudic way of dealing with Scripture was often forced
and unnatural, and so it was found necessary to draw a sharp
distinction between the traditional Talmudic interpretation
of any text, which continued to have the value of an indisputable legal authority, and the grammatical interpretation
or *P'shat*, representing that exact and natural sense of the
passage which more modern study had enabled men to determine with sharpness and precision.

The mediæval Rabbins concentrated their attention on the
plain grammatical sense of Scripture, and their best doctors,
who were the masters of our Protestant translators, rose much
above the Talmudical exegesis, although they never altogether
shook off the false principle that a good sense must be got

out of everything, and that if it cannot be got out of the text by the rules of grammar, these rules must give way. Even our own Bible, which rests almost entirely upon the better or grammatical school of Jewish interpretation, does, in some passages, show traces of the Talmudical weakness of determining to harmonise things, and get over difficulties, even at the expense of strict grammar; but this false tendency was confined within narrow limits ; and, on the whole, the influence of the Talmudists was almost completely conquered in the Protestant versions, although it is still felt in the harmonistic exegesis of the anti-critical school.[1]

A much more serious question is raised by the consideration that although we are able to correct the interpretation of the ancient Scribes, we have the text of the Hebrew Old Testament as they gave it to us ; and we must therefore inquire whether they were in a position to hand down to us the best possible text. Let me illustrate the significance of this question, by referring to the history of the text of the New Testament. The books of the New Testament circulated in manuscript copies, and it is by a comparison of such old codices as still remain to us that scholars adjust the printed texts of their modern editions. The comparison shows that

---

[1] The point in which the exegesis of the Mediæval Jews (and of King James's translators) was most defective was that they always assumed it to be possible to interpret what lay before them, and would not recognise that many difficulties arise from corruption of the text. In a book of profane antiquity, a passage that cannot be construed grammatically is at once assumed to be corrupt, and a remedy is sought from MSS. or conjecture. The Jews, and until recently the great majority of Christian scholars, refused to admit this principle for the Hebrew Scriptures. The Septuagint proves the existence of corruptions in the Hebrew text, and often supplies the correction. But many corruptions are older than the Septuagint version, and can be dealt with only by conjectural emendation. The English reader may form a fair idea of the state of the Old Testament text, and of what has been done by modern scholarship to correct it, from the notes of Professors Cheyne and Driver in the *Variorum Bible*, 3d ed., 1889 (Eyre and Spottiswoode).

Examples of the few cases where the Authorised Version has been misled by dogmatical or historical prepossessions will come before us in the course of these Lectures.

the old copies often differ in their readings. Some of the variations are mere slips of the transcriber, which any Greek scholar can correct as readily as one corrects a slip made in writing a letter; but others are more serious. Those of you who have not access to the Greek Testament, will find sufficient examples either in the small English New Testament published by Tischendorf in 1869, which gives the readings of three ancient MSS., or in that very convenient book, Eyre and Spottiswoode's *Variorum* Bible, which, on the whole, is the best edition of the English version for any one who wishes to look below the surface. Now if you consult such collections of various readings as are given in these works, you will find that, in various MSS., words, clauses, and sentences are inserted or omitted, and sometimes the insertions change the whole meaning of a passage. In one or two instances a complete paragraph appears in some copies, and is left out in others. The titles in particular offer great variations. The oldest MSS. do not prefix the name of Paul to the Epistle to the Hebrews, and they do not put the words "at Ephesus," into the first verse of the first chapter of Ephesians. Such changes as these show that the copyists of these times did not proceed exactly like law clerks copying a deed. They made additions from parallel passages, they wrote things upon the margin which afterwards got into the text; and, when copying from a rubbed or blotted page, they sometimes had to make a guess at a word. In these and other ways mistakes came in and were perpetuated; and it takes the best scholarship, combined with an acuteness developed by long practice, to determine the true reading in each case, and to eliminate all corruptions.

Of course, the old Christian scholars were quite aware that such variations existed among copies, and in later times they did their best to correct the text, and reduce it to uniformity; and so we find that, while the oldest MSS. of the New Testament show great variations, the later MSS. present a very uniform text, so that from them alone we could not guess how great was the range of readings current in the early Church. Yet no one will affirm that the shape which the New Testament ultimately took in the hands of the scholars of Antioch and Constantinople, is as near to the first hand of the Apostles as the text which a good modern editor is able to make by comparing the ol⸱⸱⸱ copies. The mere fact that a particular form of the text got the upper hand, and became generally accepted in later times, does not prove it to be the best form of the text, *i.e.* the most exact transcript of the very words that were written by the apostles and evangelists. To the critical editor the variations of early copies are far more significant than the artificial uniformity of late manuscripts.

Now as regards the Old Testament, we certainly find a great uniformity among copies. All MSS. of the Hebrew Bible represent one and the same text. There are slight variations, but these are, almost without exception, mere slips, such as might have been made even by a careful copyist, and do not affect the general state of the text. The text, therefore, was already fixed by the beginning of the tenth century after Christ, which is the age of the oldest MS. of undisputed date. But a comparison of the ancient translations carries us much further back. We may say that the text of the Hebrew Old Testament which we now have is the same as lay before Jerome 400 years after Christ ; the same as underlies certain translations into Aramaic called Targums, which took shape in Babylonia about the third century after Christ ; indeed the same text as was received by the Jews early in the second century, when the Mishna was being formed, and when the Jewish proselyte Aquila made his translation into Greek. I do not affirm that there were no various readings in the copies of the second or even of the fourth century, but the variations were slight and easily controlled, and such as would have

occurred in manuscripts carefully transcribed from one standard copy.[1]

The Jews, in fact, from the time when their national life
was finally extinguished, and their whole soul concentrated
upon the preservation of the monuments of the past, devoted
the most strict and punctilious attention to the exact transmission of the received text, down to the smallest peculiarity
of spelling, and even to certain irregularities of writing. Let me
explain this last point. We find that when the standard manuscript had a letter too big, or a letter too small, the copies made
from it imitated even this, so that letters of an unusual size
appear in the same place in every Hebrew Bible. Nay, the
scrupulousness of the transcribers went still further. In old
MSS., when a copyist had omitted a letter, and when the error
was detected, as the copy was revised, the reviser inserted the
missing letter above the line, as we should now do with a
caret. If, on the other hand, the reviser found that any superfluous letter had been inserted, he cancelled it by pricking a
dot above it. Now, when such corrections occurred in the
standard MS. from which our Hebrew Bibles are all copied,
the error and the correction were copied together, so that you
will find, even in printed Bibles (for the system has been
carried into the printed text), letters suspended above the
line to show that they had been inserted with a *caret*, and
letters "pointed" with a dot over them to show that they
form no proper part of the text.[2] It is plain that such a

---

[1] In the last century great hopes were entertained of the results to be
derived from a collation of Hebrew MSS. The collections of Kennicott (1776-
1780) and De Rossi (1784-1788) showed that all MSS. substantially represent
one text, and, so far as the consonants are concerned, recent discoveries have
not led to any new result. On the text that lay before the Talmudic doctors
compare Strack, *Prolegomena Critica in Vetus Testamentum Hebraicum*
(Leipzig, 1873). On Aquila see *supra*, p. 30, note 2 ; *infra*, p. 64. On the
Targums see Schürer, i. 115, and *infra*, p. 64, note 1.

[2] That all copies of the Hebrew text belong to a single recension, and
come from a common source, was stated by Rosenmüller in 1834 (see Stade's
Zeitschrift, 1884, p. 303). In 1853 J. Olshausen, in his commentary on the

system of mechanical transmission could not have been
carried out with precision if copying had been left to unin-
structed persons. The work of preserving and transmitting
the received text became the specialty of a guild of technic-
ally trained scholars, called the Massorets, in Hebrew *Ba'ale
hammassoreth*, or " possessors of tradition," that is, of tradition
as to the proper way of writing and reading the Bible. The
work of the Massorets extended over centuries, and they
collected many orthographical rules and great lists of
peculiarities of writing to be observed in passages where any
error was to be feared, which are still preserved either as
marginal notes and appendices to MSS. of the Bible, or in
separate works. But, what was of more consequence, the
scholars of the period after the close of the Talmud—that is,
after the sixth Christian century, or thereby—devoted themselves to preserving not only the exact writing of the received
consonantal text, but the exact pronunciation and even the
musical cadence proper to every word of the sacred text,
according to the rules of the synagogal chanting. This was
effected by means of a system of vowel points and musical
accents, consisting of small dots and apices attached to the
consonants of the Hebrew Bible. The idea of introducing

Psalms, p. 17 *sq.*, argued that there must have been, at least as far back as
the first ages of Christianity, an official recension of the text, extremely
similar to that of the Massorets, and that this text was not critical, but formed
by slavishly copying a single MS., which in many places was in very imperfect condition.   In his notes on Ps. lxxx. 14, 16 (comp. also that on Ps. xxvii.
13), he applies this view to explain the so-called "extraordinary points." In
1863, independently of Olshausen, whose observations seem to have attracted
little notice, Lagarde in his *Anmerkungen zur Griechischen Uebersetzung
der Proverbien* again maintained the origin of all Hebrew MSS. from one
archetype, using the extraordinary points to prove his thesis.   Olshausen had
explained the extraordinary points from the assumption of a single archetype,
but to him the evidence for the latter lay in comparison of the versions and
in the observation that all our authorities agree even in the most palpable
mistakes.   The doctrine of the single archetype has been accepted by Nöldeke
(whose remarks in Hilgenfeld's *Zeitschrift*, 1873, p. 444 *sqq.*, are worthy of
notice), and by other scholars. I know of no attempt to refute the arguments on which it rests.

such vowel points, which were still unknown in the time of Jerome, appears to have been borrowed from the Syrian Christians, and was developed in different directions among the Palestinian and the Babylonian Jews. The Palestinian system ultimately prevailed and is followed in all printed Bibles. The form of the pointed text which after ages received as authoritative was fixed in the tenth century by a certain Aaron, son of Moses, son of Asher, generally known as Ben Asher, whose ancestors for five previous generations were famous as *Nakdanîm,* or "punctuators." But even the first of this family, Asher "the elder," rested on the labours of earlier scholars. Some recent writers are disposed to think that the use of written vowel points and accents may have begun even in the sixth century—at all events the system must have been pretty fully worked out before 800 A.D.[1]

A remarkable feature in the work of the Massorets is that in certain cases they direct the reader to substitute another word for that which he finds written in the consonantal text. In such cases the vowel points attached to the word that is to be suppressed in reading are not its own vowels but those proper to the word to be substituted for it. The latter word is placed in the margin with the note קׁ (*i.e. Kerî,* "read thou," or *Kerê,* "read"). The word in the text which is not to be uttered is called *Kethîb* ("written"). These marginal readings are of various kinds; in a great part of them the difference between text and margin turns upon points of a purely formal character, such as varieties of orthography, pronunciation, or grammatical form; others are designed to soften expressions which it was thought indecorous to read aloud; while a small proportion of them make a change in the sense, and are either critical conjectures or readings

---

[1] See as regards Ben Asher, Baer and Strack, *Dikduke Hateamim* (Leipzig, 1879), p. ix. *sqq.*, and compare *Z. D. M. G. Jahresbericht* for 1879, p. 124; also, for the musical accents, Wickes's *Hebrew Accentuation* (Oxford, 1881), p. 1 *sqq.*

which must once have stood in the text itself. There is no reason to think that in these matters the Massorets departed from their office as conservators of old tradition; their one object was to secure that the whole Bible should be written according to the standard consonantal text and read according to the traditional use of the Synagogue service. It appears, therefore, that up to the time of the Massorets a certain small number of real variants to the written text still survived in the oral tradition of the Synagogue, and that the respect paid to the written text, great as it was, was not held to demand the suppression of these oral variants. In fact, the tradition of the right interpretation of Scripture, of which the rules of reading formed an integral part, ran, to a certain extent, a distinct course from the tradition of the consonantal text. The Targums, which are the chief monument of exegetical tradition before the work of the Massorets, generally agree with the *Keri* against the *Kethîb*.

These facts are not without importance as a corrective to the exaggerated views sometimes put forth as to the certainty of every letter of the Hebrew Text. But on the other hand, it must not be forgotten that all the real variants of the Targum and of the Massoretic notes amount to very little. A few words, or rather a few letters, were still in dispute among the traditional authorities, but the substance of the text was already fixed. There are many passages in the Hebrew Bible which cannot be translated as they stand, and where the text is undoubtedly corrupt. In a few such cases, where the corruption does not lie very deep, the marginal *Keri* or the Targum supplies the necessary correction; but for the most part the margin is silent, and the Targum, with all other versions and authorities later than the first Christian century, had exactly the same reading as the received Hebrew text. For good or for evil they all follow a single archetype, and vary from one another only in points so minute as seldom

to affect the sense. But this uniformity in the tradition of
the text does not reach back beyond the time of the Apostles.
On the contrary, there is abundant evidence that in earlier
ages Hebrew MSS. differed as much as MSS. of the New
Testament, or more. We shall have to look at the proof of
this in some detail by and by. For the present, it is enough
to point out some of the chief sources of the evidence. The
Samaritans, as well as the Jews, have preserved the Hebrew
Pentateuch, writing it in a peculiar character. Now the
copies of the Samaritan Pentateuch, which they received from
the Jews for the first time about 430 B.C., differ very considerably from our received Hebrew text. One or two of the
variations are corruptions wilfully introduced in favour of
the schismatic temple on Mount Gerizim; but others have no
polemical significance, affecting such points as the ages
assigned to the patriarchs.[1] Then, again, the old Greek
version, the Alexandrian version of the Septuagint, which, in

---

[1] Up to the time of Nehemiah's second visit to Jerusalem, there was still
a party, even among the priests, which entertained friendly relations with the
Samaritans, cemented by marriages. Nehemiah broke up this party; and an
unnamed priest, who was Sanballat's son-in-law, was driven into exile. This
priest, who would naturally flee to his father-in-law, is plainly identical with
the priest Manasseh, son-in-law of Sanballat, of whom Josephus (*Antiq.* xi. 8)
relates that he fled from Jerusalem to Samaria, and founded the schismatic
temple on Mount Gerizim, with a rival hierarchy and ritual. The account of
Josephus is confused in chronology and untrustworthy in detail; but the
main fact agrees with the Biblical narrative, and it is clear that the establishment of the rival temple was a natural consequence of the final defeat of the
Samaritans in their persistent efforts to establish relations with the Jewish
priesthood and secure admission to the temple at Jerusalem. This determines
the age of the Samaritan Pentateuch. The Samaritans cannot have got the
law before the Exile through the priest of the high place at Samaria mentioned
in 2 Kings xvii. 28. For the worship of Jehovah, as practised at Samaria
before the fall of the Northern Kingdom, was remote from the ordinances of
the law, and up to the time when the books of Kings were written the
Samaritans worshipped images, and did not observe the laws of the Pentateuch
(2 Kings xvii. 34, 41). The Pentateuch, therefore, was introduced as their
religious code at a later date; and this can only have happened in connection
with the ritual and priesthood which they received from Jerusalem through
the fugitive priest banished by Nehemiah.

part at least, was written before the middle of the third century
B.C., contains many various readings, sometimes omitting
large passages, or making considerable insertions ; sometimes
changing the order of chapters and verses; sometimes pre-
senting only minor variations, more similar to those with
which we are familiar in Greek MSS. Nay, even among
learned Jews who read Hebrew, the text was not fixed up to
the first century of our era. For the *Book of Jubilees*, a
Hebrew work which was written apparently but a few years
before the fall of the Temple, agrees with the Samaritan
Pentateuch in some of the numbers in the patriarchal
chronology, and in other readings.[1]

Now, observe the point to which we are thus brought.
After the fall of the Jewish state, when the Scribes ceased to
be an active party in a living commonwealth, and became more
and more pure scholars, gathering up and codifying all the
fragments of national literature and national life that remained
to them, we find the text of the Old Testament carefully conformed to a single archetype. But we cannot trace this text
back through the centuries when the nation had still a life of
its own. Nay, we can be sure that in these earlier centuries
copies of the Bible circulated, and were freely read even by
learned men like the author of the *Book of Jubilees*, which had
great and notable variations of text, not inferior in extent to
those still existing in New Testament MSS. In later times
every trace of these varying copies disappears. They must
have been suppressed, or gradually superseded by a deliberate
effort, which has been happily compared by Professor Nöldeke
to the action of the Caliph Othman in destroying all copies
of the Koran which diverged from the standard text that he
had adopted. There can be no question who were the instru-

---

[1] On the *Book of Jubilees*, see especially H. Rönsch, *Das Buch der Jubiläen*
(Leipzig, 1874), and Schürer, *op. cit.* vol. ii. p. 677 *sqq.* On the various
readings of the book, Rönsch, pp. 196, 514.

ments in this work. The Scribes alone possessed the necessary influence to give one text or one standard MS. a position
of such supreme authority. Moreover, we are able to explain
how it came about that the fixing of a standard text took
place about the Apostolic age, or rather a little later than
that date, and not at any earlier time. We have already
glanced at the political causes which made the power of the
Scribes greater in the time of Herod than it had ever been
before. The doctors of the Law wielded a great authority,
and were naturally eager to consolidate their legal system.
In earlier times the oral and written law went independently
side by side, and each stood on its own footing. Therefore,
variations in the text did not seriously affect any practical
question. But under Rabbi Hillel, a contemporary of Herod
the Great, and the grandfather of the Gamaliel who is
mentioned in the fifth chapter of Acts, a great change took
place. It was the ambition of Hillel to devise a system of
interpretation by which every traditional custom could be
connected with some text from the Pentateuch, no matter in
how arbitrary a way. This system was taken up and perfected
by his successors, especially by Rabbi Akiba, who was a
prominent figure in the revolt against Hadrian.[1] The new

---

[1] On Hillel and his school, see especially Derenbourg, *op. cit.* chap. xi.;
and on the development of his system by R. Ishmael and R. Akiba, *ibid.*
chap. xxiii. "Akiba adopted, not only the seven rules of Hillel, but the
thirteen of Ishmael ; even the latter did not suffice him in placing all the
halachoth, or decisions of the Rabbins, under the shield of the word of the
Pentateuch. His system of interpretation does not recognise the limits established by the usage of the language, and respected by Ishmael ; every word
which is not absolutely indispensable to express the intention of the legislator,
or the logical relations of the sentences of a law and their parts, is designed to
enlarge or restrict the sphere of the law, to introduce into it the additions of
tradition, or exclude what tradition excludes. No particle or conjunction, be
it augmentative or restrictive, escapes this singular method of exegesis."
Thus the Hebrew prefix *eth*, which marks the definite accusative, agrees in
form with the preposition *with*. Hence, when Deut. x. 20 says, "Thou shalt
fear *eth*-Jehovah thy God," Akiba interprets, "Thou shalt fear *the doctors of
the law along with* Jehovah." So Aquila, the disciple of Akiba, translates

method of exegesis laid weight upon the smallest word, and
sometimes even upon mere letters of Scripture; so that it
became a matter of great importance to the new school of
Rabbins to fix on an authoritative text. We have seen that
when this text was fixed, the discordant copies must have
been rigorously suppressed. The evidence for this is only
circumstantial, but it is quite sufficient. There is no other
explanation which will account for the facts, and the conclusion is confirmed by what took place among the Greek-
speaking Jews with reference to their Greek Bible. The
Bible of the Greek-speaking Jews, the Septuagint, had
formerly enjoyed very great honour even in Palestine, and is
most respectfully spoken of by the ancient Palestinian tradition; but it did not suit the newer school of interpretation,
it did not correspond with the received text, and was not
literal enough to fit the new methods of Rabbinic interpretation, while the Christians, on the contrary, found it a convenient instrument in their discussions with the Jews.
Therefore it fell into disrepute, and early in the second
century, just at the time when, as we have seen, the new
text of the Old Testament had been fixed, we find the Septuagint superseded among the Greek-speaking Jews by a
new translation, slavishly literal in character, made by a
Jewish proselyte of the name of Aquila, who was a disciple
of the Rabbi Akiba, and studiously followed his exegetical
methods.[1]

the mark of the accusative by σύν. See Field, *Proleg.* p. xxii. Compare on
the whole subject Schürer, *op. cit.* vol. ii. § 25.

[1] The progress of the stricter exegesis, and its influence on the treatment
of the text, may also be traced in the history of the Targums or Aramaic
paraphrases. Targum means originally the oral interpretation of the Meturgeman in the synagogue (*supra*, p. 36). The Meturgemanim did not keep close
to their text, but added paraphrastic expositions, practical applications, poetical
and romantic embellishments. But there was a restraint on individual
liberty of exegesis. The translators formed a guild of scholars, and their
interpretations gradually assumed a fixed type. By and by the current
form of the Targum was committed to writing; but there was no fixed

It was then the Scribes that chose for us the Hebrew text which we have now got. But were they in a position to choose the very best text, to produce a critical edition which could justly be accepted as the standard, so that we lose nothing by the suppression of all divergent copies? Well, this at least we can say: that if they fixed for us a satisfactory text, the Scribes did not do so in virtue of any great critical skill which they possessed in comparing MSS. and selecting the best readings. They worked from a false point of view. Their objects were legal, not philological. Their defective philology, their bad system of interpretation, made them bad critics; for it is the first rule of criticism that a good critic must be a good interpreter of the thoughts of his author. This judgment is fully borne out by the accounts given in the Talmudical books of certain small and sporadic attempts made by the Scribes to exercise something like criticism upon the text. For example, we read of three MSS. preserved in the Court of the Temple, each of which had one reading which the other MSS. did not share. The Scribes, we are told, rejected in each case the reading which had only one

edition, and those Palestinian Targums which have come down to us belong to various recensions, and contain elements added late in the Middle Ages.

This style of interpretation, in which the text was freely handled, and the exposition of the law did not stand on the level of the new science of Akiba and his associates, fell into disfavour with the dominant schools, just as the Septuagint did. The Targum is severely censured in the Rabbinical writings; and at length the orthodox party took the matter into their own hands, and framed a literal Targum, which, however, did not reach its final shape till the third Christian century, when the chief seat of Jewish learning had been moved to Babylonia. The Babylonian Targum to the Pentateuch is called the Targum of Onkelos, *i.e.* the Targum in the style of Aquila (Akylas). The corresponding Targum to the Prophets bears the name of Jonathan. As Jonathan is the Hebrew equivalent of Theodotion, this perhaps means only the Targum in the style of Theodotion. At any rate these Targums are not the private enterprise of individual scholars, but express the official exegesis of their age. The Targums to the Hagiographa have not an official character. Comp. Geiger, *Urschrift u. Uebersetzungen* (Breslau, 1857), p. 163 *sqq.*, p. 451 *sqq.*

copy for it and two against it.[1] Now, every critic knows that to accept or reject a reading merely according to the number of MSS. for or against it is a method which, if applied on a larger scale, would lead to a bad text. But further there is some evidence, though it cannot be said to be unambiguous, that the Scribes made certain changes in the text, apparently without manuscript authority, in order to remove expressions which seemed irreverent or indecorous. We have seen that in later times, after the received text was fixed, the Jewish scholars permitted themselves, in such cases, to make a change in the reading though not in the writing; but in earlier times, it would seem, the rule was not quite so strict. There is a series of passages in which, according to Jewish tradition, the expressions now found in the text depart from the form of words which ought to be used to convey the sense that was really in the mind of the sacred writers. These are referred to as the *eighteen Tikkûnê Sôpherîm* (corrections or determination of the Scribes). Thus in Job vii. 20, where the present text reads, " I am a burden to myself," the tradition explains that the expression ought to have been, " I am a burden upon thee," *i.e.* upon Jehovah. Again in Genesis xviii. 22, where our version says, " Abraham stood yet before the Lord," tradition says that this stands in place of " The Lord stood yet before Abraham." And again, in Habakkuk i. 12, where our version and the present Hebrew text read, " Art thou not from everlasting, Jehovah my God, my Holy One? We shall not die," the tradition tells us that the expression should have been, " Thou canst not die," which was changed because it seemed irreverent to mention the idea of God dying, even in order to negative it. It is sometimes maintained by Jewish scholars that the

---

[1] Geiger, *Urschrift*, p. 232; *Mas. Sôpherîm*, vi. 4. A copy of the Law was carried away by Titus among the spoils of the Temple; Josephus, *B. J.* vii. 5, § 5.

tradition as to these *Tikkûnê Sôpherîm* does not imply any tampering with the text on the part of the Scribes, but only that the sacred writers themselves disguised their thought by refusing to use expressions which they thought unseemly; but it is highly improbable that this was the original meaning of the tradition, and quite certain that the more explicit traditional accounts can have no other meaning than that the first Scribes, the so-called men of the Great Synagogue, corrected the text, and made it what we now read. It may indeed be doubted whether the details of the tradition are of any critical value. In most of the passages in question the Septuagint agrees with our present text, and the internal evidence is on the same side; while in some cases, as 2 Sam. xx. 1, where the original expression is said to have been "every man to his gods" instead of "his tents," the supposed older reading is manifestly absurd. On the other hand, in 1 Sam. iii. 13, where a *Tikkûn* is registered upon the expression "his sons made themselves vile" [Rev. V.: "did bring a curse on themselves"], there is plainly something wrong, and the Septuagint, with the change of a single letter in the Hebrew, produces the good sense "did revile God," which agrees with the Jewish tradition. On the whole, therefore, we are entitled to conclude that the Rabbins had some vague inaccurate knowledge of old MS. readings which departed from the received text. And what is more important, the tradition implies a recognition of the fact that the early guardians of the text did not hesitate to make small changes in order to remove expressions which they thought unedifying.[1] Beyond doubt, such changes were made in a good many cases of which no record has been retained. For

---

[1] The oldest list of the *Tikkûnê Sôpherîm* is in the *Mechilta*, a work of the second century, and contains only eleven passages. See also Geiger, *op. cit.* p. 309, and the full list in *Ochla w'ochla*, ed. Frensdorff, No. 168 (Hannover, 1864). On the value of this tradition comp. Nöldeke in *Gött. Gel. Anz.*, 1869, p. 2001 *sq.*

example, in our text of the books of Samuel, Saul's son and successor is called Ishbosheth, but in 1 Chronicles viii. 33, ix. 39, he is called Eshbaal. Eshbaal means "Baal's man," a proper name of a well-known Semitic type, precisely similar to such Arabic names as Imrau-l-Cais, "the man of the god Cais." We must not, however, fancy that a son of Saul could be named after the Tyrian or Canaanite Baal. The word Baal is not the proper name of one deity, but an appellative noun meaning lord or owner, which the tribes of the Northern Semites applied each to their own chief divinity. In earlier times it appears that the Israelites did not scruple to give this honorific title to their national God Jehovah. Thus the golden calves at Bethel and Dan, which were worshipped under the supposition that they represented Jehovah, were called Baalim by their devotees; and Hosea, when he prophesies the purification of Israel's religion, makes it a main point that the people shall no longer call Jehovah their Baal (Hosea ii. 16, 17; comp. xiii. 1, 2). This prophecy shows that in Hosea's time the use of the word was felt to be dangerous to true religion; and indeed there is no question that the mass of the people were apt to confound the true God with the false Baalim of Canaan, the local divinities or lords of individual tribes, towns, or sanctuaries. And so in process of time scrupulous Israelites not only desisted from applying the title of Baal to Jehovah, but taking literally the precept of Exod. xxiii. 13, "Make no mention of the name of other gods," they were wont, when they had occasion to refer to a false deity, to call him not Baal but Bosheth, "the shameful thing," as a euphemism for the hated name. The substitution of "Ishbosheth" for "Eshbaal," and other cases of the same kind, such as Mephibosheth for Meribaal (man of Baal), are therefore simply due to the scruples of copyists or readers who could not bring themselves to write or utter the hated word even in a compound proper name. Of course no

man, and certainly no king, ever bore so absurd a name as
"The man of the shameful thing," and as Chronicles still
preserves the true form, we may be pretty certain that the
change in the name in the book of Samuel was made after
he wrote, and is a veritable "correction of the Scribes."

These, then, are specimens of the changes which we can
still prove to have been made by early editors, and they are
enough to show that these guardians of the text were not
sound critics. Fortunately for us, they did not pretend to
make criticism their main business. It would have been a
very unfortunate thing for us indeed, if we had been left to
depend upon a text of the Hebrew Bible which the Scribes
had made to suit their own views. There can be no doubt,
however, that the standard copy which they ultimately
selected, to the exclusion of all others, owed this distinction
not to any critical labour which had been spent upon it, but
to some external circumstance that gave it a special reputation. Indeed, the fact, already referred to, that the very errors
and corrections and accidental peculiarities of the manuscript
were kept just as they stood, shows that it must have been
invested with a peculiar sanctity ; if indeed the meaning of
the so-called extraordinary points—that is, of those suspended
and dotted letters, and the like—had not already been forgotten when it was chosen to be the archetype of all future
copies.

Now, if the Scribes were not the men to make a critical
text, it is plain that they were also not in a position to choose,
upon scientific principles, the very best extant manuscript ;
but it is very probable that they selected an old and well-
written copy, possibly one of those which were preserved in
the Court of the Temple. Between this copy and the original
autographs of the Sacred Writers there must have been many
a link. It may have been an old manuscript, but it was not
an exorbitantly old one. Of that there are two proofs. In

the first place, it was certainly written in Aramaic characters, not very different from the "square" or "Assyrian" letters used in our modern Hebrew Bibles; but in old times the Hebrews used the quite different character usually called Phœnician. According to Jewish tradition, which is disposed to ascribe everything to Ezra which it has not the assurance to refer to Moses, the change on the character in which the sacred books were written was introduced by Ezra; but we know that this is a mistake, for the Samaritans, who acquired the Pentateuch after Ezra's publication of the Law, received it in the old Phœnician letter, which they retain in a corrupted form down to the present day. It is most improbable that the Jews adopted the Aramaic character for Biblical MSS. before the third century B.C., and that therefore would be the earliest possible date for the archetype of our present Hebrew copies.[1] Another proof that the copy was not extraordinarily old lies in the spelling. In Hebrew, as in other languages, the rules of spelling varied in the course of centuries, and as we have a genuine specimen of old Hebrew

---

[1] Tables of the forms of the Semitic alphabet at various times, by the eminent calligrapher and palæographer, Prof. Euting of Strassburg, are appended to the English translation of Bickell's *Hebrew Grammar* (1877), and to the latest edition of Kautzsch-Gesenius, *Hebr. Grammatik* (1889). Fuller tables by the same skilful hand are in Chwolson's *Corpus Inscr. Heb.* (Petersburg, 1882), and *Syrisch-nestor. Grabinschriften* (Petersburg, 1890); the last also separately, *Tabula Scripturæ Aramaicæ* (Strassburg, 1890). On the history of the Hebrew alphabet see Wright, *Lectures on the Comp. Grammar of the Sem. Languages* (Cambridge, 1890), p. 35 *sqq.*; Driver, *Notes on Samuel* (Oxford, 1890), Introduction; and comp. the plates in the *Oriental Series* of the Palæographical Society. The old character must still have been generally understood when the first Jewish coins were struck (141 B.C.); for though conservatism may explain its retention on later coins, an obsolete letter would not have been chosen by Simon when he struck Hebrew money for the first time. On the other hand, the expressions in Matt. v. 18 imply that in the time of our Lord the Aramaic script was used; for in the old character Yod ("jot") was not a very small letter. Indeed, it seems to be pretty well made out that parts, at least, of the Septuagint were translated from MSS. in the Aramaic character. See Vollers in Stade's *Zeitschrift*, 1883, p. 230 *sqq.*, and the literature there cited.

spelling in the inscription of Siloah (eighth century B.C.), and also possess a long Moabite inscription of still earlier date and many Phœnician inscriptions of different periods, evidence is not lacking to decide which of two orthographies is the older. Now, it can be proved that the copies which lay before the translators of the Septuagint in the third, and perhaps in the second, century B.C., often had an older style of spelling than existed in the archetype of our present Hebrew Bibles. It does not follow of necessity that in all respects these older MSS. were better and nearer to the original text ; but certainly the facts which we have been developing give a new importance to the circumstance that the MSS. of the LXX. often contained readings very different from those of our Hebrew Bibles, even to the extent of omitting or inserting passages of considerable length.

In this connection there is yet another point worth notice. In these times Hebrew books were costly and cumbrous, written on huge rolls of leather, not even on the later and more convenient parchment. Copies therefore were not very numerous, and, being much handled, were apt to get worn and indistinct. For not only was leather an indifferent surface to write on, but the ink was of a kind that could be washed off, a prejudice existing against the use of a mordant.[1] No single copy, therefore, however excellent, was likely to remain long in good readable condition throughout. And we have seen that collation of several copies, by which

---

[1] That the old Hebrew ink could be washed off appears from Numb. v. 23, Exod. xxxii. 33. From the former passage is derived the Rabbinic objection to the use of a mordant in ink. See *Sôpherîm*, i. 5, 6, and the notes in Müller's edition (Leipzig, 1878) ; Mishna, *Sota*, ii. 4, and Wagenseil's Commentary (Surenh., iii. p. 206 *sq.*) The Jews laid no value on old copies, but in later times prized certain MSS. as specially correct. A copy in which a line had become obliterated, or which was otherwise considerably defective, was cast aside into the *Genîza* or lumber-room (*Sôpherîm*, iii. 9). There was a difference of opinion as to touching-up faded letters (*ibid.* 8, and Müller's note). Compare Harkavy in *Mém. de l'Acad. de S. Petersbourg*, xxiv. p. 57.

defects might have been supplied, was practised to but a
small extent.   Often indeed it must have been difficult to
get manuscripts to collate, and once at least the whole
number of Bibles existing in Palestine was reduced to very
narrow limits.   For Antiochus Epiphanes (168 B.C.) caused
all copies of the Law, and seemingly of the other sacred books,
to be torn up and burnt, and made it a capital offence to
possess a Pentateuch (1 Mac. i. 56, 57; Josephus, *Ant.* xii. 5,
§ 4).   The text of books preserved only in manuscript might
very readily suffer in passing through such a crisis, and it is
most providential that before this time, the Law and other
books of the Old Testament had been translated into Greek
and were current in regions where Antiochus had no sway.
This Greek version, called the Septuagint, of which the
greater part is older than the time of Antiochus, still exists,
and supplies, as we shall see in the next Lecture, the most
valuable evidence for the early state of the Old Testament
text.

LECTURE IV

THE SEPTUAGINT [1]

WE have passed under review the vicissitudes of the Hebrew
Text, as far back as the days of Antiochus Epiphanes. We
have found that all our MSS. go back to one archetype. But
the archetype was not formed by a critical process which we
can accept as conclusive. It was not so ancient but that a
long interval lay between it and the first hand of the Biblical
authors ; and the comparative paucity of books in those early
times, combined with the imperfect materials used in writing,
and the deliberate attempt of Antiochus to annihilate the
Hebrew Bible, exposed the text to so many dangers that it
cannot but appear a most welcome and providential circumstance that the Greek translation, derived from MSS. of
which some at least were presumably older than the archetype of our present Hebrew copies, and preserved in countries
beyond the dominions of Antiochus, offers an independent
witness to the early state of the Biblical books, vindicating

---

[1] On the subject of this Lecture compare, in general, Wellhausen's article
SEPTUAGINT (*Enc. Brit.*, 9th ed.). The two books which have perhaps done
most to exemplify the right method of using the Septuagint for criticism of
the Hebrew text are Lagarde, *Anmerkungen zur Griechischen Uebersetzung der
Proverbien* (Leipzig, 1863) ; Wellhausen, *Der Text der Bücher Samuelis* (Gött.,
1871). For English students the best practical introduction to the critical
use of the LXX. is Driver, *Notes on the Hebrew Text of the Books of Samuel*
(Oxford, 1890). On the relation of the Septuagint to the Palestinian tradition compare Geiger, *op. cit.*, and Frankel, *Ueber den Einfluss der palästin-
ischen Exegese auf die Alexandrinische Hermeneutik* (Leipzig, 1851).

the substantial accuracy of the transmission of these records; while, at the same time, it displays a text not yet fixed in every point of detail, exhibits a series of important various readings, and sometimes indicates the existence of corruptions in the received Hebrew recension—corruptions which it not seldom enables us to remove, restoring the first hand of the sacred authors.

Nevertheless, there have been many scholars who altogether reject this use of the Septuagint. One of the latest representatives of this party is Keil, from whose *Introduction* (Eng. trans., vol. ii. p. 306) I quote the following sentences :—

"The numerous and strongly marked deviations [of the Septuagint] from the Massoretic text have arisen partly at a later time, out of the carelessness and caprice of transcribers. But in so far as they existed originally, almost in a mass they are explained by the uncritical and wanton passion for emendation, which led the translators to alter the original text (by omissions, additions, and transpositions) where they misunderstood it in consequence of their own defective knowledge of the language, or where they supposed it to be unsuitable or incorrect for historical, chronological, dogmatic, or other reasons ; or which, at least, led them to render it inexactly, according to their own notions and their uncertain conjectures."

If this judgment were sound, we should be deprived at one blow of the most ancient witness to the state of the text ; and certainly, at one time, the opinion advocated by Keil was generally current among Protestant scholars. We have glanced, in a previous Lecture (*supra*, p. 32), at the reasons which led the early Protestants to place themselves, on points of Hebrew scholarship, almost without reserve in the hands of the Jews. Accepting the received Hebrew text as transmitted in the Jewish schools, they naturally viewed with distrust the very different text of the Septuagint. However, the question of the real value of the Greek version was stirred early in the seventeenth century, mainly by two French scholars, one of whom was a Catholic, Jean Morin (Morinus), priest of the Oratory, the other a Protestant, Louis Cappelle (Cappellus).

The controversy raised by the publication of the *Exercitationes Biblicæ* of Morinus (Paris, 1633-1660) was unduly prolonged by the introduction of dogmatic considerations which should have had no place in a scholarly argument as to the history of the Biblical text. These considerations lost much of their force when all parties were compelled to admit the value of the various readings of MSS. and versions for the study of the New Testament; and, since theological prejudice was overcome, it has gradually become clear to the vast majority of conscientious students that the Septuagint is really of the greatest value as a witness to the early history of the text.

It is very difficult to convey, in a popular manner, a sufficiently clear idea of the arguments by which this position is established. Even the few remarks which I shall make may, I fear, seem to you somewhat tedious; but I must ask your attention for them, because it is of no slight consequence to know whether, in this, the oldest, version, we have or have not a valuable testimony to the way in which the Old Testament has been transmitted, an independent basis for a rational and well-argued belief as to the state of the Hebrew text.

In judging of the Septuagint translation, we must not put ourselves on the standpoint of a translator in these days. We must begin by realising to ourselves the facts brought out in Lecture II., that Jewish scholars, before the time of Christ, had no grammar and no dictionary; that all their knowledge of the language was acquired by oral teaching; that their exegesis of difficult passages was necessarily traditional; and that, where tradition failed them, they had for their guidance only that kind of practical knowledge of the language which they got by the constant habit of reading the sacred text, and speaking some kind of Hebrew among themselves in the schools. We must also remember that, when the Septuagint was composed, the Hebrew language was either dead or dying, and that the mother-tongue of the translators was either Greek or Aramaic. Hence we must not be surprised to find that, when tradition was silent, the Septuagint translators made many mistakes. If they came to a difficult passage, say of a prophet, of which no traditional interpretation had been handed down in the schools, or which contained words the meanings of which had not been taught them by their masters, they could do nothing better than make a guess—sometimes guided by analogies and similar words in Aramaic—sometimes by other considerations. The value of the translation does not lie in the sense which they put upon such passages, but in the evidence that we can find as to what Hebrew words lay in the MSS. before them.

Apart from the inherent defects of scholarship derived entirely from tradition, we find that the Septuagint sometimes varies from the older text for reasons which are at once intelligible when we understand the general principles of the Scribes at the time. We have already seen, for example, that the Scribes in Palestine did not hesitate occasionally to make a dogmatic correction, removing from the writing, or at least from the reading, of Scripture some expression which they thought it indecorous to pronounce in public. In like manner we find that the translators of the Septuagint sometimes changed a phrase which they thought likely to be misunderstood, or to be used to establish some false doctrine. Thus, in the Hebrew text of Exodus xxiv. 10, we read that the elders who went up towards Sinai with Moses " saw the God of Israel." This anthropomorphic expression, it was felt, could not be rendered literally without lending some countenance to the false idea that the spiritual God can be seen by the bodily eyes of men, and offering an apparent contradiction to Exodus xxxiii. 20. The Septuagint therefore changes it, and says, "They saw the place where the God of Israel had stood." One change on the text, made by the Septuagint in deference to an early and widespread Jewish scruple, is followed even in the English Bible. The ancient proper name of the God of Israel, which we are accustomed to write as Jehovah, is habitually suppressed by the Greek translators, the word ὁ κύριος (A. V. the LORD) taking its place. This agrees with the usage of the Hebrew-speaking Jews, who in reading substituted *Adonai* (the Lord), or, in certain cases, *Elohim* (God), for the "ineffable name." So strictly was this rule carried out that the true pronunciation of the name was ultimately forgotten among the Jews; though several early Christian writers had still access to authentic information on the subject. From their testimony, and from a comparison of the many old Hebrew proper names which are compounded with the sacred name, we can still make out that the true pronunciation is *Iahwè*. The vulgar form Jehovah is of very modern origin, and arises from a quite arbitrary combination of the true consonants with the vowel points which the Massorets set against the word in all passages where they meant it to be read *Adonai* and not *Elohim*. Unhappily, this spurious form is now too deeply rooted among us to be displaced, at least in popular usage.

Again, we have already seen that the interpretation of the Scribes was largely guided by the Halacha, that is, by oral tradition ultimately based upon the common law and habitual usage of the sanctuary and of Jerusalem. The same influence of the Halacha is found in the Septuagint translation. Thus, in Lev. xxiv. 7, where the Hebrew text bids frankincense be placed on the shewbread, the Septuagint makes it "frankincense and salt," because salt, as well as frankincense, was used in the actual ritual of their period.

Such deviations of the Septuagint as these need not seriously embarrass the critic. He recognises the causes from

which they came. He is able, approximately, to estimate
their extent by what he knows of Palestinian tradition, and
he is not likely, in a case of this sort, to be misled into the
supposition that the Septuagint had a different text from the
Hebrew. Once more, we find that the translators allowed
themselves certain liberties which were also used by copyists
of the time. Their object was to give the thing with perfect
clearness as they understood it. Consequently they sometimes changed a " he " into " David " or " Solomon," naming
the person alluded to; and they had no scruple in adding a
word or two to complete the sense of an obscure sentence, or
supply what appeared to be an ellipsis. Even our extant
Hebrew MSS. indicate a tendency to make additions of this
description. The original and nervous style of early Hebrew
prose was no longer appreciated, and a diffuse smoothness,
with constant repetition of standing phrases and elaborate
expansion of the most trifling incidents, was the classical
ideal of composition. The copyist or translator seldom
omitted anything save by accident; but he was often tempted
by his notions of style to venture on an expansion of the
text. Let me take a single example. In passages in the Old
Testament where we read of some one eating, a compas-
sionate editor, as a recent critic humorously puts it, was pretty
sure to intervene and give him also something to drink.
Sometimes we find the longer reading in the Septuagint,
sometimes in the Hebrew text. In 1 Samuel i. 9 the Hebrew
tells us that Hannah rose up after she had eaten in Shiloh
and after she had drunk, but the Septuagint has only the
shorter reading, "After she had eaten." Conversely, in
2 Samuel xii. 21, where the Hebrew text says only,
" Thou didst rise and eat bread," the Septuagint presents
the fuller text, " Thou didst rise and eat bread, and
drink." In cases of this sort, the shorter text is obviously
the original.

For our present purpose these three classes of variations do not come into account. First of all we must put aside the cases where, having the present Hebrew text before them, the translators failed to understand it, simply because they had no tradition to guide them. We must not say that they were ignorant or capricious, because they were not able to make a good grammatical translation of a difficult passage at a time when such a thing as grammar or lexicon did not exist even in Palestine. In the next place, we must put on one side the cases where the interpretation was influenced by exegetical considerations derived from the dogmatic theology of the time or from the traditional law. And, thirdly, we can attach no great importance to those variations in which, without changing the sense, the translator, or perhaps a copyist before him, gave a slight turn to an expression to remove ambiguity, or to gain the diffuse fulness which he loved.

But after making every allowance for these cases a large class of passages remains, in which the Septuagint presents important variations from the Massoretic text. The test by which the value of these variations can be determined is the method of retranslation. A faithful translation from Hebrew into an idiom so different as the Greek—especially such a translation as the Septuagint, the work of men who had no great command of Greek style—cannot fail to retain the stamp of the original language. It will be comparatively easy to put it back into idiomatic Hebrew, and even the mistakes of the translator will often point clearly to the words of the original which he had before him. But where the translator capriciously departs from his original, the work of retranslation will at once become more difficult. For the capricious translator is one who substitutes his own thought for that of the author, and what he thinks in Greek —even in lumbering Jewish Greek—will not so naturally

lend itself to retroversion into the Hebrew idiom. The test
of retranslation gives a very favourable impression of the
fidelity of the Alexandrian version. With a little practice
one can often put back whole chapters of the Septuagint into
Hebrew, reproducing the original text almost word for word.
The translation is not of equal merit throughout, and it is
plain that the different parts of the Bible were rendered by
men of unequal capacity; but in general, and under the
limitations already indicated, it is safe to say that the translators were competent scholars as scholarship then went, and
that they did their work faithfully and in no arbitrary way.
Now as we proceed with the work of retranslation, and when
all has gone on smoothly for perhaps a whole chapter, in
which we find no considerable deflection from the present
Hebrew, we suddenly come to something which the practised
hand has no difficulty in putting back into Hebrew, which
indeed is full of such characteristic Hebrew idiom that it is
impossible to ascribe it to the caprice of a translator thinking
in Greek, but which, nevertheless, diverges from the Massoretic
text. In such cases we can be morally certain that a various
reading existed in the Hebrew MS. from which the Septuagint
was derived. Nay, in some passages, the moral certainty
becomes demonstrative, for we find that the translator
stumbled on a word which he was unable to render into
Greek, and that he contented himself with transcribing it in
Greek letters. A Hebrew word thus bodily transferred to
the pages of the Septuagint, and yet differing from what we
now read in our Hebrew Bibles, constitutes a various reading
which cannot be explained away. An example of this is
found in 1 Sam. xx., in the account of the arrangement made
between Jonathan and David to determine the real state of
Saul's disposition towards the latter. In the Hebrew text
(ver. 19) Jonathan directs David to be in hiding "by the
stone Ezel;" and at verse 41, when the plan agreed on has

been carried out, David at a given signal emerges "from beside the Negeb." The Negeb is a district in the south of Judæa, remote from the city of Saul, in the neighbourhood of which the events of our chapter took place ; and the attempt of the English version to smooth away the difficulty is not satisfactory either in point of grammar or of sense. But the Septuagint makes the whole thing clear. At verse 19 the Greek reads "beside yonder Ergab," and at verse 41 "David arose from the Ergab." *Ergab* is the transcription in Greek of a rare Hebrew word signifying a *cairn* or rude monument of stone, which does not occur elsewhere except as a proper name (Argob). The translators transliterated the word because they did not understand it, and the reading of the Massoretic text, which involves no considerable change in the letters of the Hebrew, probably arose from similar lack of knowledge on the part of Palestinian copyists.

The various readings of the Septuagint are not always so happy as in this case ; but in selecting some further examples, it will be most instructive for us to confine ourselves to passages where the Greek gives a better reading than the Hebrew, and where its superiority can be made tolerably manifest even in an English rendering. It must, however, be remembered that complete proof that the corruption lies on the side of the Hebrew and not of the Greek can be offered only to those who understand these languages. Our first example shall be 1 Sam. xiv. 18.

Hebrew.	*Septuagint.*
And Saul said to Ahiah, Bring hither the ark of God. For the ark of God was on that day and [*not as E. V.* with] the children of Israel.	And Saul said to Ahiah, Bring hither the ephod, for he bare the ephod on that day before Israel.

The Authorised Version smooths away one difficulty of

the Hebrew text at the expense of grammar. But there are other difficulties behind. The ark was then at Gibeah of Kirjath-jearim (1 Sam. vii. 1 ; 2 Sam. vi. 3), quite a different place from Gibeah of Benjamin ; and its priest was not Ahiah, but Eleazar ben Abinadab. Besides, Saul's object was to seek an oracle, and this was done, not by means of the ark, but by the sacred lot connected with the ephod of the priest (1 Sam. xxiii. 6, 9). This is what the Septuagint actually brings out, and there can be no doubt that it preserves the right reading. The changes on the Hebrew letters required to get the one reading out of the other are far less considerable than one would imagine from the English.

Another example is the death of Ishbosheth (2 Sam. iv. 5, 6, 7) :—

Hebrew.	*Septuagint.*
[The assassins] came to the house of Ishbosheth in the hottest part of the day, while he was taking his midday siesta. (6) And hither they came into the midst of the house fetching wheat, and smote him in the flank, and Rechab and Baanah his brother escaped. (7) And they came into the house as he lay on his bed, . . . and smote him and slew him, *etc.*	They came to the house of Ishbosheth in the hottest part of the day, while he was taking his midday siesta. And lo, the woman who kept the door of the house was cleaning wheat, and she slumbered and slept, and the brothers Rechab and Baanah passed in unobserved and came into the house as Ishbosheth lay on his bed, *etc.*

In the Hebrew there is a meaningless repetition in verse 7 of what has already been fully explained in the two preceding verses. The Septuagint text gives a clear and progressive narrative, and one which no " capricious translator " could have derived out of his own head. As in the previous case, the two readings are very like one another when written in the Hebrew.

Another reading, long ago appealed to by Dathe as one which no man familiar with the style of the translator could

credit him with inventing, is found in Ahithophel's advice to
Absalom (2 Sam. xvii. 3):—

Hebrew.	*Septuagint.*
I will bring back all the people to thee. Like the return of the whole is the man whom thou seekest. All the people shall have peace.	I will make all the people turn to thee as a bride turneth to her husband. Thou seekest the life of but one man, and all the people shall have peace.

The cumbrousness of the Hebrew text is manifest. The
Septuagint, on the contrary, introduces a graceful simile,
thoroughly natural in the picturesque and poetically-coloured
language of ancient Israel, but wholly unlike the style of the
prosaic age when the translator worked.

The Books of Samuel, from which these examples are
selected, are, on the whole, the part of the Old Testament in
which the value of the Septuagint is most manifest and most
generally recognised. The Hebrew text has many obscurities
which can only be explained as due to faulty transmission,
and the variations of the Septuagint are numerous and often
good. In the Pentateuch, on the other hand, the Septuagint
seldom departs far from the Hebrew text, and its variations
seldom give a better reading. This is just what we should
expect, for from a very early date the Law was read in the
synagogues every Sabbath day (Acts xv. 21) in regular
course, the whole being gone through in a cycle of three
years. The Jews thus became so familiar with the words of
the Pentateuch that copyists were in great measure secured
from important errors of transcription; and it is also reasonable to suppose that the rolls written for the synagogue were
transcribed with special care long before the full development
of the elaborate precautions which were ultimately devised to
exclude errors from all the sacred books. Sections from the
prophetic books were also read in the synagogue (Acts xiii. 15),
but not in a complete and systematic manner. At the time

of Christ, indeed, it would seem that the reader had a certain
freedom of choice in the prophetic lessons (Luke iv. 17).
Such books as Samuel, again, had little place in the synagogue service, while the interest of the narrative caused
them to be largely read in private. But private study gave
no such guarantee against the introduction of various readings
as was afforded by use in public worship. Private readers
must no doubt have often been content to purchase or tran-
scribe indifferent copies, and a student might not hesitate to
make on his own copy notes or small additions to facilitate
the sense, or even to add a paragraph which he had derived
from another source, a procedure of which we shall find
examples by and by. Under such circumstances, and in the
absence of official supervision, the multiplication of copies
opened an easy door to the multiplication of errors; which
might, no doubt, have been again eliminated by a critical
collation, but might very easily become permanent when, as
we have seen, a single copy, without critical revision, acquired
the position of the standard manuscript, to which all new
transcripts were to be conformed.

In general, then, we must conclude, *first*, that many
various readings once existed in MSS. of the Old Testament
which have totally disappeared from the extant Hebrew
copies ; and, *further*, that the range and distribution of these
variations were in part connected with the fact that all books
of the Old Testament had not an equal place in the official
service of the synagogue. But the force of these observations
is sometimes met by an argument directed to depreciate the
value of the Septuagint variations. It is not denied that
the MSS. which lay before the Greek translators contained
various readings ; but it is urged that these MSS. were presumably of Egyptian origin, and that the Jews of Egypt had
probably to content themselves with inferior copies, transmitted and multiplied by the hands of scholars who were

neither so learned nor so scrupulous as the Scribes of
Jerusalem. Upon this view we are invited to look upon the
Septuagint as the witness to a corrupt Egyptian recension of
the text, the various readings in which deserve little attention, and afford no evidence that Palestinian MSS. did not
agree even at an early period with the present Massoretic text.

We have already seen that this view is at any rate exaggerated, for we have had cases before us in which no sober
critic will hesitate to prefer the so-called Egyptian reading.
But further it is to be observed that the whole theory of a
uniform Palestinian recension is a pure hypothesis. There is
not a particle of evidence that there was a uniform Palestinian
text in the sense in which our present Hebrew Bibles are
uniform—or, in other words, to the exclusion even of such
variations and corruptions as are found in MSS. of the New
Testament—before the first century of our era. Nay, as we
have seen, the author of the *Book of Jubilees,* a Palestinian
scholar of the first century, used a Hebrew Bible which often
agreed with the Septuagint or the Samaritan recension against
the Massoretic text (*supra,* p. 62).

But let us look at the history of the Greek translation,
and see what ground of fact there is for supposing that it was
made from inferior copies, and could pass muster only in a
land of inferior scholarship. The account of the origin of the
Septuagint version of the Law which was current in the time
of Christ, and may be read in Josephus and Eusebius, is full
of fabulous embellishments, designed to establish the authority
of the version as miraculously composed under divine inspiration. The source of these fables is an epistle purporting to be
written by one Aristeas, a courtier in Alexandria under Ptolemy
Philadelphus (283-247 B.C.).[1] This epistle is a forgery, but the

---

[1] Critical edition of the text of the letter of Aristeas to Philocrates, by M.
Schmidt, in Merx's *Archiv,* i. 241 *sq.* (Halle, 1870). It is unnecessary to
sketch its contents, for which the English reader may turn to the translations
of Eusebius and Josephus. What basis of truth underlies the fables depends

author seems to have linked on his fabulous stories to some
element of current tradition; and there is other evidence that
in the second century B.C. the uniform tradition of the Jews
in Egypt was to the effect that the Greek Pentateuch was
written for Ptolemy II. Philadelphus, to be placed in the
royal library collected by Demetrius Phalereus. This tradition is not wholly improbable, and at all events the date to
which it leads us has generally commended itself to the
judgment of scholars; it is confirmed by the fact that the
fragments of the Jew, Demetrius, who wrote a Greek history
of the kings of Judæa under Ptolemy IV. (222-205 B.C.),
betray acquaintance with the Septuagint Pentateuch. The
other books were translated later, but they probably followed
pretty fast. The author of the prologue to Ecclesiasticus,
who wrote in Egypt about 130 B.C., speaks of the law, the
prophets, and the other books of the fathers, as current in
Greek in his time. The Septuagint version, then, was made
in Egypt under the Ptolemies. Under these princes the
Jewish colony in Egypt was not a poor or oppressed body;
it was very numerous, very influential. Jews held important
posts in the kingdom, and formed a large element in the
population of Alexandria. Their wealth was so great that
they were able to make frequent pilgrimages and send many
rich gifts to the Temple at Jerusalem. They stood, therefore,
on an excellent footing with the authorities of the nation in
Palestine, and there is not the slightest evidence that they
were regarded as heretics, using an inferior Bible, or in
any way falling short of all the requisites of true Judaism.
There was, indeed, a schismatic temple in Egypt, at Leonto-
polis; but that temple, so far as we can gather, by no means
attracted to it the service and the worship of the greater part

mainly on the genuineness of the fragments of Aristobulus. See on the one
side Wellhausen-Bleek, § 279, on the other Kuenen's *Religion of Israel*, note
1 to chap. xi. For Demetrius see Schürer, *op. cit.* vol. ii. p. 730, and for
Aristobulus, *ibid.* p. 760 ; see also *ibid.* p. 697 *sqq.*, p. 819 *sqq.*

of the Greek-speaking Jews in Egypt. Their hearts still turned towards Jerusalem, and their intercourse with Palestine was too familiar and frequent to suffer them to fall into the position of an isolated and ignorant sect.

All this makes it highly improbable that the Jews of Egypt would have contented themselves with a translation below the standard of Palestine, or that they would have found any difficulty in procuring manuscripts of the approved official recension, if such a recension had then existed. But the argument may be carried further. In the time of Christ there were many Hellenistic Jews resident in Jerusalem, with synagogues of their own, where the Greek version was necessarily in regular use. We find these Hellenists in Acts vi., living on the best terms with the religious authorities of the capital. Hellenists and Hebrews, the Septuagint and the original text, met in Jerusalem without schism or controversy. Yet many of the Palestinian scholars were familiar with Greek, and Paul cannot have been the only man born in the Hellenistic dispersion, and accustomed from infancy to the Greek version, who afterwards studied under Palestinian doctors, and became equally familiar with the Hebrew text. The divergences of the Septuagint must have been patent to all Jerusalem. Yet we find no attempt to condemn and suppress this version till the second century, when the rise of the new school of exegesis, and the consequent introduction of a fixed official text, were followed by the discrediting of the old Greek Bible in favour of the new translation by Aquila. On the contrary, early Rabbinical tradition expressly recognises the Greek version as legitimate. In some passages of the Jewish books mention is made of thirteen places in which those who "wrote for Ptolemy" departed from the Hebrew text. But these changes, which are similar in character to the "corrections of the Scribes" spoken of in the last Lecture, are not

reprehended; and in one form of the tradition they are
even said to have been made by divine inspiration. The
account of these thirteen passages contains mistakes which
show that the tradition was written down after the Septuagint had ceased to be a familiar book in Palestine. It
is remarkable that the graver variations of the Egyptian
text are passed over in absolute silence, and had apparently
fallen into oblivion. But the tradition recalls a time when
Hebrew scholars knew the Greek version well, and noted
its variations in a spirit of friendly tolerance. These facts
are entirely inconsistent with the idea that the Egyptian
text was viewed as corrupt. To the older Jewish tradition
its variations appeared, not in the light of deviations from
an acknowledged standard, but as features fairly within
the limits of a faithful transmission or interpretation of
the text.[1] And so the comparison of the Septuagint with
the Hebrew Bible not merely furnishes us with fresh critical
material for the text of individual passages, but supplies
a measure of the limits of variation which were tolerated

---

[1] Compare Morinus, *Exercitatio* viii. In Mishna, *Megilla*, i. 8, we read,
"The Scriptures may be written in every tongue. R. Simeon b. Gamaliel
says they did not suffer the Scriptures to be written except in Greek." On
this the Gemara observes, " R. Judah said, that when our Rabbins permitted
writing in Greek, they did so only for the Torah, and hence arose the translation made for King Ptolemy," etc. So Josephus, though an orthodox Pharisee,
makes use of the LXX., even where it departs from the Hebrew (1 Esdras).
The thirteen variations are given in the Gemara, *ut supra*, and in *Sôpherîm*, i.
9. In both places God is said to have guided the seventy-two translators, so
that, writing separately, all gave one sense. Side by side with this favourable estimate, *Soph.* i. 8, following the glosses on *Megillath Ta'anith*, gives
the later hostile tradition, which it supposes to refer to a different version.
"That day was a hard day for Israel—like the day when they made the
golden calf," because the Torah could not be adequately translated. See
further, on the gradual growth of the prejudice against the Greek translation,
Müller's note, *op. cit.* p. 11. Jerome, following the text supplied by Jewish
tradition, will have it that the LXX. translators purposely concealed from
Ptolemy the mysteries of faith, especially the prophecies referring to the
advent of Christ. See *Quæst. in Gen.* p. 2 (ed. Lagarde, 1868), and *Praef.
in Pent.*

two hundred years after Ezra, when the version was first written, and indeed from that time downwards until the apostolic age. For in the times of the New Testament the Greek and Hebrew Bibles were current side by side; and men like the apostles, who knew both languages, used either text indifferently, or even quoted the Old Testament from memory, as Paul often does, with a laxness surprising to the reader who judges by a modern rule, but very natural in the condition of the text which we have just characterised. It may be observed in passing that these considerations remove a great part of the difficulties which are commonly felt to attach to the citations of the Old Testament in the New.

When we say that the readings of the Septuagint afford a fair measure of the limits of variation in the early history of the text, it is by no means implied that the Greek version, taken as a whole, is as valuable as the Hebrew text. A translation can never supply the place of a manuscript. There is always an allowance to be made for errors and licences of interpretation, and the allowance is necessarily large in the case of the Septuagint, which was the first attempt at a translation of the Bible, and perhaps the first considerable translation ever made. Thus, even if we possessed the Septuagint in its original form it would be necessary to use it with great caution as an instrument of textual criticism. But in reality this use of the Septuagint is made greatly more difficult and uncertain by many corruptions which it underwent in the course of transmission. The Greek text was in a deplorable state even in the days of Origen, in the first half of the third Christian century. In his Hexaplar Bible, in which the Hebrew, the Septuagint, and the later Greek versions were arranged in parallel columns, Origen made a notable attempt to purify the text, and indicate its variations from the Hebrew. But the use made of Origen's labours by later generations rather increased the mischief, and in the present day it is an affair of the most delicate scholarship to make profitable use of the Alexandrian version for the confirmation or emendation of the Hebrew. The work has often fallen into incompetent hands, and their rashness is a chief reason why cautious scholars are still apt to look with unjustifiable indifference on what, after all, is our oldest witness to the history of the text of the Old Testament.

For our present purpose it is not necessary that I should conduct you over the delicate ground which cannot be safely trodden save by the most experienced scholarship. My object will be attained if I succeed in conveying to you by a few plain examples a just conception of the methods of the ancient copyists as they stand revealed to us in the broader differences between the Hebrew and the Septuagint. It will conduce to clearness if I indicate at the outset the conclusions to which these differences appear to point, and the proof of which will be specially contemplated in the details which I shall presently set before you. I shall endeavour to show that the comparison of the Hebrew and Greek texts carries us beyond the sphere of mere verbal variations, with which textual criticism is generally busied, and introduces us to a series of questions affecting the composition, the editing, and the collection of the sacred books. This class of questions forms the special subject of the branch of critical science which is usually distinguished from the verbal criticism of the text by the name of Higher or Historical Criticism. The value of textual criticism is now admitted on all hands. The first collections of various readings for the New Testament excited great alarm, but it was soon seen to be absurd to quarrel with facts. Various readings were actually found in MSS., and it was necessary to make the best of them. But while textual criticism admittedly deals with facts, the higher criticism is often supposed to have no other basis than the subjective fancies and arbitrary hypotheses of scholars. When

critics maintain that some Old Testament writings, traditionally ascribed to a single hand, are really of composite
origin, and that many of the Hebrew books have gone through
successive redactions—or, in other words, have been edited
and re-edited in different ages, receiving some addition or
modification at the hand of each editor—it is often supposed
that these are mere idle theories unsupported by evidence.
Here it is that the Septuagint comes in to justify the critics.
The variations of the Greek and Hebrew text reveal to us a
time when the functions of copyist and editor shaded into
one another by imperceptible degrees. They not only prove
that Old Testament books were subjected to such processes
of successive editing as critics maintain, but that the work of
redaction went on to so late a date that editorial changes are
found in the present Hebrew text which did not exist in the
MSS. of the Greek translators. The details of the evidence
will make my meaning more clear, but in general what I
desire to impress upon you is this. The evidence of the
Septuagint proves that early copyists had a very different view
of their responsibility from that which we might be apt to
ascribe to them. They were not reckless or indifferent to
the truth. They copied the Old Testament books knowing
them to be sacred books, and they were zealous to preserve
them as writings of Divine authority. But their sense of
responsibility to the Divine word regarded the meaning
rather than the form, and they had not that highly-developed
sense of the importance of preserving every word and every
letter of the original hand of the author which seems natural
to us. When we look at the matter carefully, we observe
that the difference between them and us lies, not in any
religious principle, but in the literary ideas of those ancient
times. From our point of view a book is the property of the
author. You may buy a copy of it, but you do not thereby
acquire a literary property in the work, or a right to tamper

with the style and alter the words of the author even to make
his sense more distinct.   But this idea was too subtle for
those ancient times.   The man who had bought or copied a
book held it to be his own for every purpose.   He valued it
for its contents, and therefore would not disfigure these by
arbitrary changes.   But, if he could make it more convenient
for use by adding a note here, putting in a word there, or
incorporating additional matter derived from another source,
he had no hesitation in doing so.   In short, every ancient
scholar who copied or annotated a book for his own use was
very much in the position of a modern editor, with the difference that at that time there was no system of footnotes,
brackets, and explanatory prefaces, by which the insertions
could be distinguished from the original text.

In setting before you some examples of the evidence
which enables us to prove this thesis, I shall begin with the
question of the titles which are prefixed to some parts of the
Old Testament.   And here it is proper to explain that the
general titles prefixed to the several books in the English
Bible, such as "The First Book of Moses called Genesis,"
"The Book of the Prophet Isaiah," and so forth, are no part
of the Hebrew text.   Even the shorter titles of the same kind
found in our common printed Hebrew Bibles lack manuscript
authority.   The only titles that form an integral part of the
textual tradition are those which appear in the English Bible
in the body of the text itself—such titles, for example, as
are contained in Proverbs i. 1, x. 1, xxv. 1, or in Isaiah i. 1,
xiii. 1, etc. etc.   This being understood, it immediately
appears that a large proportion of the books of the Old Testament are anonymous.   The Pentateuch, for example, bears
no author's name on its front, although certain things in the
course of the narrative are said to have been written down
by Moses.   All the historical books are anonymous, with the
single exception of one of the latest of them, the memoirs of

Nehemiah, in which the author's name is prefixed to the first
chapter. This fact is characteristic. Why do the authors
not give their names? Because the literary public was interested in the substance of the history, but was not concerned
to know who had written it.

To give this observation its just weight, we must remember that most of the historical books are not contemporary
memoirs, written from personal observation, but compila-
tions, extending over long periods, for which the authors
must have drawn largely from earlier sources, or from oral
tradition. Moreover, the frequent changes of style and other
marks of composite authorship which occur in these histories
prove that the work of compilation largely consisted in
piecing together long quotations from older books. In such
circumstances a modest compiler might very well prefer to
remain anonymous; but then, according to modern ideas of
the way in which literary work should be done, he ought to
have given full and careful indications of the sources from
which he drew. In the Book of Kings reference is habitually
made, for certain particulars in the political history of each
reign, to the official chronicles of the sovereigns of Judah
and Israel, and in 2 Sam. i. 18 a poem of David is quoted
from the Book of Jashar, which is also cited in Josh. x. 13.
But for the mass of the narrative of the Earlier Prophets
(Joshua—Kings) the compilers give no indication of the
sources from which they worked. In short, the whole historical literature of Israel before the Exile is written by and
for men whose interest in the story of the nation was not
combined with any interest in the hands by which the story had
been first set forth, or from time to time reshaped. To these
ages a book was a book, to be taken or rejected on its internal
merits, without regard to the personality that lay behind it.

And this feeling was not confined to historical books.
No ancient poem excites in the modern mind a more eager

curiosity as to the personality of the author than the wonderful Book of Job. We can understand that hymns like some of the Psalms, which speak the common feelings of all pious minds, are appropriately left anonymous. But the Book of Job is an individual creation, as clearly stamped with the impress of a great personality as the prophecies of Isaiah. And yet the author is nameless and unknown.

The only part of the older Hebrew literature in which the rule of anonymity does not prevail is the prophetical books. And the reason for this is obvious. Most of the prophets—to say *all* would be to prejudge a question that must come before us presently—were preachers first of all, and writers only in the second instance. Their books are not products of the closet, but summaries of a course of public activity, in which the personality of the preacher could not be separated from his words. And so their books make no exception to the rule that in old Israel a man could not make himself known and perpetuate his name by literary labours. If a man was already prominent in the eyes of his contemporaries, and wrote, as he spoke, with the weight of a public character, he had a reason to put his name to his books, and others had a reason for remembering what he had written; but not otherwise. Even in the Book of Psalms the only names that occur in the titles are those of famous historical characters—Moses, David, Solomon; and possibly, for here the individual reference of the names is doubtful, those of the founders and ancestors of Temple choirs—Asaph, Heman, Ethan.

After the time of Ezra and Nehemiah, when the Church took the place of the State, and the scribes succeeded to the empty seat of the prophets, all this began to change. A great part of the spiritual and intellectual energy of the Jews was turned into purely literary channels; and ultimately, after the decline of the Hasmonean power, the men of books

became the acknowledged leaders of national life, and letters
the recognised means of public distinction. To the doctors
of the Law, who knew no other greatness than that of learning, all the heroes of ancient Israel, even the rude warrior
Joab, appeared in the character of book-men and students.
To this point of view the anonymity of the old literature was
a great stumbling-block. It seemed obvious to the Rabbins
that the leaders of the ancient nation must have been, above
all things, the authors of the national literature, and they
proceeded with much confidence to assign the composition of
the nameless books to Moses, Joshua, Samuel, and so forth.
Even Adam, Melchizedek, and Abraham were not excluded
from literary honours, each of them being credited with the
authorship of a psalm.[1]

In the times of the Talmud, when these strange conjectures took final shape, and were admitted into the body of
authoritative Jewish tradition, the text of the Bible was
already rigidly fixed, so that no attempt could be made to
embody them in titles prefixed to the several books. But the
tendency that culminates in the Talmudic legends is much
older than the Talmud itself, and no one, I imagine, will be
prepared to affirm on general grounds that the Jews of the
last pre-Christian centuries either lacked curiosity as to the
authorship of their sacred books, or were prepared to restrain
their curiosity within the limits prescribed by the rules of
evidence. But in these ages, as we have already seen, the
Biblical text was still in a more or less fluid state, and we
dare not say *a priori* that the introduction of a title based on
conjecture would have seemed to exceed the licence allowed
to a copyist. We know that such conjectural titles found
a place in manuscripts of the New Testament, where, for
example, many copies prefix the name of Paul to the Epistle

---

[1] See the famous passage, *Bâbâ Bâthra*, 14, *b*, quoted at length by
Driver, *Introduction*, p. xxxii. *sq.*

to the Hebrews, though it is certain that the oldest manuscripts left it anonymous. Whether something of the same sort took place in copies of the Old Testament is a question not to be answered on general grounds, but only on the evidence of facts; and the Septuagint supplies us with facts that are to the point.

The part of the Old Testament in which the system of titles has been carried out most fully is the Book of Psalms. The titles to the Psalms are to a large extent directions for their liturgical performance in the service of the Temple music; but they also contain the names of men—David, the Sons of Korah, and so forth. Are we to suppose that there is no title of a psalm in the Hebrew Bible which does not go back to the author of the psalm, or at least to a time when his name was known from contemporary evidence? Let us consult the Septuagint, and what do we find? We find, in the first place, that the Septuagint has the words " of " or " to David " in a number of psalms where the Hebrew has no author's name (Psalms xxxiii. xliii. lxvii. lxxi. xci. xciii. to xcix. civ.[1] cxxxvii.); and, conversely, it omits the name of David from four, and the name of Solomon from one, of the Psalms of Degrees (Psalms cxxii. cxxiv. cxxxi. cxxxiii. cxxvii.).[2] Now the large number of cases in which the Septuagint inserts the name of David is evidence of a tendency to ascribe to him an ever-increasing

[1] In Ps. civ., according to the Syro-Hexaplar, Aquila has " of David," so that these words may have stood in his Hebrew copy.

[2] Strack, in a review of the first edition of these Lectures (*Theol. Literaturblatt*, 1882, No. 41), takes the objection that the Sinaitic MS. has the name of David in the four Psalms of Degrees cited by me, and that the evidence of the Vatican MS. is lacking owing to a lacuna. But no one who knows the elements of textual criticism will set the evidence of the Sinaitic Codex against the overwhelming mass of MSS. on the other side, even though it is reinforced in the case of two of the four psalms by the Memphitic version. The materials given in Field's *Hexapla* show clearly that we have here to do with Hexaplar additions, *i.e.* with words added by Origen from the Hebrew, and originally marked as additions by an asterisk, which Sin. has dropped.

number of psalms. That tendency, we know, went on, till at length it became a common opinion that he was the author of the whole Psalter. We cannot therefore suppose that the Greek version, or the Hebrew MSS. on which it rested, would omit the name of David in any case where it had once stood; and the conclusion is inevitable that at least in four cases our Hebrew Bibles have the name of David where it has no right to be, and that the insertion was made by a copyist after the time when the text of the Septuagint branched off. But if this be so, it is impossible to maintain on principle that the titles of the Psalms are throughout authoritative : and if there is no principle involved, it is not only legitimate, but an absolute duty, to test every title by comparing it with the internal evidence supplied by the poem itself. I shall have occasion to return to this subject in Lecture VII.

Similar variations, leading to similar conclusions, are found in other parts of the Old Testament, and even in the prophetical books. In Jer. xxvii. 1 the Hebrew has a title which the Septuagint omits, and which every one can see to be a mere accidental repetition of the title of chap. xxvi. For the prophecy which the title ascribes to the beginning of the reign of Jehoiakim is addressed in the most explicit way to Zedekiah, king of Judah (verses 3, 12). So again the Septuagint omits the name of Jeremiah in the title to the prophecy against Babylon (chaps. l. li.), which, for other reasons, modern critics generally ascribe to a later prophet. Here, it is true, chap. li. 59-64 may seem to be a subscription establishing the traditional authorship. But a note at the end of the chapter in the Hebrew expressly says that the words of Jeremiah end with "they shall be weary,"—the close of verse 58. This note is the real subscription to the prophecy, and it is also omitted by the Septuagint.[1]

---

[1] It is argued by those who ascribe chaps. l. li. to Jeremiah, that the expression "all these words" in chap. li. 60 necessarily refers to the context

As a detailed survey of the prophetical writings does not fall within the plan of these Lectures I will take the opportunity, before passing from the subject, to make some further remarks on the titles of the prophetic books, going beyond the indications to be derived from the Septuagint. You are aware that according to the traditionally received opinion there is not in these books any such thing as an anonymous prophecy: the Books of Isaiah, Jeremiah, and Ezekiel contain prophecies by these three men alone, and in like manner the Book of the Twelve Minor Prophets, which in Hebrew is reckoned as one book, contains prophecies by the Twelve who are named in the titles and by no other hand. Modern critics reject this opinion, and maintain that various prophecies, such as chaps. xl.-lxvi. of the Book of Isaiah, chaps. l. li. of the Book of Jeremiah, and some parts of Micah and Zechariah, are not the composition of the prophets to whose works they are traditionally reckoned. It is not argued that these pieces are spurious works palmed off under a false name. They are accepted as genuine writings of true prophets, but it is maintained that their style and other characters, above all the historical situation which they presuppose, show that they are not the work of the hand and age to which current tradition refers them. Thus in the case of Isaiah xl.-lxvi. it is pointed out that the prophet addresses his words of consolation and exhortation to Israel in its Babylonian exile. This exile is to him the present situation, not an event foreseen in the far prophetic future, and therefore, it is argued, the prophecy must have been written in the days of the Captivity. It is not disputed on any hand that the custom of the prophets is to speak to the needs and

immediately preceding. But the order of Jeremiah's prophecies is greatly disturbed (*infra*, p. 109 *sq.*). No one will argue that "these words" in chap. xlv. 1 refer to chap. xliv.; yet the argument is as good in the one case as in the other. Compare Budde, "Ueber die Capitel L. und LI. des Buches Jeremia" in *Jahrbb. f. D. Theol.* vol. xxiii. p. 428 *sq.*, p. 529 *sq.*

actual situation of their contemporaries. However far their visions reach into the future, they take their start from the present. Had they failed to do this their word could not have been the direct message of God to their own contemporaries. Accordingly it is admitted by those who still argue for Isaiah as the author of Isa. xl.-lxvi. that that great prophet in his later years must have been supernaturally transported out of his own historical surroundings, and set, as it were, in vision, in the midst of the community of the Captivity, that he might write a word of prophetic exhortation, not for his own contemporaries but for the future generation of Babylonian exiles. To make this theory plausible it must further be maintained that the prophecy so written remained a sealed book for a hundred and fifty years ; for it is manifest that subsequent prophets, like Jeremiah, who were very familiar with other parts of Isaiah's teaching, had no acquaintance with this wonderful revelation. Surely there is a difficulty here which is not the creation of scepticism, but must be felt by every thoughtful reader. There is a method in Revelation as much as in Nature, and the first law of that method, which no careful student of Scripture can fail to grasp, is that God's Revelation of Himself is unfolded gradually, in constant contact with the needs of religious life. Every word of God is spoken for all time, but every word none the less was first spoken to a present necessity of God's people. The great mass of the prophecies are obviously conformed to this rule, and the burden of proof lies with those who ask us to recognise an exception to it. In the case before us we are asked to admit an exception of the most startling kind, in spite of the fact that the chapters in question are very different in style and language from the undisputed writings of Isaiah, and in spite of the fact that for a hundred and fifty years the teaching of the prophets who continued Isaiah's work remained uninfluenced by what,

on the traditional view, was the crowning achievement of
Isaiah's ministry. The defenders of tradition make no
serious attempt to remove these difficulties.[1] They seek
to cut the discussion short by two arguments—(1) that the
synagogue and the Church agree in ascribing the chapters
to Isaiah; and (2) that if they are not by Isaiah it is
impossible to explain how they could have been admitted
into his book. (See Keil, *Introduction*, Eng. trans., i. 331.)

Now as regards the testimony of the synagogue and the
Church it is true that Ecclus. xlviii. 24 (27) already cites
Isa. xl. 1 as the words of Isaiah, and from this it may be taken
as probable that five hundred years after the death of Isaiah,
when the son of Sirach wrote (*circa* 200 B.C.), the whole Book
of Isaiah was assumed to be by a single hand. But on what
authority was this assumed? The son of Sirach had no other
written sources for the literary history of the Bible than those
we still possess, and it is plain, therefore, that the opinion of
his time simply rested on the fact that the disputed prophecies
already stood in the same book with the unquestioned writings of Isaiah, and were held to be covered by the general title
in Isa. i. 1. Thus the two arguments reduce themselves to
one, the supposed incredibility that a writing not by Isaiah
could have been included in Isaiah's book. Let us understand
what this argument means. In ancient times a book meant a
separate roll or volume, and the Jewish division of the prophetic writings into four books means that they were usually
comprised in four volumes, of which the Book of Isaiah was
one, as we see from Luke iv. 17. But these volumes were

---

[1] Some trifling and totally inadequate attempts have been made to mini-
mise the differences of style, and a few passages have been pointed out in
which there are points of contact, rather in expression than in thought,
between Isa. xl. *sqq.* and prophets who lived between Isaiah and the Exile.
None of these coincidences has any force as proving the priority of the great
anonymous prophecy, and none of these petty arguments touches the broad
and decisive fact that Jeremiah and his compeers are totally uninfluenced by
the *leading ideas* of Isa. xl.-lxvi.

not constructed on the principle that each writer should have a separate roll for himself, for the twelve minor prophets formed a single book. Why then should it be inconceivable that a separate prophecy, too short to make a volume by itself, should have been placed at the end of Isaiah's volume, which, without this appendix, would have been very much shorter than the other three prophetic books? You may object that if this had been done the collector would at least have been careful to mark off the true Isaiah from the addition. But this assumption is not warranted. It may be taken as certain that a prophecy composed in the Exile, when the Jews were scattered and had no public life, was never preached, but circulated from the first in writing, passing privately from hand to hand. Under these circumstances the author was not likely to put his name to his book, and the collector of the present Book of Isaiah, who received it without a title, would transmit it in the same way. It is true that by so doing he left it possible for readers to draw a false inference as to the authorship; but every one who has handled Eastern manuscripts knows that scribes constantly copy out several works into one volume without taking the precautions necessary to prevent an anonymous piece from being ascribed to the author of the work to which it is attached. To prevent mistakes of this sort it is necessary that every piece which bears an author's name should be furnished not only with a title but with a subscription marking the point at which it ends. But in the prophetic books subscriptions are the exception not the rule; the only formal one, which professes to say where the words of a particular prophet end, is Jer. li. 64, and this, as we have already seen, is absent from the Septuagint, and presumably formed no part of the original text. We have no right, therefore, to expect a formal indication of the point at which the actual words of Isaiah end; but in point of fact the main part of the book is very clearly separated from the Babylonian chapters by the historical section, chaps. xxxvi.-xxxix.   Apart from the psalm of Hezekiah, these chapters are found also with slight variations in the Book of Kings, and the nature of the variations proves (as you may see in detail by consulting Prof. Driver's *Introduction*) that the text of Kings is the original, and that the narrative of Isaiah is extracted from that book.   These extracts form an appendix, which cannot have been added to the volume of Isaiah's prophecies till the time of the Captivity at the earliest, and Isaiah xl.-lxvi. constitutes a second and still later addition.

As another instance of the futility of the arguments from authority that are used to cut short critical discussion as to the authorship of prophetical pieces, I may take the case of Zechariah ix.-xiv.   On what authority are these declared to form part of the Book of Zechariah?   In the Hebrew Bible there is no such book.   There is not even a general title to the section of the fourth prophetic volume in which these chapters stand ; for the titles in Zech. i. 1, vii. 1, refer only to single prophecies of Zechariah delivered at particular dates.   At chapter ix. we have an entirely separate prophecy with a separate title, in which Zechariah is not named, a different historical situation, and a quite different style and manner.   Further, we must remember that the volume of Minor Prophets is a miscellaneous collection, not even arranged on chronological principles (since, for example, Hosea precedes Amos), but gathering up all the remains of prophetic literature that were not already comprised in the Books of Isaiah, Jeremiah, and Ezekiel.   Under these circumstances there is absolutely no inference to be drawn from the fact that the anonymous prophecies, Zech. ix.-xiv., stand immediately after others that bear Zechariah's name. The later Jews ascribed them to Zechariah, but that is no evidence for us ; for they did so on exactly the same absurd principle on which, in the days of Origen, they ascribed all anonymous psalms to the author of the nearest preceding psalm that bears a title.[1]

I now return to the Septuagint, and propose to call your attention to an example of editorial redaction, involving a series of changes running through the whole structure of a passage. For this purpose I select the twenty-seventh chapter of Jeremiah, the Hebrew title of which has already been shown to be an editorial insertion. We are now to see that the hand of an editor has been at work all through the chapter. Let me say at the outset that the example is a somewhat unusual one. There are not many parts of the Old Testament where the variations of the Greek and Hebrew are so extensive as in Jeremiah; but it is necessary to choose a well-marked case in order to convey a distinct conception of the limits of editorial interference. To facilitate comparison, I print a translation of the Hebrew text, putting everything in italics which is omitted by the Septuagint. The Greek has some other slight variations, which are not of consequence for our present purpose. The essential difference between the two texts is that the Hebrew, without omitting anything that is in the Greek, has a number of additional clauses and sentences.

In the reign of King Zedekiah a congress of ambassadors from the neighbouring nations was held at Jerusalem, to concert a rising against Nebuchadnezzar. The prophets and diviners encouraged this scheme; but Jeremiah was commanded by the Lord to protest against it, and declare that the empire of Nebuchadnezzar had been conferred on him by

---

[1] See for the rule as to the anonymous psalms, Origen, ii. 514 *sq.*, Rue; Jerome, *Ep.* cxl. *ad Cypr.* That the same principle was applied to the Psalter and the Book of the Minor Prophets is not a mere conjecture, but appears from Jerome's *Praef. in XII. Proph.* and the Preface to his Commentary on Malachi. In the case of the prophets, the principle was applied to settle the chronology; where the title gives no date the prophecy was delivered in the reigns of the kings mentioned in the next preceding dated title.

Jehovah's decree, and that it was vain to rebel. The prophetic message delivered in the name of the God of Israel ran thus :—

Jer. xxvii. 5.—I have made the earth, *the man and the beast which are upon the face of the earth,* by my great power and outstretched arm, and give it to whom I please. (6.) *And now* I have given all these lands [LXX. the earth] into the hand of Nebuchadnezzar. . . . (7.) *And all nations shall serve him and his son and his son's son, till the time of his land come also, and mighty nations and great kings make him their servant.* (8.) And the nation and kingdom which will not *serve him,* Nebuchadnezzar, *king of Babylon, and* put their neck under the yoke of the king of Babylon, will I punish, saith the Lord, with the sword, and with famine, *and with pestilence,* till I have consumed them by his hand. (9.) Therefore hearken ye not to your prophets, . . . which say ye shall not serve the king of Babylon. (10.) For they prophesy lies to you to remove you from your land, *and that I should drive you out and ye should perish.* . . .

(12.) And to Zedekiah, king of Judah, I spake with all these words, saying, Bring your neck *under the yoke of the king of Babylon,* and *serve him and his people, and live.* (13.) *Why will ye die, thou and thy people, by the sword, by famine, and by pestilence, as the Lord hath spoken against the nation that will not* serve the king of Babylon ? (14.) *Therefore hearken not unto the words of the prophets who speak unto you, saying, Serve not the king of Babylon* ; for they [emphatic] prophesy lies unto you. (15.) For I have not sent them, saith the Lord, and they prophesy lies in my name. . . .

(16.) And to the priests and to all this people [LXX. to all the people and the priests] I spake saying, Thus saith the Lord, Hearken not to the words of your prophets who prophesy to you, saying, Behold the vessels of the house of the Lord shall be brought back from Babylon *now quickly,* for they prophesy a lie unto you. (17.) *Hearken not unto them* [LXX. I have not sent them], *serve the king of Babylon, and live ; wherefore should this city be laid waste ?* (18.) But if they are prophets, and if the word of the Lord is with them, let them intercede with the Lord of Hosts [LXX. with me], *that the vessels which are left in the house of the Lord, and the house of the king of Judah, and in Jerusalem, come not to Babylon.* (19.) For thus saith the Lord *of Hosts concerning the pillars and the sea and the bases,* and the rest of the vessels left in this city, (20) Which *Nebuchadnezzar* the king of Babylon took not when he carried Jeconiah *son of Jehoiakim king of Judah* captive from Jerusalem *to Babylon, and all the nobles of Judah and Jerusalem ;* (21.) *For thus saith the Lord of Hosts, the God of Israel, concerning the vessels left in the house of God, and in the house of the king of Judah and Jerusalem ;* (22.) They shall be taken to Babylon, *and there shall they be unto the day that I visit them,* saith the Lord ; *then will I bring them up and restore them to this place.*

Throughout these verses the general effect of the omissions of the Septuagint is to make the style simpler, more natural, and more forcible. At verses 8, 10, 12, 13, 17, the additional matter of the Massoretic text is mere expansion of ideas fully expressed in the shorter recension ; and at verse 14 the omissions of the Septuagint give the proper oratorical value to the emphatic "they" of the original, which the prophet, in genuine Hebrew style, must have spoken with a gesture pointing to the false prophets who stood before the king. It is not to be thought that a later copyist added nerve and force to the prophecy by pruning the prolixities of the original text. Jeremiah is no mean orator and author, and the prolixities are much more in the wearisome style of the later Jewish literature.

But in some parts the two recensions differ in meaning as well as language. At verse 7 the Hebrew text inserts in the midst of Jeremiah's exhortation to submission a prophecy that the Babylonians shall be punished in the third generation. No doubt Jeremiah does elsewhere predict the fall of Babylon and the restoration of Israel. He had done so at an earlier date (xxv. 11-13). But is it natural that he should turn aside to introduce such a prediction here, in the very midst of a solemn admonition on which it has no direct bearing? And is this a thing which a copyist would be tempted to omit? Much rather was it natural for a later scribe to introduce it. Again, at verse 16, the Hebrew text modifies the prediction of the restoration of the sacred vessels made by the false prophets, by the insertion of the words "now quickly." There was no motive for the omission of these words, if they are original. But a later scribe, reflecting on the fact that the sacred vessels were restored by Cyrus, might well insert the qualification "now quickly" to deprive the false prophets of any claim to have spoken truly after all. In reality it does not need these words to prove them liars; for their prediction, taken in the context, plainly meant that the alliance should defeat Nebuchadnezzar and recover the spoil. But the words stand or fall with the prediction put into Jeremiah's mouth, in verse 22, that the vessels of the temple and the palace, including the brazen pillars, sea, and bases, should be taken indeed to Babylon, but be brought back again in the day of visitation. This is plainly the spurious insertion of a thoughtless copyist, who had his eye on chapter lii. 17. For it is true that the pillars, the sea, and the bases were carried to Babylon, but they were not and could not have been brought back. These huge masses could not have been transported entire across the mountains and deserts that separated Judæa from Babylon. And so we are expressly told in chapter lii. that they were broken up and carried off as old brass, fit only for the melting-pot. Jeremiah and his hearers knew well that they could not reach Babylon in any other form, and in his mouth the prediction which we read in the Hebrew text would have been not only false, but palpably absurd. That such a prediction now stands in the text only proves what the thoughtlessness of copyists was capable of, and makes the reading of the Septuagint absolutely certain.

We conclude, then, from a plain argument of physical impossibility, that Jeremiah did not predict the restoration of the spoils of the Temple. And by this result we remove a serious inconsistency from his religious teaching. For the restoration to which Jeremiah constantly looks is not the re-establishment of the old ritual, but the bringing in of a spiritual covenant when God's law shall be written on the hearts of the people (chap. xxxi.). No prophet thinks more lightly of the service of the Temple (chap. vii.). He denies that God gave a law of sacrifice to the people when they left Egypt. They may eat their burnt-offerings as well as the other sacrifices, and God will not condemn them (vii. 21, 22).

Even the ark of the covenant is in his eyes an obsolete symbol, which in the day of Israel's conversion shall not be missed and not be remade (iii. 16, R. V., marg.). To the false prophets and the people who followed them, the ark, the temple, the holy vessels, were all in all. To Jeremiah they were less than nothing, and their restoration was no part of his hope of salvation.[1]

[1] There is one passage in Jeremiah, as we read it, which appears inconsistent with the view I have ventured to take of the prophet's attitude to the temporary elements of the Old Testament ritual. In Jer. xxxiii. 14-26 it is predicted that the Levitical priesthood and its sacrifices shall be perpetual as the succession of day and night. This passage is also wanting in the Septuagint. No reason can be suggested for its omission ; for we know from Philo that even those Jews of Alexandria who sat most loosely to the ceremonial law regarded the Temple and its service as an essential element in religion (*De Migr. Abra.* cap. xvi.). If taken literally, the eternity of Levitical sacrifices, as expressed in xxxiii. 18, seems quite inconsistent with all else in Jeremiah's prophecies. Taken typically, the verse only fits the sacrifice of the mass, to which Roman Catholic expositors refer it ; for the sacrifices are to be offered continually in all time.

LECTURE V

THE SEPTUAGINT (*continued*)—THE COMPOSITION OF BIBLICAL BOOKS

In the last Lecture we began to examine those features of the Septuagint which bear witness to the kind of labour that was spent on the text by ancient editors. We have seen how redactors or copyists sometimes added titles to anonymous pieces, and how by a series of small editorial changes, running from verse to verse through a chapter, the form and even the meaning of an important passage were sometimes considerably modified.

We now come to another part of the subject, in which I propose to use the variations between the Greek and Hebrew text to throw light on the structure of the books of the Bible. The main point which I desire to enforce in this Lecture is that certain books which we have been wont to look upon as continuous unities are really composite in character. Some evidence to this effect, especially as regards the prophetic books, has already come before us when we looked at the question of titles. To-day we have to deal with another branch of evidence, drawn from the transpositions of the Septuagint, the entire omission of certain sections, and so forth. I hope to be able to handle these evidences in a way that will not only confirm the results at which we have already arrived, but will give us valuable insight into deeper critical questions, especially as regards the historical books.

I begin with the *transpositions* of the Septuagint text, and choose as my first example the chapters comprising Jeremiah's prophecies against the heathen nations. In our Bibles, and in the Hebrew Bible, these prophecies occupy chapters xlvi. to li. In the Septuagint they follow the 13th verse of the twenty-fifth chapter, and appear in a different order. In the Hebrew the sequence is Egypt, Philistines, Moab, Ammon, Edom, Damascus, Kedar and Hazor, Elam, Babylon. The Septuagint sequence is Elam, Egypt, Babylon, Philistines, Edom, Ammon, Kedar and Hazor, Damascus, Moab. Can we then assume that in this case the translator of the Septuagint version, having before him a fixed and certain order of all Jeremiah's oracles, took the liberty to shift the prophecies against the nations through one another, and to put them in an entirely different part of the book? From what we have seen already as to the general way in which these translators acted, such an assumption is highly improbable. Rather we are to suppose that in their copy these prophecies already occupied a different place from what they hold in the Hebrew Bible.

What does that lead us to conclude? Variations in the order of the individual pieces may very well happen in collected editions of writings originally published separately, but not in a single book of one author. And that is just what the facts lead us otherwise to suppose, for we know that Jeremiah's prophecies were not all written down at one time, or in the order in which they now stand. We learn from chap. xxxvi. that a record of the first twenty-three years of his prophetic ministry was dictated by the prophet to Baruch in the fourth year of Jehoiakim. But this book does not correspond with the first part of the present Book of Jeremiah, in which prophecies later than the reign of Jehoiakim —such as chap. xxiv.—precede others which must have stood in the original collection (chap. xxvi.). Jeremiah's book, then, as we have it, is not a continuous record of his prophecies, which he himself kept constantly posted up to date, but a compilation made up from several prophetic writings originally published separately. In this compilation the natural order is not always observed, for it is plain that chap. xlv., containing a brief prophecy addressed to Baruch, "when he wrote these words in a book at the mouth of Jeremiah in the fourth year of Jehoiakim" (ver. 1), must originally have stood at the close of the collection spoken of in chap. xxxvi. It is easy, then, to understand that, when several distinct books of Jeremiah's words and deeds were brought together into one volume, there might be variations of order in different copies of the collection, just as modern editions of the collected works of one author frequently differ in arrangement.

It is very doubtful whether this group of prophecies appears just as they were first published, either in the Septuagint or in the Hebrew. The order of the individual prophecies seems to be more suitable in the Hebrew and English texts; for chap. xxv. 15 *sq.* contains a sort of brief summary or general conspectus of Jeremiah's prophecies against the nations, and here the order agrees very closely with that in our present Hebrew text as against the Septuagint; but then, on the other hand, the summary of Jeremiah's prophecies against the nations is found in the twenty-fifth chapter, whereas in our present edition the details under this general sketch begin at chap. xlvi. Much more natural in this respect is the arrangement of the Septuagint, placing all the details in immediate juxtaposition with the general summary; so that here we seem to have a case in which neither edition of Jeremiah's prophecies is thoroughly satisfactory and in good order. But the general conclusion is that the transpositions give us a key to the way in which the book came together, showing that it was not all written and published in continuous unity by Jeremiah himself, but has the character of a collected edition of several writings originally distinct. We observe, also, that the compilers did not execute their work with perfect skill and judgment ; and so it would plainly be unreasonable to call every critic a rationalist who ventures to judge, on internal or other evidence, that the collection may possibly contain some chapters, such as l. and li., which are not from the hand of Jeremiah at all.

Another example of the important inferences that may be drawn from the transpositions of the Septuagint occurs in the Book of Proverbs. I presume that many of us have been accustomed to think of the Proverbs as a single composition, written from first to last by Solomon. But here again we find such transpositions as indicate that the book is not so much one continuous writing as a collected edition of various proverbial books and tracts. For example, the first fourteen verses of Proverbs xxx., containing the words of Agur, are placed in the Septuagint collection after the 22d verse of chap. xxiv. Then immediately upon that follows chap. xxiv. 23-34, a little section which in the Hebrew has a separate title, — " These also are [words] of the wise." After that comes chap. xxx. 15-xxxi. 9. Then comes the collection of " proverbs of Solomon " copied out by the men of King Hezekiah (xxv.-xxix.) ; and the book closes with the description of the virtuous woman (xxxi. 10-31). It is natural to explain the fact that these several small collections of proverbs are grouped in such different order in the Septuagint and in the Hebrew respectively by the hypothesis that they originally existed as separate books ; for in that case, when they came to be collected into one volume, differences of order might readily arise, which could hardly have happened if the whole had been the original composition of Solomon alone. And indeed the existence of such separate collections is more than an hypothesis, as the sub-titles of the book

show. For after the general title, chap. i. 1-6, and a long
section, not proverbial in form, containing poetical admonitions in praise of wisdom, morality, and religion (chap. i. 7-
ix. 18), we come on a collection of proverbs or aphorisms
extending from chap. x. 1 to chap. xxii. 16, and headed (in
the Hebrew) " Proverbs of Solomon." This again is followed
by a collection of " Words of the wise " (chap. xxii. 17-
xxiv. 22), with a preface of its own (chap. xxii. 17-21). Then
comes the second collection of words of the wise already
referred to, and then again the second collection of Proverbs
of Solomon, copied out by the "Men of Hezekiah." The men
of Hezekiah's time, we see, had written materials before them.
And the *corpus* of proverbs which they formed from these
must once have existed side by side with the great collection
of Proverbs of Solomon in chaps. x. *sqq.*, and in an independent
form. For the title runs : " These also are the proverbs of
Solomon, which the men of Hezekiah copied out." The word
" also " shows that this title was written when two separate
collections of Salomonic Proverbs were brought for the first
time into one volume. In like manner the title in chap.
xxiv. 23 : " These also are [words] of the wise," shows that
the preceding collection of Words of the Wise once stood by
itself without the appendix in xxiv. 23 *sqq.*, from which, in
fact, it is separated in the Septuagint.[1]

---

[1] That the two Salomonic collections were formed independently, and not
by the same hand, appears most clearly from the many cases in which the
same proverb appears in both (see the Introduction to Delitzsch's *Commentary*, § 3). Even these parts of the book, therefore, were not collected by
Solomon himself, and the title in chap. i. 1 is not from his hand, but was
added by some collector or editor. Hence there is no reason to suppose that
Solomon is the author of chaps. i.-ix. any more than of the " Words of the
Wise." The whole book bears the name of Solomon's Proverbs, because the
two great Salomonic collections are the leading element in it. Compare on
the whole subject Professor A. B. Davidson's article PROVERBS in the 9th ed.
of the *Encyclopædia Britannica* ; Professor Cheyne's *Job and Solomon* (London,
1887) ; and Professor Driver's *Introduction to the O. T.* (Edinburgh, 1891).
There are close analogies between the composition of the Book of Proverbs
and that of the Psalter. See Lecture VII.

Let us now pass on to the historical books. In these the questions of composition are more complicated, because a historian whose object is to produce a continuous narrative, covering a long period, by the aid of a series of older histories or memories, has it open to him to deal with these materials in various ways. He may content himself with choosing one good narrative for each section of the history, transcribing or abridging it, and adding little of his own except at the points where he passes from one source to another. Or while mainly following this plan, he may from time to time insert supplementary matter taken from other sources. Or, on the other hand, if he has before him several histories of the same period, he may frame from them a combined narrative. And in this case he may either recast the whole story in his own words as modern historians do, or he may take short extracts from his several sources and piece them together in a sort of mosaic, so that the language, style, and colour of each of the sources are still largely preserved, though the old fragments are reset in a new pattern and frame.

Even from the English Bible an attentive reader may satisfy himself that the history of the Hebrew kings is not a homogeneous literary composition like Macaulay's *History of England*. Many minor marks of variety in language and style that are very apparent in the Hebrew necessarily disappear in translation; but the broader characteristics of style and literary treatment survive, and these are so different in different parts of the narrative as to leave no doubt that the compiler used a number of sources and followed them closely, retaining in great measure the very words of his predecessors. Sometimes a single source is followed without interruption for a number of chapters, as in the so-called "court history" of David, 2 Sam. ix.-xx. Read this whole section continuously, and while your mind is still under the impression, look back to chap. viii. You pass in a moment from a narrative full of

life and colour to a bare chronicle of public affairs, mainly
foreign wars. Note further that to a certain extent both
narratives cover the same ground ; both speak of David's
wars with the Syrians. But the particulars given are not
the same, and the choice of particulars shows that the authors
of the two accounts had different interests. The writer of
the longer history is a student of human nature, who has
taken David and his court as his field of observation, and
loves to dwell on every incident, however trivial, that illustrates character. But he has no great interest in foreign
wars ; many of David's campaigns he passes over altogether,
and his mention of the Syrian campaigns seems to be due to
their connection with the war with Ammon, which—through
the matter of Uriah—had a very special bearing on David's
personal history. The other account is wholly interested in
the public glories of David's reign, and, brief as it is, finds
room for particulars about rich booty and tributes of voluntary homage to which the court history never alludes.

Now pass on to 1 Kings i. ii. You cannot, I think, fail
to realise that here we are again in the hands of the court
historian. The style, the manner, the character of the picturesque details is the same, and the main thread of the narrative is still that which forms the thread of most personal
histories of an Eastern court—intrigues about the succession.
Lastly, note that the two great extracts from the court
history are separated by 2 Sam. xxi.-xxiv., a series of appendices of very various content, all of which hang quite loose
from one another and from the continuous well-knit narrative
which they interrupt.

I have begun with a very simple example of the incor-
poration of an older document in the Bible history, and one
that raises no questions to alarm the most timid faith. I
now pass on to a case one degree more complex, in which,
however, we are not wholly dependent on internal evidence,

but get some assistance from the Greek version. Many of you have probably observed the way in which the history of the sovereigns of Judah and Israel is arranged in the Book of Kings. Here the narrative is concerned with the affairs of two monarchies, and has to pass backwards and forwards from the one to the other. The plan on which this is effected is to take up each king, whether of Judah or of Ephraim, in the order of his accession to the throne, and follow his reign to the end. For example, after the history of Asa of Judah we have the story of all the northern kings, from Nadab to Ahab, who came to the throne in Asa's lifetime, and then the narrative goes back to Jehoshaphat of Judah, who came to the throne in the fourth year of Ahab. For the better execution of this plan the history of each reign is, so to speak, framed in and kept apart by an introduction and conclusion of stereotyped form (2 Kings xiii. 1): " In the three and twentieth year of Joash the son of Ahaziah king of Judah Jehoahaz the son of Jehu began to reign over Israel in Samaria, and reigned seventeen years." . . . (ver. 8) " Now the rest of the acts of Jehoahaz, . . . are they not written in the book of the chronicles of the kings of Israel? And Jehoahaz slept with his fathers ; and they buried him in Samaria : and Joash his son reigned in his stead." For the kings of Judah the formula is slightly fuller but of the same type.

These set formulas constitute a chronological framework binding the whole narrative together. But the details within the framework do not form a continuous story, and are plainly not all written by one hand or on a uniform plan. One reign is full of striking episodes and picturesque incident, another is comparatively barren in detail and style, and sometimes we find sections that are distinguished not only by variety of style and phrase but by marked peculiarities of grammatical form. On closer examination we observe that each reign is furnished with a brief epitome of affairs, a mere enumeration of important events, combined with a moral judgment on the king. For some reigns we have nothing more than this meagre epitome; but even where the story is filled out by long and interesting narratives the epitome is not lacking. It forms, along with the chronological framework, a uniform feature in the history, and appears to be based on the royal chronicles or official records of the two kingdoms, to which reference is regularly made at the close of each reign. That the epitome is all by one hand is evident from the precise similarity in tone and language which marks all its moral judgments on the kings. On the other hand, the longer and richer narratives show great variety of tone and style, and in many cases it is clear from the nature of their contents that they cannot be derived from the royal chronicles. The sympathetic account of Elijah's work, for example, cannot have been recorded in the annals of his enemy Ahab. The compiler of the Book of Kings, therefore, must have had access to unofficial as well as to official sources. From the former he abstracted the brief notices that make up the skeleton of his work, but the living flesh and blood of the history he supplied by long extracts from narratives of a more popular and interesting kind.

There is no reason to doubt that most of these extracts were selected and worked in by the compiler of the epitome, who may therefore be properly called the main author of the Book of Kings. But the book did not leave his hands in absolutely fixed and final form. Many of the episodes are so loosely attached to the surrounding context that they might be moved to another place without inconvenience. In the Septuagint not a few passages are transposed, and sometimes with advantage to the reader. For example, the story of Naboth's vineyard (1 Kings xxi.) stands in the Greek before chap. xx., so that the narrative of Ahab's Syrian wars is made continuous. Again, in the history of King Solomon, which is largely made up of disjointed anecdotes and notices, the Greek order differs enormously from the Hebrew. And here we find also variations in the substance of the narrative, an omission here and an insertion there, to warn us that, in a book so loosely constructed that its parts can be freely moved about, we must also be prepared to find unauthorised additions creeping into the text. This last point is of too much consequence to be passed over without further illustration; and perhaps the best example for our purpose is found in the history of Jeroboam. The Greek, as commonly read, gives two distinct accounts of Jeroboam's elevation to the throne. One account agrees substantially with the Hebrew, supplying only a few various readings. Some of these are improvements, and enable us to emend the Hebrew text, so as to remove the discrepancy which every reader must observe between 1 Kings xii. 2, 3, 12, and verse 20. In the English version the emendations may be thus effected. Place xii. 2 before xii. 1, so as to make Jeroboam hear of Solomon's death, not of the congress at Shechem, and change the last words (by altering one letter in the Hebrew) into "Then Jeroboam returned from Egypt." In verse 3 omit the whole first part down to "came," leaving only "And they spake before Rehoboam, saying." In verse 12 omit the words "Jeroboam and." The whole is then in accord with verse 20, which implies that Jeroboam (though within reach, and probably acting as a secret instigator of the rebel leaders) was not present at Shechem.

This first account is common to the Hebrew and all Greek copies. The second Greek account, which comes in after chap. xii. 24 in many copies, goes again over the whole ground of chap. xi. 26 to xii. 24, and partly in the very same words. But the arrangement is different, and so are some of the leading incidents. Jeroboam (as the first account also hints) was engaged in a plot against Solomon before he fled to Egypt. On Solomon's death he returned to his native city, fortified by a marriage with an Egyptian princess, and put himself at the head of Ephraim. Then he convened the congress at Shechem, which issued in the revolt of all the northern tribes. But the most serious difference between the two accounts lies in the action ascribed to the prophets Ahijah and Shemaiah. In the Hebrew the promise of king-ship over ten tribes was given to Jeroboam by Ahijah at Jerusalem in the time of Solomon. In the second Greek account there is nothing of this, but a similar prophecy, with the same symbolism of the torn mantle, is put into the mouth of Shemaiah at the congress at Shechem.

The two Greek accounts of how Jeroboam became king cannot possibly have stood from the first in the same volume. They are alternative versions of a single story, and though both of them evidently rest on Hebrew originals, they repre-sent two distinct recensions of the Hebrew text. Thus it appears that, when the two versions were made, the Hebrew text was still so little fixed that one copy could ascribe to Shemaiah, at Shechem, in the days of Rehoboam, what another copy ascribed to Ahijah, at Jerusalem, in the days of Solomon. It is certain that one or other account must be wrong ; but it is probable that neither account forms any part of the original history. If the original compiler of the Book of Kings had related the story of Ahijah's tearing his garment into twelve pieces, and giving ten to Jeroboam in promise of sovereignty, it is hard to believe that a later copyist would have ventured to suppress this narrative and substitute another entirely different ; and, further, when we look at Ahijah's prophecy, as it is given in 1 Kings xi. 29-39, we cannot but feel that it fits badly into the context. At verses 26, 27 we are promised an account of a rebellion of Jeroboam against Solomon ; and verse 40, which relates that

Solomon sought to kill Jeroboam, seems to imply that some
overt act of rebellion really took place. But the intervening
verses tell only of Ahijah's prophecy, which, as we are expressly told, was a private communication to Jeroboam of
which no third party could know anything.

To all this you may object that one form of the Greek
bears out the Hebrew text, and that it is unfair to build
on the second Greek version, which may be a quite recent
interpolation. But it is certain that the second as well as
the first Greek is translated from the Hebrew, and therefore
deserves some consideration. And, further, it is noteworthy
that where Ahijah is again mentioned in the Hebrew in
chap. xiv., the Septuagint shows a blank.[1] This, indeed,
seems to be due to a transposition; for a shorter form of
the prophecy of Ahijah to Jeroboam's wife still occurs in
the second Greek, in an impossible place, wedged into the
account of the events that preceded the congress of Shechem.
But while the Hebrew of chap. xiv. distinctly refers to
Ahijah's earlier prophecy to Jeroboam, this Greek version
introduces him as a new personage who has not been heard of
before. How can we then escape the inference that both
parts of the story of Ahijah represent a fluctuating and
uncertain element in the text, which cannot be accepted with
confidence as part of old and genuine historical tradition?

Now I cannot but suppose that to some of you the idea
that a whole narrative could be interpolated into the Hebrew
text must appear both startling and extravagant. And if
the case with which we have been dealing stood alone, one
would hesitate to build on it. But there are other cases of
the same kind, where the presence of an interpolation forces
itself on our notice by manifest inconsistencies in the Hebrew
text, and where the variations of the Septuagint serve not to
create the difficulty, but to remove it. One of the most

---

[1] In some copies the blank is supplied from Aquila's version.

familiar and striking of these is the story of David and
Goliath (1 Sam. xvii.), which, as it appears in our English
Bible, presents inextricable difficulties. In chap. xvi. 14 *sqq.*
we are told how David is introduced to the court of Saul,
and becomes a favourite with the king. Then suddenly we
have in chap. xvii. the account of a campaign, and find that
David, although he was Saul's armour-bearer, did not follow
him to the field. This is singular enough, and it is not made
more intelligible by xvii. 15, which explains that David
used to go to and fro from Saul's court to feed his father's
sheep at Bethlehem (see R. V.; the translation of A. V. is
inaccurate). Presently David is sent by his father on a
message to the camp to carry supplies to his brothers. He
is also entrusted with a small gift to the captain of their
thousand, *i.e.* of the local regiment of militia to which they
belong; but he has no such gift for Saul, and does not even
present himself at headquarters to salute the king. And,
further, when he reaches the camp, his brethren treat him
with a degree of petulance not likely to be displayed even
by elder brothers to a youth who already stood well at court.
But, in fact, it appears from the close of the chapter that
David is utterly unknown at court, neither Saul nor Abner
having ever heard of him before. But in the Septuagint
version xvii. 12-31, 41, 50, and also the verses from xvii. 55
to xviii. 5 inclusive, are omitted, and when these are removed
we get a far more consistent account of the matter. We
find David in the camp (xvii. 54) and close to the person of
Saul (ver. 32), just as we should expect from chap. xvi.
When all are afraid to face the Philistine champion, he
volunteers to accept the challenge, and so springs at once
from the position of a mere apprentice in arms to that of a
celebrated warrior. On the other hand, if we take the verses
omitted in the Septuagint and read them consecutively, we
cannot fail to observe that they are fragments of an independ-

ent account which gives a different turn to the whole story. According to this account David was still an unknown shepherd lad when his father sent him to the camp with provisions for his brethren and he volunteered to fight the Philistine. After the victory he was retained at court, and Jonathan, with impulsive generosity, at once received him as his bosom friend. It is needless to insist that this account is inconsistent with that which the text of the LXX. offers, and that the slight attempt to reconcile the two which is made in xvii. 15 is totally inadequate. There are only two alternatives before us. Either we must recognise that the LXX. has preserved the true text, and that the additions of the Hebrew are interpolations, fragments of some lost history of David, which have got into the Hebrew text by accident, or else we must suppose that the shorter text is due to a deliberate omission; that is to say, the translators, or some Hebrew scribe before their time, may have felt the difficulties that encumbered the longer text, and deliberately left out a number of verses in order to make the narrative run more smoothly. But it is difficult to believe that simple omissions, made without changing a word of what was left, could produce a complete and consecutive narrative. It is obvious that verse 32 follows on verse 11 much more smoothly than verse 12 does. And it is still more remarkable that verses 12-31 are quite complete in themselves, as far as they go. They take nothing for granted that has been already mentioned in verses 1-11, but tell all about the campaign, the champion, and so forth, over again, in a way perfectly natural in an independent story, but not natural if the whole chapter, as it stands in the Hebrew, was originally a continuous narrative. Note also that xvii. 1-11 are plainly part of a history of public affairs; it is Saul and the children of Israel that occupy the foreground of the narrative. But as plainly verses 12-31 are part of a biography of David; he is the central figure whose movements are followed, and public affairs, the campaign, the champion, the king's promise to the victor, are all brought in at the point where they touch him. Thus the champion comes up and is introduced to us by name, while David is talking with his brethren, and the king's promise is first referred to in a conversation with David. Moreover, that promise itself is sufficient to show that the narrative of verses 12-31 is a fragment foreign to the main narrative of the Book of Samuel; for though David did ultimately marry the king's daughter, he did not receive her hand as a reward for slaying the Philistine, but for quite different services, as we shall see presently. On the whole, therefore, we must conclude that the verses lacking in the Septuagint are not arbitrarily omitted. They are interpolations in the Hebrew text, extracts from a lost biography of David, which some ancient reader must have inserted in his copy of the Book of Samuel. At first, we may suppose, they stood in the margin, and finally, like so many other marginal glosses on ancient books, they got into the text; but they were not found in the text that lay before the Septuagint translators.[1]

Another excellent example of the critical value of the Septuagint may be found in the account of the gradual progress of Saul's hostility to David (1 Sam. xviii.). When the women came out to meet the victorious Israelites and praised David above Saul—

1 Sam. xviii. 8.—*Saul was very wroth* and the saying displeased him [LXX. Saul], and he said, They have ascribed unto David myriads, and to me they have ascribed thousands, *and what can he have more but the kingdom ?* (9.) *And Saul eyed David from that day, and forward.* (10, 11.) *Next day Saul casts a javelin at David.* (12.) And Saul was afraid of David, *because the Lord was with him and was departed from Saul.* (13.) And *Saul* removed him from his person, and made him his captain over a thousand, and he went out and in before the people. (14.) And David was successful in all that he undertook, and the Lord

---

[1] For further remarks on this passage see additional Note A.

was with him. (15.) And when Saul saw that he was so successful, he dreaded him. (16.) But all Israel loved David, because he went out and came in before them. (17-19.) *Saul promises Merab to David, but disappoints him.* (20-27.) Michal falls in love with David, and Saul avails himself of this opportunity to put him on a dangerous enterprise in the hope that he will fall. David, however, succeeds, and marries Michal.[1] (28.) And when Saul saw, *and knew* that the Lord was with David, and that *Michal the daughter of Saul* (LXX. all Israel) loved him, (29) he came to fear David still more, *and hated David continually.* (30.) *Thereafter David again distinguishes himself in war.* (xix. 1.) Saul proposes to his son and servants to kill David.

The words and verses quoted or summarised in italics are omitted in the Septuagint. Without them the progress of the narrative is perspicuous and consistent. Saul's jealousy is first roused by the praises bestowed on David, and he can no longer bear to have him constantly attached to his person. Without an open breach of relations, he removes him from court by giving him an important post. David's conduct, and the popularity he acquires in his new and more in-dependent position, intensify Saul's former fears into a fixed dread. But there is still no overt act of hostility on the king's part; he hopes to lead David to destruction by stimulating his ambition to a desperate enterprise; and it is only when this policy fails, and David returns to court a universal favourite, with the new importance conferred by his alliance with the royal family, that Saul's fears wholly conquer his scruples, and he plans the assassination of his son-in-law. The three stages of this growing hostility are marked by the rising strength of the phrases in verses 12, 15, 29. The additions of the Hebrew text destroy the psychological truth of the narrative. Here Saul's fears reach the highest pitch as soon as his jealousy is first aroused, and on the very next day he attempts to slay David with his own hand. In the original narrative this attempt comes much later, and is accepted by David as a

---

[1] The words in 21 and 26, which refer to the incident of Merab, are not in the LXX.

warning to flee at once (xix. 10). The other additions are
equally inappropriate, and the episode of Merab is particularly unintelligible. It seems to hang together with xvii.
25, that is, with the interpolated part of the story of
Goliath; and in 2 Sam. xxi. 8, Michal, not Merab, appears
as the mother of Adriel's children. In that passage the
English version has attempted to remove the difficulty by
making Michal only the foster-mother, but the Hebrew will
not bear such a sense.

Here, then, we have another case where all probability
is in favour of the Greek text, and a fresh example of
the principle alluded to in the last Lecture, that, where
there are two recensions of a passage, the shorter version
is in most cases to be recognised as that which is nearest
to the hand of the original author. Sometimes, indeed,
we meet with an insertion which is valuable because derived from an ancient source, such as the quotation from
the Book of Jashar, preserved in the Septuagint of 1
Kings viii. 53. But seldom indeed did a copyist, unless
by sheer oversight, omit anything from the copy that lay
before him.[1]

A remarkable case of variations between the Hebrew and
the Greek is found, where we should least expect it, within
the Pentateuch itself. The translation of the Law is the
oldest part of the Septuagint, and in the eyes of the Jews
was much the most important. And as a rule the variations
are here confined within narrow limits, the text being already
better fixed than in the historical books. But there is one
considerable section, Exod. xxxv.-xl., where extraordinary
variations appear in the Greek, some verses being omitted
altogether, while others are transposed and knocked about
with a freedom very unlike the usual manner of the
translators of the Pentateuch. The details of the varia-

---

[1] See further, on this subject, additional Note B.

tions need not be recounted here; they are fully exhibited
in tabular form in Kuenen's *Onderzoek*, 2d ed., vol. i. p. 77,
and in Driver's *Introduction*, p. 37 *sq*. The variations
prove either that the text of this section of the Pentateuch
was not yet fixed in the third century before Christ, or
that the translator did not feel himself bound to treat it
with the same reverence as the rest of the Law. But
indeed there are strong reasons for suspecting that the
Greek version of these chapters is not by the same hand
as the rest of the Book of Exodus, various Hebrew words
being represented by other Greek equivalents than those
used in the earlier chapters. And thus it seems possible
that this whole section was lacking in the copy that lay
before the first translator of the Law. It is true that the
chapters are not very essential, since they simply describe,
almost in the same words, the execution of the directions
about the tabernacle and its furniture already given in
chaps. xxv.-xxxi. Most modern critics hold chaps. xxxv.-
xl. for a late addition to the text, and see in the variations
between the Hebrew and the Greek proof that the form
of the addition underwent changes, and was not finally
fixed in all copies when the Septuagint version was made.
In favour of this view several considerations may be adduced which it would carry us too far to consider here.
But in any case those who hold that the whole Pentateuch
dates from the time of Moses, and that the Septuagint
translators had to deal with a text that had been fixed
and sacred for a thousand years, have a hard nut to
crack in the wholly exceptional freedom with which the
Greek version treats this part of the sacrosanct Torah.

These examples must suffice as indications of what may
be learned from the Septuagint with regard to the way in
which the Biblical books were originally compiled, and
the changes which the text underwent at the hand of

later editors. There is yet another important matter—the history of the Old Testament Canon—which may be most conveniently approached by comparing the Hebrew and Greek Bibles, but this subject I propose to defer to another Lecture. The lessons which we have already learned from the Septuagint have applications of a far-reaching kind that have not yet been considered, and to which we may profitably turn our attention before we pass on to a new topic.

The variations between the Hebrew and the Greek give us a practical insight into the kind of changes to which the Old Testament text was exposed in the course of transmission, and the kind of work which compilers and editors did in the way of retouching the text, rearranging its component parts, and introducing new matter. But, after all, the Hebrew text only represents one manuscript and the Septuagint another. By direct comparison of the two we learn broadly how great the variations between copies still were in the third century B.C. or later, and we get also a general and most instructive insight into the cause of these differences. But two copies are not enough to give us a full knowledge of all the variations that were still found in MSS. at the time when the Septuagint version was made; much less are they enough to enable us to determine all the vicissitudes through which each book had passed in earlier ages. It is to be presumed that the same causes which make the Septuagint so different from the Hebrew had always been at work in the transmission of the text; and we have no right to suppose that, in all passages which they affected, one or other of the two copies before us must have preserved the original hand of the first author. In some cases the Hebrew text is evidently better than the Greek, in others the converse is true ; but both give us a text which has passed through the hands of many editors and copyists, who dealt very freely

with the materials before them, and sometimes added matter
of doubtful authority, derived from inferior sources. Now
the genealogy of manuscripts is like the genealogy of men;
the copy used by the Septuagint and the copy represented by
our Hebrew Bible are cousins, and to judge by their general
resemblance not very distant cousins. At all events, as
cousins they have a common ancestor, or as critics would say,
a common archetype, a manuscript from which both texts
have descended through successive generations of copies and
copies of copies. It is not probable that this archetype was
separated by many generations from the time of the Septuagint translators; it would be a very bold thing to suppose
that for any part of the Old Testament the two recensions
had branched off before the time of Ezra. To any changes
that may have been made on the text before the date of
the common archetype the comparison of the Greek and the
Hebrew can afford no clue; yet the older books must have
been copied and recopied many times before that archetype
was written, and every time they were copied there was at
any rate a possibility that changes would creep into the text
—changes of the same general kind as now separate the two
extant recensions. *To the way in which the text was treated in
the earliest times, before the date of the common archetype of the
Greek and Hebrew, we have no clue except internal evidence.*
"Very good," says the conservative school; "and that being
so, there is an end of the matter. For internal evidence is
notoriously uncertain and delusive, and so our best course is
quietly to acquiesce in what we have received by tradition."
This is a convenient counsel, and appeals to the indolence that
forms a part of every man's nature, even though he be bound
by the most sacred vows, and by the responsibility of high
office in the churches, to give the strength of his life to the
study of divine truth. To such men, above all others, a short
and easy argument, which can be learned and repeated in an

armchair, and which serves the double purpose of furnishing a plausible reply to suspicious innovations and dispensing the man who uses it from making a fresh and laborious study of the Bible, comes either as a godsend or as a temptation of the flesh. I leave it to the consciences of those dignitaries and leaders of the English and Scottish churches who have refused and still refuse to study the modern criticism, to determine whether their lofty indifference to matters that have been to every diligent student of the Scriptures the cause of great searchings of heart, is indeed a fruit of surer faith and truer insight than is given to those who bear the burden and heat of the day in the field of Biblical study; but to plain men, who desire to know the truth and are willing to look it in the face, I cannot think that an airy contempt for all internal evidence will be apt to commend itself in the view of the facts that have already come before us. You propose (do you?) to acquiesce in the received tradition and to ask no questions as to the history of the Biblical books beyond the point for which you have a direct witness in the divergence of the Greek and Hebrew texts. That would be very well if the comparison of these two texts had taught you that, as far back as the third century before Christ, editors and copyists scrupulously abstained from touching a letter of the books they received as holy. But we have learned the very opposite of this. We know that changes were made as far back as we can follow the history of the text by external evidence. To shut our eyes to the probability that similar changes were made before that time, and to do this under the name of faith, is to confound faith with agnosticism. Those of us who do care to know the truth for its own sake, and not simply as much of the truth as is consistent with going on smoothly in our old ruts, will surely remember that in all other branches of ancient history internal evidence has a recognised value, that for many points in the history of the Biblical records no other evidence is attainable, and that to reject it for this history while it is accepted for all others is to place the study of the Bible at a disadvantage, which in the long run can only end in its entire exclusion from the field of sober historical research.

The test of all this lies in the application. And to bring the matter to an issue in brief compass I will not occupy your time on minor matters. It would be easy to show that the common archetype of the Greek and Hebrew texts already contained verbal corruptions, that the text was already in some instances contaminated by glosses, and so forth. But these things are comparatively trivial. We have seen that in later manuscripts variations occurred of a far more serious type. In the story of Goliath, as we read it in Hebrew and in English, two narratives are mixed up together which differ in essential particulars. The one is not a mere supplement to the other, but if one is true the other must be regarded as containing serious errors. In that case, and in the similar case of the history of David's estrangement from Saul, we still have direct evidence from the Greek that one of the two inconsistent stories has inferior authority and came into the text at a late date. Let us ask whether there is convincing internal evidence that in like manner some passages which are older than the common archetype, and appear both in the Greek and in the Hebrew, are nevertheless of no better authority than the interpolated story of David and Goliath.

To reduce this inquiry to the simplest form I will separate it as far as may be from all questions as to how and when discrepant accounts of the same event came into the text, and will simply address myself to prove that the Bible does in certain cases give two accounts of the same series of occurrences, and that both accounts cannot be followed. The cases in point may again be divided into two classes.

(1.) Those in which the two accounts are still quite separate, so that we have no more to do than to put the one against the other.

(2.) Cases where the present context of the narrative already presents an attempt to reconcile two accounts originally distinct and discordant, by working the two (or parts of them) into a consecutive story. The first class of cases is obviously the easiest to deal with, and I propose, therefore, to begin with examples drawn from it.

(1.) A very simple case is the twofold explanation of the proverb, "Is Saul also among the prophets?" (1 Sam. x. 12 ; *ibid.* xix. 24). The same proverb cannot have two origins, but nothing is commoner than to find two traditions about the origin of a single saying. The compiler of the Book of Samuel had two such traditions before him, and thought it best to insert both, without deciding which deserved the preference. And here it may be noticed further that 1 Sam. xix. 24 is inconsistent with 1 Sam. xv. 35, which tells us that Samuel never saw Saul after the death of Agag. The English Version departs from its usual fidelity when it softens this absolute statement and writes that "Samuel came no more to see Saul."

An example on a larger scale is supplied by the two accounts of the conquest of Canaan, and especially of southern Canaan. According to Joshua x. the conquest of all southern Canaan from Gibeon to Kadesh-barnea was effected in a single campaign, undertaken by Joshua in person at the head of the united forces of all Israel, immediately after the defeat of the five kings before Gibeon. The conquest was complete, for the enemy was exterminated, not a soul being left alive. But according to Judges i. the land of Judah was conquered not by all Israel under Joshua, but by Judah and Simeon alone. As the narrative now stands we learn from Judges i. 1 that the separate campaign of Judah and Simeon took place after the death of Joshua. Yet the events of the campaign in-

cluded the taking of Hebron and Debir, which, according to
the other account, had been already taken by Joshua, and
their inhabitants utterly destroyed. The difference in details
is insuperable; but still more important is the fundamental
difference between the two accounts as regards the whole
method of the conquest. In Judges i. (with which agree
certain isolated passages of Joshua that stand out very clearly
from the surrounding narrative) the conquest of Canaan is
represented as a very gradual process, carried out by each
tribe fighting for its own hand; whereas the Book of Joshua
depicts a series of great campaigns in which all Israel fought
as a united host, with the result that the Canaanites were
swept out of existence through the greater part of the
country, and their vacant lands divided by lot among the
tribes. It is impossible that both these accounts can be
correct. If Joshua had merely overrun the country, the
serious work of driving out the Canaanites and occupying
their land might have remained for the next generation; but
the account in Joshua excludes any such view, and says in
the strongest way that the Canaanites were exterminated, and
their lands occupied peaceably. (See especially Josh. x. xi.
and xxi. 43-45.)

Plainly we have here two accounts of the conquest, which
were originally quite distinct and have been united only in
the most artificial manner by the note of time ("and it came
to pass after the death of Joshua"), which has been inserted
by a later hand in Judges i. 1. Of the two accounts that in
Judges is the plain historical version, while the other has this
characteristic mark of a later and less authoritative narrative,
that it gathers up all the details of slow conquest and local
struggle in one comprehensive picture with a single hero in
the foreground. In precisely the same way the later accounts
of the establishment of the Saxons in England extend the
sphere of Hengest's original conquests far beyond the narrow

region to which they are confined by older and more authentic tradition.

As a last example under this head I will take the case of the death of Sisera, for which we have a prose narrative in Judges iv. and the statements of a contemporary poem in Judges v. In the prose narrative Jael kills Sisera in his sleep by hammering a wooden tent-peg into his forehead—an extraordinary proceeding, for the peg must have been held with one hand and hammered with the other, which is not a likely way to drive a blunt tent-peg through and through a man's skull without awakening him. But in the poem we read—

> " He asked water, and she gave him milk ;
> She brought forth sour milk in an ample bowl."

Then, while Sisera, still standing, buried his face in the bowl, and for the moment could not watch her actions—

> " She put her hand to the peg,
> And her right hand to the workmen's hammer ;
> And she hammered Sisera, she broke his head,
> And crushed and pierced his temples.
> Between her feet he sank down, he fell, he lay :
> Between her feet he sank down, he fell :
> Where he sank, there he fell overcome."

All this is perfectly plain if we note that, according to the manner of Hebrew parallelism, " she put her hand to the peg " or pin, *i.e.* the handle of the hammer, means the same thing as " and her right hand to the hammer." The act by which Jael gained such renown was not the murder of a sleeping man, but the use of a daring stratagem which gave her a momentary chance to deliver a courageous blow. But the word " peg " suggested a tent-peg, and so the later prose story took it, and thereby misunderstood the whole thing.

(2.) I now pass to a more complicated class of cases, where two independent accounts have been woven together by a later editor so that it requires some dissection to separate them. The most important series of such cases is found in the Pentateuch and the Book of Joshua, and will engage our attention in some detail at a later point in our course. For the present I will cite only one simple instance from this portion of the history, viz. the account of the taking of Ai given in Joshua viii. The capture of this city was effected by stratagem, Joshua and the main body of the host of Israel drawing the enemy away from their city by a feigned retreat, so that it was left an easy prey to an ambush that lay concealed on the west side of the town. But of the setting of this ambush we have two inconsistent accounts. According to verse 3 the ambush consisted of thirty thousand men, and was sent out from Gilgal by night to take up its post behind Ai, while Joshua and the mass of the host did not leave Gilgal till the following morning (verses 9, 10). But in verse 12 the ambush consists of but five thousand men, and is not sent from Gilgal, but detached from the main army after Joshua has taken up his position in front of Ai. These are two versions of the same occurrence, for in both accounts the place of ambush is the same, viz. the west side of the city between Bethel and Ai, and the subsequent verses speak only of one ambush. We conclude, therefore, that the editor used, and to some extent fused together, two separate accounts of the taking of Ai ; and this conclusion is confirmed when we observe that verses 20 and 21 also tell the same thing twice over with slight variations of detail and expression such as would naturally occur in two independent stories.

In the books that follow Joshua, cases where two narratives are worked together to form a mosaic of small fragments become less frequent, but something of the kind can still be traced in parts of the Book of Samuel, especially in the history of Saul, where, as we have already seen, the Septuagint some-

times helps us to dissect out late additions to the story. There
are other doublets (double versions) of passages in Saul's
history which are common to the Hebrew and the Greek, and
can be recognised only by internal evidence. Such, for
example, are the two accounts of Saul's rejection by Samuel
at Gilgal, of which one is found in 1 Sam. xv. and the other
from 1 Sam. xiii. 7 (second half) to ver. 15 (first half), a passage
to which chap. x. 8 must once have formed the introduction.
Any one who reads chap. xv. with care must see that the
writer of this narrative knew nothing of an earlier rejection
of Saul. And further, the Gilgal episode in chap. xiii. gives
no reasonable sense. Saul had waited for Samuel the full
time appointed; it was a matter of urgency to delay military
operations no longer, and according to ancient usage the war
had to be opened with religious ceremonies. What was the
crime of performing these without Samuel's presence ? There
is not a word in the story to imply that no one but Samuel
could do acceptable sacrifice, or that the king's offence lay in
an encroachment on the prerogatives of the priesthood. The
sin, if there was a sin, lay in Saul's presuming to begin a
necessary war without Samuel's express orders. But it is
plain from the whole history that the kings of Israel never
were mere puppets in the hands of the prophets, and that the
prophets never claimed the right to make them so. The
story is unhistorical, and nothing more than an early and
unauthorised interpolation, as appears from the fact that both
xiii. 7 b-15 a, and the associated verse, x. 8, dislocate the context
of the passages in which they are inserted.[1] Here we have
two versions of a passage in Saul's history which have been
allowed to stand side by side without any attempt to work
them into unity. But in the history of Saul's appointment

---

[1] See Wellhausen, *Composition* (1889), p. 247 *sq.* ; Budde, *Richter und
Samuel*, p. 191 *sqq.* The mention of Gilgal in 1 Sam. xiii. 4 seems to have
been added along with the greater interpolation, for Gilgal is an impossible
rendezvous for an army gathering to meet a Philistine invasion.

as king, where there are also two accounts, each is broken up
and passages of the one are intercalated in the other.   This
may be shown by a table as follows—[1]

Acct. A,	1 Sam. ix., x. 1-16.		xi. 1-11.		xi. 15.
Acct. B, 1 Sam. viii.		x. 1-24 (25-27 ?).		(xi. 12, 13 ?).	
Editor.		(x. 25-27 ?).		(xi. 12, 13 ?). xi. 14.	

The main clues to this analysis are two.   In the first
place, the status of Samuel is different in chaps. viii. and ix. ;
in the former he is the acknowledged judge of all Israel, in
the latter he is a seer of great local reputation, but hardly
known outside of his own district.   In the second place,
chap. xi. presents Saul to us as still a private person.   The
messengers from Jabesh do not come specially to seek him,
and he acts by no public authority, but on his own initiative
under the impulse of the Divine Spirit.   But in chap. ix. he
has already been made king amidst the acclamations of the
whole nation.   Other points of difference I leave you to note
for yourselves ; the best justification of the analysis is to
sketch the two stories, and show that each is complete in
itself.

According to the older story (A) the establishment of the
kingship in Israel was not of man's seeking but of God.
The Hebrews were hard pressed by the Philistines and other
foes, against whom they could make no head for want of
organisation and a recognised captain.   Only one man in
Israel, the seer Samuel, who in this narrative appears as
little known beyond his own district, saw by divine revelation that the remedy lay in the appointment of a king, and
was guided to recognise the leader of Israel in a young man,
the son of a Benjamite noble, who came to consult him on a
trivial affair of lost asses.   Seizing his opportunity, Samuel
took Saul aside and anointed him king in the name of
Jehovah, commanding him to return home and await an

---

[1] I borrow the plan of this table from Driver's tables of the analysis of the
Hexateuch.

occasion to prove his vocation by deeds: "Do as thy hand shall find; for God is with thee." Saul obeyed the command, and silently returned to the daily work of his father's estate; but God had changed his heart; Samuel's words burned within him, and his neighbours, though they knew not the cause, saw that he was a different man from what he had been. A month later (1 Sam. x. 27, Sept.; see the margin of R. V.) the opportunity of action arrived. Jabesh-gilead was threatened by Nahash the Ammonite, and the messengers whom the Gileadites sent through the land to demand succour were everywhere received with tears of helpless sympathy. "But the Spirit of God came upon Saul when he heard these things, and his wrath was kindled greatly. And he took a yoke of oxen, and hewed them in pieces, and sent them throughout all the coasts of Israel by the hands of messengers, and said, Whoso cometh not forth after Saul [and after Samuel], so shall it be done unto his oxen. And the fear of the Lord fell upon the people, and they came out as one man." Nahash was defeated, the Israelites knew that they had found a leader, and with one consent they went to Gilgal and made Saul king before the Lord.

In the second account (B) all this vivid concrete picture disappears, and we find in its place a meagre skeleton of narrative only just sufficient to support an exposition, in the form of speeches, of the author's judgment upon the Hebrew kingship as an institution not strictly compatible with the ideal of Jehovah's sovereignty in Israel. In this narrative Samuel appears as the recognised head and supreme judge of all Israel. In his old age, when he has delegated part of his functions to his sons and they prove corrupt judges, the people insist on the appointment of a king. Samuel remonstrates, but is divinely instructed to grant their wish, after warning them that to seek a human king is to depart from Jehovah, and that they will repent too late of their disobedience, when they experience the heavy hand of despotism. But as they persist in their wish a solemn convocation is called at Mizpeh, and appeal is made to the sacred lot to determine the tribe, the family, and the man on whom Jehovah's choice falls. When the lot falls on Saul he is nowhere to be found, till a second oracle reveals that he is hidden among the baggage. "And they ran and fetched him thence: and when he stood among the people, he was higher than any of the people from his shoulders and upward. And Samuel said to all the people, See ye him whom the Lord hath chosen, that there is none like him among all the people? And all the people shouted, and said, God save the king."

It is not so easy, nor is it necessary for our present purpose, to follow the double thread of the narrative farther. All critics agree that the immediate sequel of the first account is found in chaps. xiii. xiv., while, on the other hand, chaps. xii. and xv. stand in close connection with the second account. Further, xi. 14, which speaks of renewing the kingdom, is an editorial addition designed to harmonise the two narratives by suggesting that Saul was crowned twice. But it is not quite clear whether x. 25-27, xi. 12, 13, are also editorial additions (Budde) or fragments of the second narrative. On the latter view we must, I think, suppose that that narrative contained an account of the war with Nahash in a different form, associating Samuel with the campaign, and making Saul act at the head of the valiant men whose hearts God had touched (x. 26). It is unreasonable to expect to attain certainty on such minor points; nor do they affect the broad lines of our analysis and the broad contrast between the first account, in which the events unfold themselves naturally, so that the Divine Spirit in Samuel and Saul guides the action of human forces without suppressing or distorting them, and the second account, in which the supernatural element is far more mechanical, and, if I may venture to use such a word, *unreal.* In saying this I do not mean that the second account is a deliberate fiction ; the incident of Saul's hiding in the baggage is evidently traditional, and indeed has close parallels in Arabian folk-lore.[1] But the two traditions cannot both be equally genuine, and there can be no doubt which is the older and better one. In the second account we already see the distorting influence on historical tradition of that mechanical conception of Jehovah's rule in Israel which prevailed more and more among the later Jews, and ultimately destroyed all feeling for historical reality, and at the same time all true insight into the methods of divine governance.

According to the prophets and apostles God's government in Israel differs from His government of the rest of the world in so far as Israel had greater privileges and greater responsibilities (Amos iii. 2, ix. 7, 8 ; Acts xvii. 30 ; Rom. ii. 12) ; a thesis which by no means involves, but rather implicitly excludes, the notion that the boundaries of Canaan formed a magic circle, within which the ordinary laws of Providence were suspended, and the sequence of well-doing and prosperity, sin and punishment, was determined by a special and immediate operation of divine sovereignty. But it requires insight and faith to see the hand of God in the ordinary processes of history, whereas extraordinary coincidences between conduct and fortune are fitted to impress the dullest minds. Hence, when the religious lesson of any part of history has been impressed on the popular mind, there is

---

[1] See the story about Mohammed in Ibn Hishâm, p. 116, and that about Mosailima in Ibn Sa'd, ed. Wellhausen, No. 101. These stories may be influenced by the Bible, but it is remarkable that both of them bring out the point of the incident more clearly than the passage of Samuel expresses it. The man who stays behind with the baggage is the youngest or obscurest of the company. Saul remained there because " he was little in his own sight " (1 Sam. xv. 17). Compare the similar incidents in the story of David, 1 Sam. xvi. 11, xvii. 28.

always a tendency to reshape the story in such a way as to bring the point out sharply and drop all details that have not a direct religious significance.   There are a hundred examples of this in modern history : the story of the Armada, for example, is habitually told in a way that accentuates the providential interposition which preserved English Protestantism—"afflavit Deus et dissipati sunt," as the commemorative medal has it—by laying too little weight on the action of human forces in which God's providence was not less truly, though it was less strikingly, present.   The history of the Old Testament, taken as a whole, forms so remarkable a chain of evidence establishing the truth of what the prophets had taught as to the laws of God's government on earth, that we cannot be surprised to find that in the circles influenced by prophetic ideas all parts of the historical tradition came to be studied mainly in the spirit of religious pragmatism. That is to say, religious students of the past times of the nation concentrated their attention in an increasing degree, and ultimately in an exclusive way, on the explanation of events by religious considerations.   The effect of this, especially after the establishment of the post-exile theocracy, was that the parts and incidents of the history which did not admit of a direct religious interpretation fell out of sight, and that the story of Israel's past ultimately resolved itself into a mechanical sequence of sin and punishment, obedience and prosperity.   The point of view which Jesus condemns in Luke xiii. 1-4, in speaking of the Galileans whose blood Pilate had mingled with their sacrifices, is that from which later Judaism looks at the whole sacred history, with the result that the manifold variety of God's workings among men shrivels up into a tedious repetition of lifeless formulas.

That this is true as regards the Rabbinical literature no one will attempt to deny; but the example that has come before us leads us to consider whether, in a less degree, something of the same tendency may not have to be allowed for in interpreting parts of the Bible.

The chief case in point, upon which critics have come to a very definite conclusion, is that of the Chronicles as compared with the Book of Kings. Our traditional education, and our hereditary way of looking at the Bible, incline us to suppose that all books of the Old Testament are of equal value as historical authorities; and that, when Kings and Chronicles appear to differ, it is as legitimate to read the older history in the light of the newer as *vice versâ*. In dealing with sources for profane history, however, we should never dream of putting books of such different age on the same footing; the Book of Kings was substantially complete before the Exile, in the early years of the sixth century B.C., while the Chronicler gives genealogies that go down at least six generations after Zerubbabel, and probably reach to contemporaries of Alexander the Great.[1] This is an interval of at least two hundred and fifty years; and it must also be remembered that the Book of Kings is largely made up of verbal extracts from much older sources, and for many purposes may be treated as having the practical value of a contemporary history. Hence, according to the ordinary laws of research, the Book of Kings is a source of the first class, and the Chronicles have a very secondary value. It is the rule of all historical study to begin with the records that stand

[1] The genealogy of the descendants of Zerubbabel in 1 Chron. iii. 19 *sqq.* is somewhat confused, but it seems to be impossible by any fair treatment of the text to get less than six generations (Hananiah, Shechaniah, Shemaiah, Neariah, Elioenai, Hodaiah and his brethren). The text of the Septuagint gives eleven generations, and this may be the true reading, for it removes the obscurity that attaches to the Hebrew text by the very slight correction, four times reading בנו for בני, and once adding בנו before ובני (at the end of verse 21). But further it is almost certain that Chronicles-Ezra-Nehemiah once formed a single book (*infra*, p. 182 *sq.*), and in Nehemiah we have mention of Darius Codomannus and of Jaddua, who was high priest at the time of the Macedonian conquest (Neh. xii. 22). See further Driver, *Introduction*, p. 486, p. 511 *sq.*

nearest to the events recorded and are written under the living impress of the life of the time described. Many features of old Hebrew custom, which are reflected in lively form in the Former Prophets, were obsolete long before the time of the Chronicler, and could not be revived except by archæological research. The whole life of the old kingdom was buried and forgotten ; Israel was no longer a nation, but a church. No theory of inspiration, save the theory of the Koran, which boasts that its fabulous legends were supernaturally conveyed to Mohammed without the use of documents or tradition, can affirm that a history written under these conditions is a primary source for the study of the ancient kingdom.[1] It is manifest that the Chronicler, writing at a time when the institutions of Ezra had universal currency, had no personal knowledge of the greatly different praxis of Israel before the Exile, and that the general picture which he gives of the life and worship of the Hebrews under the old monarchy cannot have the same value for us as the records of the Book of Kings. These considerations alone are sufficient to condemn the use made of the Chronicles by a certain school of theologians, who, finding that the narrative of that book comes closer to their own traditional ideas than the record of the ancient histories, seek to explain away everything in the latter which the younger historian does not homologate. The Book of Kings, for example, contains a mass of evidence that the best monarchs of Judah before the Captivity countenanced practices inconsistent with the Pentateuchal Law. Thus we are told in 1 Kings xv. 14, xxii. 43, that Asa and Jehoshaphat did not abolish the high places. The Chronicler, on the contrary, says that they did abolish them (2 Chron. xiv. 5, xvii. 6)—a flat contradiction. There

---

[1] Mohammed boasts of his fabulous version of the story of Joseph, that he had it by direct revelation, not having known it before (Sura xii. 3). The Bible historians never made such a claim, which to thinking minds is one of the clearest proofs of Mohammed's imposture.

is an end to historical study if in such a case we accept the
later account against the earlier; for it is evident that the
Chronicler, writing at a time when every one was agreed in
rejecting high places as idolatrous, was unable to conceive
that good kings could have tolerated them.[1] We shall see,
however, in Lecture VIII., that a mass of concurrent evidence,
derived from the prophets as well as the historical books,
shows that there was no feeling against the high places even
in the most enlightened circles in Israel till long after the
time of Asa and Jehoshaphat.

The cases where the Chronicler flatly contradicts the
Book of Kings are pretty numerous; but there is not one of
them where an impartial historical judgment will decide in
favour of the later account. It is true that the Chronicler
had access to some old sources now lost, especially for the
genealogical lists which form a considerable part of his
work.[2] But for the history proper, his one genuine source
was the series of the Former Prophets, the Books of Samuel
and especially of Kings. These books he read in manuscripts
which occasionally preserved a good reading that has been
corrupted in the Massoretic text (supra, p. 68), but where
he adds to the narrative of Kings or departs from it, his
variations are never such as to inspire confidence. In large
measure these variations are simply due to the fact that,
as we have already seen in the example of the high places
he takes it for granted that the religious institutions of his
own time must have existed in the same form in old Israel.
Hence he assumes that the Levitical organisation of his own

---

[1] That here the Chronicler is arbitrarily changing the record appears
incidentally from 2 Chron. xv. 17, xx. 33, where he is inconsiderate enough
to copy the opposite statement of 1 Kings in connection with some other
particulars which he has occasion to transfer from that book to his own.

[2] The genealogies are not all of equal value, but the great historical importance of some of them has been demonstrated by Wellhausen in his
Habilitationschrift, De Gentibus et Familiis Judaeis, Gött., 1870. Only a
summary of the results is reproduced in his Prolegomena.

time, and especially the three choirs of singers, were established by David. Of all this the old history has not a word,
and the Books of Ezra and Nehemiah show that even after
the restoration, a much simpler system was in force, and
was only gradually elaborated into the form described in
Chronicles (*infra*, Lecture VII.). But, indeed, the text of
Chronicles contains distinct internal evidence that the author
is really describing later institutions, although he brings his
description into the life of David. The gates, etc., mentioned
in 1 Chron. xxvi. presuppose the existence of a temple, and
as the gate Parbar bears a Persian name, it is clear that he is
thinking of the second Temple.[1] And this case does not
stand alone. In 2 Chron. xiii. 10 *sqq.* Abijah boasts against
Jeroboam of the superior legitimacy of the ritual of Jerusalem,
which was conducted according to all the rules of the Law.
But the ritual described is that of the second Temple, for
reference is made to the golden candlestick. In Solomon's
Temple there was not one golden candlestick in front of the
oracle, but ten (1 Kings vii. 49). Further, Abijah speaks of
the morning and evening holocausts. But there is a great
concurrence of evidence that the evening sacrifice of the
first Temple was not a holocaust, but a cereal oblation
(1 Kings xviii. 36, *Heb.* ; 2 Kings xvi. 15 ; Ezra ix. 4, *Heb.*).[2]

[1] A curious point, remarked by Ewald (*Lehrbuch*, § 274 *b*), and more
clearly brought out by Wellhausen, is that six heads of the choir of the
guild of Heman bear the names—(1) I have given great (2) and lofty help
(3) to him that sat in distress ; (4) I have spoken (5) a superabundance of
(6) prophecies (1 Chron. xxv. 4). As actual names of men, in the time of
David, these designations are impossible. But the words seem to form an
anthem in which six choirs of singers may well have had parts, and these
may have received names from their parts. In like manner Jeduthun, which,
if the description of the Temple music is literal history of David's time, must
be the name of a chief singer, is really, as we see from the titles of the Psalms,
a musical term.

[2] Cp. Kuenen, *Religion of Israel*, chap. ix. note 1. Note also, as
characteristic of the freedom used with facts in the speeches in Chronicles,
that in 2 Chron. xiii. 7 Abijah says that Jeroboam's rebellion took place
when Rehoboam was a lad and soft-hearted, and could not pluck up courage

So again, in 2 Chron. v. 4, the ark is borne by Levites, according to the rule of the Levitical law ; but the parallel passage
of 1 Kings viii. 3 says that it was borne by the priests, and
the latter statement is in accordance with Deut. xxxi., and
with all the references to the carrying of the ark in the pre-
exilic histories (Josh. iii. 3, vi. 6, viii. 33 ; 2 Sam. xv.
24, 29). Once more, in 2 Kings xi., Jehoiada's assistants in
the revolution which cost Athaliah her life are the foreign
bodyguard, which we know to have been employed in the
sanctuary up to the time of Ezekiel (*infra*, p. 262). But
in 2 Chron. xxiii. the Carians and the footguards are replaced
by the Levites, in accordance with the rule of the second
Temple, which did not allow aliens to approach so near to the
holy things.

These examples are enough to show that the Chronicler
is no authority in any point that touches difference of usage
between his own time and that of the old monarchy ; but
further, he does not hesitate to make material changes in the
tenor of narratives that do not agree with his doctrine of
the uniformity of religious institutions before and after the
Exile. Of this one example must suffice. In 2 Kings xxiii.
Josiah's action against the high places is represented as
taking place in the eighteenth year of his reign, as the immediate result of his repentance on hearing the words of the
Law found in the Temple, and in pursuance of the covenant
of reformation made on that occasion. But in 2 Chron. xxxiv.
the reformation begins in Josiah's twelfth year, that is, as
soon as he emerged from his minority.[1] Josiah was a good

to withstand the rebels. But according to 1 Kings xiv. 21 the "lad" was
forty-one years old, and he certainly did not lose his kingdom for softness of
heart.

[1] Josiah came to the throne when he was eight years old, so that in his
twelfth year he would be nineteen years old. He began to seek God, says the
Chronicler, in the eighth year of his reign, *i.e.* at the age of fifteen. According to the Mishna (*Aboth*, v. 21) a boy should begin to learn Talmud at
fifteen, marry at eighteen, and pursue business at twenty.

king, and therefore the Chronicler felt that there must be a
mistake in the account which made him wield an independent sceptre for many years before he touched the idolatrous
abuses of his land. That the result of this is to put the
solemn repentance and covenant of reformation ten years
after the reformation itself is an inconsistency which seems
never to have struck him.

The tendency to construct history according to a mechanical rule, which we meet with in this example, is only one side
of the general tendency of later Judaism, already characterised,
to sacrifice all interest in the veritable facts of sacred history
to a mechanical conception of God's government of the world
at large, and of Israel in particular. Another side shows
itself in the Book of Chronicles in the constant endeavour to
make the divine retribution act immediately, after the fashion
of the falling of the tower of Siloam. This is sometimes
spoken of as a moralising tendency, and the name is not
amiss if we make it clear to ourselves that it is moralising of
a different kind from what we find in the prophets. To
prophets like Amos and Isaiah, the retributive justice of God
is manifest in the general course of history. The fall of the
Hebrew nation is the fruit of sin and rebellion against
Jehovah's moral commands; but God's justice is mingled
with long-suffering, and the prophets do not for a moment
suppose that every sin is promptly punished, and that temporary good fortune is always the reward of righteousness.
But a very large part of the novel additions made in the
Chronicles to the old history is meant to show that in Israel
retribution followed immediately on good or bad conduct,
and especially on obedience or disobedience to prophetic
warnings. Some good remarks on this head, with a list of
illustrative passages, will be found in Driver's *Introduction*,
p. 494; I must here content myself with one or two conspicuous examples out of many.

In 1 Kings xxii. 48 we read that Jehoshaphat built
Tarshish ships (*i.e.* such great ships as the Phœnicians used
in their trade with southern Spain) at Ezion-geber for the
South Arabian gold trade ; but the ships were wrecked before
starting.   For this the Chronicler seeks a religious reason ;
and, as 1 Kings goes on to say that, after the disaster, Ahaziah
of Israel offered to join Jehoshaphat in a fresh enterprise, and
the latter declined, we are told in 2 Chron. xx. 37 that the
king of Israel was partner in the ships that were wrecked,
and that Jehoshaphat was warned by a prophet of the certain
failure of an undertaking in which he was associated with
the wicked Ahaziah.   That this is a mere pragmatical inference from the story in Kings, and does not rest on some
good independent source, is confirmed by the fact that the
Chronicler misunderstands the words of 1 Kings, and changes
"Tarshish ships" into "ships to go to Tarshish," as if ships
for the Mediterranean trade could possibly be built on the
Gulf of Akaba in the Red Sea!   On the other hand, in
2 Kings iii., we read of a war with Moab, in which Jehoshaphat was associated with the wicked house of Ahab, and
came off scatheless.   In Chronicles this war is entirely
omitted, and in its place we have a war of Jehoshaphat alone
against Moab, Ammon, and Edom, in which the Jewish king,
having begun the campaign with suitable prayer and praise,
has no further task than to spoil the dead of the enemy who
have fallen by one another's hands.   The idea of this easy
victory is taken from the story of the real war with Moab
(2 Kings iii. 21 *sq.*), where we learn that the Moabites fell into
a trap by imagining that their enemies of Israel, Judah, and
Edom had quarrelled and destroyed one another.   Let me
ask you, taking this hint with you, to read 2 Kings iii. and
2 Chron. xx. carefully through, and consider the difference
between the old and the new conception of the supernatural
in Israel's history.   In reading the old account observe that

verses 16, 17, 20 describe the way in which the underground water descending from the Edomite mountains can still be obtained, by digging water pits, in the Wâdy el-Ahsâ ("valley of water pits"), on the southern frontier of Moab, which was the scene of the events in question.[1]

In Chronicles the kings undergo alternate good and bad fortune, according to their conduct immediately before. Rehoboam is first good and strong, then he forsakes the Law, and Shishak invades the land; then he repents, and the rest of his reign is prosperous. And so it goes with all his successors. According to 1 Kings xv. 14 Asa's heart was perfect with the Lord all his days. But in his old age he had a disease in his feet (1 Kings xv. 23). Accordingly the Chronicler tells us that for three years before this misfortune (2 Chron. xvi. 1, 12) he had done several wicked things, one of which, his alliance with Damascus, is also recounted in Kings, but without the slightest hint that there was anything in it displeasing to God. To bring this incident into the place that fits his *theodicea*, the Chronicler has to change the chronology of Baasha's reign (2 Chron. xvi. 1 compared with 1 Kings xv. 33). Similarly the misfortunes of Jehoash, Amaziah, Azariah are all explained by sins of which the old history knows nothing, and Pharaoh Necho himself is made a prophet, that the defeat and death of Josiah may be due to disobedience to revelation (2 Chron. xxxv. 21, 22), while, on the other hand, the wicked Manasseh is converted into a penitent to justify his long reign. All this is exactly in the style of the Jewish Midrash; it is not history but Haggada, moralising romance attaching to historical names

---

[1] See Wellhausen, *Composition*, p. 287, with Wetzstein in Delitzsch, *Genesis*, ed. 4, p. 567 as there cited. Cp. further Doughty, *Travels*, i 26 *sq.*, and for the kind of bottom, yielding water under the sand, implied in the name el-Ahsâ (el-Hisâ, el-Hisy), Yâcût, i. 148; Zohair, ed. Landberg, p. 95; Ibn Hishâm, *Sîra*, p. 71, l. 9. The point of the miracle lies in the copiousness of the supply obtained by the use of ordinary means.

and events. And the Chronicler himself gives the name of *Midrash* (E. V. " story ") to two of the sources from which he drew (2 Chron. xiii. 22, xxiv. 27), so that there is really no mystery as to the nature of his work when it departs from the old canonical histories.

I have dwelt at some length on this topic, because the practice of using the Chronicles as if they had the same historical value as the older books has done more than any other one cause to prevent a right understanding of the Old Testament and of the Old Dispensation. To admit what I think has been proved in the previous pages involves a serious shock to received ideas of the equal authority of the whole Hebrew Canon; but if the thing is true—and the proofs that it is true may be greatly added to—the consequences must be faced. Moreover, we shall see in the next Lecture that the difficulty as to admitting the truth which is supposed to arise from the history of the Canon is really imaginary, and that no sacred authority binding on the Christian conscience fixes the precise limits of the Canon, and excludes all criticism of its contents.

LECTURE VI

THE HISTORY OF THE CANON

In this Lecture I propose to discuss the main points in the history of the Old Testament Canon; inquiring what books were accepted by the Jews as Sacred Scriptures; at what date the list of canonical books was closed; and on what principles the list was formed.[1] Here I would again ask you to begin by comparing the Hebrew Bible with the Greek.

The Hebrew Bible has twenty-four books, arranged in three great sections—the Law, the Prophets, and the Hagiographa. The first section consists of the Pentateuch, or, as the Hebrews call it, the "Five-Fifths of the Law." The second section has two subdivisions—(a) The old histories, which were believed to have prophets for their authors, and are called the "Earlier Prophets," or, more exactly, the "Former Prophets"; and (b) the prophetic books proper, which are called the "Latter Prophets." In these designations, the words "Former" and "Latter" cannot refer to the date of composition, but must be taken to indicate the order of the books in the canonical collection. Each subdivision of the Prophets contains four books; for the Hebrews count

[1] On the subject of this Lecture see especially the excellent little book of Professor G. Wildeboer of Groningen (*Die Entstehung des Alttestamentlichen Kanons*, ed. 2, Gotha, 1891). Many points of detail to which it was impossible to refer in the present volume are lucidly discussed by Dr. Wildeboer, and by my friend Prof. Ryle, whose *Canon of the O. T.* (London, 1892) reaches me as these sheets are passing through the press.

but one book of Samuel and one of Kings, and the Twelve Minor Prophets are reckoned as one book. The third section of the Hebrew Bible consists of what are called the Hagiographa, or " Kethûbîm," that is [sacred] writings. At the head of these stand three poetical books—Psalms, Proverbs, and Job. Then come the five small books of Canticles, Ruth, Lamentations, Ecclesiastes, and Esther, which the Hebrews name the Megillôth, or "rolls." They have this name because they alone among the Hagiographa were used on certain annual occasions in the service of the synagogue, and for this purpose were written each in a separate volume. Last of all, at the end of the Hebrew Bible, stand Daniel, Ezra with Nehemiah (forming a single book), and the Chronicles, also forming a single book. As the contents of these books are historical and prophetical, we should naturally have expected to find them in the section of Prophets. The reason why they hold a lower place will fall to be examined later. This number of twenty-four books, and the division into the Law, the Prophets, and the Hagiographa, were perfectly fixed during the Talmudic period, that is, from the third to the sixth century of our era.[1] The order in each division was to some extent variable.[2] The number of twenty-four books seems

---

[1] The scheme of the Hebrew Canon may be put thus :—

I. The five-fifths of the Law   5
II. The Prophets—
    Earlier Prophets : Joshua, Judges, Samuel, Kings .   .   .   4
    Later Prophets : Isaiah, Jeremiah, Ezekiel, The Twelve   .   .   4
III. Hagiographa or Ketûbîm—
    Poetical Books : Psalms, Proverbs, Job   3
    The Megilloth : Canticles, Ruth, Lamen., Eccles., Esther .   .   5
    Daniel, Ezra-Nehemiah, Chronicles   3
                                              —
                                           24

[2] The fundamental passage in the Babylonian Gemara, *Bâbâ Bâthra*, ff. 14, 15, says, "The order of the prophets is Joshua and Judges, Samuel and Kings, Jeremiah and Ezekiel, Isaiah and the Twelve. Hosea is the first because it is written, 'the beginning of the word of the Lord by Hosea' (Hos. i. 2). . . . But, because his prophecy is written along with the latest prophets, Haggai, Zechariah, and Malachi, he is counted with them. Isaiah is earlier than Jeremiah and Ezekiel. . . . But because Kings ends with

to be found in the Second (or Fourth) Book of Esdras, towards the close of the first Christian century.[1]

Another division into twenty-two books is adopted in the earliest extant list of the contents of the Hebrew Bible, that given by Josephus in his first book against Apion, chap. viii. This scheme was still well known in the time of Jerome, who prefers to reckon twenty-two books, joining Ruth to Judges, and Lamentations to Jeremiah ; although he also mentions the Talmudic enumeration of twenty-four books, and a third scheme which reckons twenty-seven, dividing Samuel, Kings, Chronicles, and Ezra-Nehemiah, as is done in our modern Bibles, and separating Jeremiah from Lamentations. It is proper to observe that the scheme of twenty-two books is conformed to the number of letters in the Hebrew alphabet. Jerome draws a parallel between this arrangement and the alphabetical acrostics in the Psalms, Lamentations, and Proverbs xxxi. 9-31, and there can be little doubt that it is artificial. Nor is there any clear evidence that it had an established place in Palestinian tradition.[2]

destruction and Jeremiah is all destruction, while Ezekiel beginning with destruction ends in consolation and Isaiah is all consolation, destruction is joined to destruction and consolation to consolation. The order of the Hagiographa is Ruth and Psalms and Job and Proverbs, Ecclesiastes, Canticles, and Lamentations, Daniel and Esther, Ezra and Chronicles." Compare Müller's note on *Sôpherîm*, iii. 5. Isaiah follows Ezekiel in some MSS. (Lagarde, *Symmicta*, i. 142), and the order of the Hagiographa varies considerably ; comp. Driver, *Introd.* p. xxviii., and Ryle, pp. 229, 281.

[1] Even after Professor Bensly's researches the Latin text of 4 Esdras xiv. 44, 46 remains obscure. Nor is the evidence of the Oriental versions quite unambiguous. But on the whole it can hardly be doubted that the original text spoke of ninety-four books, of which seventy were esoteric, leaving twenty-four published and canonical books. (See *infra*, p. 168.)

[2] See the three enumerations in Jerome, *Prol. Galeat.* His order for the Hagiographa is Job, David, Proverbs, Ecclesiastes, Canticles, Daniel, Chronicles, Ezra, Esther. On the Canon of Josephus see below, p. 164 and note. I agree with Wildeboer that it is very doubtful whether the division into twenty-two books ever had an established place in Palestine. Jerome himself in his preface to Daniel says that the Jews reckon five books of the Law, eight Prophets, and eleven Hagiographa ; the testimony of Origen, *ap.* Eus. *H. E.* vi. 25, is plainly not an unmixed reflex of Palestinian tradition, since it

It is often taken for granted that the list of Old Testament books was quite fixed in Palestine at the time of our Lord, and that the Bible acknowledged by Jesus was precisely identical with our own. But it must be remembered that we have no list of the sacred books earlier than the time of Josephus, who wrote at the very end of the first century. Before this date the nearest approach to a catalogue is the panegyric on the famous men of Israel in Ecclesiasticus xliv.-l., in which authors are expressly included. The writer takes up the Pentateuch, Joshua, Judges, Samuel, Kings, Isaiah, Jeremiah, Ezekiel, and the twelve Minor Prophets in order. He also mentions the psalms of David, and the songs proverbs and parables of Solomon. Daniel and Esther are passed over in silence, and Nehemiah is mentioned without Ezra. Neither Philo nor the New Testament enables us to make up a complete list of Old Testament books, for there are some of the Hagiographa (Esther, Canticles, Ecclesiastes) which are quoted neither by the apostles nor by their Alexandrian contemporary. On the other hand, there is no reason to believe that any books were received in Palestine at the time of Christ which have now fallen out of the Canon.

When we turn to the Septuagint we find, in the first place, a very different arrangement of the books. There is no division into Law, Prophets, and Hagiographa; but the

includes not only Lamentations but the Epistle of Jeremiah in the Book of Jeremiah ; and no weight can be laid on Epiphanius, *De Mens. et Pond.* 4 (ed. Lagarde, p. 156), whose division into four pentateuchs and two odd books stands quite by itself. Finally, the statement that the Book of Jubilees reckoned twenty-two books is not borne out by the extant (Ethiopic) text, but rests on a doubtful inference from Syncellus (p. 5, Bonn ed.) and Cedrenus (p. 9, Bonn ed.), where the citation from the Leptogenesis (Book of Jubilees) may refer only to the parallel between the twenty-two works of creation and the twenty-two generations from Adam to Jacob (against Rönsch, *Buch der Jub.* (1874), p. 527 *sq.*) As Josephus does not follow the Hebrew division or arrangement of the books, it is not safe, when the other authorities thus break down, to assume that he had Hebrew authority for the number twenty-two.

Law and the historical books come first, the poetical and
didactic books follow, and the prophets stand at the end as
in our English Bibles. But there is another difference.
MSS. and editions of the Septuagint contain, interspersed
through the books of the Hebrew Canon, certain additional
writings which we call Apocrypha. The Apocrypha of the
Septuagint are not precisely identical with those given in the
English Authorised Version. The apocalyptic book called
Second (or Fourth) Esdras is not extant in Greek. The
Prayer of Manasseh is not in all copies of the Septuagint, but
is found in the collection of hymns or Canticles which some
MSS. append to the Psalms. All our MSS. of the LXX. are
of Christian origin, and these Canticles comprise the Magni-
ficat and other New Testament hymns. On the other hand,
the Septuagint reckons four books of Maccabees, while the
English Apocrypha have only two.

The additional books contained in the Septuagint may be
divided into three classes :—

I. Books translated from the Hebrew. Of these 1 Maccabees and Ecclesiasticus were still extant in Hebrew in the time
of Jerome, and the Books of Tobit and Judith were translated
or corrected by him from Aramaic copies. Baruch, in his
day, was no longer current among the Hebrews.

II. Books originally composed in Greek by Hellenistic
Jews, such as the Second Book of Maccabees, the principal
part of which is an epitome of a larger work by Jason of
Cyrene, and the Wisdom of Solomon, which, though it professes to be the work of the Hebrew monarch, is plainly the
production of an Alexandrian Jew trained in the philosophy
of his time.

III. Books based on translations from the canonical
books, but expanded and embellished with arbitrary and
fabulous additions. In the Greek Book of Esther the " Additions " given in the English Apocrypha form an integral part

of the text. Similarly, the Septuagint Daniel embodies
Susanna, the Song of the Three Children, and Bel and the
Dragon; but these are perhaps later additions to the Greek
version. 1 Esdras is based on extracts from Chronicles, Ezra,
and Nehemiah, but treats the text freely, and adds the
fabulous history of Zerubbabel.

The style of literature to which this third class of Apocrypha belongs was also known in Palestine; and we still
possess many Rabbinical books of similar character, containing popular reproductions of the canonical books interwoven
with fabulous additions. This kind of literature is a branch
of the Midrash, or treatment of the sacred books for purposes
of popular edification. It seems to have had its origin in the
Synagogue, where the early Meturgemans and preachers did
not confine themselves to a faithful reproduction of Bible
teaching, but added all manner of Haggada, ethical and
fabulous, according to the taste of the time. But in Palestine the Haggadic Midrash was usually kept distinct from
the text, and handed down either orally or in separate books.
In Alexandria, on the contrary, the Jews seem to have been
content, in certain instances, to receive books through a
Midrash instead of an exact version, or to admit Midrashic
additions to the text.

From the fact that the Apocrypha stand side by side with
the canonical books in the MSS. and editions of the Septuagint, some have leaped to the conclusion that the Canon of
the Alexandrian Jews contained all these books, or, in other
words, that they were recognised in Alexandria as being
divine and inspired in the same sense as the Law, the
Prophets, and the Psalms. There are, however, several
reasons which should make us hesitate to draw such an inference. In the first place, we observe that the number of
Apocryphal books is not identical in all copies, and that some
of the books are found in two recensions with very consider-

able variations of form.[1]   This in itself is a strong reason for
doubting the existence of a fixed Alexandrian Canon.   In
the second place, all our manuscripts of the Septuagint are of
Christian origin.   The presence of an Apocryphon in a Christian MS. shows that it had a certain measure of recognition
in the Church, but does not prove that full canonical authority
was ascribed to it in the Synagogue.   Again, in the third
place, the books must have been current one by one before
they were collected into a single volume.   We learn from
the prologue to Ecclesiasticus and the subscription to the
Apocryphal Book of Esther that some of them at least were
translated by private enterprise without having any official
sanction.   Whatever position, then, they ultimately attained,
they were not translated as part of an authoritative Canon.
And finally, Philo, the greatest of Jewish Hellenists, who
flourished in the time of our Lord, knew the Apocrypha
indeed, for he seems sometimes to borrow the turn of a phrase
from them, but he never quotes from them, much less uses
them for the proof of doctrine as he habitually uses most of
the books in our Old Testament.   There are, then, sufficient
reasons for hesitating to believe that the Alexandrian Jews
received all these books as authoritative, in the same sense as
the Law and the Prophets.   But, on the other hand, we are
bound to explain how such books ever came to stand so
closely associated with the canonical books as they do in our
Greek copies.   If the line of demarcation between canonical
and uncanonical books had been sharply fixed, it is hard to
see how they could have got into the Septuagint at all.   And
how did it come to pass that certain of the Hagiographa were
not used in Alexandria in their canonical form, but only in
the shape of Haggadic reproductions?   These phenomena

[1] Two Greek recensions of Esther and Tobit exist.   See for the former
book Lagarde's edition of the Septuagint (Gött., 1883), where the two recensions are printed on opposite pages, and for Tobit, Swete's edition, where the
recension of the Sinaiticus stands under the text of the Vaticanus.

point to a time when the idea of canonicity was not yet fixed, and when certain books, even of the Hebrew Canon, were only pushing their way gradually towards universal recognition. In Alexandria, for example, the Book of Esther cannot have been accepted as beyond dispute ; for instead of a proper translation we find only a Midrash, circulating in two varying recensions, and not claiming by its subscription to be more than a private book brought to Alexandria in the fourth year of Ptolemy and Cleopatra by one Dositheos, who called himself a priest.

These facts force us to inquire upon what principles the Jews separated the sacred writings from ordinary books. But, before doing this, let me ask you to look at the Apocrypha as they appear to us in the light of history. All the books of the Apocrypha are comparatively modern. There is none of them, on the most favourable computation, which can be supposed to be older than the latest years of the Persian empire. They belong, therefore, to the age when the last great religious movement of the Old Testament under Ezra had passed away—when prophecy had died out, and the nation had settled down to live under the Law, looking for guidance in religion, not to a continuance of new revelation, but to the written Word, and to the interpretations of the Scribes. To place these books on the same footing with the Law and the Prophets is quite impossible to the historical student. They belong to a new literature which rose in Judæa after the cessation of prophetic originality, when the law and the tradition were all in all, when there was no man to speak with authority truths that he had received direct from God, but the whole intellect of Israel was either concentrated on the development of legal Halacha, or, in men of more poetical imagination, exercised itself in restating and illustrating the old principles of religion in ethical poetry, like that of Ecclesiasticus, or in romance and fable of a re-

ligious complexion, like the Books of Judith and Tobit.
Halacha, Midrash, and Haggada became the forms of all
literary effort ; or if any man tried a bolder flight, and sought
for his work a place of higher authority, he did so by assuming the name of some ancient worthy. This last class of
pseudepigraphic works, as they are called, consists largely of
pseudoprophetic books in apocalyptic form, like 2 (4) Esdras.[1]

It is plain, then, on broad historical considerations,
without entering into any matters of theological dispute, as
to the nature of inspiration and so forth, that there is a distinct line of demarcation between the Apocrypha and the
books which record the progress of Israel's religion during
the ages when prophets and righteous men still looked for
their guidance in times of religious need not to a written book
and its scholastic interpreters, but to a fresh word of revelation. But how far was this understood by those who separated out the books of our Hebrew Bible as canonical, and

---

[1] The line between the old literature and the new cannot be drawn with
chronological precision. The characteristic mark of canonical literature is
that it is the record of the progress of fresh truths of revelation, and of the
immediate reflection of these truths in the believing heart. The Psalms are,
in part, considerably later than Ezra, but they record the inner side of the
history of his work of reformation, and show us the nature of the faith with
which Israel apprehended the Law and its institutes. This is a necessary
and most precious element of the Old Testament record, and it would be
arbitrary to attempt to fix a point of time at which this part of Old Testament Scripture must necessarily have closed. But the direct language of
faith held by the psalmists is intrinsically different from such artificial reflection on the law, in the manner of the schools, as is found in Ecclesiasticus.
The difference can be felt rather than defined, and a certain margin of uncertainty must attach to every determination of the limits of what is
canonical. But, on the whole, the instinct that guided the formation of the
Hebrew Canon was sound, because the theories of the schools affected only
certain outlying books, while the mass of the collection established itself in
the hearts of all the faithful in successive generations, under historical circumstances of a sifting kind. The religious struggle under the Maccabees,
which threw the people of God upon the Scriptures for comfort when the
outward order of the theocracy was broken, doubtless was for the later books
of the Canon a period of proof such as the Captivity was for the older
literature.

rejected all others? The Jews had a dim sort of consciousness after the time of Ezra that the age of revelation was
past, and that the age of tradition had begun. The feeling
that new revelation had almost ceased is found even in the
latest prophecies of the Old Testament. In Zechariah xiii.
the prophet predicts the near approach of a time when every
one who calls himself a prophet, and puts on a prophet's
garment, shall be at once recognised as a deceiver, and his
own father and mother shall be the first to denounce the
imposture. And, in the last verse of the prophetic books of
the Old Testament, Malachi does not look forward to a constant succession of prophets, such as is foretold in Deuteronomy. He sees no hope for the corrupt state of his times,
except that the old prophet Elijah shall return to bring back
the hearts of the fathers with their children, and the hearts
of the children with their fathers, lest God come and smite
the earth with a curse. As time rolled on, the feeling that
there was no new revelation among the people became still
more strong. In 1 Maccabees ix. 27 we read that "there
was great sorrow in Israel, such as there had not been since
the days that prophets ceased to appear among them;" and,
according to Josephus, the strict succession of prophets ended in
the reign of Artaxerxes Longimanus. The Scribes thoroughly
sympathised with this view. Even when they made innovations, they always professed to do so as mere interpreters,
claiming nothing more than to restore, to expound, or to fence
in, the law given by Moses. Their position is aptly described
in the phrase of the New Testament, where Jesus is said to
teach "as one having authority, and not as the scribes." But,
while the Jews had a general feeling that the age of revelation was past, they had no such clear perception of the reason
of the change as we can have in the light of the New Testament; they did not see, as we can do, that no further development of spiritual religion was possible without breaking

through the legal forms and national limitations of Judaism ; and they continued to look, not for a new revelation super- seding the old covenant, but for the reappearance of prophets working in the service of the law and its ritual.   In 1 Macca- bees iv. 46 they put aside the stones of the polluted altar, not knowing what to do with them, but waiting till a prophet shall arise in Israel to tell it; and again (chap. xiv. 41), they agree to make Simon high priest until such time as a true prophet shall appear.   The revival of prophecy was still looked for, but the idea of the function of prophecy was narrowed to things of no moment.   Malachi had looked for a prophet to bring back to God the hearts of fathers and children alike ; in the days of the Maccabees the true nature of prophecy had been so far forgotten that it was thought that the business of a prophet was to tell what should be done with the stones of a polluted altar, or which family was to hold the dignity of the high priesthood.   Where the mean- ing of prophecy was so little understood, it is not surprising that a sporadic reappearance of prophets was not thought impossible.   Josephus, in a curious passage of his *Jewish War*, says that John Hyrcanus was the only man who united in his person the three highest distinctions, being at once the ruler of his nation, and high priest, and gifted with prophecy; "for the Divinity so conversed with him that he was cognisant of all things that were to come" (*B. J.* Bk. i. chap. ii. 8; compare the similar expressions of John xi. 51). Moreover, although the Scribes in general did not consider that they had the spirit of revelation, we find the author of Ecclesi- asticus (chap. xxiv. 31, 32) claiming for his book an almost prophetic authority : " I will yet make instruction to shine as the morning, and will send forth her light afar off.   I will pour forth doctrine as prophecy, and leave it unto eternal generations" (comp. i. 30, li. 13 *sq.*).   The author is fully conscious that his whole wisdom is derived from the study of the law (xxiv. 30). He does not pretend that he or other scholars are the vehicles of new truths of revelation (chaps. xxxviii. xxxix.); but he is evidently not conscious that this circumstance constitutes an absolute difference between the teaching which, by his own admission, was nothing more than an enforcement of the principles of the law of Moses, and the old creative prophecy of Isaiah or Jeremiah. This unclearness of view rested upon an error which not only was fatal to the Jews, but has continued to exercise a pernicious influence even on Christian theology down to our own day. The Jews, as we have already seen, identified religion with the Law, and the Law with the words of Moses.

All revelation was held to be comprised in the Torah. According to the Son of Sirach, the sacred Wisdom, created before the world and enduring to all eternity, which is established in Sion and bears sway in Jerusalem, the all-sufficient food of man's spiritual life, is identical with the book of the Covenant of God most High, the Law enjoined by Moses (Ecclesiasticus xxiv.). The secrets of this law are infinite, and all man's wisdom is a stream derived from this unfailing source. This doctrine of the pre-existent and eternal Law, comprising within itself the sum of all wisdom and all possible revelation, runs through the whole Jewish literature. It is brought out in a very interesting way in the old Jewish commentaries on Deut. xxx. 12 :—"The law is not in the heavens." "Say not," says the commentary, "another Moses shall arise and bring another law from heaven : there is no law left in heaven;" that is, according to the position of the Jews, the law of Moses contained the whole revelation of God's goodness and grace which had been given or which ever could be given.[1]

---

[1] *Midrash Rabba*, p. 529 (Leipzig, 1864). For the law as everlasting, see Baruch, iv. 1. The pre-existence of the law (Ecclus. xxiv. 9) follows from its being identified with wisdom as described in Prov. viii. Compare further Weber, *Altsynagogale Theologie*, p. 18 *sq.* The Rabbinical theory of revela-

What place, then, was left for the Prophets, the Psalms, and the other books? They were inspired and authoritative interpretations and applications of the law of Moses, and nothing more. They were, therefore, simply the links in tradition between the time of Moses and the time of Ezra and the Scribes. And so clearly was this the Jewish notion, that the same word—*Kabbala*, doctrine traditionally received —is applied indifferently to all the books of the Old Testament except the Pentateuch, and to the oral tradition of the Scribes. The Pentateuch alone is *Mikra*, "reading," or, as we should call it, "Scripture." The Prophets, the Psalms, and the rest of the old Testament, in common with the oral tradition of the Scribes, are mere Kabbala or traditional doctrine. From these premises it necessarily follows that the other books are inferior to the Law. This consequence was drawn with full logical stringency. The Law and the Prophets were not written on the same roll, and, in accordance with a legal principle which forbade a less holy thing to be purchased with the price of one more holy, the Mishna directs that a copy of the other books may no more be bought with the price of a Pentateuch than part of a street may be bought with the price of a synagogue.[1]

I need not interrupt the argument to prove at length that this is a view which cannot be received by any Christian. It was refuted, once for all, by the apostle Paul when he pointed out, in answer to the Pharisees of his time, that the permanent value of all revelation lies, not in Law, but in Gospel. Now, it is certain that the prophetical books are far richer than the

tion has exercised an influence on history far beyond the limits of the Jewish community through its adoption in Islam.

[1] On the term *Kabbala* see Zunz, *Gottesdienstliche Vorträge*, p. 44, where the evidence from Jewish authorities is carefully collected. Compare Weber, *op. cit.* p. 79 *sq.* Mishna, *Megilla*, iii. 1: "If the men of a town sell a Torah they may not buy with its price the other books of Scripture; if they sell Scriptures they may not buy a cloth to wrap round the Torah; if they sell such a cloth they may not buy an ark for synagogue rolls; if they sell an ark they may not buy a synagogue; nor if they sell a synagogue may they buy a street" (an open ground for devotion; cp. Matt. vi. 5).

Law in evangelical elements. They contain a much fuller declaration of those spiritual truths which constitute the permanent value of the Old Testament Revelation, and a much clearer adumbration of the New and Spiritual Covenant under which we now live. There is more of Christ in the Prophets and the Psalms than in the Pentateuch, with its legal ordinances and temporary precepts adapted to the hardness of the people's hearts; and therefore no Christian can for a moment consent to accept that view of the pre-eminence of the Law which was to the Jews the foundation of their official doctrine of the Canon. What, then, is the inference from these facts? We found, in Lecture II., that the early Protestants, for reasons very intelligible at their time, were content simply to accept the Canon as it came to them through the hands of the Jews. But it appears that, in defining the number and limits of the sacred books, the Jewish doctors started with a false idea of the test and measure of sacredness. Their tradition, therefore, does not conclusively determine the question of the Canon; and we cannot permanently acquiesce in it without subjecting their conclusions to a fresh examination by sounder tests.

Before we proceed to examine in detail the definitions of the Rabbins on this matter, let me say at once that the part played by the Scribes and their erroneous theories in determining the compass of the Hebrew Scriptures was after all very limited. A Canon, deliberately framed on the principles of the Scribes and Pharisees, could hardly have been satisfactory; but in reality the essential elements in the Canon were not determined by official authority. The mass of the Old Testament books gained their canonical position because they commended themselves in practice to the experience of the Old Testament Church and the spiritual discernment of the godly in Israel. For the religious life of Israel was truer than the teaching of the Pharisees. The Old Testament religion was the religion of revelation; and the highest spiritual truths then known did not dwell in the Jewish people without producing, in practical life, a higher type of religious experience, and a truer insight into spiritual things, than was embodied in the doctrines of the Scribes. When the Jewish doctors first concerned themselves with the preparation of an authoritative list of sacred books, most of the Old Testament books had already established themselves in the hearts of the faithful with an authority that could neither be shaken nor confirmed by the decisions of the schools. The controversy as to the limits of the Canon was confined to a few outlying books which, by reason of their contents or of their history, were less universally read and valued than the Prophets and the Psalms. In the ultimate decision as to the canonicity of these books the authority and theories of the Scribes played an important part; but for the rest of the Old Testament the Scribes did nothing more than accept established facts, bringing them into conformity with their theories by hypotheses as to the prophetic authorship of anonymous books and other arbitrary assumptions of which we shall find examples as we proceed.

In looking more narrowly at the constitution of the Jewish Canon we may begin by recurring to the account of the matter given by Josephus towards the close of the first century. There is little doubt that the twenty-two books of Josephus are those of our present Hebrew Canon; but the force of this evidence is disguised by the controversial purpose of the writer, which leads him to put his facts in a false light. The aim of Josephus in his work against Apion is to vindicate the antiquity of the Hebrew nation, and the credibility of its history as recorded in his own *Archæology*. In this connection he maintains that the Oriental nations kept official annals long before the Greeks, and that the Jews in particular charged their chief priests and prophets with the duty of preserving a regular record of contemporary affairs, not permitting any private person to meddle in the matter. This official record

is contained in the twenty-two books of the Old Testament.
The older history, communicated by revelation, is found in the
Pentateuch along with the legal code.   The other books, with
the exception of four containing hymns and precepts of life,
which may be identified with the Psalms, Proverbs, Ecclesiastes, and the Song of Solomon, are made to figure as a
continuous history written by an unbroken succession of
prophets, each of whom recorded the events of his own time,
down to the reign of Artaxerxes Longimanus, when the succession of prophets failed, and the sacred annals stopped short.[1]
As Josephus places Ezra and Nehemiah under Xerxes, and
identifies his son Artaxerxes with the Ahasuerus of Esther,
he no doubt views Esther as the latest canonical book.   The
number of thirteen prophetico-historical books from Joshua
to Esther is made up by reckoning Job as a history, and con-
joining Ruth with Judges and Lamentations with Jeremiah, in
the manner mentioned by Jerome.   As the Song of Solomon
figures as a didactic book, it must have been taken allegorically.[2]

According to Josephus, the close of the Canon is distinctly

---

[1] Josephus, *Contra Apion.* lib. I. cap. vii. *sq.* (§§ 37-41, Niese ; cp. Eus.
H. E. iii. 10).—"Not every one was permitted to write the national records,
nor is there any discrepancy in the things written ; but the prophets alone
learned the earliest and most ancient events by inspiration from God, and
wrote down the events of their own times plainly as they occurred.   And so
we have not myriads of discordant and contradictory books, but only two-and-
twenty, containing the record of all time, and rightly believed in [as divine :
Eus.].   And of these five are the books of Moses, comprising the laws, and
the tradition from the creation of mankind down to his death.   But from the
death of Moses till the reign of Artaxerxes, king of Persia, who succeeded
Xerxes, the prophets that followed Moses compiled the history of their
own times in thirteen books.   The other four contain hymns to God and
precepts of life for men.   But from Artaxerxes to our times all events
have indeed been written down ; but these later books are not deemed
worthy of the same credit, because the exact succession of prophets was
wanting."

[2] The allegorical interpretation of Canticles, Israel being identified with the
spouse, first appears in 2 (4) Esdras, v. 24, 26 ; vii. 26, and may very well
have been known to Josephus.   It is, however, right to say that some
scholars doubt whether Ecclesiastes and Canticles were included in the Canon
of Josephus.   So still Lagarde, *Mittheilungen*, iv. (1891), p. 345.

marked by the cessation of the succession of prophets in the time of Artaxerxes. On this view there never was or could be any discussion as to the number and limits of the canonical collection, which had from first to last an official character. Each new book was written by a man of acknowledged authority, and was added to the collection precisely as a new page would be added to the royal annals of an Eastern kingdom. It is plain that this view is not in accordance with facts. The older prophets were not official historiographers working in harmony with the priests for the regular continuance of a series of Temple annals; they were often in opposition to the sacred as well as the civil authorities of their nation. Jeremiah, for example, was persecuted and put in the stocks by Pashur the son of Immer, priest and chief governor of the Temple. Again, it is clear that there was no regular and unbroken series of sacred annals officially kept up from the time of Moses onwards. In the time of Josiah, the Law, unexpectedly found in the house of the Lord, appears as a thing that had been lost and long forgotten. Even a glance at the books of the Old Testament is enough to refute the idea of a regular succession of prophetic writers, each taking up the history just where the last had left it. In fact, Josephus in this statement simply gives a turn, for his own polemical purposes, to that theory of tradition which was current among the Pharisees of his time and is clearly expressed at the beginning of the treatise of the Mishna called *Pirkê Aboth*. In it we read that "Moses received the Torah from Sinai and delivered it to Joshua, Joshua delivered it to the elders, the elders to the prophets, and the prophets to the men of the Great Synagogue," from whom it passed in turn to the Zûgôth, as the Hebrews called them,—that is, the pairs of great doctors who, in successive generations, formed the heads of the Scribes. This whole doctrine of the succession of tradition is a dogmatical theory, not an historical fact; and in like manner Josephus's account of the Canon is a theory, and a theory inconsistent with the fact that we find no complete formal catalogue of Scriptures in earlier writers like the son of Sirach, who, enumerating the literary worthies of his nation, had every motive to give a complete list, if he had been in a position to do so; inconsistent also with the fact that questions as to the canonicity of certain books were still undecided within the lifetime of Josephus himself.

But the clearest evidence that the notion of canonicity was not fully established till long after the time of Artaxerxes lies in the Septuagint. The facts that have come before us are not to be explained by saying that there was one fixed Canon in Palestine and another in Alexandria. That would imply such a schism between the Hellenistic and Palestinian Jews, between the Jews who spoke Greek and those who read Hebrew, as certainly did not exist, and would assign to the Apocrypha an authority among the former which there is no reason to believe they ever possessed. The true inference from the fact is, that the Canon of the Old Testament was of gradual formation, that some books now accepted had long a doubtful position, while others were for a time admitted to a measure of reputation which made the line of demarcation between them and the canonical books uncertain and fluctuating. In short, we must suppose a time when the Old Testament Canon was passing through the same kind of history through which we know the New Testament Canon to have passed. In the early ages of the Christian Church we find the books of the New Testament divided into the so-called *Homologumena*, or books universally acknowledged, and the *Antilegomena*, or books acknowledged in some parts of the Church but spoken against in others. The *Homologumena* included those books which, either from their very nature or from their early and wide circulation, never could be questioned—books of ad-

mitted and undoubted apostolic authority, such as the
Gospels and the great Epistles of Paul.   The *Antilegomena*
consisted of other books, some of which are now in our New
Testament, but which for some reason were not from the
first broadly circulated over the whole Church.   Along with
these, there were other books, not now held canonical, which
in some parts of the Church were read in public worship,
and received a certain amount of reverence.   The history of
the Canon unfolds the gradual process by which the number
of *Antilegomena* was narrowed; either by the Church,
through all its length and breadth, coming to be persuaded
that some book not at first undisputed was yet worthy to
be universally received as apostolic, or, conversely, by the
spread of the conviction that other books, which for a time
had been used in certain churches, were not fit to be put on
a level with the Gospels and the great Epistles.   We must
suppose that a similar process took place with regard to the
books of the Old Testament.   About many of them there
could be no dispute.   Others were *Antilegomena* — books
spoken against — and the number of such *Antilegomena*,
which were neither fully acknowledged nor absolutely rejected, was naturally a fluctuating quantity up to a comparatively late date, when such a measure of practical
agreement had been reached as to which books were really
of sacred authority, that the theological heads of the nation
could, without difficulty, cut short further discussion, and
establish an authoritative list of Scriptures.   The reason
why a greater number of books of disputed position is
preserved in Greek than in Hebrew is that the Rabbins
of Palestine, from the close of the first century, when the
Canon was definitely fixed, sedulously suppressed all Apocrypha, and made it a sin to read them.

This account of the origin of the Canon is natural in itself
and agrees with all the facts, especially with the circumstance

that the canonicity of certain books was a moot-point among
Jewish theologians till after the fall of the Temple. This
fact gave no trouble to the Jews, who accepted the decision
of R. Akiba and his compeers as of undisputed authority.
But Christian theology could not give weight to Rabbinical
tradition, and it is thus very natural that many attempts
have been made to prove that an authoritative Canon was
fixed in the days of Ezra and Nehemiah, while the last
prophets still lived.

Among the ancient fathers it was a current opinion that
Ezra himself rewrote by inspiration the whole Old Testament,
which had been destroyed or injured at the time of the
Captivity. The source of this opinion is a fable in 2 (4)
Esdras xiv. Esdras, according to this story, prayed for the
Holy Spirit that he might rewrite the law that had been
burned. His prayer was granted; and, retiring for forty
days, with five scribes to write to his dictation, he produced
ninety-four (?) books. "And when the forty days were completed, the Most High spake, saying, Publish the first books
which thou hast written, that the worthy and the unworthy
may read them; but conserve the last seventy, and deliver
them to the wise men of thy people." To understand what
this means, we must remember that this Book of Esdras professes to be a genuine prophecy of Ezra the scribe. The
author was aware that when he produced his book, which
was not written till near the close of the first Christian
century, it would be necessary to meet the objection that it
had never been known before. Accordingly he and other
forgers of the same period fell back on the assertion that
certain of the sacred writings had always been esoteric books,
confined to a privileged circle. The whole fable is directed
to this end, and is plainly unworthy of the slightest attention.
We have no right to rationalise it, as some have done, and
read it as a testimony that Ezra may at least have collected

and edited the Old Testament. But no doubt the currency which Fourth Esdras long enjoyed helped to fix the impression on men's minds that in some shape Ezra had a part in settling the Canon, and drove them to seek arguments for this view in other quarters.

Accordingly we find that a new form of the theory started up in the sixteenth century, and gained almost undisputed currency in the Protestant Churches. According to this view, the Canon was completed by a body of men known as the Great Synagogue. The Great Synagogue plays a considerable part in Jewish tradition; it is represented as a permanent council, under the presidency of Ezra, wielding supreme authority over the Jewish nation; and a variety of functions are ascribed to it. But the tradition never said that the Great Synagogue fixed the Canon. That opinion, current as it once was, is a mere conjecture of Elias Levita, a Jewish scholar contemporary with Luther. Not only so, but we now know that the whole idea that there ever was a body called the Great Synagogue holding rule in the Jewish nation is pure fiction. It has been proved in the clearest manner that the origin of the legend of the Great Synagogue lies in the account given in Neh. viii.-x. of the great convocation which met at Jerusalem and subscribed the covenant to observe the law. It was therefore a meeting, and not a permanent authority. It met once for all, and everything that is told about it, except what we read in Nehemiah, is pure fable of the later Jews.[1]

[1] On the legend of the Great Synagogue, Kuenen's essay *Over de Mannen der Groote Synagoge*, in the proceedings of the Royal Society of Amsterdam, 1876, is conclusive. An abstract of the results in Wellhausen-Bleek, § 274. Kuenen follows the arguments of scholars of last century, and especially Rau's *Diatribe de Synagoga Magna* (Utrecht, 1725); but he completes their refutation of the Rabbinical fables by utilising and placing in its true light the important observations of Krochmal, as to the connection between the Great Synagogue and the Convocation of Neh. viii.-x., which, in the hands of Jewish scholars, had only led to fresh confusion. See, for example, Graetz (*Kohelet*, Anh. i. Leipzig, 1871) for a model of confused reasoning on the Great

Two, then, of the traditions which seem to refer the whole Canon to Ezra and his time break down; but a third, found in 2 Maccabees, has received more attention in recent times, and has frequently been supposed, even by cautious scholars, to indicate at least the first steps towards the collection of the Prophets and the Hagiographa :—

" 2 Mac. ii. 13.—The same things [*according to another reading*, these things] were related in the records, and in the memoirs of Nehemiah, and how, founding a library, he collected the [writings] about the kings and prophets, and the [writings] of David, and letters of kings concerning sacred offerings. (14.) In like manner Judas collected all the books that had been scattered in consequence of the war that came on us, and we have them by us; of which if ye have need, send men to fetch them."

This passage stands in a spurious epistle, professedly addressed to the Jews in Alexandria by the Palestinian Jews. The epistle is full of fabulous details, which claim to be taken from written sources. If this claim is not pure fiction, the sources must have been apocryphal. The Memoirs of Nehemiah, to which our passage appeals, are one of these worthless sources, containing, as we are expressly

Synagogue and the Canon. Krochmal's discovery that the Great Synagogue and the Great Convocation are identical rests on the clearest evidence. See especially the Midrash to Ruth. "What did the men of the Great Synagogue do? They wrote a book and spread it out in the court of the temple. And at dawn of day they rose and found it sealed. This is what is written in Neh. ix. 38" (Leipzig ed. of 1865, p. 77). According to the tradition of the Talmud, *Bábá Báthra, ut supra,* the men of the Great Synagogue wrote Ezekiel, the Minor Prophets, Daniel, and Esther; and Ezra wrote his own book and part of the genealogies of Chronicles. This has nothing to do with the Canon; it merely expresses an opinion as to the date of these books. Further, the *Aboth of Rabbi Nathan* (a post-Talmudic book) says that the Great Synagogue arose and explained Proverbs, Canticles, and Ecclesiastes, which had previously been thought apocryphal. Such is the traditional basis for the famous conjecture of Elias Levita in his *Massoreth hammassoreth* (Venice, 1538), which took such a hold of public opinion that Hottinger, in the middle of the seventeenth century, could say : "Hitherto it has been an unquestioned axiom among the Jews and Christians alike, that the Canon of the Old Testament was fixed, once and for all, with Divine authority, by Ezra and the men of the Great Synagogue" (*Thes. Phil.*, Zürich, 1649, p. 112). At p. 110 he says that this is only doubted by those *quibus pro cerebro fungus est.*

told, the same fables, and therefore altogether unworthy of credence. But, in fact, the transparent object of the passage is to palm off upon the reader a whole collection of forgeries, by making out that the author and his friends in Palestine possess, and are willing to communicate, a number of valuable and sacred books not known in Egypt. Literary forgery had an incredible attraction for a certain class of writers in those ages. It was practised by the Hellenistic Jews as a regular trade, and it is in the interests of this fraudulent business that our author introduces the story about Nehemiah and his library. Even if Nehemiah did collect a library, which is likely enough, as he could not but desire to possess the books of the ancient prophets, that after all was a very different thing from forming an authoritative Canon.

Scholars have sometimes been so busy trying to gather a grain of truth out of these fabulous traditions, that they have forgotten to open their eyes and simply look at the Bible itself for a plain and categorical account of what Ezra and Nehemiah actually did for the Canon of Scripture. From Neh. viii.-x. we learn that Ezra did establish a Canon, that is, that he did lead his people to accept a written and sacred code as the absolute rule of faith and life ; but the Canon of Ezra was the Pentateuch. The people entered into a covenant to keep the Law of Moses, which Ezra brought with him from Babylon (Ezra vii. 14). That was the establishment of the Pentateuch as the canonical and authoritative book of the Jews, and that is the position which it holds ever afterwards. So we have seen that to the author of Ecclesiasticus the Pentateuch, and no larger Canon, is the book of the Covenant of God most high, and the source of all sacred wisdom ; while, to all Jewish theology, the Pentateuch stands higher than the other books in sanctity, and is viewed as containing within itself the whole compass of possible revelation. In the strictest sense of the word the Torah is not merely the Canon of Ezra, but remained the Canon of the Jews ever after, all other books being tested by their conformity with its contents.

That does not mean that the Divine authority of the Prophets was not recognised at the time of Ezra. Undoubtedly it was recognised, but it was not felt to be necessary to collect the prophetic books into one authoritative volume with the Law. Indeed, Ezra and Nehemiah could not have undertaken to make a fixed and closed collection of the Prophets, unless they had known that no other prophets were to rise after their time; and we have no reason to believe that they had such knowledge, which could only have come to them by special revelation. The other sacred books, after the time of Ezra, continued to be read and to stand each on its own authority, just as the books of the apostles did in the times of early Christianity. To us this may seem highly inconvenient. We are accustomed to regard the Bible as one book, and it seems to us an awkward thing that there should not have been a fixed volume comprising all sacred writings. The Jews, I apprehend, could not share these feelings. The use of a fixed Canon is either for the convenience of private reading, or for the limitation of public ecclesiastical lessons, or for the determination of appeals in matter of doctrine. And in none of these points did the Jews stand on the same ground with us. In these days the Bible was not a book, but a whole library. The Law was not written on the same skins as the Prophets, and each prophetical book, as we learn from Luke iv. 17, might form a volume by itself. In one passage of the Talmud, a volume containing all the Prophets is mentioned as a singularity. Very few persons, it may be presumed, could possess all the Biblical books, or even dream of having them in a collected form.[1]

---

[1] In the Talmudic times it was matter of controversy whether it was

Then, again, no part of the canonical books, except the Pentateuch, was systematically read through in the Synagogue. The Pentateuch was read through every three years. Lessons from the prophetical books were added at an early date, but up to the time of the Mishna this was not done on a fixed system, while the Hagiographa had no place in the Synagogue lessons until a comparatively late period, when the Book of Esther, and still later the other four Megilloth, came to be used on certain annual occasions.[1] And, finally, in matters of doctrine, the appeal to the Prophets or Hagiographa was not sharply distinguished from appeal to the oral law. Both alike were parts of the *Kabbala*, the traditional and authoritative interpretation of the Pentateuch, which stood as the supreme standard above both.

It is true that the whole doctrine of oral tradition arose gradually and after the time of Ezra. But the one-sided legalism on which it rests could never have been developed if the books of the prophets had been officially recognised, from the time of Ezra downwards, as a part of public revelation, co-ordinate and equally fundamental with the law

legitimate to write the Law, the Prophets, and the Hagiographa in a single book. Some went so far as to say that each book of Scripture must form a separate volume. See *Sôpherîm*, iii. 1, and Müller's note. It appears that the old and predominant custom was in favour of separation. Boethos, whose copy of the eight prophets in one volume is referred to in *Bâbâ Bâthra* and *Sôpherîm*, iii. 5, lived about the close of the second Christian century. Some doctors denied that his copy contained all the books "joined into one." *Sôpherîm*, iii. 6, allows all the books to be united in inferior copies written on the material called diphthera, but not in synagogue rolls ; a compromise pointing to the gradual introduction in post-Talmudic times of the plan of treating the Bible as one volume.

[1] For the want of system in the public lessons from the Prophets in early times, see Luke iv. 17, and *supra*, p. 36, note 2. According to *Sôpherîm*, xiv. 18, Esther was read at the feast of Purim, Canticles at the Passover, Ruth at Pentecost. The reading of Lamentations is mentioned, *ibid*. xviii. 4. It is noteworthy that there is still no mention of the use of Ecclesiastes in the Synagogue. Compare further Zunz, *op. cit.* p. 6. The Jews of Nehardea in Babylonia used to read lessons from the Hagiographa in the Sabbath afternoon service, *B. Shabbath*, f. 116 *b*.

of Moses. The Prophets, in truth, with the other remains of
the old sacred literature, were mainly regarded as books of
private edification. While the Law was directly addressed
to all Israel in all ages, the other sacred writings had a
private origin, or were addressed to special necessities. Up
to the time of the Exile, the godly of Israel looked for
guidance to the living prophetic word in their midst, and the
study of written prophecies or histories, which, according to
many indications, was largely practised in the circles where
the living prophets had most influence, was rather a supplement to the spoken word than a substitute for it. But in
the time of the Exile, when the national existence with
which the ancient religion of Israel was so closely inter-
twined was hopelessly shattered, when the voice of the
prophets was stilled, and the public services of the sanctuary
no longer called the devout together, the whole continuance
of the spiritual faith rested upon the remembrance that the
prophets of the Lord had foreseen the catastrophe, and had
shown how to reconcile it with undiminished trust in
Jehovah, the God of Israel. The written word acquired a
fresh significance for the religious life, and the books of the
prophets, with those records of the ancient history which
were either already framed in the mould of prophetic thought,
or were cast in that mould by editors of the time of the
Exile, became the main support of the faithful, who felt, as
they had never felt before, that the words of Jehovah were
pure words, silver sevenfold tried, a sure treasure in every
time of need.

The frequent allusions to the earlier prophets in the
writings of Zechariah show how deep a hold their words
had taken of the hearts of the godly in Israel; but the very
profundity of this influence, belonging as it did to the sphere
of personal religion rather than the public order of the
theocracy, made it less necessary to stamp the prophetic

series with the seal of public canonicity. These books had no need to be brought from Babylon with the approval of a royal rescript, or laid before the nation by the authority of a Tirshatha. The only form of public recognition which was wanting, and which followed in due course, was the practice of reading from the Prophets in the public worship of the synagogue. It required no more formal process than the natural use made of this ancient literature, to bring it little by little into the shape of a fixed collection, though, as we have seen in the example of Jeremiah, there was no standard edition up to a comparatively late date. In the time of Daniel we already find the prophetic literature referred to under the name of "the books" or Scriptures (Dan. ix. 2). The English version unfortunately omits the article, and loses the force of the phrase.

The ultimate form of the prophetic collection is contained in the Former and Latter Prophets of the Hebrew Bible, of which only the second group consists mainly of prophecies, while the first is made up of historical books. We have seen that by the Jews the name of "Former Prophets" was justified by the unhistorical assumption that the old historical books were written by a succession of prophets. But I apprehend that the association of histories and prophecies in one collection is older than the designation Former and Latter Prophets, and rested on a correct perception (instinctive rather than critical) that the histories formed a necessary part of the record of the prophets' work. Without the histories the prophetical books proper would be almost unintelligible. And further, though there is no reason to think that the mass of the histories was actually written by the hand of prophets, they were certainly written, or at least edited and brought into their present form, by men who stood under the influence of the great prophets and sought to interpret the vicissitudes of Israel's fortunes in accordance

with the laws of God's governance which the prophets had
laid down. There was therefore good reason for placing the
old histories in the same collection with the written words of
the prophets. The authority of this collection, which was
inextricably interlaced with the profoundest experiences of
the spiritual life of Israel, was practically never disputed,
and its influence on the personal religion of the nation was
doubtless in inverse ratio to the preference assigned to the
Pentateuch as the public and official code of Ezra's theocracy.[1]

Equally undisputed was the position of the Psalter, the
hymn-book of the second Temple. The Psalter, as we shall
see in a future Lecture, has a complicated history, and, along
with elements of great antiquity, contains many pieces of a
date long subsequent to the Exile, or even to Ezra. In its
finished form the collection is clearly later than the prophetical writings. But no part of the Old Testament appeals
more directly to the believing heart, and none bears a clearer
impress of inspiration in the individual poems, and of divine
guidance in their collection. That the book containing the
subjective utterance of Israel's faith, the answer of the

---

[1] The only prophetic book as to which any dispute seems to have occurred
was Ezekiel. The beginning of this book—the picture of the *Merkaba*, or
chariot of Jehovah's glory (1 Chron. xxviii. 18)—has always been viewed as a
great mystery in Jewish theology, and is the basis of the *Kabbala* or esoteric
theosophy of the Rabbins. The closing chapters were equally puzzling, because
they give a system of law and ritual divergent in many points from the
Pentateuch. Compare Jerome's *Ep. to Paulinus*:—"The beginning and end
of Ezekiel are involved in obscurities, and among the Hebrews these parts,
and the exordium of Genesis, must not be read by a man under thirty."
Hence, in the apostolic age, a question was raised as to the value of the book;
for, of course, nothing could be accepted that contradicted the Torah. We
read in the Talmud (*Hagiga*, 13 *a*) that "but for Hananiah, son of Hezekiah,
they would have suppressed the Book of Ezekiel, because its words contradict
those of the Torah. What did he do? They brought up to him three
hundred measures of oil, and he sat down and explained it." Derenbourg,
op. cit. p. 296, with Graetz, *Geschichte*, vol. iii. p. 561, is disposed to hold
that the scholar who reconciled Ezekiel with the Pentateuch at such an
expenditure of midnight oil was really Eleazar, the son of Hananiah.

believing heart to the word of revelation, continued to grow
after the prophetic voice was still, and the written law had
displaced the living word, was natural and necessary. In
the Psalter we see how the ordinances of the new theocracy
established themselves in the hearts of the people, as well as
in the external order of the community at Jerusalem, and the
spiritual aspects of the Law which escaped the legal subtilty
of the Scribes are developed in such Psalms as the 119th,
with an immediate force of personal conviction which has
supplied a pattern of devotion to all following ages.

Thus three great masses of sacred literature, comprising
those elements which were most immediately practical under
the old dispensation, and make up the chief permanent value
of the Old Testament for the Christian Church, took shape
and attained to undisputed authority on broad grounds of
history, and through processes of experimental verification
which made it unnecessary to seek complicated theological
arguments to justify their place in the Canon. The Law, the
Prophets, and the Psalms were inseparably linked with the
very existence of the Old Testament Church. Their authority was not derived from the schools of the Scribes, and
needed no sanction from them. And, though the spirit of
legalism might mistake the true connection and relative importance of the Law and the other books, no Pharisaism was
able to undermine the influence of those evangelical and
eternal truths which kept true spirituality alive in Israel,
while the official theology was absorbed in exclusive devotion
to the temporary ordinances of the Law.

The Law, the Prophets, and the Psalms are the substance
and centre of the Old Testament, on which the new dispensation builds, and to which our Lord Himself appeals as the
witness of the Old Covenant to the New. The exegesis
which insists, against every rule of language, that the Psalms
in Luke xxiv. 44 mean the Hagiographa as a whole misses

the point of our Lord's appeal to the preceding history of revelation, and forgets that Ecclesiastes, Canticles, and Esther are not once referred to in the New Testament, and were still *antilegomena* in the apostolic age.

The Law, the Prophets, and the Psalms, form an intelligible classification, in which each element has a distinctive character. And this is still the case if we add to the Psalter the other two poetical Books of Job and Proverbs, which stand beside the Psalms in our Hebrew Bibles. But the collection of the Hagiographa, as a whole, is not homogeneous. Why does not Daniel stand among the later prophets, Ezra and Chronicles among the historical books? Why is it that the Hagiographa were not read in the synagogue? With regard to the Psalms this is intelligible. They had their original place, not in the synagogue, but in the Temple service. So, too, the Books of Job and Proverbs, which belong to the philosophy of the Hebrews, and were specially adapted for private study, might seem less suitable for public reading— Job, in particular, requiring to be studied as a whole if one is to grasp its true sense. But this explanation does not cover the whole Hagiographa. Their position can only be explained by the lateness of their origin, or the lateness of their recognition as authoritative Scriptures. The miscellaneous collection of Hagiographa appended to the three great poetical books is the region of the Old Testament *antilegomena*, and in them we no longer stand on the ground of undisputed authority acknowledged by our Lord, and rooted in the very essence of the Old Testament dispensation.

The oldest explicit reference to a third section of sacred books is found in the prologue to Ecclesiasticus, written in Egypt about 130 B.C. The author speaks of "the many and great things given to us through the Law and the Prophets, and the others who followed after them"; and again, of "the Law and the Prophets, and the other books of the fathers," as the study of his grandfather and other Israelites, who aimed at a life conformed to the Law.

When the other books of the fathers are said to have been written by those who followed after the prophets, the sense may either be that their authors were later in time, or that they were subordinate companions of the prophets. In either case the author plainly regards these books as in some sense secondary to the prophetic writings; nor does it appear that in his time there was a distinct and definite name for this collection, or perhaps that there was a formal collection at all. The overplus of God-given literature, after the Law and the Prophets are deducted, is an inheritance from the fathers. We must not infer from this statement that all ancient books not comprised in the Law and the prophets were accepted without criticism as a gift of God, and formed a third class of sacred literature. The author of Chronicles had still access to older books which are now lost; and the Book of Ecclesiastes, xii. 11 *sq.*, warns its readers against the futility of much of the literature of the time, and admonishes them to confine their attention to the words of the wise, the teachings of the masters of assemblies, *i.e.* the sages met in council, the experienced " circle of elders," praised in Ecclesiasticus vi. 34. There were many books in those days which claimed to be the work of ancient worthies, and such of them as we still possess display a very different spirit and merit from the acknowledged Hagiographa. There must have been a sifting process applied to this huge mass of literature, and the Hagiographa are the result. But it is not so easy to explain how this sifting took place and led to the collection which we now receive.

One thing is clear. The very separation of the Hagiographa from the books of cognate character which stand in the second section of the Hebrew Canon proves that the third collection was formed after the second had been closed.

And since the prophetic collection was itself a gradual formation, fixed not by external authority but by silent consent, this brings the collection of the Hagiographa down long after the time of Ezra. With this it agrees that some of the books of the Hagiographa did not originate till the very end of the Persian period at earliest. The genealogies in Chronicles and Nehemiah give direct proof of this fact, and the Book of Ecclesiastes can hardly be dated before the Chronicles; while even the most conservative critics now begin to admit that Daniel did not exist (at least in its present form) till the time of the Maccabees. Neither Esther nor Daniel, nor indeed Ezra, is alluded to in the list of worthies in Ecclesiasticus.

The determination of the collection of the Hagiographa must therefore have taken place at an epoch when the tradition of the Scribes was in full force, and we cannot assert that their false theories had no influence on the work. If they had a share in determining the collection, we can tell with tolerable certainty what principles they acted on. For to them all sacred writings outside the Torah were placed on one footing with the oral law. In substance there was no difference between written books and oral tradition. Both alike were divine and authoritative expositions of the law. There was traditional Halacha expanding and applying legal precepts, but there was also traditional Haggada, recognised as a rule of faith and life, and embracing doctrinal topics, practical exhortation, embellishments and fabulous developments of Bible narratives.[1] The difference between these traditions and the sacred books lay only in the form. Tradition was viewed as essentially adapted for oral communication. Every attempt to reduce it to writing was long discouraged by the Scribes. It was a common possession of the learned,

[1] It is sometimes said that the Haggada had no sacred authority. So Zunz, *op. cit.* p. 42; Deutsch's *Remains*, p. 17; but compare, on the other hand, Weber, *op. cit.* p. 94 *sq.* Certain Haggadoth share with the Halacha the name of *Midda*, rule of faith and life.

which no man had a right to appropriate and fix by putting it in a book of his own. The authority of tradition did not lie with the man who uttered it, but in the source from which it had come down; and any tradition not universally current and acknowledged as of old authority had to be authenticated by evidence that he who used it had heard it from an older scholar, whose reputation for fidelity was a guarantee that he in turn had received it from a sure source. The same test would doubtless be applied to a written book. Books admittedly new had no authority. Nothing could be accepted unless it had the stamp of general currency, or was authenticated by the name of an ancient author dating from the period antecedent to the Scribes. All this, as we see from the pseudepigraphic books, offered a great temptation to forgery, but it offered also a certain security that doubtful books would not be admitted till they had passed the test of such imperfect criticism as the Scribes could apply. And, besides all this, the ultimate criterion to which every book was subjected lay in the supreme standard of the Law. Nothing was holy which did not agree with the teaching of the Pentateuch.

For some of the Hagiographa the test of old currency was plainly conclusive. It does not appear that the Book of Job was ever challenged, and the vague notices of a discussion about the Proverbs that are found in Jewish books are not of a kind to command credence.[1] The same thing holds good of the Lamentations, which in all probability were ascribed to Jeremiah as early as the time of the Chronicler.[2]

---

[1] *Aboth of R. Nathan*, c. 1.—"At first they said that Proverbs, Canticles, and Ecclesiastes are apocryphal. They said they were parabolic writings, and not of the Hagiographa . . . till the men of the Great Synagogue came and explained them." Cp. *B. Shabbath* 30 *b*; Ryle, p. 194 *sq.*

[2] "In 2 Chron. xxxv. 25 we read that Jeremiah pronounced a dirge over Josiah, and that the death of Josiah was still referred to according to stated usage in the dirges used by singing men and women in the author's day, and collected in a volume of *Kînôth*—the ordinary Jewish name of our book."

Ruth, again, is treated by Josephus as an appendix to Judges, and though this reckoning cannot be shown to have had Palestinian authority, there is no reason to doubt that the book was generally accepted as a valuable supplement to the history of the period of the Judges. The case of the other books is not so clear, and for all of them (except Daniel, whose case is peculiar) we have evidence that their position was long disputed, and only gradually secured.

The book of Ezra-Nehemiah has a special value for the history of the Old Covenant, and contains information absolutely indispensable, embodying contemporary records of the close of the productive period of Israel's history. Yet we find that the Alexandrian Jews were once content to receive it in the form of a Midrash (1 Esdras of the LXX., 3 Esdras of the English Apocrypha), with many fabulous additions and a text arbitrarily mangled. The Chronicles, according to all appearance, were once one book with Ezra and Nehemiah, from which they have been so rudely torn that 2 Chronicles now ends in the middle of a verse, which reappears complete at the beginning of Ezra. But the Chronicles now stand after Ezra-Nehemiah, as if it were an afterthought to admit them to equal authority. When the Greek Book of Esdras was composed of extracts from Chronicles, as well as from Ezra and Nehemiah, the three books

Josephus says that the dirge of Jeremiah on this occasion was extant in his days (*Ant.* x. 5. 1), and no doubt means by this the canonical Lamentations. Jerome on Zech. xii. 11 understands the passage of Chronicles in the same sense; but modern writers have generally assumed that, as our book was certainly written after the fall of Jerusalem, the dirges alluded to in Chronicles must be a separate collection. This, however, is far from clear. The *Kinôth* of the Chronicler had, according to his statement, acquired a fixed and statutory place in Israel, and were connected with the name of a prophet. In other words, they were canonical as far as any book outside the Pentateuch could be so called in that age. Moreover, the allusion to the king, the anointed of Jehovah, in Lam. iv. 20, though it really applies to Zedekiah, speaks of him with a warmth of sympathy which later ages would not feel for any king after Josiah."—*Encyc. Brit.*, 9th ed., art. LAMENTATIONS, following Nöldeke, *Alttestamentliche Literatur* (1868), p. 144.

were probably still read as one work.[1] From these facts it is reasonable to infer that in spite of their close agreement with the conceptions of the Scribes, it was long held to be doubtful whether the Chronicles deserved a place among the Scriptures or should be relegated to a lower sphere. The first decision must have been to accept only that part of the book which embodied the autobiographies of Ezra and Nehemiah.

For Daniel, the facts point to late origin rather than late admission. Daniel is not mentioned among the worthies in Ecclesiasticus, and had his book been known in old times it would surely have stood with the prophets.

The authority of the Book of Esther, which is not used by Philo or the New Testament, is necessarily connected with the diffusion of the feast of Purim. Now, the book contains two ordinances on this head—the observance of the feast proper (Esther ix. 22), and the celebration of a memorial fast preceding it (Esther ix. 31). According to Jewish usage, the fast falls on the 13th of Adar. But this was the day when Judas Maccabæus defeated and slew Nicanor in the battle of Bethhoron, and was kept as a joyful anniversary in Palestine from that time onward (1 Mac. vii. 48). The day of Nicanor is still placed among the anniversaries on which fasting is forbidden in the *Megillath Ta'anîth*, after the death of Trajan. In Palestine, therefore, at the time of our Lord, the fast of Purim was not observed, and it may well be doubted whether even the subsequent feast was universally acknowledged. The Palestinian Talmud still contains traditions of opposition to its introduction; while the other Talmud (*B. Megill.* 7 *a*, *Sanh.* 100 *a*) names certain eminent Rabbins who denied that Esther " defiles the hands," *i.e.* is canonical.

---

[1] The most palpable argument for the original unity of Chronicles, Ezra, and Nehemiah is that mentioned in the text. But further, the parts of Ezra-Nehemiah which are not extracts from documents in the hands of the editor display all the characteristic peculiarities of the Chronicles in style, language, and manner of thought. See Driver, *Introduction*, chap. xii.

And, again, it is a notable circumstance that the book is so freely handled in the two Greek recensions of the text.

The Book of Esther was not undisputed in the early Christian Church; and, according to Eusebius, Melito, Bishop of Sardis in the third quarter of the second century, journeyed to Palestine to ascertain the Jewish Canon of his time, and brought back a list, from which Esther was excluded.[1]

The last stage in the history of the Jewish Canon is most clearly exhibited in the case of Ecclesiastes and the Song of Solomon, which were still controverted up to the very end of the first Christian century. In earlier times, as we have seen, no urgent necessity was felt to determine the precise compass of the sacred books. But in the apostolic age more than one circumstance called for a definite decision on the subject of the Canon. The school of Hillel, with its new and more powerful exegetical methods, directed to find a Scripture proof for every tradition, was naturally busied with the compass, as well as the text, of the ancient Scriptures. R. Akiba, a rigid spirit averse to all compromise, would admit no middle class between sacred books and books which it was a sin to read. "Those who read the outside books have no part in the life to come."[2] Such books were to be buried

---

[1] Eusebius, *Hist. Eccles.* Lib. iv. cap. 26. It is certainly very hard to understand what Jewish authorities could omit Esther at so late a date, but the statement of Eusebius is precise. In the fourth century Athanasius and Gregory of Nazianzus still omit Esther from the Canon. The ordinance of the fast of Purim (Esther ix. 31), which we see not to have been observed in Palestine in the time of Christ, is lacking in the Greek text of Esther, and in Josephus, *Ant.* xi. 6. 13, where, however, we are told that the feast was celebrated by the Jews throughout the world. On the origin of the feast of Purim, see Lagarde, *Purim* (Gött., 1887; *Abhandlungen* of the Göttingen Academy, vol. xxxiv.), who connects it with the Persian Fûrdigân, and Zimmern in Stade's *Zeitschrift f. AT. W.* (1891), p. 157 *sqq.*, who argues for a connection with the Babylonian New Year Feast. That the observance of Purim began not in Palestine, but in the Eastern Dispersion, is probable almost to certainty. On the *Megillath Ta'anith*, or list of days on which the Jews are forbidden to fast, consult Derenbourg, p. 439 *sq.*

[2] Mishna, *Sanhedrin*, xi. 1 (ed. Suren., vol. iv. p. 259).—"All Israelites have a share in the world to come, except those who deny the resurrection of

—thrust away in the rubbish-room to which condemned
synagogue rolls were relegated. But the immediately practical
call for a precise definition of the compass of the sacred books
arose from the circumstance that this question came to be
necessarily associated with a point of ritual observance. The
Rabbins, always jealous for the ceremonial sanctity of sacred
things, were concerned to preserve copies of the Scriptures
from being lightly handled or used for common purposes.
They therefore devised, in accordance with their principle of
hedging in the law, a Halacha to the effect that the sacred
books communicate ceremonial uncleanness to hands that
touch them, or to food with which they are brought in contact.
This ordinance was well devised for the object in view, for it
secured that such books should be kept in a place by themselves, and not lightly handled. But it now became absolutely necessary to know which books defile the hands. The
Mishna contains a special treatise on "hands" (*Iadaim*), and
here we find authentic information on the controversies to
which the ordinance gave rise. Two books were involved.
The schools of Shammai and Hillel were divided as to
Ecclesiastes. But there was also discussion as to the Song
of Solomon, and both points came up for decision at
a great assembly held in Iamnia (*ca.* 90 A.D. ?), where R.
Akiba took a commanding place. Some of the doctors must
have hinted that the canonicity of Canticles was a moot-point.
But Akiba struck in with his wonted energy, and silenced all
dispute. "God forbid!" he cried. "No one in Israel has
ever doubted that the Song of Solomon defiles the hands.
For no day in the history of the world is worth the day when

the dead, those who say that the Torah is not from God, and the Epicureans.
R. Akiba adds those who read in outside books, and him who whispers over
a wound the words of Exod. xv. 26,"—a kind of charm, the sin of which,
according to the commentators, lay in the fact that these sacred words were
pronounced after spitting over the sore. Compare on the "outside books"
Geiger, p. 200 *sq.*

the Song of Solomon was given to Israel. For all the Hagiographa are holy, but the Song of Solomon is a holy of the
holies. If there has been any dispute, it referred only to
Ecclesiastes." [1]

In the characteristic manner of theological partisanship,
Akiba speaks with most confident decision on the points
where he knew his case to be weakest. So far was it from
being true that no one had ever doubted the canonicity of
Canticles that he himself had to hurl an anathema at those
who sang the Song of Solomon with quavering voice in the
banqueting house as if it were a common lay. The same
tendency to cover the historical weakness of the position of
disputed books by energetic protestations of their superla-
tive worth appears in what the Palestinian Talmud relates of
the opinions of the Doctors as to the roll of Esther. While
some Rabbins, appealing to Deuteronomy v. 22, maintained

---

[1] Mishna, *Iadaim*, iii. 5.—"All the Holy Scriptures defile the hands:
the Song of Solomon and Ecclesiastes defile the hands. R. Judah says, The
Song of Solomon defiles the hands, and Ecclesiastes is disputed. R. Jose
says, Ecclesiastes does not defile the hands, and the Song of Solomon is disputed. R. Simeon says, Ecclesiastes belongs to the light things of the
school of Shammai, and the heavy things of the school of Hillel [*i.e.* on this
point the school of Shammai is less strict]. R. Simeon, son of Azzai, says, I
received it as a tradition from the seventy-two elders on the day when they
enthroned R. Eliezer, son of Azariah [as President of the Beth Dîn at Iamnia,
which became the seat of the heads of the Scribes after the fall of Jerusalem],
that the Song of Solomon and Ecclesiastes defile the hands. R. Akiba said,
God forbid! No one in Israel has ever doubted that the Song of Solomon
defiles the hands. For no day in the history of the world is worth the day
when the Song of Solomon was given to Israel. For all the Hagiographa are
holy, but the Song of Solomon is a holy of the holies. If there has been any
dispute, it referred only to Ecclesiastes. . . . So they disputed, and so they
decided."

Eduioth, v. 3.—"Ecclesiastes does not defile the hands according to the
school of Shammai, but does so according to the school of Hillel."

For the disputes as to Ecclesiastes, compare also Jerome on chap. xii. 13,
14. "The Hebrews say that this book, which calls all God's creatures vain,
and prefers meat, drink, and passing delights to all else, might seem worthy
to disappear with other lost works of Solomon; but that it merits canonical
authority, because it sums up the whole argument in the precept to fear God
and do His commandment."

that a day must come when the Hagiographa and the Prophets
would become obsolete, and only the Law remain ; nay, says
Rabbi Simeon, Esther and the Halachoth can never become
obsolete (Esther ix. 28).[1]

In speaking of these Old Testament *Antilegomena* I have
confined myself to a simple statement of facts that are not
open to dispute. It is matter of fact that the position of
several books was still subject of controversy in the apostolic
age, and was not finally determined till after the fall of the
Temple and the Jewish state. Before that date the Hagiographa did not form a closed collection with an undisputed
list of contents, and therefore the general testimony of Christ
and the Apostles to the Old Testament Scriptures cannot be
used as certainly including books like Esther, Canticles, and
Ecclesiastes, which were still disputed among the orthodox
Jews in the apostolic age, and to which the New Testament
never makes reference. These books have been delivered to
us ; they have their use and value, which are to be ascer-
tained by a frank and reverent study of the texts themselves;
but those who insist on placing them on the same footing
with the Law, the Prophets, and the Psalms, to which our
Lord bears direct testimony, and so make the whole doctrine
of the Canon depend on its weakest part, sacrifice the true
strength of the evidence on which the Old Testament is
received by Christians, and commit the same fault with Akiba
and his fellow Rabbins, who bore down the voice of free
inquiry with anathemas instead of argument.

---

[1] Akiba's anathema in *Tosef. Sanhedrin*, c. 12 ; R. Simeon's utterance in
Talmud Jer. *Megilla*, i. 5 (Krotoschin ed. of 1866, f. 70 *b*).

LECTURE VII

THE PSALTER

UP to this point we have been occupied with general discussions as to the transmission of the Old Testament among the Jews, and the collection of its books into a sacred Canon. In the remaining part of our course we must deal with the origin of individual books; and as it is impossible in six Lectures to go over the whole field of the Old Testament literature, I shall confine myself to the discussion of some cardinal problems referring to the three great central masses of the Old Testament, the Law, the Prophets, and the Psalms. The present Lecture will deal with the Book of Psalms.

The Psalter, as we have it, unquestionably contains Psalms of the Exile and the new Jerusalem. It is also generally held to contain Psalms of the period of David, thus embracing within its compass poems extending over a range of some five hundred years. How did such a collection come together? How was it formed, and how were the earlier Psalms preserved up to the date when they were embodied in our present Psalter?

In discussing this question, let us begin by looking at the nature and objects of the Psalter. The Book of Psalms is a collection of religious and devotional poetry. It is made up mainly of prayers and songs of praise, with a certain number of didactic pieces. But it is not a collection of all the religious

poetry of Israel. That is manifest from the circumstance
that, with one exception (2 Sam. xxii. = Psalm xviii.), the
poems preserved in the old historical books are not repeated
in the Psalter. Nor, again, was the collection formed with
an historical object. It is true that there are some titles
which contain historical notes, but on the other hand there
are many Psalms whose contents naturally suggest an inquiry
as to the historical situation in which they were composed, but
where we have no title or hint of any sort to answer that
question. Again, although the Psalms represent a great range
of personal religious experience, it is to be noticed that they
avoid such situations and expressions as are of too unique a
character to be used in the devotion of other believers. The
feelings expressed in the Psalter are mainly such as can be
shared by every devout soul, if not in every circumstance,
yet at least in circumstances which frequently recur in human
life. Some of the Psalms are manifestly written from the
first with a general devotional purpose, as prayers or praises
which can be used in any mouth. In others, again, the poet
seems to speak, not in his private person, but in the name of
the people of God as a whole ; and even the Psalms more
directly individual in occasion have so much catholicity of
sentiment that they have served with the other hymns of the
Psalter as a manual of devotion for the Church in all ages of
both dispensations.[1]

[1] Some recent writers go so far as to maintain that in all (or almost all)
the Psalms, the speaker is Israel, the church-nation personified, so that the
" I " and " me " of the Psalms throughout mean " we," " us," the community
of God's grace and worship. So especially Smend in Stade's *Zeitschrift*, viii.
49 *sqq.* (1888). Few will be disposed to go so far as Smend ; but the view
that many Psalms are spoken in the name of the community is no novelty,
and can hardly be disputed. There is, of course, room for much difference of
opinion as to the limits within which this method of interpreting the " I "
and " me " of the Psalms is to be applied. Driver, *Introduction*, p. 366 *sq.*,
would confine it to a few Psalms, while Cheyne (whose remarks on the bearing of the question on the use of the Psalter in the Christian Church will
repay perusal) gives it a much larger range. (*Origin of the Psalter*, 1891,
Lecture VI.)

The Psalms, then, are a collection of religious poetry, chosen with a special view to the edification of the Old Testament Church. But further, the purpose immediately contemplated in the collection is not the private edification of the individual Israelite, but the public worship of the Old Testament Church in the Temple, and necessarily (since some of the Psalms are later than the Exile), in the second Temple. This appears most clearly in the latter part of the book, where we meet with many Psalms obviously composed from the first for liturgical use. Some are doxologies ; others are largely made up of extracts from earlier Psalms, in a way very natural in a liturgical manual of devotion, but not so natural in a poet merely composing a hymn for his personal use. The liturgical element is specially prominent in those Psalms (from civ. onwards) which begin or end with the phrase Hallelujah, " Praise ye the Lord." This phrase connects the Hallelujah Psalms with the part of the Temple service called the *hallel*, which denotes a jubilant song of praise executed to the accompaniment of Levitical music, and the blare of the priestly trumpets (1 Chron. xvi. 4 *sqq.*, xxv. 3 ; 2 Chron. v. 12 *sq.*, xxix. 27-30). By the later Jews the term *hallel* is mainly applied to Psalms cxiii.-cxviii., which were sung at the great annual feasts, at the encænia (the feast spoken of in John x. 22), and at the new moons. Again, throughout the Psalms, the Temple, Zion, the Holy City, are kept in the foreground. Once more, the same destination appears in the titles. The musical titles are full of technical terms which occur again in the Book of Chronicles in descriptions of the Levitical Psalmody of the Temple. The proper names in the titles have a similar reference. The sons of Korah were a guild of Temple musicians ; Asaph was the father and patron of a similar guild ; Heman and Ethan are named in the Chronicles as Temple singers of the time of David. Finally, the very name of the Psalter in the Hebrew

Bible leads to the same conclusion. The Psalms are called
Tehillîm, hymns, from the same root as Hallelujah, and with
the same allusion to the Temple service of praise.[1]

The fact that the Psalter is a hymnal at once elucidates
some important features in the book, and suggests certain
rules for its profitable use and study. The liturgical character
of the Psalms explains their universality, and justifies the
large use made of them in the Christian Church. As a
liturgical collection, the Psalter expresses the feelings and
hopes, the faith, the prayers and the praises of the Old Testament Church, their sense of sin, and their joyful apprehension of God's salvation. These are the subjective elements
of religion, the answer of the believing heart to God. And
precisely in these elements the religion of all ages is much
alike. The New Testament revelation made a great change
in the objective elements of religion. Old ideas and forms
passed away, and new things took their place; but through
all this growth of the objective side of revelation, the devotion
of the faithful heart to God remains essentially one and the
same. Our faith, our sense of sin, our trust upon God and
His salvation, the language of our prayers and praises, are
still one with those of the Old Testament Church. It is true
that not a little of the colouring of the Psalms is derived
from the ritual and order of the old dispensation, and has
now become antiquated; but practical religion does not refuse

---

[1] The later Jews were not completely informed as to the liturgical use of
the Psalter in the Temple services. There is even some uncertainty as to
what parts of the Hallelujah Psalms are included in the *Hallel*, presumably
because several selections from this part of the Psalter were used. Of the daily
Psalms, sung at the morning sacrifice, the following list, which has every
appearance of authenticity, is given in the Mishna *Tamîd*, vii. 4 (Surenh.,
v. 10): Sunday, Ps. 24; Monday, Ps. 48; Tuesday, Ps. 82; Wednesday,
Ps. 94; Thursday, Ps. 81; Friday, Ps. 93; Sabbath, Ps. 92. Ps. 92 is
assigned to the Sabbath in the title, and the titles in the Septuagint also
confirm the statements of the Mishna, except as regards Pss. 81 and 82, the
former of which must originally have been written for some great feast (see
verse 3 [Heb. 4]). According to tradition it was sung at the Feast of
Trumpets (Numb. xxix. 1), as well as at the ordinary Thursday service.

those bonds of connection with the past. The believing soul
is never anxious to separate its own spiritual life from the
spiritual life of the fathers. Rather does it cling with special
affection to the links that unite it to the Church of the Old
Testament; and the forms which, in their literal sense, are
now antiquated, become to us an additional group of figures
in the rich poetic imagery of the Hebrew hymnal.

But the Psalter and the Old Testament in general are to
us not merely books of devotion, but sources of study for the
better knowledge of the whole course of God's revelation. It
is a law of all science that, to know a thing thoroughly, we
must know it in its genesis and in its growth. To understand the ways of God with man, and the whole meaning of
His plan of salvation, it is necessary to go back and see His
work in its beginnings, examining the rudimentary stages of
the process of revelation; and for this the Psalms are invalu-
able, for they give us the first answer of the believing heart
to God under a dispensation where the objective elements of
revelation were far less fully developed, and where spiritual
processes were in many respects more naïve and childlike.
While the simple Christian can always take up the Psalm-
book and use it for devotion, appropriating those elements
which remain the same in all ages, those who are called upon
to study the Bible systematically, and who desire to learn all
that can be learned from it, will also look at the Psalms from
another point of view. Recognising the fact that many of
them have an historical occasion, and that they express the
life of a particular stage of the Old Testament Church, they
will endeavour to study the history of the collection, and
ascertain what can be learned of the epoch and situation in
which each Psalm was written.

In entering upon this study, it is highly important to
carry with us the fact that the Psalms are preserved to us,
not in an historical collection, but in a hymn-book specially

adapted for the use of the second Temple. The plan of a hymn-book does not secure that every poem shall be given exactly as it was written by the first author. The practical object of the collection makes it legitimate and perhaps necessary that there should be such adaptations and alterations as may secure a larger scope of practical utility in ordinary services.

In a book which contains Psalms spreading over a period of perhaps five hundred years, such a period as that which separates Chaucer from Tennyson, or Dante from Manzoni, changes of this kind could hardly be avoided ; and so in fact we find not a few variations in the text and indica-tions of the hand of an editor retouching the original poems. Between Psalm xviii. and 2 Samuel xxii. there are some seventy variations not merely orthographical. The Psalter itself repeats certain poems with changes. Psalm liii. is a copy of Ps. xiv. with variations of text ; Psalm lxx. repeats Ps. xl. 13-17 ; Ps. cviii. is verses 7-11 of Ps. lvii., followed by Ps. lx. 5-12. Another clear sign that we have not every Psalm in its original text lies in the alphabetical acrostics, Psalms ix.-x. xxv. xxxiv. xxxvii. cxi. cxii. cxix. cxlv., in which the initial letters of successive half verses, verses, or larger stanzas make up the alphabet. It is of the nature of an acrostic to be perfect. An acrostic poem which misses some letter or puts it in a false place is a failure ; and there-fore, when we find that some of these acrostics are now incomplete, we must conclude that the text has suffered. In some cases it is still easy to suggest the slight change neces-sary to restore the original scheme. Elsewhere, as in the beautiful acrostic now reckoned as two Psalms (ix. and x.), the corruption in the text, or possibly the intentional change made to adapt the poem for public worship, is so considerable that the original form cannot be recovered.[1]

---

[1] Another case where one Psalm has been made two is xlii.-xliii., where, by taking the words "O my God" from the beginning of xlii. 6 to the end of

In general, then, we conclude that the oldest text of a
sacred lyric is not always preserved in the Psalter. And so,
again, we must not suppose that the notes of authors' names
in a hymn-book have the same weight as the statements of
an historical book. In a liturgical collection the author's
name is of little consequence, and the editors who altered the
text of a poem cannot be assumed *a priori* to have taken
absolute care to preserve a correct record of its origin. But
to this subject we shall recur presently.

Let us now look at the collection somewhat more closely;
and, in the first place, let us take note of the traditional
division of the Psalter into five smaller books, each terminating with a doxology. In most modern Hebrew Bibles, and
also in the English Revised Version, the five books are
marked off by short titles, which are not found in most manuscripts, are devoid of Massoretic authority, and are rightly
absent from the Authorised Version. But the division itself
rests on an ancient Jewish tradition which was already
known to Hippolytus at the beginning of the third Christian
century. Mediæval Jewish opinion, following the Midrash
on Psalm i., ascribed the partition to David, and the majority
of modern scholars regard the terminal doxologies (which are
also found in the Septuagint) as sufficient evidence that a
fivefold arrangement of the Psalter, presumably on the
model of the Pentateuch, was actually designed by the collector of the book.[1] Before we discuss how far this opinion

---

the previous verse, and making a single change in the division of the words,
we get a poem of three stanzas, with an identical refrain to each. Conversely
Ps. cxliv. 12 *sqq.* seems to have no connection with the poem (verses 1-11) to
which it is now attached.

[1] The witness of Hippolytus is found in the Greek (ed. Lag., p. 193;
closely followed by Epiphanius, *De Mens. et Pond.* § 5; see Lagarde, *Symmicta*, ii. 157), in a passage of which the genuineness has been questioned;
but the same doubt does not attach to the Syriac form of Hippolytus's testimony (Lagarde, *Analecta Syriaca*, 1858, p. 86). The Greek speaks of a
division into five books (βιβλία), the Syriac of five parts or sections (mĕnawâthê).
The latter expression agrees best with Jerome's statement in the *Prologus*

is sound it will be convenient to present a table showing
the scheme of the traditional division :—

Book I. Psalms 1-41.—All ascribed to David, except 1, 2, 10 [which
is part of 9], 33 [ascribed to David in the LXX.] *Doxology*—
Blessed be Jehovah, God of Israel, from everlasting and to everlasting. Amen and Amen.

Book II. Psalms 42-72.—42-49, Korahite [43 being part of 42]; 50,
Asaph; 51-71, David, except 66, 67, 71, which are anonymous;
72, Solomon. *Doxology*—Blessed be Jehovah God, the God of
Israel, who alone doeth wondrous things. And blessed be His
name of glory for ever: and let the whole earth be filled with
His glory. Amen and Amen. *Subscription*—The prayers of
David the son of Jesse are ended.

Book III. Psalms 73-89.—73-83, Asaph; 84, 85, 87, 88, Korahite;
86, David; 88, Heman; 89, Ethan. *Doxology*—Blessed be
Jehovah for ever. Amen and Amen.

Book IV. Psalms 90-106.—90, Moses; 101, 103, David; the rest
anonymous. *Doxology*—Blessed be Jehovah, God of Israel, from
everlasting and to everlasting. *And let all the people say*, Amen :
Hallelujah.

Galeatus, "David, quem quinque incisionibus et uno volumine compre-
hendunt" [*scil*. Hebraei]. In the Preface to his *Psalt. iuxta Hebraeos* Jerome
refuses to allow the expression "five books," which some used. For the
Jewish recognition of the fivefold partition of the Psalter most writers refer
only to the later Midrash on the Psalms, from which Kimchi draws in the
Preface to his Commentary. But there is much older Jewish evidence to
confirm that of the Christian authorities. Mr. Schechter refers me to *B.
Kiddâshîn*, 33 *a*, where R. Simeon, son of Rabbi, says, complaining of a pupil,
"I taught him two-fifths of the Book of Psalms, and he did not rise up before
me (out of respect when I entered the place where he was seated)." The
expression "fifths" is commonly used of the books of the Pentateuch, but it
occurs also in *J. Megillah*, ii. 4, in connection with the Book of Esther
(Müller, *Sôpherîm*, p. 34), and is not a sufficient justification for speaking of
five books (ספרים) of the Psalms. In *Sôpherîm*, ii. 4, where a blank of four
lines is prescribed between each book of the Torah, and a blank of three
lines between each of the twelve Minor Prophets, nothing is said of the
sections of the Psalter. There are, however, traces of a later rule by which
two lines are to be left between each section of the Psalms; but the rule is
very imperfectly followed in MSS. The first Massoretic Bible (that of Jacob
b. Chayyim) notes the commencement of Bks. 2, 3, 4, 5 in the margin, or in
vacant spaces in the text, in smaller characters (ספר שני and so forth), and
similar titles are found in some MSS.

We learn from Hippolytus and Jerome that the doxologies, or rather the
double Amen of the doxologies, furnished the argument for the fivefold
division. In Ps. cvi. 48 Jerome appears to have read a double γένοιτο in the
Greek (as many MSS. do), and also (against the present Massoretic text) a
double אמן in the Hebrew. (See the critical apparatus in Lagarde's edition.)

Book V. Psalms 107-150.—108-110, 122,[1] 124,[1] 131,[1] 133,[1] 138-145,
David ; 127,[1] Solomon ; 120-134, Pilgrimage songs. The book
closes with a group of doxological Psalms, but there is no such
special doxology as in the previous books.

The first three doxologies plainly form no part of the
Psalms to which they are attached, but mark the end of each
book after the pious fashion, not uncommon in Eastern literature, to close the composition or transcription of a volume
with a brief prayer or words of praise. In Psalm cvi. the
case is different. For here we find a liturgical direction that
all the people shall say, "Amen, Hallelujah," which seems to
imply that this doxology was actually sung at the close of
the Psalm. And so it is taken in 1 Chron. xvi., where the
Psalm is quoted. For here (ver. 36) the imperatives are
changed to perfects, "and all the people said, Amen, and
praised the Lord."

This essential difference in character between the three
first doxologies and the fourth appears to be fatal to the
theory that the collector of the whole Psalter disposed his
work in five sections, and added a doxology to each. Nor
can this theory be mended by joining Books IV. and V., and
supposing the collector to have aimed at a fourfold division.
For it is not conceivable that, after writing formal doxologies
to three sections of his work, the collector would have left
the close of the whole Psalter unprovided with a similar
formula. We conclude, therefore, that the three first doxologies are older than the final collection ; and, as they evidently
mark actual subdivisions in the Psalm-book, it naturally
occurs to us to inquire whether these subdivisions are not
the boundaries of earlier collections, of which the first three
books of our present Psalter are made up.[2]

---

[1] Not so in LXX.

[2] An illustration of the way in which the limits of an older collection may
be revealed by the retention of the doxological subscription is supplied by the
Dîwân of the Hodhalite poets. At the close of the 236th poem (according to

A closer examination confirms this conjecture. The first
book, Psalms i.-xli., is all Davidic, every Psalm bearing the
title of David except Psalms i. ii. x. xxxiii. Now Psalm i.
is clearly a preface to the collection. But in Talmudic times
Psalm ii. was reckoned as forming one section with Psalm i.,
and so it is actually cited as the first Psalm in the correct
text of Acts xiii. 33. Again, Psalm x. is the second part of
the acrostic Psalm ix., and Psalm xxxiii. is certainly a late
piece, and probably came into this part of the Psalter afterwards. The first book, therefore, is a formal collection of
Psalms ascribed to David. So, again, in the second book, the
Psalms ascribed to David stand apart from the Korahite and
Asaphic Psalms, and form a connected group, though they
include some anonymous pieces, and also one hymn (Psalm
lxxii.), which is entitled "of Solomon," but was perhaps
viewed, as our version takes it, as a prayer of David for his
son. In Book III. only Psalm lxxxvi. bears the name of
David, and this title is unquestionably a mistake, for the
Psalm is a mere cento of reminiscences from older parts of
Scripture, and the prayer in verse 11, "Unite my heart to
fear thy name," is based on the promise (Jer. xxxii. 39), "I
will give them one heart . . . to fear me continually." It is
the law of the religious life that prayer is based on promise,
and not conversely.[1] It cannot be accident that has thus
disposed the Davidic Psalms of Books I.-III. in two groups.
But if the final collector had gathered these poems together
for the first time, he would surely have made one group, not
two. Nor can he have added the subscription to Psalm
lxxii., "The prayers of David are ended," unless, indeed, we
suppose that the titles ascribing Psalms of the fourth and
fifth books to David are all additions of later copyists after

Wellhausen's enumeration) occurs the subscription, *tamma hâdhâ walillâhi
'l-hamdu*, etc., showing that the collection once ended at this point.

[1] See additional Note C.

the collection was closed. We conclude, then, that the first book once existed as a separate collection, and that the subscription to Psalm lxxii., with the doxology, marks the close of another once separate collection of Davidic Psalms.

Another evidence that the first three books of the Psalter contain collections formed by more than one editor, lies in the names of God. Books I. IV. and V. of the Psalter use the names of God in the same way as most other parts of the Old Testament, where Jehovah is the prevailing term, and other names, such as Elohim (God), occur less frequently. But in the greater part of Books II. and III. (Psalms xlii.-lxxxiii.) the name of Jehovah is rare, and Elohim takes its place even where the substitute reads very awkwardly. For example, a common Old Testament phrase is " Jehovah my God," " Jehovah thy God," based upon Exodus xx. 2, where, in the preface to the Ten Commandments, we have, " I am Jehovah thy God." Some later writers seem to have avoided the name Jehovah, in accordance with a tendency which ultimately became so prevalent among the Jews that they now never pronounce the word Jehovah (Iahwè), but read Adonai (Lord) in its place (*supra*, p. 77). Such writers do not use the phrase " Jehovah my God," but simply say, " my God." In the Elohim Psalms, however, and nowhere else in the Old Testament, we find the peculiar phrase " God my God," with Elohim in place of Jehovah. And so, even in Psalm l. 7, where the words of Exodus xx. 2 are actually quoted, we read " I am God thy God." Clearly this is no accident. The Psalms in which the name Elohim is habitually used instead of Jehovah hang together. And, when we look more closely at the matter, we see that they not only hang together, but that the phenomenon of the names of God is due, not to the original authors of the Psalms, but to the collector himself; for some of these Elohim Psalms occur also in the earlier Jehovistic part of the Psalter. Psalm liii.

is identical with Psalm xiv.; Psalm lxx. with part of Psalm
xl.; and here, among other variations of text, we find Jehovah
six times changed to Elohim, and only one converse change.
That is a clear proof that the Elohim Psalms have been
formed by an editor who, for some reason, preferred to suppress, as far as possible, the name Jehovah.

Now let us look a little more closely at this Elohistic
collection. It forms the main part of the second and third
Psalm-books. The Psalms that remain look like an appendix,
containing some supplementary Korahite Psalms, and one
Psalm ascribed to David, which we have seen to be late, and
which may fairly be judged to be no part of the original
Davidic collections. If we set the appendix on one side, we
find in Books II. and III. a single Elohistic collection with a
well-marked editorial peculiarity running through it. This
Elohistic Psalm-book consists of two kinds of elements. It
contains, in the first place, Levitical Psalms—that is, Psalms
ascribed to Levitical choirs, the sons of Korah and Asaph;
and, further, a collection of Davidic Psalms, marked off as a
distinct section by the subscription at the end of Psalm lxxii.
and the accompanying doxology. As now arranged, the
Davidic collection is wedged in between two masses of Levitical Psalms, and even separates the Asaphic Psalm l. from
the body of the Asaphic collection, Psalms lxxiii.-lxxxiii. It
is not probable that this was the original order, for if we
simply take Psalms xlii.-l., and lift them into the place between Psalms lxxii. and lxxiii., we get a complete and natural
arrangement. We thus have a book containing, first, a
collection of Davidic Psalms with a subscription, and then
two collections of Levitical Psalms, the first Korahitic and
the last Asaphic. We may fairly accept this as the older
arrangement, which possibly was changed by the final collector in order that he might show by a distinct mark that the
two Davidic collections in his work were originally separate.

Perhaps, also, he may have been influenced by the fact that Psalms l. and li. are both suitable for the service of sacrifices of praise. Such is the account it seems reasonable to give of Books II. and III.

We come next to Books IV. and V. They also are really one book, for the doxology of Psalm cvi. belongs to the Psalm, and there is no clear mark of difference in subject, character, or editorial treatment in the Psalms which precede and follow it. But, taken as a unity, Books IV. and V. are marked by a liturgical character more predominant than in the other books. They are also of later collection than the Elohistic Psalm-book, for Psalm cviii. is made up of two Elohim Psalms (lvii. 7-11, lx. 5-12), retaining the predominant use of Elohim, al-though the other Psalms of the last two books are Jehovistic. As the Elohim Psalms got their peculiar use of the names of God from the collector, and not from their authors, we may safely affirm that Books II. and III. existed in their collected form before Psalm cviii. was composed.

Thus the five books of the Psalms reduce themselves to three collections (with subdivisions in the case of the second), which may be thus exhibited in tabular form :—

First Collection
(Bk. I.)   DAVID   Pss. 1-41
                        Doxology

Second Collection
(Bks. II. and III.)

        Part i.   DAVID   Pss. 51-72   ⎫
                        Doxology and Subscription   ⎪ ELOHIM
        Part ii. *a.* KORAH   Pss. 42-49   ⎬ Psalms
                b. ASAPH   Pss. 50, 73-83   ⎭
        Appendix. MISCELLANEOUS   Ps. 84-89
                        Doxology

Third Collection
(Bks. IV. and V.) MAINLY ANONYMOUS Ps. 90-150

In accordance with these results we can distinguish the following steps in the redaction :—

(a) The formation of the *first* Davidic collection with a closing doxology (1-41).

(b) The formation of the *second* Davidic collection, with doxology and subscription (51-72).

(c) The formation of a twofold Levitical collection (42-49 ; 50, 73-83).

(d) An Elohistic redaction and combination of (b) and (c).

(e) The addition to (d) of a non-Elohistic supplement and doxology (84-89).

(f) The formation of the Third Collection (90-149).

Finally, the anonymous Psalms i. and ii. may have been prefixed after the whole Psalter was completed.

A process of collection which involves so many stages must plainly have taken a considerable time, and the question arises whether we can fix a limit for its beginning and end, or can assign a date for any particular stages of the process.

An inferior limit for the final form of the collection is given by the Septuagint translation. But the traditions examined in Lecture IV., which fix the middle of the third century B.C. as the probable date of the Greek translation of the Law, tell us nothing about the translation of the Hagiographa. We know, however, from the prologue to Ecclesiasticus that certain Hagiographa, and doubtless, therefore, the Psalter, were current in Egypt in a Greek version about 130 B.C. or a little later. And the Greek Psalter, though it adds one apocryphal Psalm at the end, is essentially the same as the Hebrew ; there is nothing to suggest that the Greek was first translated from a less complete Psalter and afterwards extended to agree with the received Hebrew. It is therefore reasonable to hold that the Hebrew Psalter was completed and recognised as an authoritative collection long enough before 130 B.C. to allow of its passing to the Hellenistic Jews

of Alexandria.   There does not appear to be any unambiguous
external evidence to carry the close of the collection farther
back than this.   For though 1 Chron. xvi. and 2 Chron. vi. 41,
42, contain a series of passages from Psalms of the Third Collection (Pss. xcvi. cv. cvi. cxxxii.), there is no proof that the
Chronicler read these hymns in their place in the present Psalter,
or even that in his days Ps. cvi. existed in its present form.

In this scarcity of external evidence we are thrown back
on internal indications, and above all on the evidence of the
titles.   But here you must permit me to draw a distinction.   We
have already seen (*supra*, p. 95 *sqq.*) that there are variations
between the Greek and Hebrew tradition of the titles, and
that there was among the later Jews a marked tendency to
attach known and famous names to anonymous pieces.   The
titles, therefore, viewed as evidence to the authorship of
individual Psalms, are not to be accepted without reserve.
But the use which I now propose to make of them is of
another kind.   Except in the Third Collection, where anonymity is the rule, authors' names occurring only sporadically, and in the appendix to the Second Collection, which
has a miscellaneous character, the titles run in series and
correspond very closely with the limits of the old collections
of Psalms of which the present Psalter is made up.   It is
plain that such connected series of titles have quite a
different value from the scattered titles in the last division
of the Psalter.   They form a system, and cannot be looked
upon as the arbitrary conjectures of successive copyists.
To doubt that the consecutive Psalms xlii.-xlix., each of which
bears a title assigning it to the sons of Korah, or the Psalms
lxxiii.-lxxxiii., which are similarly assigned to Asaph, hang
together, would be irrational scepticism.   By far the most
probable view is that each of the groups, with the addition
in the case of the Asaphic Psalms of the now disjoined
Psalm l., once formed separate hymn-books, bearing a general

title, which in the one case was "of the sons of Korah," and in the other "of Asaph." When these small hymn-books were merged in a larger collection it would obviously be convenient to repeat the title before each Psalm. Apart from its general plausibility, this conjecture derives strong support from the series of fifteen Psalms, cxx.-cxxxiv., which bear in the Authorised Version the title of Songs of Degrees. According to the Mishna (*Middoth*, ii. 5) and other Jewish traditions, these Psalms were sung by the Levites, at the Feast of Tabernacles, on the fifteen steps or degrees that led from the women's to the men's court of the Temple. But when we read the Psalms themselves, we see that originally they must have been sung not by Levites but by the laymen who came up to Jerusalem at the great feasts; and the word which Jewish tradition renders by "degree" or "step" ought rather to be translated "going up" to Jerusalem (cf. the Hebrew of Ezra vii. 9), so that the Songs of Degrees ought rather to be called "Pilgrimage Songs." But now the curious thing is that, according to the laws of Hebrew grammar, the title prefixed to each of these hymns must be translated not "a song of Pilgrimage," but "the songs of Pilgrimage." In other words, each title is properly the collective title of the whole fifteen Psalms, which must once have formed a separate hymnal for the use of pilgrims; and when the collection was taken into the greater Psalter, this general title was set at the head of each of the hymns.

I take it, then, the Asaph and Korah Psalms were at one time the hymn-books of two Levitical choirs or guilds. In all probability the titles tell us no more than this; they do not name the authors of the Psalms, but they refer us to a period when the Temple psalmody was in the hands of two hereditary choirs, which, after the fashion of ancient Eastern guilds, called themselves sons of Asaph and of

Korah respectively. Now in the time of the Chronicler, who (as we have seen in Lecture V.) describes the ordinances of his own time in what he tells us about the Temple music, there were not two Levitical guilds but three, named not after Asaph and Korah, but after Asaph, Heman, and Ethan (1 Chron. vi. 31 *sqq.*), or Asaph, Heman, and Jeduthun (1 Chron. xxv. 1). These three guilds were reckoned to the three great Levitical houses of Gershon, Kohath, and Merari, and the genealogy of Heman was traced to Kohath through Korah. But in the time of the Chronicler the name of Korahites designated a guild not of singers but of porters (1 Chron. ix. 19, xxvi. 1, 19). The Chronicler assumes that this organisation of the singers dated from David; but in reality it was quite modern. At the time of the first return from the Exile "singers" and "sons of Asaph" were equivalent terms (Ezra ii. 41; Neh. vii. 44), and the singers were distinct from the Levites. This distinction seems still to have been recognised nearly a century later, in the days of Ezra and Nehemiah (Ezra x. 23, 24; Neh. vii. 1, 73, etc.). But by this time the distinction had lost the greater part of its meaning; for at the dedication of Nehemiah's wall (Neh. xii. 27, 28) the musical service was divided between the Levites and the "sons of the singers," *i.e.* the Asaphites. From this there is only a step to the order of the Elohistic Psalm - book, where there are two guilds of singers, the Asaphites and the sons of Korah.[1] But the first unam-

---

[1] The oldest attempt to incorporate the Asaphites with the Levites seems to be found in the priestly part of the Pentateuch, where Abiasaph, "the father of Asaph," or in other words, the eponym of the Asaphite guild, is made one of the three sons of Korah (Exod. vi. 24). In the ultimate system of Levitical organisation Asaph belongs not to Korah and Kohath but to Gershon (1 Chron. vi.). In Ezra and Nehemiah the singers, like the porters and the Nethinim, are habitually named after the Levites, as an inferior class of Temple ministers. In the time of the Chronicler this inferiority has disappeared, and ultimately, in the last days of the Temple, the singers claimed,

biguous appearance of three guilds of singers is found in
Neh. xii. 24, in a passage which does not belong to Nehemiah's memoirs, and refers to the time of Darius Codomannus
and of Jaddua, the high priest contemporary with Alexander
the Great.[1] The legitimate inference from these facts
appears to be that the Asaphic and Korahitic Psalms were
collected for use in the Temple service between the time
of Nehemiah and the fall of the Persian empire, or, speaking
broadly, in the second century after the return from Babylon
(*circa* 430-330 B.C.). It is quite possible that the formation
of the Elohistic Psalter, in which the two Levitical hymn-
books are fused together with a non-Levitical book (the
second Davidic collection), may be connected with the re-
modelling of the singers in three choirs; at any rate, the
appendix with which the Second Collection closes already
presupposes the new order, for Heman and Ethan are mentioned in the titles of Pss. lxxxviii. lxxxix.

The contents of the Korah and Asaph Psalms agree well,
on the whole, with these conclusions. We must bear in
mind that a Psalm may have been written long before it was
taken into one of the Temple hymn-books, and that two
Levitical Psalms, liii. and lxx., actually repeat, in Elohistic
form, pieces that appear also in the First Collection. But
the very fact that there was an older collection, and that only
two pieces in it reappear in the Second Collection, makes it
probable that most of the Levitical Psalms belong to the
period of the two choirs, *i.e.* to the time between Ezra's

and obtained from Agrippa II., the privilege of wearing garments of priestly
linen (Jos. *Antt.* xx. 9, § 6).

[1] The threefold division of singers appears in the Hebrew text of Neh. xi.
17, in a list which is not part of Nehemiah's memoirs, but is probably older
than chap. xii. 22-26. But the Septuagint does not give the triple division,
and the mention of Jeduthun as a man instead of a musical term is not in
favour of the Hebrew form of the text. The term sons of Korah, as designat-
ing a guild of singers, was evidently obsolete in the Chronicler's time, but was
still used in the Midrashic source of 2 Chron. xx. 19 ; cf. verse 14, where the
sons of Asaph are also mentioned.

reformation and the Greek Conquest of Asia. And this presumption is in accord with the general character of the Psalms in question. One of the most remarkable features common to the Asaph and Korah Psalms is that they contain little or no recognition of present national sin,—though they confess the sins of Israel in the past—but are exercised with the observation that prosperity does not follow righteousness either in the case of the individual (xlix., lxxiii.) or in that of the nation, which suffers notwithstanding its loyalty to God, or even on account thereof. Now problems about God's righteousness as it appears in his dealings with individual men first emerge in the Books of Jeremiah and Ezekiel, while the confident assertion of national righteousness is a characteristic mark of pious Judaism from the time of Ezra downwards, when the Pentateuchal Law was practically enforced, but not earlier. Malachi, Ezra, and Nehemiah, like Haggai and Zechariah, are still far from holding that the national sins of Israel lie all in the past.[1] It was only after the great reformation of 444 B.C. that the pious Israelite could say, what is said in Psalm xliv. and practically repeated elsewhere, that the people, in spite of their afflictions, have not forgotten God or been false to his covenant, that they are persecuted not because of their sins but for God's sake and because of their adherence to Him.

Thus far the contents of the Levitical Psalms are entirely consistent with the conclusion as to the date of their collection indicated by the titles. The mass of these Psalms cannot be earlier than the time of Ezra and Nehemiah, when Israel first became a law-abiding people. But when we seek to fix an

---

[1] In Ezekiel's time the people complained that they were punished for the sins of their fathers (Ezek. xviii.), and in Malachi's days the complaint was heard that it was vain to serve God, and that there was no profit in observing his ordinances (Mal. iii. 14). But both Ezekiel and Malachi refuse to admit that their contemporaries were innocent sufferers, and so take up quite a different standpoint from the Levitical Psalms.

inferior limit for the collection there is more difficulty in
bringing the evidence of the contents into harmony with the
titles. A considerable number of these Psalms (xliv. lxxiv.
lxxix. lxxx.) point to an historical situation which can be
very definitely realised. They are post-exile in their whole
tone, and belong to a time when prophecy had ceased and the
synagogue worship was fully established (lxxiv. 8, 9). But
the Jews are no longer the obedient slaves of Persia; there
has been a national rising, and armies have gone out to battle.
Yet God has not gone forth with them; the heathen have been
victorious; blood has flowed like water round Jerusalem; the
Temple has been defiled; and these disasters assume the
character of a religious persecution. These details would fit
the time of Antiochus Epiphanes, to which, indeed, Psalm
lxxiv. is referred (as a prophecy) in 1 Mac. vii. 16 *sq.* But
against this reference there is the objection that if these
Psalms are of the age of the Maccabees they can have been
no original part of the Elohistic Psalter. And even if we
suppose, what is not absolutely inconceivable, that three or
four pieces were inserted among the Levitical hymns at a
later date, there is still the difficulty that these Psalms are
written in a time of deepest dejection, and yet are Psalms of
the Temple choirs. Now when the Temple was reopened for
worship after its profanation by Antiochus the Jews were
victorious, and a much more joyous tone was appropriate.
On the whole, therefore, though many of the best modern
writers on the Psalter accept a Maccabee date at least for
Pss. xliv. lxxiv. lxxix., I feel a difficulty in admitting that
any of these pieces is later than the Persian period. Our
records of the history of the Jews in the last century of
Persian rule are very scanty; but we know that under
Artaxerxes Ochus (*circa* 350 B.C.) there was a widespread
rebellion in Phœnicia and other western parts of the empire,
which was put down with great severity. And in this

rebellion the Jews had a part, for many of them were led captive by the Persian king and planted in Hyrcania on the shores of the Caspian. That the rising of the Jews against Ochus took a religious character, like all the later rebellions against Greece and Rome, is highly probable; indeed it is impossible that the leaders could have had any other programme than the establishment of a theocracy. The desecration of the Temple referred to in Psalm lxxiv. is in accordance with the usual practice of the Persians towards the sanctuaries of their enemies ; and there is some independent evidence that in the reign of Ochus the sanctity of the Temple was violated by the Persians, and humiliating conditions attached to the worship there.[1]

Let us next consider the Third Collection (Bks. IV. and V.). We have seen that this collection was formed after the Elohistic redaction of the Second Collection (*supra*, p. 200), so that if our argument up to this point is sound the last part of the Psalter must be thrown into the Greek period, and probably not the earliest part thereof. This conclusion is borne out by a variety of indications. First of all, the language of some of the Psalms points to a very late date indeed. Even in the time of Nehemiah the speech of the Jews was in danger of being corrupted by the dialects of their neighbours (Neh. xiii. 24), but the restorers of the law fought against this tendency with vigour and with so much success that very tolerable Hebrew—coloured by Aramaic influences, but still real Hebrew—was written at least a century later. But in Ps. cxxxix. the language is not merely coloured by Aramaic, it is a jargon of Hebrew and Aramaic mixed together; which in a hymn accepted for use in the Temple shows the Hebrew speech to have reached the last stage of decay.

Another notable feature in the Third Collection is the

[1] See additional Note D.

entire disappearance of the musical titles "upon Neginoth,"
"upon Sheminith," and so forth, which are so frequent in the
earlier collections.   That is to say, the old technical terms of
the Temple music have fallen out of use, presumably because
they were already unintelligible, as they were to the Septuagint translators.   This implies a revolution in the national
music, and is probably connected with that influence of
Hellenic culture which from the time of the Macedonian
conquest began to work such changes in the whole civilisation
and art of the East.

A curious and interesting feature in the musical titles in
the earlier half of the Psalter is that many of them indicate
the tune to which the Psalm was set, by quoting phrases like
Aijeleth [hash-]shahar, or Jonath elem rechokim, which are
evidently the names of familiar songs.[1]   Of the song which
gave the title Al-taschith, "Destroy not," a trace is still
preserved in Isa. lxv. 8.   "When the new wine is found in
the cluster," says the prophet, "men say, 'Destroy it not, for a
blessing is in it.'"   These words in the Hebrew have a distinct
lyric rhythm.   They are the first line of one of the vintage
songs so often alluded to in Scripture.   And so we learn that
the early religious melody of Israel had a popular origin, and
was closely connected with the old joyous life of the nation.
In the time when the last books of the Psalter were composed,
the Temple music had passed into another phase, and had
differentiated itself from the melodies of the people, just as
we should no longer think of using as church music the
popular airs to which Psalms and hymns were set in Scotland
at the time of the Reformation.

[1] Similarly the ancient Syrian hymn-writers prefix to their compositions
such musical titles as "To the tune of ('al qâlâ dh') 'I will open my mouth
with knowledge.'" See the hymns of Ephræm *passim*. The same usage is
found in the fragments of Palestinian hymnology published by Land,
Anecdota Syriaca, iv. 111 *sqq.*, but here "to the tune of" is expressed by the
preposition 'al alone. The titles of the Hebrew Psalms also use the simple
preposition 'al, but even this is sometimes omitted.

Turning, now, to the contents of Books IV. and V., we observe that the general tone of large parts of this collection is much more cheerful than that of the Elohistic Psalm-book. It begins with a Psalm (xc.) ascribed in the title to Moses, and seemingly designed to express feelings appropriate to a situation analogous to that of the Israelites when, after the weary march through the wilderness, they stood on the borders of the promised land. It looks back on a time of great trouble and forward to a brighter future. In some of the following Psalms there are still references to deeds of oppression and violence, but more generally Israel appears as happy under the law with such a happiness as it did enjoy under the Ptolemies during the third century B.C. The problems of divine justice are no longer burning questions; the righteousness of God is seen in the peaceful felicity of the pious (xci. xcii., etc.). Israel, indeed, is still scattered and not triumphant over the heathen, but even in the dispersion the Jews are under a mild rule (cvi. 46), and the commercial activity of the nation has begun to develop beyond the seas (cvii. 23 *sq.*). The whole situation and vein of piety here are strikingly parallel to those shown in Ecclesiasticus, which dates from the close of the Ptolemaic sovereignty in Palestine.

But some of the Psalms carry us beyond this peaceful period to a time of struggle and victory. In Ps. cxviii. Israel, led by the house of Aaron—this is a notable point— has emerged triumphant from a desperate conflict and celebrates at the Temple a great day of rejoicing for the unhoped-for victory; in Ps. cxlix. the saints are pictured with the praises of God in their throat and a sharp sword in their hands to take vengeance on the heathen, to bind their kings and nobles, and exercise against them the judgment written in prophecy. Such an enthusiasm of militant piety, plainly based on actual successes of Israel and the house of Aaron,

can only be referred to the first victories of the Maccabees,
culminating in the purification of the Temple in 165 B.C.
This restoration of worship in the national sanctuary,
under circumstances that inspired religious feelings very
different from those of any other generation since the return
from Babylon, might most naturally be followed by an ex-
tension of the Temple psalmody; it certainly was followed
by some liturgical innovations, for the solemn service of
dedication on the twenty-fifth day of Chisleu was made the
pattern of a new annual feast (that mentioned in John x.
22). Now in 1 Mac. iv. 54 we learn that the dedication was
celebrated with hymns and music. In later times the Psalms
for the encænia or feast of dedication embraced Ps. xxx. and
the *hallel* Pss. cxiii.-cxviii. There is no reason to doubt that
these were the very Psalms sung in 165 B.C., for in the title
of Ps. xxx. the words "the song for the dedication of the
house," which are a somewhat awkward insertion in the
original title, are found also in the LXX., and therefore are
probable evidence of the liturgical use of the Psalm in the
very first years of the feast. But no collection of old Psalms
could fully suffice for such an occasion, and there is every
reason to think that the *hallel,* which especially in its closing
part contains allusions that fit no other time so well, was
first arranged for the same ceremony. The course of the
subsequent history makes it very intelligible that the Psalter
was finally closed, as we have seen from the date of the
Greek version that it must have been, within a few years at
most after this great event.[1] From the time of Hyrcanus
downwards the ideal of the princely high priests became
more and more divergent from the ideal of the pious in
Israel, and in the Psalter of Solomon (about 50 B.C.) we see

---

[1] The final redaction may have taken place under Simon ; compare the
closing series of Hallelujah Psalms (cxlvi.-cl.) with 1 Mac. xiii. 50 *sqq.* The
title of Ps. cxlv. "a Davidic Tehilla," is probably meant to cover all the
Psalms that follow and designate them as one great canticle.

religious poetry turned against the lords of the Temple and its worship.

We are thus led by a concurrence of arguments to assign the collection of Psalms xc.-cl. and the completion of the whole Psalter to the early years of Maccabee sovereignty It by no means follows that all the Psalms in the last great section of the Psalter were written in the Greek period ; for the composition of a poem and its introduction into the Temple liturgy do not necessarily go together except in the case of hymns written with a direct liturgical purpose. In the fifteen Pilgrimage Songs already referred to we have a case in point. All these songs are plainly later than the Captivity, but some of them are surely older than the close of the Elohistic Psalm-book, and the simple reason why they are not included in it is that they were hymns of the laity, describing the emotions of the pilgrim when his feet stood within the gates of Jerusalem, when he looked forth on the encircling hills, when he felt how good it was to be camping side by side with his brethren on the slopes of Zion (cxxxiii.),[1] when a sense of Jehovah's forgiving grace and the certainty of redemption for Israel triumphed over all the evils of the present and filled his soul with humble and patient hope.

When I say that the fifteen Pilgrimage Psalms are all later than the Captivity, I do not forget that the Hebrew titles ascribe four of them to David and one to Solomon. But these titles are lacking in the Septuagint, although the general

---

[1] The point of Ps. cxxxiii. is missed in all the commentaries I have looked at. The good and pleasant thing (ver. 1) is that those who are brethren also (גם) dwell together, *i.e.* not that they live in harmony, but that, in the solemn feast which has brought them together to Zion, the scattered brethren of one faith enjoy the privilege of being near one another. The following verses describe the scene under a figure. The long lines of the houses of Jerusalem, and the tents of the pilgrims, flow down the slopes of the Temple hill even to the base, like the oil on Aaron's garments—a blessed sight. Nay, this gathering of all the piety of Israel is as if the fertilising dews of great Hermon were all concentrated on the little hill of Zion.

tendency of that version is to give David more Psalms than bear his name in the Hebrew (*supra*, p. 96). In Psalm cxxii. the title seems to have been suggested by verse 5, and from the English version one would at least conclude that the Psalm was written under the Davidic dynasty. But the true translation in verses 4, 5, is "whither the tribes went up," and "for there were set thrones of judgment, the thrones of the house of David." To the Psalmist, therefore, the Davidic dynasty is a thing of the past. Better attested, because found in the Greek as well as the Hebrew, are the titles which assign Ps. xc. to Moses and Pss. ci. ciii. cviii.-cx. cxxxviii.-cxlv. to David. But where did the last collectors of the Psalter find such very ancient pieces, which had been passed over by all previous collectors, and what criterion was there to establish their genuineness ? The Psalms ascribed to David in the earlier parts of the Psalter form well-marked groups bearing internal evidence that they once formed separate collections. But in the Third Collection and in the appendix to the Elohistic Psalm-book authors' names occur only sporadically, and there is no evidence that the titles were taken over along with the Psalms from some older book. No canon of literary criticism can assign value to an attestation which first appears so many centuries after the supposed date of the poems, especially when it is confronted by facts so conclusive as that Ps. cviii. is made up of extracts from Pss. lvii. and lx. ; that in Ps. cxliv. 10 the singer expressly distinguishes himself from David (" O thou . . . that didst save David from the hurtful sword, save me "), and that Psalm cxxxix. is marked by its language as one of the latest pieces in the whole book. The only possible question for the critic is whether all these titles rest on editorial conjecture, or whether some of the Psalms exemplify the habit, so common in later Jewish literature, of writing in the name of ancient worthies. In the case of Ps. xc. at least it seems probable that the

Psalmist designs to speak, dramatically, in the name of Moses.

We have now seen that for the later stages in the history of the Psalter there is an amount of circumstantial evidence pointing to conclusions of a pretty definite kind. The approximate dates which their contents suggest for the collection of the Elohistic Psalm-book and of Books IV. and V. confirm one another and are in harmony with such indications as we obtain from external sources. But, in order to advance from the conclusions already reached to a view of the history of the Psalter as a whole, we have still to consider the two great groups of Psalms ascribed to David in Books I. and II. Both these groups appear once to have formed separate collections and to have been ascribed to David in their separate form; for in Book I. every Psalm, except the introductory poems i. and ii. and the late Ps. xxxiii., which may have been added as a liturgical sequel to Ps. xxxii., bears the title " of David," and in like manner the group Pss. li.-lxxii. is essentially a Davidic hymn-book, which has been taken over as a whole into the Elohistic Psalter, even the subscription lxxii. 20 not being omitted. Moreover, the collectors of Books I.-III. knew of no Davidic Psalms outside of these two collections; for Ps. lxxxvi., in the appendix to the Elohistic collection, is merely a cento of quotations from Davidic pieces with a verse or two from Exodus and Jeremiah. These two groups, therefore, represented to the collectors the oldest tradition of Hebrew psalmody; they are either really Davidic or they passed as such. This fact is important; but its weight may readily be over-estimated, for the Levitical Psalms comprise poems of the last half-century of the Persian empire, and the final collection of Books II. and III. may fall a good deal later. Thus the tradition as to the authorship of the second Davidic Collection comes to us, not exactly from the time of the Chronicler, but certainly from the time when the view of Hebrew history which he expresses was in the course of formation. And that view—which to some extent appears in the historical Psalms of the Elohistic Psalter [1]— implies such incapacity to understand the difference between old Israel and later Judaism as to make almost anything possible in the way of the ascription of comparatively modern pieces to ancient worthies. It is true that the collectors of the Elohistic Psalm-book did not invent the titles and subscription of the group of Davidic Psalms which they included in their work ; but evidence that these titles are older than the beginning of the Greek period, and that the Elohistic collectors accepted them as genuine, goes but a very little way towards proving that they really are derived by continuous tradition from the time of David himself. As regards the first Davidic Collection, the evidence carries us a little farther back. That collection is not touched by the Elohistic redaction (the habitual substitution of *Elohim* for *Iahwè*) which the second Davidic Collection has undergone. Now the formation of the Elohistic Psalter must have been an official act directed to the consolidation of the liturgical material used in the Temple services; and if it left the First Collection untouched the reason presumably was that this collection already had a fixed liturgical position which could not be meddled with. In other words, Pss. i.-xli. form the oldest extant Temple hymn-book, while there is no evidence that Pss. li.-lxxii. had a fixed liturgical position before the last years of the Persian Empire.

At this point I think that we may simplify the argument by dropping for a moment the question of the Davidic Collec-

---

[1] In Ps. lxxviii. the final rejection of the house of Joseph is co-ordinated with the fall of the sanctuary of Shiloh and the rise of Zion and the Davidic house in a way that comes very close to the Chronicler's attitude to the northern kingdom. We have already seen (*supra*, p. 205, note) that one of the Midrashim drawn on by the Chronicler seems to have been written at the time when the singers were still divided into Asaphites and Korahites (2 Chron. xx. 14, 19).

tions as wholes and looking at individual Psalms. Our
estimate of the value of the tradition which ascribes whole
groups of Psalms to David must necessarily be lowered if we
find individual Psalms bearing David's name which cannot
possibly be his. And this is undoubtedly the case as regards
both the Davidic Collections; for not only are many of the
titles certainly wrong, but they are wrong in such a way as
to prove that they date from an age to which David was
merely the abstract psalmist, and which had no idea whatever of the historical conditions of his time. For example,
Pss. xx. xxi. are not spoken by a king but addressed to a
king by his people; Pss. v. xxvii. allude to the Temple
(which did not exist in David's time), and the author of the
latter Psalm desires to live there continually. Even in the
older Davidic Psalm-book there is a whole series of hymns
in which the writer identifies himself with the poor and
needy, the righteous people of God suffering in silence at the
hands of the wicked, without other hope than patiently to
wait for the interposition of Jehovah (Pss. xii. xxv. xxxvii.
xxxviii. etc.). Nothing can be farther removed than this
from any possible situation in the life of the David of the
Books of Samuel. Most of these Psalms are referred by the
defenders of the titles to the time when David was pursued
by Saul. But it is quite unhistorical to represent Saul as a
man who persecuted and spoiled all the quiet and godly souls
in Israel ; and David and his friends were never helpless
sufferers—the quiet or timid in the land (xxxv. 20), dumb
amidst all oppression (xxxviii. 13, 14). And such a Psalm
as xxxvii., where the Psalmist calls himself an old man,
must, on the traditional view, be spoken by David late in his
prosperous reign ; yet here we have the same situation—the
wicked rampant, the righteous suffering in silence, as if
David were not a king who sat on his throne doing justice
and judgment to all his people (2 Sam. viii. 15). If Psalms

ix. x. xxxvii. represent the state of things in the time of
David, the Books of Samuel are the most partial of histories,
and the reign of the son of Jesse was not the golden age
which it appeared to all subsequent generations. The case
is still clearer in the second Davidic Collection, especially
where we have in the titles definite notes as to the historical
occasion on which the poems are supposed to have been
written. To refer Ps. lii. to Doeg, Ps. liv. to the Ziphites,
Ps. lix. to David when watched in his house by Saul, implies
an absolute lack of the very elements of historical judgment.
Even the bare names of the old history were no longer
correctly known when Abimelech (the Philistine king in the
stories of Abraham and Isaac) could be substituted in the
title of Ps. xxxiv. for Achish, king of Gath. In a word, the
ascription of these two collections to David has none of the
characters of a genuine historical tradition.[1]

Against the certainty that all the Psalms ascribed to
David in Books I.-III. cannot really be his, and that the
historical notes ascribing particular Psalms to special events
in his life are often grotesquely impossible, we have still to
set the fact that the name of David was attached to the
oldest collection of hymns used in the Temple. The facts
that have come before us are sufficient to disprove the idea

---

[1] Psalm lii. is said to refer to Doeg. It actually speaks of a rich and
powerful man, an enemy of the righteous in Israel, whom God will lay low,
whilst the psalmist is like a green olive tree in the house of God, whose mercy
is his constant support. Psalm liv. is said to be spoken against the Ziphites.
In reality it speaks of strangers and tyrants, standing Old Testament names
for foreign oppressors. In Psalm lv. the singer lives among foes in a city
whose walls they occupy with their patrols, exercising constant violence
within the town, from which the psalmist would gladly escape to the desert.
The enemy is in alliance with one who had once been an associate of the
psalmist, and joined with him in the service of the sacred feasts. Hence the
Psalm is often applied to Ahithophel ; but the whole situation is as different
as possible. In Psalm lix. we are asked to find a Psalm composed by David
when he was watched in his house by Saul. In reality the singer speaks of
heathen foes encircling the city, *i.e.* Jerusalem, whom God is prayed to cast
down, that His power may be manifest over all the earth.

that even in the First Collection every Psalm ascribed to
David was really his.   But the example of the fifteen
Pilgrimage Songs has made it probable to us that when these
Davidic Collections existed separately the name of David may
not have been attached to every Psalm, and that the titles, as
we now have them, may have been drawn from a general title
which originally stood at the head of the whole collection.
And just as the whole Book of Proverbs, though it contains
elements of various dates, now appears as the Proverbs of
Solomon, it is conceivable that the titles "Psalms of David,"
prefixed to Pss. i.-xli. li.-lxxii., originally stood in front of
collections consisting of Psalms of David and other hymns.
And so it may be argued that though the titles taken one by
one are of deficient authority, their combined evidence is
strong enough to prove that in both Davidic Collections, or at
any rate in the first, there is a substantial element that really
goes back to David.   This is a contention worth examining;
whereas those who argue for more than this are already put
out of court by the evidence before us.   But it is evident that
the force of the presumption that a substantial number of
Psalms are from David's pen must in great measure depend
on the date at which the First Collection was brought together.
We have seen reason to believe that Pss. i.-xli. are the oldest
part of the Temple liturgy; but can we suppose that the
oldest Temple liturgy was collected before the Exile and used
in the worship of the first Temple ?   To answer this question I must begin by bringing together the scanty notices
that have reached us as to religious music and hymns in the
old kingdom.

We have it in evidence that music and song accompanied
the worship of the great sanctuaries of northern Israel in the
eighth century B.C. (Amos v. 23), but from the context it
appears probable that the musicians were not officers of the
Temple but rather the worshippers at large (compare Amos

vi. 5). So it certainly was in the days of David (2 Sam. vi. 5), and even of Isaiah (xxx. 29); the same thing is implied in the song of Hezekiah (Isa. xxxviii. 20); and in Lam. ii. 7 the noise within the sanctuary on a feast-day affords a simile for the shouts of the victorious Chaldeans, which suggests the untrained efforts of the congregation rather than the disciplined music of a Temple choir. The allusion to "chambers of singers" in Ezek. xl. 44 is omitted in the Septuagint, and this is justified by the context; so that the first certain allusion to a class of singers among the sacred ministers is at the return from Babylon (Ezra ii. 41). The way in which these singers, the sons of Asaph, are spoken of may be taken as evidence that there was a guild of Temple singers before the Exile; but if they had been very conspicuous we should have heard more of them. The historical books are fond of varying the narrative by the insertion of lyrical pieces, and one or two of these—the "passover song" (Exod. xv.) and perhaps the song from the Book of Jashar ascribed to Solomon (*supra*, p. 124)—look as if they were sung in the first Temple; but they are not found in the Psalter, and, conversely, no piece from the Psalter is used to illustrate the life of David except Ps. xviii., and it occurs in a section which interrupts the original sequence of the history (*infra*, p. 222). These facts seem to indicate that even Book I. of the Psalter did not exist during the Exile, when the editing of the historical books was completed, and that in psalmody as in other matters the ritual of the second Temple was completely reconstructed. Indeed the radical change in the religious life of the nation caused by the Captivity could not fail to influence the psalmody of the sanctuary more than any other part of the worship; the Book of Lamentations marks an era of profound importance in the religious poetry of Israel, and no collection formed before these dirges were first sung could have been an adequate hymn-book for the

second Temple. In point of fact the notes struck in the
Lamentations and in Isa. xl.-lxvi. meet our ears again in not
a few Psalms of Book I., *e.g.* Pss. xxii. xxv., where the closing
prayer for the redemption of Israel in a verse additional to
the acrostic perhaps gives, as Lagarde suggests, the characteristic post-exile name Pedaiah as that of the author; Ps.
xxxi., with many points of resemblance to Jeremiah; Pss.
xxxiv. xxxv., where the "servant of Jehovah" is the same
collective idea as in Isaiah xl.-lxvi.; and Pss. xxxviii. xli.
The key to many of these Psalms is that the singer is not an
individual but, as in Lam. iii., the true people of God represented as one person; and only in this way can we do justice
to expressions which have always been a stumbling-block to
those who regard David as the author. But, at the same
time, other Psalms of the collection treat the problems of
individual religion in the line of thought first opened by
Jeremiah. Such a Psalm is xxxix., and above all Ps. xvi.
Other pieces, indeed, may well be earlier. When we compare Ps. viii. with Job vii. 17, 18, we can hardly doubt that
the Psalm lay before the writer who gave its expressions so
bitter a turn in the anguish of his soul, and Pss. xx. xxi.
plainly belong to the old kingdom. But on the whole it is
not the pre-exilic pieces that give the tone to the collection;
whatever the date of this or that individual poem, the collection as a whole—whether by selection or authorship—is
adapted to express a religious life of which the exile is the
presupposition. Only in this way can we understand the
conflict and triumph of spiritual faith, habitually represented
as the faith of a poor and struggling band, living in the midst
of oppressors and with no strength or help but the consciousness of loyalty to Jehovah, which is the fundamental
note of the whole book.

The contents of the First Collection suggest a doubt
whether it was originally put together by the Temple ministers,

whose hymn-book it ultimately became. The singers and
Levites were ill provided for, and consequently irregular in
their attendance at the Temple, till the time of Nehemiah,
who made it his business to settle the revenues of the clergy
in such a way as to make regular service possible. With
regular service a formal liturgy would be required, and in
the absence of direct evidence it may be conjectured that the
adoption of the first part of the Psalter for this purpose took
place in connection with the other far-reaching reforms of
Ezra and Nehemiah, which first gave a stable character to
the community of the second Temple. In any case these
Psalms, full as they are of spiritual elements which can never
cease to be the model of true worship, are the necessary com-
plement of the law as published by Ezra, and must be always
taken along with it by those who would understand what
Judaism in its early days really was, and how it prepared the
way for the gospel.

The second Davidic Collection, which begins with a Psalm
of the Exile (Ps. li. ;[1] see the last two verses), contains some
pieces which carry us down to a date decidedly later than that
of Nehemiah. Thus Ps. lxviii. 27 represents the worshipping
congregation as drawn partly from the neighbourhood of
Jerusalem and partly from the colony of Galilee. In several
Psalms of this collection, as in the Levitical Psalms with
which it is coupled, we see that the Jews have again begun
to feel themselves a nation and not a mere municipality,
though they are still passing through bitter struggles ; and
side by side with this there is a development of Messianic
hope, which in Ps. lxxii. takes a sweep as wide as the vision
of Isaiah xl.-lxvi. All these marks carry us down for this, as
for the other parts of the Elohistic Psalter, to the last days
of the Achæmenian empire, when the great revolt of the
West broke the tradition of passive obedience to the Persian.

[1] See additional Note E.

Several points indicate that this collection was not originally formed as part of the Temple liturgy. The title, as preserved in the subscription of Psalm lxxii. 20, was not "Psalms" but "Prayers of David." Again, while the Levitical Psalms were sung in the name of righteous Israel, of which, according to the theory of the second Temple, the priests and Levites were the special holy representatives, the Davidic Psalms contain touching utterances of contrition and confession (Pss. li. lxv.). And while there are direct references to the Temple service, these are often made from the standpoint, not of the ministers of the sanctuary, but of the laity who came up to join in the solemn feasts or appear before the altar to fulfil their vows (Pss. liv. 6, lv. 14, lxvi. 13, etc.). Moreover, the didactic element so prominent in the Levitical Psalms is not found here.

When we have learned that the two Davidic Collections are in the main the utterance of Israel's faith in the time of the second Temple, the question whether some at least of the older poems are really David's becomes more curious than important. There is no Psalm which we can assign to him with absolute certainty and use to throw light on his character or on any special event in his life. One Psalm indeed (xviii.) is ascribed to David not only by the title but in 2 Sam. xxii., and if this attestation formed part of the ancient and excellent tradition from which the greater part of the narrative of 2 Samuel is derived there would be every reason to accept it as conclusive. But we have already seen (*supra*, p. 114) that 2 Sam. xxi.-xxiv. is an appendix, of various contents, which breaks the original continuity of the court history. Originally Samuel and Kings were a single history, and 1 Kings i. followed directly on 2 Sam. xx. The appendix which now breaks the connection must have been inserted after the history was divided into two books, not earlier than the Captivity, and possibly a good deal later; and so this evidence does not help us to prove that any Psalm was assigned to David by ancient and continuous tradition.

On the whole, then, it cannot be made out that the oldest Psalm-book bore the name of David because it was mainly from his hand, or even because it contained a substantial number of hymns written by him. And on the other hand, there is evidence that the association of David's name with the Temple psalmody originally referred to the music and execution rather than to the hymns themselves. In the memoirs of Nehemiah we do not read of Psalms of David, but we learn that the singers used the musical instruments of David the man of God (Neh. xii. 36). So, too, the expression "the sweet psalmist of Israel," in 2 Sam. xxiii. 1, refers in the Hebrew not to the composition of psalms but to musical execution. Though the old histories do not speak of David as a Psalm-writer they dwell on his musical skill, and 2 Sam. vi. 5, 14, tells how he danced and played before the ark as it was brought up with joy to Jerusalem. Dancing, music, and song are in early times the united expression of lyrical inspiration, and the sacred melodies were still conjoined with dances at the time of the latest Psalms (cxlix. 3, cl. 4). We have every right, therefore, to conclude that the talents of Israel's most gifted singer were not withheld from the service of Jehovah, which King David placed high above all considerations of royal dignity (2 Sam. vi. 21). On the other hand, a curious passage of the Book of Amos (vi. 5), "they devise for themselves instruments of music like David," makes David the chosen model of the dilettanti nobles of Samaria, who lay stretched on beds of ivory, anointed with the choicest perfumes, and mingling music with their cups in the familiar fashion of Oriental luxury. These two views of David as a musician are not irreconcilable if we remember that in old Israel religion was not separated from ordinary life, and that the gladness of the believing heart found natural utterance in sportful forms of unconstrained mirth. At a much later date, as we have seen, chants for the Temple service were borrowed from the joyous songs of the vintage, and so it was possible that David should give the pattern alike for the melodies of the sanctuary and for the worldly airs of the nobles of Samaria. The sacred music of Israel was of popular origin, and long retained its popular type, and of this music David was taken to be father and great master. The oldest psalmody of the second Temple was still based on the ancient popular or Davidic model, and this seems to be the real reason why the oldest Psalm-book came to be known as "David's." The same name was afterwards extended to the other lay collection of "Prayers of David," while the collections that were formed from the first for use in the Temple were simply named from the Levitical choirs, or in later times bore no distinctive title.

The conclusion of this long and complicated investigation takes from us one use of the Psalter which has been a favourite exercise for pious imaginations. It is no longer possible to treat the psalms as a record of David's spiritual life through all the steps of his chequered career. But if we lose an imaginary autobiography of one Old Testament saint, we gain in its place something far truer and far richer in religious lessons; a lively image of the experience of the Old Testament Church set forth by the mouth of many witnesses, and extending through the vicissitudes of a long history. There is nothing in this change to impoverish the devotional use of the Psalms; for even a life like David's is a small thing compared with the life of a whole nation, and of such a nation as Israel. It is a vain apprehension which shrinks from applying criticism to the history of the Psalter out of fear lest the use of edification should suffer; for what can be less edifying than to force an application to David's life upon a psalm that clearly bespeaks for itself a different origin?

No sober commentator is now found to maintain the traditional titles in their integrity; and it is puerile to try to
conserve the traditional position by throwing this and that
title overboard, instead of frankly facing the whole critical
problem and refusing to be content till we have got a clear
insight into the whole history of the Psalter, and a solid
basis for its application not merely to purposes of personal
devotion but to the systematic study of the ancient dispensation.

LECTURE VIII

THE TRADITIONAL THEORY OF THE OLD TESTAMENT HISTORY [1]

THE Book of Psalms has furnished us with an example of what can be learned by critical study in a subject of limited compass, which can be profitably discussed without any wide digression into general questions of Old Testament history. The criticism of the Prophets and the Law opens a much larger field, and brings us face to face with fundamental problems.

We know, as a matter of historical fact, that the Pentateuch, as a whole, was put into operation as the rule of Israel's life at the reformation of Ezra, with a completeness which had never been aimed at from the days of the conquest

---

[1] On the subject of this and the following Lectures the most important book is Wellhausen's *Geschichte Israels* (Erster Band, Berlin, 1878). The later editions appeared under the title of *Prolegomena zur Gesch. Israels* (1883, 1888); Eng. trans., Edinburgh, 1885. The view set forth in this volume, which makes the Priestly Legislation the latest stage in the development of the Law, is often called Wellhausenianism, but this designation is illegitimate, and conveys the false impression that the account of the Pentateuch with which Wellhausen's name is associated is a revolutionary novelty which casts aside all the labours of earlier critics. In point of fact Wellhausen had many forerunners even in Germany (George, Vatke, Reuss, Graf, etc.); while in Holland the lines of a sound historical criticism of the Pentateuch had been firmly traced by the master hand of Kuenen, and the results for the history of the religion of Israel had been set forth in his *Godsdienst van Israel* (Haarlem, 1869-70). But it was reserved for Wellhausen to develop the whole argument with such a combination of critical power and historical insight as bore down all opposition. Even Dillmann, who still maintains the pre-exilic origin of the main body of the Priestly Code, defends this view only on the assump-

of Canaan (*supra*, p. 43).   From this time onwards the Pentateuch, in its ceremonial as well as its moral precepts, was the
acknowledged standard of Israel's righteousness (Neh. xiii.;
Ecclus. xlv.; 1 Mac. *passim*; Acts xv. 5).   According to the
theory of the later Jews, which has passed into current Christian theology, it had always been so.   The whole law of the
Pentateuch was given in the wilderness, or on the plains of
Moab, and Moses conveyed to the Israelites, before they
entered Canaan, everything that it was necessary for them to
know as a revelation from God, and even a complete system
of civil laws for the use of ordinary life.   The law was a rule
of absolute validity, and the keeping of it was the whole of
Israel's religion.   No religion could be acceptable to God
which was not conformed to the legal ordinances.   On this
theory the ceremonial part of the law must always have been
the prominent and most characteristic feature of the Old
Covenant.   In the Levitical legislation, the feasts, the sacrificial ritual, the ordinances of ceremonial purity, are always
in the foreground as the necessary forms in which alone the
inner side of religion, love to God and man, can find acceptable expression.   Not that religion is made up of mere forms,

---

tion that the work was an ideal or theoretical sketch, from a priestly point
of view, of a system of ordinances for the Hebrew theocracy based on Mosaic
principles and modified by the conditions of the author's time.   "As such
it had a purely private character, and possessed no authority as law" (*Num.,
Deut., und Jos.*, 1886, p. 667).

The most complete introduction to the Pentateuch on the lines of the
newer criticism is Kuenen's *Historisch-Kritisch Onderzoek*, 2d ed., vol. i.   The
first part of this volume, embracing the Hexateuch, was published in 1884,
and has been translated into English (London, 1886).   A shorter book,
learned, sober, and lucid, which contains all that most students can require,
is Professor Driver's *Introduction to the Lit. of the O. T.* (Edinburgh, 1891).   It
ought to be added that the new criticism does not reject the work that had
been done by older scholars, but completes it.   Those scholars were mainly
busied in separating, by linguistic and literary criteria, the several sources of
the Pentateuch; and this work retains its full value.   The weak point in the
old criticism was that it failed to give the results of literary analysis their
proper historical setting.

but everything in religion is reduced to rule and has some
fixed ceremonial expression. There is no room for religious
spontaneity.

According to this theory, it is not possible to distinguish
between ceremonial and moral precepts of the law, as if the
observance of the latter might excuse irregularity in the
former. The object of God's covenant with Israel was to
maintain a close and constant bond between Jehovah and His
people, different in kind from the relations of mankind in
general to their Creator. Israel was chosen to be a holy
people. Now, according to the Pentateuch, holiness is not
exclusively a moral thing. It has special relation to the
observances of ritual worship and ceremonial purity. "Ye
shall distinguish between clean beasts and unclean, and not
make yourselves abominable by any beast, fowl, etc., which I
have separated from you as unclean. And ye shall be holy
unto me : for I Jehovah am holy, and have severed you from
the nations to be mine" (Lev. xx. 25, 26). If a sacrifice is
eaten on the third day, "it is abominable ; it shall not be
accepted. He that eateth it shall bear his guilt, for he hath
profaned Jehovah's holy thing : that soul shall be cut off from
his people" (Lev. xix. 8). "That which dieth of itself, or is
torn of beasts, no priest may eat to defile himself therewith.
I am Jehovah ; and they shall keep my ordinance and not
take sin on themselves by profaning it and die therein. I
Jehovah do sanctify them" (Lev. xxii. 8, 9). No stronger
words than these could be found to denounce the gravest
moral turpitude.

The whole system is directed to the maintenance of holiness in Israel, as the condition of the benefits which Jehovah
promises to bestow on his people in the land of Canaan. And
therefore every infringement of law, be it merely in some
point of ceremony which we might be disposed to think
indifferent, demands an atonement, that the relation of God

to His people may not be disturbed. To provide such atonement is the great object of the priestly ritual which culminates in the annual ceremony of the day of expiation.
Atonement implies sacrifice, the blood or life of an offering
presented on the altar before God. " It is the blood that
atones by the life that is in it" (Lev. xvii. 11; Hebrews ix.
22). But the principle of holiness demands that the sacrificial act itself, and the altar on which the blood is offered,
be hedged round by strict ritual precautions. At the altar,
Jehovah, in His awful and inaccessible holiness, meets with
the people, which is imperfectly holy and stands in need of
constant forgiveness. There is danger in such a meeting.
Only the priests, who live under rules of intensified ceremonial purity, and have received a peculiar consecration
from Jehovah Himself, are permitted to touch the holy
things, and it is they who bear the sins of Israel before God
to make atonement for them (Lev. x. 17). Between them
and Israel at large is a second cordon of holy ministers, the
Levites. It is death for any but a priest to touch the altar,
and an undue approach of ordinary persons to the sanctuary
brings wrath on Israel (Num. i. 53). Accordingly, sacrifice,
atonement, and forgiveness of sin are absolutely dependent
on the hierarchy and its service. The mass of the people
have no direct access to their God in the sanctuary. The
maintenance of the Old Testament covenant depends on the
priestly mediation, and above all on that one annual day of
expiation when the high priest enters the Holy of Holies and
" cleanses the people that they may be clean from all their
sins before Jehovah" (Lev. xvi. 30). The whole system, you
perceive, is strictly knit together. The details are necessary
to the object aimed at. The intermission of any part of the
ceremonial scheme involves an accumulation of unforgiven
sin, with the consequence of divine wrath on the nation and
the withdrawal of God's favour.

To complete this sketch of the theory of the Pentateuch it is only necessary to add that the hierarchy has no dispensing power. If a man sins, he has recourse to the sacramental sacrifice appointed for his case. The priest makes atonement for him, and he is forgiven. But knowingly and obstinately to depart from any ordinance is to sin against God with a high hand, and for this there is no forgiveness. "He hath despised the word of the Lord and broken his commandment: that soul shall be cut off in his guilt" (Num. xv. 30, 31).

Such is the system of the law as contained particularly in the middle books of the Pentateuch, and practically accepted from the days of Ezra. It is not strange that the later Jews should have received it as the sum of all revelation, for manifestly it is a complete theory of the religious life. Its aim is to provide everything that man requires to live acceptably with God, the necessary measure of access to Jehovah, the necessary atonement for all sin, and the necessary channel for the conveyance of God's blessing to man. It is, I repeat, a complete theory of the religious life, to which nothing can be added without an entire change of dispensation. Accordingly, the Jewish view of the law as complete, and the summary of all revelation, has passed into Christian theology, with only this modification, that, whereas the Jews think of the dispensation of the law as final, and the atonement which it offers as sufficient, we have learned to regard the dispensation as temporary and its atonement as typical, prefiguring the atonement of Christ. But this modification of the Jewish view of the Torah does not diminish the essential importance of the law for the life of the old dispensation. The ceremonies were not less necessary because they were typical ; for they are still to be regarded as divinely appointed means of grace, to which alone God had attached the promise of blessing.

Now, as soon as we lay down the position that the system of the ceremonial law, embracing, as it does, the whole life of every Jew, was completed and prescribed as an authoritative code for Israel before the conquest of Canaan, we have an absolute rule for measuring the whole future history of the nation, and the whole significance of subsequent revelation under the Old Testament.

On the one hand, the religious history of Israel can be nothing else than the history of the nation's obedience or disobedience to the law. Nothing could be added to the law and nothing taken from it till the time of fulfilment, when the type should pass away and be replaced by the living reality of the manifestation of Christ Jesus. So long as the old dispensation lasted, the law remained an absolute standard. The Israelite had no right to draw a distinction between the spirit and the letter of the law. The sacrifices and other typical ordinances might not be of the essence of religion. But obedience to God's word undoubtedly was so, and that word had in the most emphatic manner enjoined the sacrifices and other ceremonies, and made the forgiveness of Israel's sins to depend on them. The priestly atonement was a necessary part of God's covenant. "The priest shall make atonement for him, and he shall be forgiven." To neglect these means of grace is, according to the Pentateuch, nothing less than the sin committed with a high hand, for which there is no forgiveness.

Again, on the other hand, the position that the whole legal system was revealed to Israel at the very beginning of its national existence strictly limits our conception of the function and significance of subsequent revelation. The prophets had no power to abrogate any part of the law, to dispense with Mosaic ordinances, or institute new means of grace, other methods of approach to God in lieu of the hierarchical sacraments. For the Old Testament way of atonement is set forth in the Pentateuch as adequate and efficient. According to Christian theology, its efficiency as a typical system was conditional on the future bringing in of a perfect atonement in Christ. But for that very reason it was not to be tampered with until Christ came. The prophets, like the law itself, could only point to a future atonement; they were not themselves saviours, and could do nothing to diminish the need for the temporary provisions of the hierarchical system; and, as a matter of fact, the prophets did not abolish the Pentateuch or any part of the Levitical system. Nay, it is just as their work closes that we find the Pentateuchal code solemnly advanced, in the reformation of Ezra, to a position of public authority which it had never held before.

Hence the traditional view of the Pentateuch necessarily regards the prophets as ministers and exponents of the law. Their business was to enforce the observance of the law on Israel and to recall the people from backsliding to a strict conformity with its precepts. According to the Jewish view, this makes their work less necessary and eternal than the law. Christian theologians avoid this inference, but they do so by laying stress on the fact that the reference to a future and perfect atonement, which lay implicitly in the typical ordinances of the ceremonial law, was unfolded by the prophets in the clear language of evangelical prediction. We have been taught to view the prophets as exponents of the spiritual elements of the law, who showed the people that its precepts were not mere forms but veiled declarations of the spiritual truths of a future dispensation which was the true substance of the shadows of the old ritual. This theory of the work of the prophets is much more profound than that of the Rabbins. But it implies, as necessarily as the Jewish view, that the prophets were constantly intent on enforcing the observance of the ceremonial as well as the moral pre-

cepts of the Pentateuch. Neglect of the ritual law was all
the more culpable when the spiritual meaning of its precepts
was made plain.

I think that it will be admitted that in this sketch I have
correctly indicated the theory of the Old Testament dispensation which orthodox theologians derive from the traditional
view as to the date of the Pentateuch. I ask you to observe
that it is essentially the Rabbinical view supplemented by a
theory of typology; but I also ask you to observe that it is
perfectly logical and consistent in all its parts. It is, so far
as one can see, the only theory which can be built on the
premisses. It has only one fault. The standard which it
applies to the history of Israel is not that of the contemporary historical records, and the account which it gives of
the work of the prophets is not consistent with the writings
of the prophets themselves.

This may seem a strong statement, but it is not lightly
made, and it expresses no mere personal opinion, but the
growing conviction of an overwhelming weight of the most
earnest and sober scholarship. The discrepancy between the
traditional view of the Pentateuch and the plain statements
of the historical books and the Prophets is so marked and so
fundamental that it can be made clear to every reader of
Scripture. It is this fact which compels us, in the interests
of practical theology—nay, even in the interests of Christian
apologetic—to go into questions of Pentateuch criticism. For
if the received view which assigns the whole Pentateuch
to Moses is inconsistent with the concordant testimony of
the Earlier and Later Prophets, we are brought into this
dilemma :—Either the Old Testament is not the record of a
self-consistent scheme of revelation, of one great and continuous work of a revealing and redeeming God, or else the
current view of the origin of the Pentateuch must be given
up. Here it is that criticism comes in to solve a problem

which in its origin is not merely critical, but springs of necessity from the very attempt to understand the Old Testament
dispensation as a whole. For the contradiction which cannot
be resolved on traditional assumptions is at once removed
when the critic points out within the Pentateuch itself clear
marks that the whole law was not written at one time, and that
the several documents of which it is composed represent successive developments of the fundamental principles laid down
by Moses, successive redactions of the sacred law of Israel
corresponding to the very same stages in the progress of
revelation which are clearly marked in the history and the
prophetic literature. Thus the apparent discordance between
the several parts of the Old Testament record is removed, and
we are able to see a consistent divine purpose ruling the
whole dispensation of the Old Covenant, and harmoniously
displayed in every part of the sacred record. To develop this
argument in its essential features, fitting the several parts of
the record into their proper setting in the history of revelation, is the object which I propose for our discussion of the
Law and the Prophets. Of the critical or constructive part
of the argument I can give only the main outlines, for many
details in the analysis of the Pentateuch turn on nice questions of Hebrew scholarship. But the results are broad and
intelligible, and possess that evidence of historical consistency
on which the results of special scholarship are habitually
accepted by the mass of intelligent men in other branches of
historical inquiry.

Such, then, is the plan of our investigation; and, first of
all, let us compare the evidence of the Bible history with the
traditional theory already sketched. In working out this
part of the subject I shall confine your attention in the first
instance to the books earlier than the time of Ezra, and in
particular to the histories in the Earlier Prophets, from
Judges to Second Kings. I exclude the Book of Joshua

because it in all its parts hangs closely together with the Pentateuch. The difficulties which it presents are identical with those of the Books of Moses, and can only be explained in connection with the critical analysis of the law. And, on the other hand, I exclude the narrative of Chronicles for reasons which have been sufficiently explained at the close of Lecture V. The tendency of the Chronicler to assume that the institutions of his own age existed under the old kingdom makes his narrative useless for the purpose now in hand, where we are expressly concerned with the differences between ancient and modern usage. Let me observe, however, that the proposal to test the traditional theory of the Pentateuch by the old historical books is one which no fair controversialist can refuse, even if he has not made up his mind as to the value of the testimony of the Chronicler; for, in all historical questions, the ultimate appeal is to contemporary sources, or to those sources which approach most nearly to the character of contemporary witnesses.

Every reader of the Old Testament history is familiar with the fact that from the days of the Judges down to the Exile the law was never strictly enforced in Israel. The history is a record of constant rebellion and shortcomings, and the attempts at reformation made from time to time were comparatively few and never thoroughly carried out. The deflections of the nation from the standard of the Pentateuch come out most clearly in the sphere of worship. In the time of the Judges the religious condition of the nation was admittedly one of anarchy. The leaders of the nation, divinely-appointed deliverers like Gideon and Jephthah, who were zealous in Jehovah's cause, were as far from the Pentateuchal standard of righteousness as the mass of the people. Gideon erects a sanctuary at Ophrah, with a golden ephod—apparently a kind of image —which became a great centre of illegal worship (Jud.

viii. 24 *sqq.*); Jephthah offers his own daughter to Jehovah; the Lord departs from Samson, not when he marries a daughter of the uncircumcised, but when his Nazarite locks are shorn.

The revival under Samuel, Saul, and David was marked by great zeal for Jehovah, but brought no reform in matters of glaring departure from the law. Samuel sacrifices on many high places, Saul builds altars, David and his son Solomon permit the worship at the high places to continue, and the historian recognises this as legitimate because the Temple was not yet built (1 Kings iii. 2-4). In Northern Israel this state of things was never changed. The high places were an established feature in the kingdom of Ephraim, and Elijah himself declares that the destruction of the altars of Jehovah—all illegitimate according to the Pentateuch—is a breach of Jehovah's covenant (1 Kings xix. 10). In the Southern Kingdom it was not otherwise. It is recorded of the best kings before Hezekiah that the high places were not removed by them; and in the eighth century B.C. the prophets describe the worship of Ephraim and Judah in terms practically identical. Even the reforms of Hezekiah and Josiah were imperfectly carried through; and important points of ritual, such as the due observance of the Feast of Tabernacles, were still neglected (Neh. viii. 17). These facts are not disputed. The question is how we are to interpret them.

The prophets and the historical books agree in representing the history of Israel as a long record of disobedience to Jehovah, of which captivity was the just punishment. But the precise nature of Israel's sin is often misunderstood. We are accustomed to speak of it as idolatry, as the worship of false gods in place of Jehovah; and in a certain sense this corresponds with the language of the sacred books. In the judgment of the prophets of the eighth century the mass of the Israelites, not merely in the Northern Kingdom but equally in Judah, had rebelled against Jehovah, and did not pay Him worship in any true sense. But that was far from being the opinion of the false worshippers themselves. They were not in conscious rebellion against Jehovah and His covenant. On the contrary, their religion was based on two principles, one of which is the fundamental principle of Old Testament revelation, while the second is the principle that underlies the whole system of ritual ordinance in the Pentateuch. The first principle in the popular religion of Israel, acknowledged by the false worshippers as well as by the prophets, was that Jehovah is Israel's God, and that Israel is the people of Jehovah in a distinctive sense. And with this went a second principle, that Israel is bound to do homage to its God in sacrifice, and to serve Him diligently and assiduously according to an established ritual.

Let me explain this point more fully. There is no doubt that the worship of heathen deities, such as the Tyrian Baal or the Sidonian Astarte, and the local gods and goddesses of lesser Canaanite sanctuaries, was not unknown in ancient Israel. Solomon and Ahab even went so far as to erect temples to foreign gods (1 Kings xi. 4 *sqq.* compared with 2 Kings xxiii. 13; 1 Kings xvi. 32) out of complaisance to their foreign wives; and though these shrines seem to have been primarily designed for the convenience of the heathen princesses and their countrymen resident in the land of Israel, they were not exclusively frequented by foreigners. But as a rule, an Israelite who bowed the knee to a strange god did not suppose that in so doing he was renouncing his allegiance to Jehovah as his national God and the chief object of his homage. Even Ahab, of whose Baal-worship we hear so much, never proposed to give up the God of Israel for the god of Tyre. The state religion was still Jehovah-worship, and it was Jehovah's prophets

that were consulted in affairs of state (1 Kings xxii.). Moreover, the foreign worship introduced by Ahab had only a
temporary vogue. The mass of the people soon came to
regard it, with the prophets Elijah and Elisha, as an
apostasy from Jehovah, who would tolerate no rival within
his land; and in Jehu's revolution the alien temple was
destroyed and its worshippers ruthlessly put to death.
Most certainly, then, the national disobedience with which
the prophets charge their countrymen was not denial that
Jehovah is Israel's God, with a paramount claim to the
service and worship of the nation. On the contrary, the
prophets represent their contemporaries as full of zeal for
Jehovah, and confident that they have secured His help
by their great assiduity in His service (Amos iv. 4 *sq.*, v.
18 *sq.* ; Hosea vi.; Isa. i. 11 *sq.*; Micah iii. 11; Jer. vii.).

To obtain a precise conception of what this means, we
must look more closely at the notion of worship under
the Old Testament dispensation. To us worship is a
spiritual thing. We lift up our hearts and voices to God
in the closet, the family, or the church, persuaded that
God, who is spirit, will receive in every place the worship
of spirit and truth. But this is strictly a New Testament
conception, announced as a new thing by Jesus to the
Samaritan woman, who raised a question as to the disputed prerogative of Zion or Gerizim as the place of
acceptable worship. Under the New Covenant neither
Zion nor Gerizim is the mount of God. Under the Old
Testament it was otherwise. Access to God—even to
the spiritual God—was limited by local conditions. There
is no worship without access to the deity before whom
the worshipper draws nigh to express his homage. We
can draw near to God in every act of prayer in the
heavenly sanctuary, through the new and living way which
Jesus has consecrated in His blood. But the Old Testament

worshipper sought access to God in an earthly sanctuary
which was for him, as it were, the meeting-place of heaven
and earth. Such holy points of contact with the divine
presence were locally fixed, and their mark was the altar,
where the worshipper presented his homage, not in purely
spiritual utterance, but in the material form of an altar
gift. The promise of blessing, or, as we should now call
it, of answer to prayer, is in the Old Testament strictly
attached to the local sanctuary. "In every place where I
set the memorial of my name, I will come unto thee and
bless thee" (Exod. xx. 24). Every visible act of worship
is subjected to this condition. In the mouth of Saul,
"to make supplication to Jehovah" is a synonym for
doing sacrifice (1 Sam. xiii. 12). To David, banishment
from the land of Israel and its sanctuaries is a command
to serve other gods (1 Sam. xxvi. 19 ; compare Deut.
xxviii. 36, 64). And the worship of the sanctuary imperatively demands the tokens of material homage, the gift
without which no Oriental would approach even an earthly
court. "None shall appear before me empty" (Exod.
xxiii. 15). Prayer without approach to the sanctuary is
not recognised as part of the "service of Jehovah" ; and
for him who is at a distance from the holy place, a vow,
such as Absalom made at Geshur in Syria (2 Sam. xv. 8),
is the natural surrogate for the interrupted service of the
altar. The essence of a vow is a promise to do sacrifice
or other offering at the sanctuary (Deut. xii. 6 ; Lev. xxvii. ;
1 Sam. i. 21 ; compare Gen. xxviii. 20 *sq.*).

This conception of the nature of divine worship is the
basis alike of the Pentateuchal law and of the popular
religion of Israel described in the historical books and
condemned by the prophets. The sanctuary of Jehovah,
the altar and the altar gifts, the sacrifices and the solemn
feasts, the tithes and the free-will offerings, were never

treated with indifference (Amos iv. 4, viii. 5; Hosea viii. 13; Isa. i. 11 *sq.*; Jer. vii.). On the contrary, the charge which the prophets constantly hurl against the people is that they are wholly absorbed in affairs of worship and ritual service, and think themselves to have secured Jehovah's favour by the zeal of their external devotion, without the practice of justice, mercy, and moral obedience.

The condition of religious affairs in Northern Israel is clearly described by the prophets Amos and Hosea. These prophets arose under the dynasty of Jehu, the ally of Elisha and the destroyer of Baal-worship, a dynasty in which the very names of the kings denote devotion to the service of Jehovah. Jehovah was worshipped in many sanctuaries and in forms full of irregularity from the standpoint of the Pentateuch. There were images of Jehovah under the form of a calf or steer in Bethel and Dan, and probably elsewhere. The order of the local sanctuaries, and the religious feasts celebrated at them, had much in common with the idolatry of the Canaanites. Indeed many of the high places were old Canaanite sanctuaries. Nevertheless these sanctuaries and their worship were viewed as the fixed and normal provision for the maintenance of living relations between Israel and Jehovah. Hosea predicts a time of judgment when this service shall be suppressed. "The children of Israel shall sit many days without sacrifice and without *maççēba*, without ephod and teraphim." This language expresses the entire destruction of the religious order of the nation, a period of isolation from all access to Jehovah, like the isolation of a faithful spouse whom her husband keeps shut up, not admitting her to the privileges of marriage (Hos. iii.).[1]

---

[1] The English version of Hosea iii. does not clearly express the prophet's thought. Hosea's wife had deserted him for a stranger. But though she is thus "in love with a paramour, and unfaithful," his love follows her, and he buys her back out of the servile condition into which she appears to have

It appears, then, that sacrifice and *maççēba*, ephod and teraphim, were recognised as the necessary forms and instruments
of the worship of Jehovah.   They were all old traditional
forms, not the invention of modern will - worship.   The
maççēba, or consecrated stone, so often named in the Old
Testament where our version unfortunately renders "image,"
is as old as the time of Jacob, who set up and consecrated
the memorial stone that marked Bethel as a sanctuary.   It
was the necessary mark of every high place, Canaanite as
well as Hebrew, and is condemned in the Pentateuchal laws
against the high places along with the associated symbol of
the sacred tree or pole (*ashēra*, E. V. *grove*), which was also
a feature in the patriarchal sanctuaries.   (The oak of Moreh,
Gen. xii. 6, 7; the tamarisk of Beersheba, Gen. xxi. 33; Gen.
xxxi. 45, 54; Gen. xxxiii. 20, with xxxv. 4; Jos. xxiv. 26;
Hos. iv. 13.)   The ephod is also ancient.   It must have been
something very different from the ephod of the high priest,
but is to be compared with the ephods of Gideon and Micah
(Judges viii. 27, xvii. 5), and with that in the sanctuary of
Nob (1 Sam. xxi. 9).   Finally, teraphim are a means of
divination (Ezek. xxi. 21; Zech. x. 2) as old as the time of
Jacob, and were found in Micah's sanctuary and David's
house (1 Sam. xix. 13; E. V. *image*).[1]

It appears, then, that the national worship of Jehovah,
under the dynasty of Jehu, was conducted under traditional

---

fallen.   She is brought back from shame and servitude, but not to the
privileges of a wife.   She must sit alone by her husband, reserved for him,
but not yet restored to the relations of wedlock.   So Jehovah will deal with
Israel, when by destroying the state and the ordinances of worship He breaks
off all intercourse, not only between Israel and the Baalim, but between
Israel and Himself.

[1] On the ephod, see Vatke, *Bibl. Theologie* (1835), p. 267 *sq.*; Studer on
Judges viii. 27.   The passages where teraphim are mentioned in the Hebrew
but not in the English version are, Gen. xxxi. 19, 34, 35; 1 Sam. xv. 23,
xix. 13, 16; 2 Kings xxiii. 24; Zech. x. 2.   Compare, as to their nature,
Spencer, *De Legibus Ritualibus Hebræorum*, Lib. iii. c. 3, § 2 *sq.*   On the
maççēba and *ashera* see my *Religion of the Semites*, vol. i. (1889), Lect. 5.

forms which had a fixed character and general recognition.
These forms were ancient. There is no reason to think that
the worship of the northern shrines had undergone serious
modifications since the days of the Judges. The sanctuaries
themselves were of ancient and, in great part, of patriarchal
consecration. Beersheba, Gilgal, Bethel, Shechem, Mizpah,
were places of the most venerable sanctity, acknowledged by
Samuel and earlier worthies. Of the sanctuary at Dan we
know the whole origin and history. It was founded by the
Danites who carried off Micah's Levite and holy things ; and
the family of the Levite, who was himself a grandson of
Moses, continued in office through the age of David and
Samuel down to the Captivity (Jud. xviii. 30). It was a
sanctuary of purely Israelite origin, originally instituted by
Micah for the service of Jehovah, and equipped with every
regard to the provision of an acceptable service. " Now I
know," said Micah, " that Jehovah will do me good, since I
have got the Levite as my priest." This trait indicates an
interest in correct ritual which never died out. In truth,
ritual is never deemed unimportant in a religion so little
spiritual as that of the mass of Israel. All worships that
contain heathenish elements are traditional, and nothing is
more foreign to them than the arbitrary introduction of forms
for which there is no precedent of usage.

That this traditional service and ritual was not Levitically
correct needs no proof. Let us rather consider the features
which mark it as unspiritual and led the prophets to condemn
it as displeasing to God.

In the first place, we observe that though Jehovah was
worshipped with assiduity, and worshipped as the national
God of Israel, there was no clear conception of the fundamental difference between Him and the gods of the nations.
This appears particularly in the current use of images, like
the golden calves, which were supposed to be representations

or symbols of Jehovah. But, indeed, the whole service is represented by the prophets as gross, sensual, and unworthy of a spiritual deity (Amos ii. 7, 8; Hosea iv. 13, 14). We know that many features in the worship of the high places were practically identical with the abominations of the Canaanites, and gave no expression to the difference between Jehovah and the false gods. Thus it came about that the Israelites fell into what is called *syncretism* in religion. They were unable sharply to distinguish between the local worship of Jehovah and the worship of the Canaanite Baalim. The god of the local sanctuary was adored as Jehovah, but a local Jehovah was practically a local Baal. This confusion of thought may be best illustrated from the Madonna - worship of Roman Catholic shrines. Every Madonna is a representation of the one Virgin; but practically each Virgin has its own merits and its own devotees, so that the service of these shrines is almost indistinguishable from polytheism, of which, indeed, it is often an historical continuation. In Phœnicia one still sees grottoes of the Virgin Mary which are old shrines of Astarte, bearing the symbols of the ancient worship of Canaan. So it was in those days. The worship of the one Jehovah, who was Himself addressed in old times by the title of Baal or Lord (*supra*, p. 68), practically fell into a worship of a multitude of local Baalim, so that a prophet like Hosea can say that the Israelites, though still imagining themselves to be serving the national God, and acknowledging His benefits, have really turned from Him to deities that are no gods.

In this way another fault came in. The people, whose worship of Jehovah was hardly to be distinguished from a gross polytheism, could not be fundamentally averse to worship other gods side by side with the national deity. Thus the service of Astarte, Tammuz, or other deities that could not even in popular conception be identified with

Jehovah, obtained a certain currency, at least in sections of the nation. This worship was always secondary, and was put down from time to time in movements of reformation which left the high places of Jehovah untouched (1 Sam. vii. 3 ; 1 Kings xv. 12 *sq.*; 2 Kings x. 28, 29, xi. 18).

This sketch of the popular religion of Israel is mainly drawn from the Northern Kingdom. But it is clear from the facts enumerated that it was not a mere innovation due to the schism of Jeroboam. Jeroboam, no doubt, lent a certain *éclat* to the service of the royal sanctuaries, and the golden calves gave a very different conception of Jehovah from that which was symbolised by the ark on Zion. But the elements of the whole worship were traditional, and were already current in the age of the Judges. Gideon's golden ephod and the graven image at Dan prove that even image-worship was no innovation of Jeroboam. And it is certain that the worship of the Judæan sanctuaries was not essentially differ-ent from that of the northern shrines. The high places flourished undisturbed from generation to generation. The land was full of idols (Isa. ii.). Jerusalem appears to Micah as the centre of a corrupt Judæan worship, which he parallels with the corrupt worship of Samaria (Micah i. 5, iii. 12, v. 11 *sq.*, vi. 16).

Where, then, did this traditional worship, so largely diffused through the mass of Israel, have its origin, and what is its historical relation to the laws of the Pentateuch? No doubt many of its corrupt features may be explained by the in-fluence of the Canaanites; and from the absolute standard of spiritual religion applied by the prophets it might even be said that Israel had forsaken Jehovah for the Baalim. But from the standpoint of the worshippers it was not so. They still believed themselves loyal to Jehovah. Their great sanctuaries were patriarchal holy places like Bethel and Beersheba, or purely Hebrew foundations like Dan. With

all its corruptions, their worship had a specifically national
character.   Jehovah never was a Canaanite God, and the
roots of the popular religion, as we have already seen, were
that acknowledgment of Jehovah as Israel's God, and of the
duty of national service to Him, which is equally the basis
of Mosaic orthodoxy.[1]   These are principles which lie behind
the first beginnings of Canaanite influence.   But in the
Pentateuch these principles are embodied in a ritual altogether diverse in system and theory, as well as in detail,
from the traditional ritual of the high places.   The latter
service is not merely a corrupt copy of the Mosaic system,
with elements borrowed from the Canaanites.   In the Levitical ritual the essentials of Jehovah-worship are put in a
form which made no accommodation to heathenism possible,
which left no middle ground between the pure worship of
Jehovah, as maintained by the Aaronic priesthood in the one
sanctuary, and a deliberate rejection of Israel's God for the
idols of the heathen.

To understand this point we must observe that according
to the Levitical system God is absolutely inaccessible to man,
except in the priestly ritual of the central sanctuary.   Controversial writers on the law of the one sanctuary have often
been led to overlook this point by confining their attention
to the law of the sanctuary in Deuteronomy, which speaks of

---

[1] After the conclusive remarks of Kuenen (*Godsdienst*, i. 398 *sq.*) it is unnecessary to spend words on the theory, which still crops up from time to
time, that the Hebrews borrowed the worship of Jehovah (or *Iahwè*, as the
name should rather be pronounced) from the Canaanites.   Further, the judgment pronounced by Baudissin in 1876 (*Studien*, vol. i. No. 3), and confirmed
by Kuenen in 1882 (*Hibbert Lectures*, p. 311), still holds its ground ; there
is no valid evidence that a god bearing the name of Iahwè (or some equivalent
form such as Iahu) was known to any other Semitic people.   See further on
this point and on other questions connected with the name a paper by
Professor Driver in *Studia Biblica*, i. (Oxford, 1885).   The statement of
Professor Sayce, *Fresh Light* (1890), p. 63, that the form Iahwè or Yahveh,
as it is often written, is incompatible with the form Yahu (-iahu, -iah) which
appears in proper names [*e.g.* Hiskiyahu, the Hezekiah of our Bibles], is due
to haste or to ignorance.

the choice of one place in Canaan where Jehovah will set
His name as a practical safeguard against participation in
the worship of Canaanite high places. But if the whole
Pentateuch is one Mosaic system, the law of Deuteronomy
must be viewed in the light of the legislation of the Middle
Books. Here the theory of the one sanctuary is worked out
on a basis independent of the question of heathen shrines.
According to the Old Testament, worship is a tryst between
man and God in the sanctuary, and the question of the
legitimate sanctuary is the question of the place where
Jehovah has promised to hold tryst with His people, and
the conditions which He lays down for this meeting. The
fundamental promise of the Levitical legislation is Exod.
xxix. 42 *sq.* The place of tryst is the Tent of Tryst or
Meeting, incorrectly rendered in the Authorised Version,
"The tabernacle of the congregation." "There will I hold
tryst with the children of Israel, and it shall be sanctified by
my glory. And I will sanctify the tent of meeting and the
altar, and I will sanctify Aaron and his sons to do priestly
service to me. And I will dwell in the midst of the children
of Israel, and will be their God." The tent of meeting is
God's *mishkan*, His dwelling-place, which He sets in the
midst of Israel (Lev. xxvi. 11). The first condition of divine
blessing in Lev. xxvi. is reverence for the Sabbath and the
sanctuary, and the total rejection of idols and of the *maççĕba*
which was the mark of the high places. There is no local
point of contact between heaven and earth, no place where
man can find a present God to receive his worship, save this
one tent of meeting, where the ark with the Cherubim is the
abiding symbol that God is in the midst of Israel, and the
altar stands at the door of the tabernacle as the legitimate
place of Israel's gifts. This sanctuary with its altar is the
centre of Israel's holiness. It is so holy that it is hedged
round by a double cordon of sacred ministers. For the

presence of Jehovah is a terrible thing, destructive to sinful man. The Old Testament symbol of Jehovah's manifestation to His people is the lightning flash from behind the thunder cloud, fire involved in smoke, an awful and devouring brightness consuming all that is not holy. Therefore the dreadful spot where His holiness dwells may never be approached without atoning ritual and strict precautions of ceremonial sanctity provided for the priests, and for none other. Even the Levites may not touch either ark or altar, lest both they and the priests die (Num. xviii. 3). Still less dare the laity draw near to the tabernacle (Num. xvii. 13 [28]). It is only the sons of Aaron who, by their special consecration, can bear with impunity "the guilt of the sanctuary" (xviii. 1); and so every sacred offering of the Israelite, every gift which expresses the people's homage, must pass through their hand and pay toll to them (Num. xviii. 8 *sq.*). Thus the access of the ordinary Israelite to God is very restricted. He can only stand afar off while the priest approaches Jehovah as his mediator, and brings back a word of blessing. And even this mediate access to God is confined to his visits to the central sanctuary. The stated intercourse of God with His people is not the concern of the whole people, but of the priests, who are constantly before God, offering up on behalf of the nation the unbroken service of the continual daily oblations. This is a great limitation of the freedom of worship. But it is no arbitrary restriction. On the Levitical theory, the imperfection of the ordinary holiness of Israel leaves no alternative open. For the holiness of God is fatal to him who dares to come near His dwelling-place.

On this theory the ritual of the sanctuary is no artificial system devised to glorify one holy place above others, but the necessary scheme of precaution for every local approach to God. Other sanctuaries are not simply less holy, places of less solemn tryst with Jehovah; they are places where His holiness is not revealed, and therefore are not, and cannot be, sanctuaries of Jehovah at all. If Jehovah were to meet with man in a second sanctuary, the same consequences of inviolable holiness would assert themselves, and the new holy place would again require to be fenced in with equal ritual precautions. In the very nature of the covenant, there is but one altar and one priesthood through which the God of Israel can be approached.

The popular religion of Israel, with its many sanctuaries, proceeds on a theory diametrically opposite. Opportunity of access to Jehovah is near to every Israelite, and every occasion of life that calls on the individual, the clan, or the village, to look Godwards is a summons to the altar. In the family every feast was an eucharistic sacrifice. In affairs of public life it was not otherwise. The very phrases in Hebrew for "making a covenant" or "inaugurating war" point to the sacrificial observances that accompanied such acts. The earlier history relates scarcely one event of importance that was not transacted at a holy place. The local sanctuaries were the centres of all Hebrew life. How little of the history would remain if Shechem and Bethel, the two Mizpahs and Ophra, Gilgal, Ramah, and Gibeon, Hebron, Bethlehem, and Beersheba, Kedesh and Mahanaim, Tabor and Carmel, were blotted out of the pages of the Old Testament.[1]

---

[1] In some of these cases, evidence that the place was a sanctuary may be demanded. Kedesh is proved to be so by its very name, with which it agrees that it was a Levitical city and a consecrated asylum. Accordingly it formed the *rendezvous* of Zebulon and Naphtali under Barak and Deborah. Mahanaim was the place of a theophany, from which it had its name. It was also a Levitical city, and Cant. vi. 13 alludes to the "dance of Mahanaim," which was probably such a festal dance as took place at Shiloh (Jud. xxi. 21). As a holy place the town was the seat of Ishbosheth's kingdom, and the headquarters of David's host during the revolt of Absalom. Tabor, on the frontiers of Zebulon and Issachar, seems to be the mountain alluded to in Deut. xxxiii. 18, 19, as the sanctuary of these tribes, and it appears along with Mizpah, as a seat of degenerate priests, in Hos. v. 1. The northern Mizpah is identical with Ramoth Gilead and with the sanctuary of Jacob (Gen. xxxi. 45 *sq.*).

This different and freer conception of the means of access to God, the desire which it embodies to realise Jehovah's presence in acts of worship, not at rare intervals only but in every concern of life, cannot be viewed as a mere heathenish corruption of the Levitical system. This fact comes out most clearly in the point which brings out the contrast of the two systems in its completest form.

In the traditional popular Jehovah-worship, to slay an ox or a sheep for food was a sacrificial act, and the flesh of the victim was not lawful food unless the blood or life had been poured out before Jehovah. The currency of this view is presupposed in the Pentateuchal legislation. Thus in Lev. xvii. it appears as a perpetual statute that no domestic animal can be lawfully slain for food, unless it be presented as a peace-offering before the central sanctuary, and its blood sprinkled on the altar. One has no right to slay an animal on other conditions. The life, which lies in the blood, comes from God and belongs to Him. The man who does not recognise this fact, but eats the flesh with the blood, "hath shed blood, and shall be cut off from his people" (ver. 4; comp. Gen. ix. 4). In Deuteronomy this principle is pre-supposed, but relaxed by a formal statute. Those who do not live beside the sanctuary may eat flesh without a sacrificial act, if they simply pour out the blood upon the ground (Deut. xii. 20 *sq.*). The old rule, it would seem, might still hold good for every animal slain within reach of the holy place. Now, under the conditions of Eastern life, beef and mutton are not everyday food. In Canaan, as among the Arabs at this day, milk is the usual diet (Prov. xxvii. 26, 27; Jud. iv. 19). The slaughter of a victim for food marks a festal occasion, and the old Hebrew principle modified in Deuteronomy means that all feasts are religious, that sacred occasions and occasions of natural joy and festivity are identical.[1] Under

[1] Except at a feast, or to entertain a guest, or in sacrifice before a local

the full Levitical system this principle was obsolete, or at least could assert itself only in the vicinity of the sanctuary, and in connection with the three great festive gatherings at Passover, Pentecost, and the Feast of Tabernacles. But in the actual history of the nation the principle was not yet obsolete. Thus in 1 Sam. xiv., when the people, in their fierce hunger after the battle of Michmash, fly on the spoil and, slaying beasts on the ground, eat them with the blood—*i.e.* as we see from Lev. xvii., without offering the blood to Jehovah —Saul rebukes their transgression, erects a rude altar in the form of a great stone, and orders the people to kill their victims there. A feast and a sacrifice are still identical in the Book of Proverbs, which speaks the ordinary language of the people. Compare Prov. xv. 17 with xvii. 1, and note the inducement offered to the foolish young man in chap. vii. 14. In Hosea ii. 11 all mirth is represented as connected with religious ceremonies. But the most conclusive passage is Hosea ix. 3 *sq.*, where the prophet predicts that in the Exile all the food of the people shall be unclean, because sacrifice cannot be performed beyond the land of Israel. They shall eat, as it were, the unclean bread of mourners, " because their necessary food shall not be presented in the house of Jehovah." In other words, all animal food not presented at the altar is unclean ; the whole life of the people becomes unclean when they leave the land of Jehovah to dwell in an "unclean land" (Amos vii. 17). We see from this usage how closely the practice of sacrifice in every corner of the land was inter-

shrine, the Bedouin tastes no meat but the flesh of the gazelle or other game. This throws light on Deut. xii. 16, 22, which shows that in old Israel game was the only meat not eaten sacrificially. That flesh was not eaten every day even by wealthy people appears very clearly from Nathan's parable and from the Book of Ruth. The wealthy man, like the Arab sheikh, ate the same fare as his workmen. According to *MI Noctes* (Calcutta edition, ii. 276), eating flesh is one of the three elements of high enjoyment.

The rule that all legitimate slaughter is sacrificial is not confined to old Israel. Distinct traces of the same view survived in Arabia down to the time of Mohammed ; see Wellhausen, *Arab. Heidenthum*, p. 114.

woven with the whole life of the nation, and how absolute
was the contrast between the traditional conception of sacrificial intercourse between Jehovah and His people and that
which is expressed in the Levitical law. But we see also
that the popular conception is not a new thing superadded to
the Levitical system from a foreign source, but an old traditional principle of Jehovah-worship prior to the law of
Deuteronomy. When did this principle take root in the
nation? Not surely in the forty years of wandering, when,
according to the express testimony of Amos v. 25, sacrifices
and offerings were not presented to Jehovah.

But let this pass in the meantime. We are not now
concerned to trace the history of the ordinances of worship
in Israel, but only to establish a clear conception of the
essential difference between the old popular worship and the
finished Levitical system. The very foundation of revealed
religion is the truth that man does not first seek and find
God, but that God in His gracious condescension seeks out
man, and gives him such an approach to Himself as man
could not enjoy without the antecedent act of divine self-
communication. The characteristic mark of each dispensation of revealed religion lies in the provision which it makes
for the acceptable approach of the worshipper to his God.
Under the Levitical dispensation all approach to God is
limited to the central sanctuary, and passes of necessity
through the channel of the priestly mediation of the sons of
Aaron. The worshipping subject is, strictly speaking, the
nation of Israel as a unity, and the function of worship is
discharged on behalf of the nation by the priests of God's
choice. The religion of the individual rests on this basis. It
is only the maintenance of the representative national service
of the sanctuary which gives to every Israelite the assurance
that he stands under the protection of the national covenant
with Jehovah, and enables him to enjoy a measure of such

personal spiritual fellowship with God as can never be lacking in true religion.   But the faith with which the Israelite
rested on God's redeeming love had little direct opportunity
to express itself in visible acts of homage.   The sanctuary
was seldom accessible, and in daily life the Hebrew believer
could only follow with an inward longing and spiritual
sympathy the national homage which continually ascended
on behalf of himself and all the people of God in the stated
ritual of the Temple.   Hence that eager thirst for participation in the services of the sanctuary which is expressed in
Psalms like the forty-second: " My soul thirsteth for God the
living God; when shall I come and appear before the face of
God ? "   " Send forth thy light and thy truth; let them guide
me; let them bring me to thy holy mountain, even unto thy
dwelling-place."   This thirst, seldom satiated, which fills the
Psalter with expressions of passionate fervour in describing
the joys of access to God's house, was an inseparable feature
of the Levitical system.   After the Exile, the necessity for
more frequent acts of overt religion was partly supplied by
the synagogues; but these, in so far as they provided a sort
of worship without sacrifice, were already an indication that
the dispensation was inadequate and must pass away.   All
these experiences are in the strongest contrast to the popular
religious life before the Captivity.   Then the people found
Jehovah, and rejoiced before Him, in every corner of the
land, and on every occasion of life.

This contrast within the Old Testament dispensation presents no difficulty if we can affirm that the popular religion was
altogether false, that it gave no true access to Jehovah, and
must be set on one side in describing the genuine religious
life of Israel.   But it is a very different thing if we find that
the true believers of ancient Israel—prophets like Samuel,
righteous men like David—placed themselves on the standpoint of the local sanctuaries, and framed their own lives on

the assumption that God is indeed to be found in service non-Levitical. If the whole Pentateuchal system is really as old as Moses, the popular worship has none of the marks of a religion of revelation; it sought access to God in services to which He had attached no promise. And yet we shall find, in the next Lecture, that for long centuries after Moses, all the true religion of Israel moved in forms which departed from the first axioms of Levitical service, and rested on the belief that Jehovah may be acceptably worshipped under the popular system, if only the corruptions of that system are guarded against. It was not on the basis of the Pentateuchal theory of worship that God's grace ruled in Israel during the age of the Judges and the Kings, and it was not on that basis that the prophets taught.

LECTURE IX

THE LAW AND THE HISTORY OF ISRAEL BEFORE
THE EXILE

In the last Lecture I tried to exhibit to you the outlines of
the popular worship of the mass of Israel in the period before
the Captivity, as sketched in the Books of Kings and in the
contemporary prophets. In drawing this sketch I directed
your attention particularly to two points. On the one hand,
the popular religion has a basis in common with the Pentateuchal system: both alike acknowledge Jehovah as the God
of Israel, who brought His people out of the land of Egypt;
both recognise that Israel's homage and worship are due to
Jehovah, and that the felicity of the people in the land of
Canaan is dependent on His favour. But along with this we
found that between the popular worship and the system
of the Pentateuch there is a remarkable contrast. In the
Levitical system access to God is only to be attained through
the mediation of the Aaronic priests at the central sanctuary.
The whole worship of Israel is narrowed to the sanctuary of
the ark, and there the priests of God's consecration conduct
that representative service which is in some sense the worship
of the whole people. The ordinary Israelite meets with God
in the sanctuary only on special occasions, and during the
great part of his life must be content to stand afar off, following with distant sympathy that continual service which is

going on for him at Jerusalem in the hands of the Temple priests. In the popular religion, on the contrary, the need of constant access to God is present to every Israelite. Opportunities of worship exist in every corner of the land; and every occasion of importance, whether for the life of the individual or for the family, village, or clan, is celebrated by some sacrificial rite at the local sanctuary. We saw, further, that, as these two types of religion are separated by a fundamental difference, so also it is impossible to suppose that the popular worship is merely a corruption of the Levitical theory under the influence of Canaanite idolatry. It is indeed very natural to suppose that the system of the Law, the distance that it constitutes between Jehovah and the ordinary worshipper, was too abstract for the mass of Israel. It may well be thought that the mass of the people in those days could not be satisfied with the kind of representative worship conducted on their behalf in the one sanctuary, and that they felt a desire to come themselves into immediate contact with the Deity in personal acts of service embodied in sacrifice. But if the Levitical theory was the starting-point it is pretty clear that this would rather lead the unspiritual part of Israel to worship other gods side by side with Jehovah, local and inferior deities, just as in the Roman Catholic Church the distance between God and the ordinary layman leads the mass of the people to approach the saints and address themselves to them as more accessible helpers. But that is not what we find in Israel. We do not find that a sense of the inaccessibility of Jehovah, as represented in the system of the Pentateuch, led Israel for the most part to serve other gods, although that also happened in special circumstances. They held that Jehovah Himself could be approached and acceptably worshipped at a multitude of sanctuaries not acknowledged in the system of the Law, and at which, according to that system, God had given no promise whatever to meet with His people. It can hardly be questioned that the idea of meeting with Jehovah at the local sanctuaries and of doing acceptable service to Him there had survived from a time previous to the enactment of the law of the middle books of the Pentateuch. This is confirmed by the fact that the lineaments of the popular religion as displayed in the historical books have much that is akin to the worship of the patriarchs, and in particular that many of the sanctuaries of Israel were venerated as patriarchal shrines.

Nevertheless, if Moses left the whole Levitical system as a public code, specially entrusted to the priests and leaders of the nation, that code must have influenced at least the *élite* of Israel. Its provisions must have been kept alive at the central sanctuary, and, in particular, the revealing God, who does not contradict Himself, must have based upon the law His further communications to the people, and His judgment upon their sins spoken through His prophets. He cannot have stamped with His approval a popular system entirely ignoring the fundamental conditions of His intercourse with Israel. And the history must bear traces of this. God's word does not return unto Him void without accomplishing that which He pleaseth, and succeeding in the thing whereto He sends it (Isa. lv. 11).

Now it is certain that the first sustained and thorough attempt to put down the popular worship, and establish an order of religion conformed to the written law, was under King Josiah. An essay in the same direction had been made by Hezekiah at the close of the eighth century B.C. (2 Kings xviii. 4, 22). Of the details of Hezekiah's reformation we know little. It was followed by a violent and bloody reaction under his successor Manasseh, and in Josiah's time the whole work had to be done again from the beginning. Hezekiah evidently acted in harmony with Isaiah and his fellow-prophets ; but neither in the history nor in their writings is

anything said of the written law as the rule and standard of
reformation. In the case of Josiah it was otherwise. The
reformation in his eighteenth year (621 B.C.) was based on
the Book of the Law found in the Temple, and was carried
out in pursuance of a solemn covenant to obey the law, made
by the king and the people in the house of Jehovah. This
is an act strictly parallel to the later covenant and reformation under Ezra. But it did not amount, like Ezra's reformation, to a complete establishment of the whole ritual system
of the Pentateuch. The Book of Nehemiah expressly says
as much with respect to the Feast of Tabernacles. And the
same fact comes out in regard to the order of the priestly
ministrations at the Temple. For, while Josiah put to death
the priests of the high places of Ephraim, he brought the
priests of the Judæan high places to Jerusalem, where they
were not allowed to minister at the altar, but " ate unleavened
bread in the midst of their brethren" (2 Kings xxiii. 8, 9).
The reference here is to the unleavened bread of the Temple
oblations, which, on the Levitical law, was given to the sons
of Aaron, to be eaten in the court of the sanctuary (Lev. vi.
14-18; Num. xviii. 9). It appears, then, that the priests of
the local high places were recognised as brethren of the
Temple priests, and admitted to a share in the sacred dues,
though not to full altar privileges. This was unquestionably
a grave Levitical irregularity, for, though it appears from
Ezek. xliv. 10 *sqq.* that the priests of the high places were
Levites, it is not for a moment to be supposed that they were
all sons of Aaron (compare Neh. vii. 63 *sq.*). This point
will come up again along with other indications that the
worship in the Temple at Jerusalem was not established by
Josiah in full conformity with the Levitical system. All
that I ask you to carry with you at present is that Josiah's
reformation, although based upon the Book, and explicitly
taking it as the standard, did not go the whole length of that

17

Pentateuchal system which we now possess. In truth, when we compare the reformation of Josiah, as set forth in Second Kings, with what is written in the Pentateuch, we observe that everything that Josiah acted upon is found written in one or other part of Deuteronomy. So far as the history goes, there is no proof that his "Book of the Covenant" was anything more than the law of Deuteronomy, which, in its very form, appears to have once been a separate volume.[1]

No one can read 2 Kings xxii. xxiii. without observing how entirely novel was the order of things which Josiah introduced. Before the Book of the Law was read to him, Josiah was interested in holy things, and engaged in the work of restoring the Temple. But the necessity for a thorough overturn of the popular sanctuaries came on him as a thing entirely new. It is plain, too, that he had to consider established privileges and a certain legitimate status on the part of the priests of the high places. There was in Judæa a

---

[1] Critics distinguish in Deuteronomy the legislative code (chaps. xii.-xxvi.) and the framework, which appears to contain pieces by more than one hand. As the book now stands the laws are preceded by two introductory discourses, Deut. i. 1-iv. 43, Deut. v.-xi. To the second of these is prefixed a title, chap. iv. 44-49, which is evidently meant to cover the code of chaps. xii.-xxvi., while again the verses xxvi. 16-19 form a sort of subscription or colophon to the code. In all probability, therefore, the code once stood, along with the second introduction, in a separate book corresponding to Deut. iv. 44-xxvi. 19, to which Kuenen would add, as a sort of appendix from the hand of the original author, xxvii. 9, 10, ch. xxviii. (*Onderzoek*, i. 111, 122). There is no evidence that Josiah had more than this book, and it is by no means certain that the code, when it fell into his hands, was already provided with the parenetic introduction and appendices ; see Wellhausen, *Composition* (1889), p. 189 *sqq.*, p. 352. Even the Fathers identify the book found in the Temple with Deuteronomy. So Jerome, *Adv. Jovin.* i. 5 ; Chrysostom, *Hom. in Mat.* ix. p. 135 B. The relation of Josiah's reformation to Deuteronomy may be shown thus :—

2 Kings xxiii.	3-6	.	.	.	.	Deut.	xii. 2.
,,	,,	7				,,	xxiii. 17, 18.
,,	,,	8, 9	.	.	.	,,	xviii. 6-8.
,,	,,	10	.	.	.	,,	xviii. 10.
,,	,,	11	.	.	.	,,	xvii. 3.
,,	,,	14	.	.	.	,,	xvi. 21, 22.
,,	,,	21	.	.	.	,,	xvi. 5.
,,	,,	24	.	.	.	,,	xviii. 11.

class of irregular priests called *Chemarim,* instituted by royal authority (A. V. *idolatrous priests,* 2 Kings xxiii. 5), whom he simply put down. But the priests of the popular high places were recognised priests of Jehovah, and, instead of being punished as apostates, they received support and a certain status in the Temple (xxiii. 9). We now see the full significance of the toleration of the high places by the earlier kings of Judah. They were not known to be any breach of the religious constitution of Israel. Even the Temple priests knew of no ordinance condemning them. The high places were not interfered with by King Jehoash when his conduct was entirely directed by the high priest Jehoiada (2 Kings xii. 2, 3). Yet Jehoiada had every motive for suppressing the local sanctuaries, which diminished the dues of the central altar, and he could hardly have failed to move in this direction if he had had the law at his back.

These facts do not mean, merely, that the law was disobeyed. They imply that the complete system of the Pentateuch was not known in the period of the kings of Judah, even as the theoretical constitution of Israel. No one, even among those most interested, shows the least consciousness that the Temple and its priesthood have an exclusive claim on all the worship of Israel. And the local worship, which proceeds on a diametrically opposite theory, is acknowledged as a part of the established ordinances of the land.

Here, then, the question rises, Was the founding of the Temple on Zion undertaken as part of an attempt to give practical force to the Levitical system? Was this, at least, an effort to displace the traditional religion and establish the ordinances of the Pentateuch? The whole life of Solomon answers this question in the negative. His royal state, of which the Temple and its service were a part, was never conformed to the law. He not only did not abolish the local sanctuaries, but built new shrines, which stood till the time

of Josiah, for the gods of the foreign wives whom, like his
father David (2 Sam. iii. 3), he married against the Pentateuchal law (1 Kings xi.; 2 Kings xxiii. 13). And when the
Book of Deuteronomy describes what a king of Israel must
not be, it reproduces line for line the features of the court
of Solomon (Deut. xvii. 16 *sq.*). Even the ordinances of
Solomon's Temple were not Levitically correct. The two
brazen pillars which stood at the porch (1 Kings vii. 21)
were not different from the forbidden *maççēba*, or from the
twin pillars that stood in front of Phœnician and Syrian
sanctuaries;[1] and 1 Kings ix. 25 can hardly bear any other
sense than that the king officiated at the altar in person
three times a year. That implies an entire neglect, on his
part, of the strict law of separation between the legitimate
priesthood and laymen ; but the same disregard of the exclusive sanctity of the Temple priesthood, and of that twofold
cordon of Aaronites and Levites which the law demands to
protect the Temple from profanation, reappears in later times,
and indeed was a standing feature in the whole history of
Solomon's Temple. The prophet Ezekiel, writing after the
reforms of King Josiah, and alluding to the way in which the
Temple service was carried on in his own time, complains
that uncircumcised foreigners were appointed as keepers of
Jehovah's charge in His sanctuary (Ezek. xliv. 6 *sq.*).[2] Who

[1] Two huge pillars stood in the *propylæa* of the temple of Hierapolis
(Lucian, *De Syria Dea*, chap. 16, 28), and in front of the temple at Paphos,
of which we have representations on coins (see *Rel. of the Semites*, p. 468).
Similarly Strabo (iii. 5. 5) tells us that in the temple of Gades there
were brazen columns eight cubits high. The context shows that here also a
pair of columns is meant.

[2] This passage is so important that I give it in a translation, slightly corrected after the versions in verses 7, 8. The corrections are obvious, and
have been made also by Smend (*Der Prophet Ezechiel erklärt*, Leipzig, 1880).

Ezek. xliv. 6. O house of Israel ! Have done with all your abominations, (7) in that ye bring in foreigners uncircumcised in heart and flesh to
be in my sanctuary, polluting my house, when ye offer my bread, the fat and
the blood ; and so ye break my covenant in addition to all your abominations,
(8) and keep not the charge of my holy things, but appoint them as keepers

were these foreigners, uncircumcised in flesh and uncircumcised in heart, by whom the sanctity of the Temple was
habitually profaned ? The history still provides details which
go far to answer this question.

There was one important body of foreigners in the service
of the kings of Judah from the time of David downwards,
viz. the Philistine bodyguard (2 Sam. xv. 18; 2 Kings i. 38).
These foreign soldiers were a sort of janissaries attached to
the person of the sovereign, after the common fashion of
Eastern monarchs, who deem themselves most secure when
surrounded by a band of followers uninfluenced by family
connections with the people of the land. The constitution of
the bodyguard appears to have remained unchanged to the
fall of the Judæan state. The prophet Zephaniah, writing
under King Josiah, still speaks of men connected with the
court, who were clad in foreign garb and leaped over the
threshold. To leap over the threshold of the sanctuary is a
Philistine custom (1 Sam. v. 5); and when the prophet adds
that these Philistines of the court fill their master's house

of my charge in my sanctuary. Therefore, (9) thus saith the Lord, No
foreigner uncircumcised in heart and flesh shall enter my sanctuary—no
foreigner whatever, who is among the children of Israel.   (10) But the
Levites, because they departed from me when Israel went astray, when they
went astray from me after their idols, even they shall bear their guilt, (11)
and be ministers in my sanctuary, officers at the gates of the house, and
ministers of the house ; it is they who shall kill the burnt-offering and the
sacrifice for the people, and it is they who shall stand before them to minister
unto them.   (12) Because they ministered unto them before their idols, and
were a stumbling-block of guilt to the house of Israel, therefore I swear concerning them, saith the Lord God, that they shall bear their guilt, (13) and
shall not draw near to me to do the office of a priest to me, or to touch any
of my holy things—the most holy things ; but they shall bear their shame
and their abominations which they have done.   (14) And I will make them
keepers of the charge of the house for all the service thereof, and for all that
is to be done about it.   (15) But the Levite priests, the sons of Zadok, who
kept the charge of my sanctuary when the children of Israel went astray from
me—they shall come near unto me to minister unto me, and they shall stand
before me to offer unto me the fat and the blood, saith the Lord God. They
shall enter into my sanctuary and approach my table, ministering unto me,
and keep my charge.

with violence and fraud, we recognise the familiar characters
of Oriental janissaries (Zeph. i. 8, 9).

The foreign guards, whom we thus see to have continued
to the days of Zephaniah, had duties in the Temple identical
with those of Ezekiel's uncircumcised foreigners.   For the
guard accompanied the king when he visited the sanctuary
(1 Kings xiv. 28), and the Temple gate leading to the palace
was called "the gate of the foot-guards" (2 Kings xi. 19).
Nay, so intimate was the connection between the Temple and
the palace that the royal bodyguard were also the Temple
guards, going in and out in courses every week (2 Kings xi.
4 *sqq.*).   It was the centurions of the guard who aided Jehoiada
in setting King Jehoash on the throne ; and 2 Kings xi. 11,
14, pictures the coronation of the young king while he stood
by a pillar, "according to custom," surrounded by the foreign
bodyguard, who formed a circle about the altar and the front
of the shrine, in the holiest part of the Temple court (compare Joel ii. 17).[1]   Thus it appears that as long as Solomon's

-----

[1] In 2 Sam. xv. 18 the foreign guards consist of the Cherethites, the
Pelethites, and the Gittites, or men of Gath.   More commonly we read of
the Cherethites and the Pelethites, but in 2 Sam. xx. 23 the *Kethîb* has "the
Carite and the Pelethite."   The Carites reappear in 2 Kings xi. 4 (Hebrew
and R. V.) as forming part of the guard at the coronation of King Jehoash.
The Cherethites lived on the southern border of Canaan (1 Sam. xxx. 14),
and seem to have been reckoned as Philistines (Zeph. ii. 5 ; Ezek. xxv. 16) ;
this name and that of the Carites have been plausibly conjectured to indicate
that the Philistines, who were immigrants into Canaan from Caphtor (Amos
ix. 7), which seems to be a place over the sea (Jer. xlvii. 4, R. V.), were
originally connected with Crete and Caria.   Pelethite is probably a mere
variation of the name Philistine.

There is, I think, good ground for supposing that the slaughtering of
sacrifices, which Ezekiel expressly assigns in future to the Levites, was
formerly the work of the guards.   It was the king who provided the ordinary Temple sacrifices (2 Chron. viii. 13, xxxi. 3 ; Ezek. xlv. 17), and there
can be little doubt that the animals killed for the royal table were usually
offered as peace offerings at the Temple (Deut. xii. 21).   In Saul's time, at
least, an unclean person could not sit at the royal table, which implies that
the food was sacrificial (1 Sam. xx. 26 ; Lev. vii. 20 ; Deut. xii. 22).   Now
the Hebrew name for "captain of the guard" is "chief slaughterer" (*rab
hattabbâchîm*)—an expression which, so far as one can judge from Syriac and
Arabic as well as Hebrew, can only mean slaughterer of cattle (comp. מטבח

Temple stood, and even after the reforms of Josiah, the function of keeping the ward of the sanctuary, which by Levitical
law is strictly confined to the house of Levi, on pain of
death to the stranger who comes near (Num. iii. 38), devolved
upon uncircumcised foreigners, who, according to the law,
ought never to have been permitted to set foot within the
courts of the Temple. From this fact the inference is inevitable, that under the first Temple the principles of Levitical
sanctity were never recognised or enforced. Even the high
priests had no conception of the fundamental importance
which the middle books of the Pentateuch attach to the
concentric circles of ritual holiness around and within the
sanctuary, an importance to be measured by the consideration
that the atoning ritual on which Jehovah's forgiving grace
depends presupposes the accurate observance of every legal
precaution against profanation of the holy things. This being
so, we cannot be surprised to find that the priests of the
Temple were equally neglectful, or rather equally ignorant, of
the correct system of atoning ordinances, which forms the
very centre of the Levitical Law, and to which all other
ordinances of sanctity are subservient. The Levitical sin
offering and the trespass offering are not once mentioned
before the Captivity.[1] On the other hand, we read of an
established custom in the time of the high priest Jehoiada
that sin money and trespass money were given to the priests
(2 Kings xii. 16; comp. Hosea iv. 8, Amos ii. 8). This
usage, from a Levitical point of view, can be regarded as

in a Carthaginian inscription *C. I. S.* No. 175, 1, and מבח, *ibid.* 237, 5;
238, 2, *etc.*). So the bodyguard were also the royal butchers, an occupation
not deemed unworthy of warriors in early times. Eurip. *Electra*, 815;
Odys. A. 108. In Lev. i. 5, 6 it is assumed that every man kills his own
sacrifice, and so still in the Arabian desert every person knows how to kill
and dress a sheep.

[1] In the older books the atoning function of sacrifice is not attached to a
particular class of oblation, but belongs to all offerings, to *zebach* and *mincha*
(1 Sam. iii. 14, xxvi. 19), and still more to the whole burnt offering (Micah
iv. 6, 7; comp. 1 Sam. vii. 9, Job i. 5).

nothing but a gross case of simony, the secularising for the advantage of the priests of one of the most holy and sacred ordinances of the Levitical system. Yet this we find fixed and established, not in a time of national declension, but in the days of the reforming king and high priest who extirpated the worship of Baal.

In truth, the first Temple had not that ideal position which the law assigns to the central sanctuary. It did not profess to be the one lawful centre of all worship, and its pre-eminence was not wholly due to the ark, but lay very much in the circumstance that it was the sanctuary of the kings of Judah, as Bethel, according to Amos vii. 13, was a royal chapel of the monarchs of Ephraim. The Temple was the king's shrine; therefore his bodyguard were its natural servants, and the sovereign exercised a control over all its ordinances, such as the Levitical legislation does not contemplate and could not approve. We find that King Jehoash introduced changes into the destination of the Temple revenues. In his earlier years the rule was that the priests received pecuniary dues and gifts of various kinds so different from those detailed in the Pentateuch, that it is impossible for us to explain each one; but, such as they were, the priests appropriated them subject to an obligation to maintain the fabric of the Temple. King Jehoash, however, found that while the priests pocketed their dues nothing was done for the repair of the Temple, and he therefore ordained that all moneys brought into the Temple should be paid over for the repairs of the house, with the exception of the trespass and sin money, which remained the perquisite of the priests. Such interference with the sacred dues is inconceivable under the Levitical system, which strictly regulates the destination of every offering.

But, indeed, the kings of Judah regarded the treasury of the Temple as a sort of reserve fund available for political purposes, and Asa and Hezekiah drew upon this source when their own treasury was exhausted (1 Kings xv. 18 ; 2 Kings xviii. 15).

With this picture before us, we are no longer surprised to find that the priest Urijah, or Uriah, whom the prophet Isaiah took with him as a faithful witness to record (Isa. viii. 2), co-operated with King Ahaz in substituting a new altar, on a pattern sent from Damascus, for the old brazen altar of Solomon, and in general allowed the king to regulate the altar service as he pleased (2 Kings xvi. 10 *sq.*). The brazen altar, which, according to the Book of Numbers, even the Levites could not touch without danger of death, was reserved for the king to inquire by.

The force of these facts lies in the circumstance that they cannot be explained as mere occasional deviations from Levitical orthodoxy. The admission of uncircumcised strangers as ministers in the sanctuary is no breach of a spiritual precept which the hard heart of Israel was unable to follow, but of a ceremonial ordinance adapted to the imperfect and unspiritual state of the nation. An interest in correct ritual is found in the least spiritual religions, and there is ample proof that it was not lacking in Israel, even in the barbarous times of the Judges. The system of ceremonial sanctity was calculated to give such *éclat* to the Temple and its priesthood that there was every motive for maintaining it in force if it was known at all. But in reality it was violated in every point. All the divergences from Levitical ritual lie in the same direction. The sharp line of distinction between laymen's privileges and priestly functions laid down in the Law has its *rationale* in the theory and practice of atonement. In the Temple we find irregular atonements, a lack of precise grades of holiness, incomplete recognition of the priestly prerogative, subordination of the priesthood to the palace carried so far that Abiathar is deposed from the priesthood, and Zadok, who was not of the old priestly family of Shiloh, set in his place, by a mere fiat of King Solomon.[1] And, along with this want of clear definition in the inner circles of ceremonial holiness, we naturally find that the exclusive sanctity of the nation was not understood in a Levitical sense ; for not only Solomon but David himself intermarried with heathen nations. Nay, Absalom, the son of a Syrian princess, was the recognised heir to the throne, which implies that his mother was regarded as David's principal wife. All these facts hang together ; they show that the priests of the Temple, and righteous kings like David, were as ignorant of the Levitical theory of sanctity as the mass of the vulgar and the unrighteous kings.

The Temple of Solomon never stood forth, in contrast to the popular high places, as the seat of the Levitical system, holding up in their purity the typical ordinances of atonement which the popular worship ignored. The very features which separate the religion of the ritual law from the traditional worship of the high places are those which the guardians of the Temple systematically ignored.

Let us now go back beyond the age of Solomon to the

---

[1] According to 1 Sam. ii. 27-36 the whole clan or "father's house" of Eli, the family which received God's revelation in Egypt with a promise of everlasting priesthood, is to lose its prerogative and sink to an inferior position, in which its survivors shall be glad to crouch before the new high priest for a place in one of the inferior priestly guilds which may yield them a livelihood. As 1 Kings ii. 27 regards this prophecy as fulfilled in the substitution of Zadok for Abiathar, it is plain that the former did not belong to the high-priestly family chosen in the wilderness. That his genealogy is traced to Aaron and Eleazar in 1 Chron. vi. 50 *sq.* does not disprove this, for among all Semites membership of a guild is figured as sonship. Thus in the time of the Chronicles sons of Eleazar and Ithamar respectively would mean no more than the higher and lower guilds of priests. The common theory that the house of Eli was not in the original line of Eleazar and Phinehas is inconsistent with Num. xxv. 13 compared with 1 Sam. ii. 30. The Chronicler places Ahimelech son of Abiathar in the lower priesthood of Ithamar (1 Chron. xxiv. 3, 6), but Abiathar himself is not connected with Ithamar by a genealogical line. The deposition of the father reduces the son to the lower guild.

period of the Judges, and the age of national revival which
followed under Samuel, Saul, and David. We need not again
dwell on the fact that the whole religion of the time of the
Judges was Levitically false. Even the divinely chosen
leaders of the nation knew not the law (*supra*, p. 235
sq.). What is important for our argument is to observe that
breaches of the law were not confined to times of rebellion
against Jehovah. From the standpoint of the Pentateuchal
ritual, Israel's repentance was itself illegal in form. Acts of
true worship, which Jehovah accepted as the tokens of a
penitent heart and answered by deeds of deliverance, were
habitually associated with illegal sanctuaries. At Bochim
the people wept at God's rebuke and sacrificed to the Lord
(Judges ii. 5). Deborah and Barak opened their campaign
at the sanctuary of Kedesh. Jehovah Himself commanded
Gideon to build an altar and do sacrifice at Ophrah, and this
sanctuary still existed in the days of the historian (Judges
vi. 24). Jephthah spake all his words " before the Lord " at
Mizpah or Ramoth Gilead, the ancient sanctuary of Jacob,
when he went forth in the spirit of the Lord to overthrow
the Ammonites (Judges xi. 11, 29 ; Gen. xxxi. 45 *sqq.*), and his
vow before the campaign was a vow to do sacrifice in Mizpah.

We are accustomed to speak of the sacrifices of Gideon
and Manoah as exceptional, and, no doubt, they were so if
our standard is the law of the Pentateuch. But in that case
all true religion in that period was exceptional; for all God's
acts of grace mentioned in the Book of Judges, all His calls
to repentance, and all the ways in which He appears from
time to time to support His people, and to show Himself their
living God, ready to forgive in spite of their disobedience, are
connected with this same local worship. The call to repentance is never a call to put aside the local sanctuaries and
worship only before the ark at Shiloh. On the contrary, the
narrator assumes, without question, the standpoint of the

popular religion, and never breathes a doubt that Jehovah was acceptably worshipped in the local shrines. In truth, no other judgment on the case was possible ; for through all this period Jehovah's gracious dealings with His people expressed His acceptance of the local worship in unambiguous language. If the Pentateuchal programme of worship and the rules which it lays down for the administration of the dispensation of grace existed in these days, they were at least absolutely suspended. It was not according to the Law that Jehovah administered His grace to Israel during the period of the Judges.

Nevertheless the fundamental requisites for a practical observance of the Pentateuchal worship existed in those days. The ark was settled at Shiloh ; a legitimate priesthood ministered before it. There is no question that the house of Eli were the ancient priesthood of the ark. It was to the clan, or *father's house*, of Eli, according to 1 Sam. ii. 27 *sq.*, that Jehovah appeared in Egypt, choosing him as His priest from all the tribes of Israel. The priesthood was legitimate, and so was the sanctuary of Shiloh, which Jeremiah calls Jehovah's place, where He set His name at the first (Jer. vii. 12). Here therefore, if anywhere in Israel, the law must have had its seat ; and the worship of Shiloh must have preserved a memorial of the Mosaic ritual.

We have an amount of detailed information as to the ritual of Shiloh which shows the importance attached to points of ceremonial religion. Shiloh was visited by pilgrims from the surrounding country of Ephraim, not three times a year according to the Pentateuchal law, but at an annual feast. This appears to have been a vintage feast, like the Pentateuchal Feast of Tabernacles, for it was accompanied by dances in the vineyards (Judges xxi. 21), and, according to the correct rendering of 1 Sam. i. 20, 21, it took place when the new year came in, that is, at the close of the

agricultural year, which ended with the ingathering of the
vintage (Exod. xxxiv. 22). It had not a strictly national
character, for in Judges xxi. 19 it appears to be only locally
known, and to have the character of a village festival. Indeed
a quite similar vintage feast was observed at the Canaanite
city of Shechem (Judges ix. 27).[1]

There was, however, a regular sacrifice performed by each
worshipper in addition to any vow he might have made (1
Sam. i. 21), and the proper due to be paid to the priests on
these offerings was an important question. The great offence
of Eli's sons was that they "knew not Jehovah and the
priests' dues from the people." They made irregular ex-
actions, and, in particular, would not burn the fat of the
sacrifice till they had secured a portion of uncooked meat (1
Sam. ii. 12 *sq.* R. V., marg.). Under the Levitical ordinance
this claim was perfectly regular ; the worshipper handed over
the priest's portion of the flesh along with the fat, and part of
the altar ceremony was to wave it before Jehovah (Lev. vii.
30 *sq.*, x. 15). But at Shiloh the claim was viewed as illegal
and highly wicked. It caused men to abhor Jehovah's offering, and the greed which Eli's sons displayed in this matter is
given as the ground of the prophetic rejection of the whole
clan of priests of Shiloh (1 Sam. ii. 17, 29).

The importance attached to these details shows how essential to the religion of those days was the observance of all
points of established ritual. But the ritual was not that of

---

[1] 1 Sam. i. 20, 21. "When the new year came round, Hannah conceived and bare a son, and named him . . . and Elkanah went up with his
whole household to sacrifice to Jehovah the yearly sacrifice and his vow."
The date of the new year belongs to the last of this series of events. Compare Wellhausen, *Prolegomena*, pp. 95, 109, and Driver's notes on the passage.
The autumn feast was also the great feast at Jerusalem (1 Kings viii. 2),
and in the Northern Kingdom (1 Kings xii. 32).

In Judges ix. 27 read, "They trode the grapes and made *hillûlîm* (a
sacred offering in praise of God from the fruits of the earth, Lev. xix. 24),
and went into the house of their god and feasted," etc.

the Levitical law.   Nay, when we look at the worship of
Shiloh more closely, we find glaring departures from the very
principles of the Pentateuchal sanctuary.   The ark stood, not
in the tabernacle, but in a Temple with doorposts and folding-
doors, which were thrown open during the day (1 Sam. i. 9,
iii. 15).   In the evening a lamp burned in the Temple (1 Sam.
iii. 3), but contrary to the Levitical prescription (Exod. xxvii.
21 ; Lev. xxiv. 3) the light was not kept up all night, but was
allowed to go out after the ministers of the Temple lay down
to sleep.   Access to the Temple was not guarded on rules of
Levitical sanctity.   According to 1 Sam. iii. 3, Samuel, as a
servant of the sanctuary who had special charge of the doors
(ver. 15), actually slept " in the temple of Jehovah where
the ark of God was."   To our English translators this statement seemed so incredible, that they have ventured to change
the sense against the rules of the language.   One can hardly
wonder at them ; for, according to the Law, the place of the
ark could be entered only by the high priest once a year, and
with special atoning services.   And, to make the thing more
surprising, Samuel was not of priestly family.   His father
was an Ephrathite or Ephraimite (1 Sam. i. 1, R. V.), and he
himself came to the Temple by a vow of his mother to dedicate
him to Jehovah.   By the Pentateuchal law such a vow could
not make Samuel a priest.   But here it is taken for granted
that he becomes a priest at once.   As a child he ministers
before Jehovah, wearing the ephod which the law confines to
the high priest, and not only this, but the high priestly mantle
(*me'îl*, A. V. coat, 1 Sam. ii. 18, 19).   And priest as well as
prophet Samuel continued all his life, sacrificing habitually
at a variety of sanctuaries.   These irregularities are sufficiently startling.   They profane the holy ordinances, which,
under the Law, are essential to the legitimate sanctuary.
And, above all, it is noteworthy that the service of the great
day of expiation could not have been legitimately performed

in the Temple of Shiloh, where there was no awful seclusion of
the ark in an inner *adyton,* veiled from every eye, and inaccessible on ordinary occasions to every foot.   These things
strike at the root of the Levitical system of access to God.
But of them the prophet who came to Eli has nothing to
say.   He confines himself to the extortions of the younger
priests.

The Law was as little known in Shiloh as among the mass
of the people, and the legitimate priesthood, the successors of
Moses and Aaron, are not judged by God according to the
standard of the Law.   Where, then, during this time was the
written priestly Torah preserved ?   If it lay neglected in some
corner of the sanctuary, who rescued it when the Philistines
destroyed the Temple after the battle of Ebenezer?   Was it
carried to Nob by the priests, who knew it not, or was it
rescued by Samuel, who, in all his work of reformation,
never attempted to make its precepts the rule of religious
life ?

The capture of the ark, the fall of Shiloh, and the exten-
sion of the Philistine power into the heart of Mount Ephraim,
were followed by the great national revival successively headed
by Samuel, Saul, and David.   The revival of patriotism went
hand in hand with zeal for the service of Jehovah.   In this
fresh zeal for religion, affairs of ritual and worship were not
neglected.   Saul, who aimed at the destruction of necromancy,
was also keenly alive to the sin of eating flesh with the blood
(1 Sam. xiv. 33); the ceremonially unclean might not sit at
his table (1 Sam. xx. 26) ; and there are other proofs that
ritual observances were viewed as highly important (1 Sam.
xxi. 4 *sq.* ; 2 Sam. xi. 4), though the details agree but ill with
the Levitical ordinances.   The religious patriotism of the period
finds its main expression in frequent acts of sacrifice.   On every
occasion of national importance the people assemble and do
service at some local sanctuary, as at Mizpah (1 Sam. vii. 6,

9), or at Gilgal (x. 8, xi. 15, xiii. 4, 9, etc.).   The seats of
authority are sanctuaries, Ramah, Bethel, Gilgal (vii. 16, 17 ;
comp. x. 3), Beersheba (viii. 2; comp. Amos v. 5, viii. 14),
Hebron (2 Sam. ii. 1, xv. 12).   Saul builds altars (1 Sam. xiv.
35) ; Samuel can make a dangerous visit most colourably by
visiting a local sanctuary like Bethlehem, with an offering in
his hand (1 Sam. xvi.) ; and in some of these places there are
annual sacrificial feasts (1 Sam. xx. 6).   At the same time the
ark is settled on the hill (Gibeah) at Kirjath-jearim, where
Eleazar ben Abinadab was consecrated its priest (1 Sam. vii.
1).   The priests of the house of Eli were at Nob, where there
was a regular sanctuary with shewbread, and no less than
eighty-five priests wearing a linen ephod (1 Sam. xxii. 18).

It is quite certain that Samuel, with all his zeal for
Jehovah, made no attempt to bring back this scattered
worship to forms of legal orthodoxy.   He continued to
sacrifice at a variety of shrines; and his yearly circuit to
Bethel, Gilgal, and Mizpah, returning to Ramah, involved
the recognition of all these altars (1 Sam. vii. 16 ; comp.
x. 3, xi. 15, vii. 6, 9, ix. 12).

In explanation of this it is generally argued that the age
was one of religious interregnum, and that Jehovah had not
designated a new seat of worship to succeed the ruined
sanctuary of Shiloh.   This argument might have some
weight if the law of the one sanctuary and the one priesthood rested only on the Book of Deuteronomy, which puts
the case as if the introduction of a strictly unified cultus was
to be deferred till the peaceful occupation of Palestine was
completed (Deut. xii. 8 *sq.*).   But in the Levitical legislation
the unification of cultus is not attached to a fixed place in the
land of Israel, but to the movable sanctuary of the ark and to
the priesthood of the house of Aaron.   All the law of sacrificial observances is given in connection with this sanctuary,
and on the usual view of the Pentateuch was already put into

force before the Israelites had gained a fixed habitation. In the days of Samuel the ark and the legitimate priesthood still existed. They were separated, indeed,—the one at Kirjath-jearim, the other at Nob. But they might easily have been reunited; for the distance between these towns is only a fore-noon's walk. Both lay in that part of the land which was most secure from Philistine invasion, and formed the centre of Saul's authority. For the Philistines generally attacked the central mountain district of Canaan from Aphek in the northern part of the plain of Sharon. The roads leading from this district into the country of Joseph are much easier than the routes farther south that lead directly to the land of Benjamin; and hence Saul's country was the rallying ground of Hebrew independence. Yet it is just in this narrow district, which a man might walk across in a day, that we find a scattered worship, and no attempt to concentrate it on the part of Samuel and Saul. There was no plea of necessity to excuse this if Samuel knew the Levitical law. Why should he go from town to town making sacrifice in local high places from which the sanctuary of Nob was actually visible? The Law does not require such tribute at the hands of individuals. Except at the great pilgrimage feasts the private Israelite is not called upon to bring any other sacrifice than the trespass or sin offering when he has committed some offence. But Samuel's sacrifices were not sin offerings; they were mere peace offerings, the material of sacrificial feasts which under the law had no urgency (1 Sam. ix. xvi.). What was urgent on the Levitical theory was to re-establish the stated burnt offering and the due atoning ritual before the ark in the hands of the legitimate priesthood and on the pattern of the service in the wilderness. But in place of doing this Samuel falls in with the local worship as it had been practised by the mass of the people while Shiloh still stood. He deserts the legal ritual for a service which, on the usual theory, was mere will-worship. The truth plainly is that Samuel did not know of a systematic and exclusive system of sacrificial ritual confined to the sanctuary of the ark. He did not know a model of sacred service earlier than the choice of Shiloh, which could serve the people when Shiloh was destroyed. His whole conduct is inexplicable unless, with the prophet Jeremiah, he did not recognise the Levitical law of stated sacrifice as part of the divine ordinances given in the time of Moses (Jer. vii. 22, " I spake not with your fathers, nor commanded them in the day that I brought them out of the land of Egypt, concerning burnt offerings and sacrifices "). Grant with Jeremiah that sacrifice is a free expression of Israel's homage, which Jehovah had not yet regulated by law, and at once the conduct of Samuel is clear, and Jehovah's acceptance of his service intelligible.

At length, in the reign of David, the old elements of the central worship were reunited. The ark was brought up from Kirjath-jearim to Jerusalem, and Abiathar, the representative of the house of Eli, was there as priest. Israel was again a united people, and there was no obstacle to the complete restitution of the Levitical cultus, had it been recognised as the only true expression of Israel's service. But still we find no attempt to restore the one sanctuary and the exclusive privilege of the one priesthood. According to the Law, the consecration of the priesthood is not of man but of God, and Jehovah alone can designate the priest who shall acceptably approach Him. The popular religion has another view. To offer sacrifice is the privilege of every Israelite. Saul though a layman had done so, and if his sacrifice at Gilgal was a sin, the offence lay not in the presumption of one who was not of the house of Aaron, but in the impatience which had moved without waiting for the promised presence of the prophet (1 Sam. xiii. 8 sq.; comp. xiv. 35). The priest, therefore, was the people's

delegate; his consecration was from them not from Jehovah
(Judges xvii. 5, 12; 1 Sam. vii. 1). In this respect David
was not more orthodox than Saul. When he brought up
the ark to Jerusalem he wore the priestly ephod, offered
sacrifices in person, and, to make it quite clear that in
all this he assumed a priestly function, he blessed the
people as a priest in the name of Jehovah (2 Sam. vi. 14,
18). Nor were these irregularities exceptional; in 2 Sam.
viii. 18 we read that David's sons were priests. This
statement, so incredible on the traditional theory, has led
our English version, following the Jewish tradition of the
Targum, to change the sense, and substitute "chief rulers"
for priests. But the Hebrew word means priests, and can
mean nothing else. Equally irregular was David's relation
to the high places. His kingdom was first fixed at the
sanctuary of Hebron, and long after the ark was brought
up to Jerusalem he allowed Absalom to visit Hebron in
payment of a sacrificial vow (2 Sam. xv. 8, 12). But in
fact the Book of Kings expressly recognises the worship
of the high places as legitimate up to the time when the
Temple was built (1 Kings iii. 2 *sq.*). The author or final
editor of the history, who carries the narrative down to
the Captivity, occupied the standpoint of Josiah's reformation. He knew how experience had shown the many
high places to be a constant temptation to practical
heathenism; and though he is aware that *de facto* the
best kings tolerated the local shrines for centuries after
the Temple was built, he holds that the sanctuary of Zion
ought to have superseded all other altars. But before the
Temple the high places were in his judgment legitimate.
This again is intelligible enough if he was guided by the
law of Deuteronomy, and understood the one sanctuary of
Deuteronomy to be none other than the Temple of Jerusalem.
But it is not consistent with the traditional view of the

Levitical legislation as a system completed and enforced from the days of the wilderness in a form dependent only on the existence of the Aaronic priesthood and the ark. And so we actually find that the author of Chronicles, who stands on the basis of the Levitical legislation and the system of Ezra's reformation, refuses to accept the simple explanation that the high places were necessary before the Temple, and assumes that in David's time the only sanctuary strictly legitimate was Gibeon, at which he supposes the tabernacle and the brazen altar to have stood (1 Chron. xvi. 39 *sq.*, xxi. 29 *sq.*; 2 Chron. i. 3 *sq.*). Of all this the author of Kings knows nothing. From his point of view the worship of the high places had a place and provisional legitimacy of its own without reference to the ark or the brazen altar.[1]

The result of this survey is that, through the whole period from the Judges to Ezekiel, the Law in its finished system and fundamental theories was never the rule of Israel's worship, and its observance was never the condition of the experience of Jehovah's grace. Although many individual points of ritual resembled the ordinances of the Law, the Levitical tradition as a whole had as little force in the central sanctuary as with the mass of the people. The contrast between true and false worship is not the contrast between the Levitical and the popular systems. The freedom of sacrifice which is the basis of the popular worship is equally the basis of the faith of Samuel, David, and Elijah. The reformers of Israel strove

---

[1] Some other examples of irregularities in the ritual of Israel before the Captivity have been noticed above, p. 143 *sq.*, in the discussion of the narrative of Chronicles (morning and evening sacrifice; carrying of the ark). To these one more may be added here. Under the Law the Levites and priests had a right of common round their cities, but this pasture ground was inalienable (Lev. xxv. 34), so that 1 Kings ii. 26, Jer. xxxii. 7, where priests own and sell fields, are irregular.

against the constant lapses of the nation into syncretism or the worship of foreign gods, but they did not do so on the ground of the Levitical theory of Israel's absolute separation from the nations or of a unique holiness radiating from the one sanctuary and descending in widening circles through priests and Levites to the ordinary Israelite. The history itself does not accept the Levitical standard. It accords legitimacy to the popular sanctuaries before the foundation of the Temple, and represents Jehovah as accepting the offerings made at them.   With the foundation of the Temple the historian regards the local worship as superseded, but he does so from the practical point of view that the worship there was in later times of heathenish character (2 Kings xvii.).   Nowhere does the condemnation of the popular religion rest on the original consecration of the tabernacle, the brazen altar, and the Aaronic priesthood, as the exclusive channels of veritable intercourse between Jehovah and Israel.

A dim consciousness of this witness of history is preserved in the fantastic tradition that the Law was lost, and was restored by Ezra.   In truth the people of Jehovah never lived under the Law, and the dispensation of Divine grace never followed its pattern, till Israel had ceased to be a nation.   The history of Israel refuses to be measured by the traditional theory as to the origin and function of the Pentateuch.   In the next Lecture we must inquire whether the prophets confirm or modify this result.

LECTURE X

THE PROPHETS

A SPECIAL object of the finished Pentateuchal system, as enforced among the Jews from the days of Ezra, was to make the people of Jehovah visibly different from the surrounding nations. The principle of holiness was a principle of separation, and the ceremonial ordinances of holiness, whether in daily life or in the inner circles of the Temple worship, were so many visible and tangible fences set up to divide Israel, and Israel's religion, from the surrounding Gentiles and their religion. Artificial as this system may appear, the history proves that it was necessary. The small community of the new Jerusalem was under constant temptations to mingle with the "people of the land." Intermarriages, such as Ezra and Nehemiah suppressed by a supreme effort, opened a constant door to heathen ideas and heathen morality. The religion of Jehovah could not be preserved intact without isolating the people of Jehovah from their neighbours, and this again could only be done through a highly developed system of national customs and usages, enlisting in the service of religious purity the force of habit, and the natural conservatism of Eastern peoples in all matters of daily routine. Long before the time of Christ the ceremonial observances had so grown into the life of the Jews that national pride, inborn prejudice, a disgust at foreign habits sucked in with his mother's milk, made the Israelite a peculiar person, naturally averse to contact with the surrounding Gentiles, and quite insensible to the temptations which had drawn his ancestors into continual apostasy. The hatred of the human race, which, to foreign observers, seemed the national characteristic of the Jews under the Roman Empire, was a fault precisely opposite to the facility with which the Israelites, before the Captivity, had mingled with the heathen and served their gods. This change was undoubtedly due to the discipline of the Law, the strict pedagogue, as St. Paul represents it, charged to watch the steps of the child not yet fit for liberty. Without the Law the Jews would have been absorbed in the nations, just as the Ten Tribes were absorbed and disappeared in their captivity.

But we have seen in the last two Lectures that this legal discipline of ceremonial holiness was not enforced in Israel before Josiah, nor, indeed, in all its fulness, at any time before Ezra. The ordinary life of Israel was not guarded against admixture with the nations. David married the Princess Maacah of Geshur; Solomon took many strange wives; Jehoram, in his good father's lifetime, wedded the half-heathen Athaliah; and people of lower estate were not more concerned to keep themselves apart from the Gentiles. Great sections of the nation were indeed of mixed blood. The population of Southern Judah was of half-Arab origin, and several of the clans in this district bear names which indicate their original affinity with Midian or Edom;[1] while

---

[1] See Wellhausen, *De Gentibus et Familiis Judæorum* (Göttingen, 1870). The Jerahmeelites and Calibbites of the Judæan Negeb (the southern steppes; A. V. "the south") were not fully identified with Judah proper in the time of David (1 Sam. xxvii. 10, xxx. 14); see also Josh. xv. 13, where Caleb receives a lot "among the children of Judah." Caleb, therefore, the eponym of the Calibbites, was not a Judæan by blood; he was, in fact, a Kenizzite (Josh. xiv. 6). Now the Kenizzites (or Kenaz) are one of the clans of Edom (Gen. xxxvi. 15, 42).

we know that in the time of the Judges, and later, many
cities, like Shechem, had still a Canaanite population which
was not exterminated, and must therefore have been gradually
absorbed among the Israelites.   This free intermixture of
races shows an entire absence of the spirit of religious ex-
clusiveness which was fostered in later Judaism under the
discipline of the Law.   And it could hardly have taken place
if there had been a wide difference between the social ordinances of the Hebrews and their neighbours.   But in fact we
find in old Israel traces of various social customs inconsistent
with the Pentateuchal law, and precisely identical with the
usages of the heathen Semites.   Marriage with a half-sister,
a known practice of the Phœnicians and other Semites, had
the precedent of Abraham in its favour, was not thought
inadmissible in the time of David (2 Sam. xiii. 13), and was
still a current practice in the days of Ezekiel (xxii. 11).   I
choose this instance as peculiarly striking, but it is not an
isolated case.   Another example, not less remarkable, will
come before us in Lecture XII. (*infra*, p. 369).[1]   In short,
neither the religious nor the social system of the nation was
as yet consolidated on distinctive principles.   I am now
speaking of practice, not of theory, and I apprehend that
even those who maintain that the whole Pentateuch was
then extant as a theoretical system must admit that before
the Exile the pedagogic ordinances of that system were not
the practical instrument by which the distinctive relation of
Israel to Jehovah was preserved, and the people hindered
from sinking altogether into Canaanite heathenism.

It was through an instrumentality of a very different kind
that Israel, with all its backslidings, was prevented from
wholly forgetting its vocation as the people of Jehovah, that
a spark of higher faith was kept alive in all times of national

[1] For the subject here touched on see in general an essay on *Animal-
worship*, etc., in the *Journal of Philology*, ix. 75 *sq.*, and especially my
Kinship and Marriage in Early Arabia (Cambridge, 1885).

declension, and the basis laid for that final work of reformation which at length made Israel the people of the Law not
only in name but in reality. That instrumentality was the
word of the prophets.

The conception that in Jehovah Israel has a national God
and Father, with a special claim on its worship, is not in
itself a thing peculiar to revealed religion. Other Semitic
tribes had their tribal gods. Moab is the people of Chemosh,
and the members of the nation are called sons and daughters
of the national deity even in the Israelite lay, Numbers xxi.
29 (compare Malachi ii. 11). All religion was tribal or
national. "Thy people," says Ruth, "shall be my people, and
thy God my God" (Ruth i. 16). "Hath any nation changed
its god?" asks Jeremiah (ii. 11). Jehovah Himself, according to Deut. iv. 19, has appointed the heavenly host and other
false deities to the heathen nations, while conversely He is
Himself the "portion of Jacob" (Jer. x. 16 ; comp. Deut. xxix.
26). In the early times, to be an Israelite and to be a
worshipper of Jehovah is the same thing. To be banished
from the land of Israel, the inheritance of Jehovah, is to be
driven to serve other gods (1 Sam. xxvi. 19).

These are ideas common to all Semitic religions. But in
Semitic heathenism the relation between a nation and its god
is natural. It does not rest on choice either on the nation's
part or on the part of the deity. The god, it would appear,
was frequently thought of as the physical progenitor or first
father of his people. At any rate, the god and the worshippers formed a natural unity, which was also bound up with
the land they occupied. It was deemed necessary for settlers
in a country to "know the manner of the god of the land"
(2 Kings xvii. 26). The dissolution of the nation destroys
the national religion, and dethrones the national deity. The
god can no more exist without his people than the nation
without its god.

The mass of the Israelites hardly seem to have risen above this conception. The Pentateuch knows the nation well enough to take it for granted that in their banishment from "the land of Jehovah," where He can no longer be approached in the sanctuaries of the popular worship, they will serve other gods, wood and stone (Deut. xxviii. 36 ; comp. Hosea ix.). Nay, it is plain that a great part of Israel imagined, like their heathen neighbours, that Jehovah had need of them as much as they had need of Him, that their worship and service could not be indifferent to Him, that He must, by a natural necessity, exert His power against their enemies and save His sanctuaries from profanation. This indeed was the constant contention of the prophets who opposed Micah and Jeremiah (Micah iii. 11; Jer. vii. 4 *sq.*, xxvii. 1 *sq.*); and from their point of view the captivity of Judah was the final and hopeless collapse of the religion of Jehovah. The religion of the true prophets was very different. They saw Jehovah's hand even in the fall of the state. The Assyrian and the Babylonian were His servants (Isa. x. 5 *sq.*; Jer. xxvii. 6), and the catastrophe which overwhelmed the land of Israel, and proved that the popular religion was a lie, was to the spiritual faith the clearest proof that Jehovah is not only Israel's God, but the Lord of the whole earth. As the death and resurrection of our Saviour are the supreme proof of the spiritual truths of Christianity, so the death of the old Hebrew state and the resurrection of the religion of Jehovah, in a form independent of the old national life, is the supreme proof that the religion of the Old Testament is no mere natural variety of Semitic monolatry, but a dispensation of the true and eternal religion of the spiritual God. The prophets who foresaw the catastrophe without alarm and without loss of faith stood on a foundation diverse from that of natural religion. They were the organs of a spiritual revelation, who had stood, as they themselves say, in the secret council of Jehovah (Amos iii.

7; Jer. xxiii. 18, 22), and knew the law of His working, and
the goal to which He was guiding His people. It was not the
law of ordinances, but the living prophetic word in the midst
of Israel, that separated the religion of Jehovah from the
religion of Baal or Chemosh, and gave it that vitality which
survived the overthrow of the ancient state and the banishment of Jehovah's people from His land.

The characteristic mark of a true prophet is that he has
stood in the secret council of Jehovah, and speaks the words
which he has heard from His mouth. "The Lord Jehovah,"
says Amos, "will not do anything without revealing his secret
to his servants the prophets. The lion hath roared, who will
not fear? The Lord Jehovah hath spoken, who can but
prophesy?" But the prophets do not claim universal fore-
knowledge. The secret of Jehovah is the secret of His
relations to Israel. "The secret of Jehovah belongs to them
that fear him, and he will make them know his covenant"
(Psalm xxv. 14). "If they have stood in my secret council,
let them proclaim my words to my people, that they may
return from their evil way" (Jer. xxiii. 22). The word secret
or privy council (sôd) is that used of a man's intimate
personal circle. The prophets stand in this circle. They are
in sympathy with Jehovah's heart and will, their knowledge
of His counsel is no mere intellectual gift but a moral thing.
They are not diviners but intimates of Jehovah. Balaam, in
spite of his predictions, is not in the Old Testament called a
prophet. He is only a soothsayer (Josh. xiii. 22).

Why has Jehovah a circle of intimates within Israel,
confidants of His moral purpose and acquainted with what
He is about to do? The prophets themselves supply a clear
answer to this question. There are personal relations between
Jehovah and His people, analogous to those of human friend-
ship and love. "When Israel was a child I loved him, and
called my son out of Egypt. . . . I taught Ephraim to go,

holding them by their arms. . . . I drew them with human
bands, with cords of love" (Hosea xi. 1). "You alone have
I known," says Jehovah through Amos, "of all the families
of the earth" (Amos iii. 2). This relation between Jehovah
and Israel is not a mere natural unintelligent and physically
indissoluble bond such as unites Moab to Chemosh. It rests
on free love and gracious choice. As Ezekiel xvi. 6 puts it,
Jehovah saw and pitied Jerusalem, when she lay as an infant
cast forth to die, and said unto her, Live. The relation is
moral and personal, and receives moral and personal expression. Jehovah guides His people by His word, and admits
them to the knowledge of His ways. But He does not speak
directly to every Israelite (Deut. xviii. 15 *sq.*). The organs of
His loving and personal intercourse with the people of His
choice are the prophets. "By a prophet Jehovah brought
Israel out of Egypt, and by a prophet he was preserved"
(Hosea xii. 13). "I brought you up from the land of Egypt,
and led you in the wilderness forty years to possess the land
of the Amorites. And I raised up of your sons for prophets,
and of your young men for Nazarites" (Amos ii. 10, 11). The
prophets, you perceive, regard their function as an essential
element in the national religion. It is they who keep alive
the constant intercourse of love between Jehovah and His
people which distinguishes the house of Jacob from all other
nations; it is their work which makes Israel's religion a
moral and spiritual religion.

To understand this point we must remember that in the
Old Testament the distinctive features of the religion of
Jehovah are habitually represented in contrast to the religion
of the heathen nations. It is taken for granted that the
religion of the nations does in a certain sense address itself to
man's legitimate needs. The religion of Israel would not be
the all-sufficient thing it is, if Israel did not find in Jehovah
the true supply of those wants for which other nations turn

to the delusive help of the gods who are no gods.   Now, in
all ancient religions, and not least in Semitic heathenism, it
is a main object of the worshipper to obtain oracles from his
god.   The uncertainties of human life are largely due to man's
ignorance.   His life is environed by forces which he cannot
understand or control, and which seem to sport at will with
his existence and his happiness.   All these forces are viewed
as supernatural, or rather—for in these questions it is important to eschew metaphysical notions not known to early
thinkers—they are divine beings, with whom man can enter
into league only by means of his religion.   They are to be
propitiated by offerings, and consulted by enchantments and
soothsayers.   In Semitic heathenism the deity whom a tribe
worships as its king or lord (Baal) is often identified
with some supreme power of nature, with the mighty sun,
the lord of the seasons, or with the heavens that send down
rain, or with some great planet whose stately march through
the skies appears to regulate the cycles of time.   These are
the higher forms of ethnic religion.   In lower types the deity
is more immediately identified with earthly objects,—animals,
trees, or the like.   But in any case the god is a member of
the chain of hidden natural agencies on which man is continually dependent, and with which it is essential to establish
friendly relations.   Such relations are attainable, for man
himself is physically connected with the natural powers.
They produced him; he is the son of his god as well as his
servant; and so the divinity, if rightly questioned and carefully propitiated, will speak to the worshipper and aid him
by his counsel as well as his strength.   In all this there is,
properly speaking, no moral element.   The divine forces of
nature seem to be personified, for they hear and speak.   But,
strictly speaking, the theory of such religion is the negation
of personality.   It is on the physical side of his being that
man has relations to the godhead.   Readers of Plato will

remember how clearly this comes out in the *Timæus*, where
the faculty of divination is connected with the appetitive and
irrational part of man's nature.[1]   That, of course, is a philosophical explanation of popular notions.   But it indicates a
characteristic feature in the religion of heathenism.   It is not
as an intellectual and moral being that man has fellowship
with deities that are themselves identified with physical
powers.   The divine element in man through which he has
access to his god lies in the mysterious instincts of his lower
nature; and paroxysms of artificially-produced frenzy, dreams,
and diseased visions are the accepted means of intercourse
with the godhead.

Accordingly an essential element in the religion of the
heathen Semites was divination in its various forms, of which
so many are enumerated in Deut. xviii. 10, 11.[2]   The diviner
procured an oracle, predicting future events, detecting secrets,
and directing the worshipper what choice to make in difficult
points of conduct.   Such oracles were often sought in private
life, but they were deemed altogether indispensable in the
conduct of the state, and the soothsayers were a necessary
part of the political establishment of every nation.   The Old
Testament takes it for granted that Jehovah acknowledges

---

[1] Plato, *Timæus*, cap. xxxii. p. 71, D.   The mantic faculty belongs to the
part of the soul settled in the liver, because that part has no share in reason
and thought.   "For inspired and true divination is not attained to by any
one when in his full senses, but only when the power of thought is fettered by
sleep or disease or some paroxysm of frenzy."

This view of inspiration is diametrically opposite to that of St. Paul
(1 Cor. xiv. 32), and the complete self-consciousness and self-control of the
prophets taught in that passage belong equally to the spiritual prophecy of
the Old Testament.   Plato's theory, however, was applied to the prophets by
Philo, the Jewish Platonist, who describes the prophetic state as an ecstasy
in which the human νοῦς disappears to make way for the divine Spirit (*Quis
rerum div. heres*, § 53, ed. Richter, iii. 58; *De Spec. Leg.* § 8, Richter, v.
122).   Something similar has been taught in recent times by Hengstenberg
and others,—substituting, as we observe, the pagan for the Biblical conception
of revelation.

[2] On the various forms of divination and magic enumerated in these verses,
see two papers in the *Journal of Philology*, xiii. 273 *sqq.*, and xiv. 113 *sqq.*

and supplies in Israel the want which in other nations is met
by the practice of divination. The place of the soothsayer is
supplied by the prophets of Jehovah. "These nations, which
thou shalt dispossess, hearken unto soothsayers and diviners ;
but as for thee, Jehovah thy God suffereth thee not to do so.
A prophet from the midst of thee, of thy brethren, like unto
me, will Jehovah thy God raise up unto thee; unto him
shall ye hearken" (Deut. xviii. 14 *sq.*).

In the popular religion, where the attributes of Jehovah
were not clearly marked off from those of the heathen Baalim,
little distinction was made between prophet and soothsayer.
The word prophet, *nabî*, is not exclusively Hebrew. It
appears to be identical with the Assyrian Nebo, the spokes-
man of the gods, answering to the Greek Hermes. And we
know that there were prophets of Baal, whose orgies are
described in 1 Kings xviii., where we learn that they sought
access to their god in exercises of artificial frenzy carried so
far that, like modern fanatics of the East, they became insensible to pain, and passed into a sort of temporary madness,
to which a supernatural character was no doubt ascribed, as
is still the case in similar religions. This Canaanite pro-
phetism, then, was a kind of divination, based, like all
divination, on the notion that the irrational part of man's
nature is that which connects him with the deity. It
appears that there were men in Israel calling themselves
seers or prophets of Jehovah, who occupied no higher standpoint. Saul and his servant went to Samuel with the fourth
part of a shekel as fee to ask him a question about lost asses,
and the story is told as if this were part of the business of a
common seer. In the time of Isaiah, the stay and staff of
Jerusalem, the necessary props of the state, included not only
judges and warriors but prophets, diviners, men skilled in
charms, and such as understood enchantments (Isa. iii. 2, 3,
Heb.). Similarly Micah iii. 5 *sq.* identifies the prophets and

the diviners, and places them alongside of the judges and the priests as leaders of the nation. " The heads thereof give judgment for bribes, and the priests give legal decisions for hire, and the prophets divine for money; yet they lean upon Jehovah and say, Is not Jehovah among us? none evil can come upon us." You observe that this false prophecy, which is nothing else than divination, is practised in the name of Jehovah, and has a recognised place in the state. And so, when Amos appeared at Bethel to speak in Jehovah's name, the priest Amaziah identified him with the professional prophets who were fed by their trade (Amos vii. 12), and formed a sort of guild, as the name "sons of the prophets" indicates.

With these prophets by trade Amos indignantly refuses to be identified. "I am no prophet," he cries, "nor the member of a prophetic guild, but an herdsman, and a plucker of sycomore fruit. And Jehovah took me as I followed the flock, and said unto me, Go, prophesy unto my people Israel." These words of the earliest prophetic book clearly express the standpoint of spiritual prophecy. With the established guilds, the official prophets, if I may so call them, the men skilled in enchantment and divination, whose business was a trade involving magical processes that could be taught and learned, Amos, Isaiah, and Micah have nothing in common; they declaim against the accepted prophecy of their time, as they do against all other parts of the national religion which were no longer discriminated from heathenism. They accept the principle that prophecy is essential to religion. They admit that Jehovah's guidance of His people must take the form of continual revelation, supplying those needs which drive heathen nations and the unspiritual masses of Israel to practise divination. But the method of true revelation has nothing in common with the art of the diviner. "When they say unto you, Seek counsel of ghosts and of familiar spirits that peep and mutter: should not a people consult its God? shall they go to the dead on behalf of the living?" (Isa. viii. 19). The wizards, by their ventriloquist arts, professed to make their dupes hear the voice of ghosts and gibbering spirits rising from the underground abodes of the dead (see Isa. xxix. 4; 1 Sam. xxviii.); but Jehovah is a living God, a moral and personal being. He speaks to His prophets, not in magical processes or through the visions of poor phrenetics, but by a clear intelligible word addressed to the intellect and the heart. The characteristic of the true prophet is that he retains his consciousness and self-control under revelation. He is filled with might by the spirit of Jehovah (Micah iii. 8). Jehovah speaks to him as if He grasped him with a strong hand (Isa. viii. 11). The word is within his heart like a burning fire shut up in his bones (Jer. xx. 9), so that he cannot remain silent. But it is an intelligible word, which speaks to the prophet's own heart and conscience, forbidding Isaiah to walk in the way of the corrupt nation, filling Micah with power to declare unto Jacob his transgression, supporting the heart of Jeremiah with an inward joy amidst all his trials (Jer. xv. 16). The first condition of such prophecy are pure lips and a heart right with God. Isaiah's lips are purged and his sin forgiven before he can go as Jehovah's messenger (Isa. vi.); and to Jeremiah the Lord says, " If thou return, then will I bring thee back, and thou shalt stand before me : and if thou take forth the precious from the vile, thou shalt be as my mouth : let them—the sinful people—turn to thee, but turn not thou to them " (Jer. xv. 19). Thus the essence of true prophecy lies in moral converse with Jehovah. It is in this moral converse that the prophet learns the divine will, enters into the secrets of Jehovah's purpose, and so by declaring God's word to Israel keeps alive a constant spiritual intercourse between Him and His people.

According to the prophets this spiritual intercourse is the essence of religion, and the "word of Jehovah," in the sense now explained, is the characteristic and distinguishing mark of His grace to Israel. When the word of Jehovah is withdrawn, the nation is hopelessly undone. Amos describes as the climax of judgment on the Northern Kingdom a famine not of bread but of hearing Jehovah's word. Men shall run from end to end of the land to seek the word of Jehovah, and shall not find it. In that day the fair virgins and the young men shall faint for thirst, and the guilty people shall fall to rise no more (Amos viii. 11 *sq.*). Conversely the hope of Judah in its adversity is that "thine eyes shall see thy teacher, and thine ears shall hear a word behind thee saying, This is the way, walk ye in it, when ye turn to the right hand or the left" (Isa. xxx. 20). And so the function of the prophet cannot cease till the days of the new covenant, when Jehovah shall write His revelation in the hearts of all His people, when one man "shall no more teach another saying, Know Jehovah: for they shall all know me from the least of them unto the greatest of them, saith Jehovah: for I will forgive their iniquity, and remember their sin no more" (Jer. xxxi. 33 *sq.*). When we compare this passage with Isaiah vi., we see that under this new covenant the prophetic consecration is extended to all Israel, and the function of the teacher ceases, because all Israel shall then stand in the circle of Jehovah's intimates, and see the king in His beauty as Isaiah saw Him in prophetic vision (Isa. xxxiii. 17). The same thought appears in another form in Joel ii. 28, where it is represented as a feature in the deliverance of Israel that God's spirit shall be poured on all flesh, and young and old, freemen and slaves, shall prophesy. But nowhere is the idea more clear than in the last part of the Book of Isaiah, where the true people of Jehovah and the prophet of Jehovah appear as identical. "Hearken unto me, ye that know the right, *the people in whose hearts my revelation dwells*; fear ye not the reproach of man, neither be ye afraid of their revilings. . . . *I have put my words in thy mouth,* and I have covered thee in the shadow of my hand, planting the heavens and laying the foundation of the earth, and saying to Zion, Thou art my people" (Isa. li. 7, 16).

We see, then, that the ideal of the Old Testament is a dispensation in which all are prophets. "Would that all the people of Jehovah were prophets," says Moses in Num. xi. 29, "and that Jehovah would put his spirit upon them." If prophecy were merely an institution for the prediction of future events, this wish would be futile. But the essential grace of the prophet is a heart purged of sin, and entering with boldness into the inner circle of fellowship with Jehovah. The spirit of Jehovah, which rests on the prophet, is not merely a spirit of wisdom and understanding, a spirit of counsel and might, but a spirit to know and fear the Lord (Isa. xi. 2). The knowledge and fear of Jehovah is the sum of all prophetic wisdom, but also of all religion; and the Old Testament spirit of prophecy is the forerunner of the New Testament spirit of sanctification. That this spirit, in the Old Covenant, rests only upon chosen organs of revelation, and not upon all the faithful, corresponds to the limitations of the dispensation, in which the primary subject of religion is not the individual but the nation, so that Israel's personal converse with Jehovah can be adequately maintained, like other national functions, through the medium of certain chosen and representative persons. The prophet is thus a mediator, who not only brings God's word to the people but conversely makes intercession for the people with God (Isa. xxxvii. 4; Jer. xiv. 11, xv. 1, etc.).

The account of prophecy given by the prophets themselves involves, you perceive, a whole theory of religion, pointing in the most necessary way to a New Testament fulfilment. But

the theory moves in an altogether different plane from the
Levitical ordinances, and in no sense can it be viewed as a
spiritual commentary on them.   For under the Levitical
system Jehovah's grace is conveyed to Israel through the
priest; according to the prophets it comes in the prophetic
word.   The systems are not identical; but may they at least
be regarded as mutually supplementary?

In their origin priest and prophet are doubtless closely
connected ideas.   Moses is not only a prophet but a priest
(Deut. xviii. 15 ; Hos. xii. 13 ; Deut. xxxiii. 8; Psalm xcix.
6).   Samuel also unites both functions; and there is a priestly
as well as a prophetic oracle.   In early times the sacred lot
of the priest appears to have been more looked to than the
prophetic word.   David ceases to consult Gad when Abiathar
joins him with the ephod.   (Comp. 1 Sam. xiv. 18, xxii. 10,
xxiii. 9, xxviii. 6 with xxii. 5.)   Indeed, so long as sacrificial
acts were freely performed by laymen, the chief distinction of
a priest doubtless lay in his qualification to give an oracle.
The word which in Hebrew means priest is in old Arabic the
term for a soothsayer (kôhen, kâhin), and in this, as in other
points, the popular religion of Israel was closely modelled on
the forms of Semitic heathenism, as we see from the oracle in
the shrine of Micah (Judges xviii. 5.   Comp. 1 Sam. vi. 2 ; 2
Kings x. 19).[1]   The official prophets of Judah appear to have

---

[1] In ancient times the priestly oracle of Urim and Thummim was a sacred
lot ; for in 1 Sam. xiv. 41 the true text, as we can still restore it from the
LXX., makes Saul pray, "If the iniquity be in me or Jonathan, give Urim ;
but if in Israel, give Thummim." This sacred lot was connected with the
ephod, which in the time of the Judges was something very like an idol
(supra, p. 241).   Spencer therefore seems to be right in assuming a resemblance in point of form between the priestly lot of the Urim and Thummim
and divination by Teraphim (De Leg. Rit. lib. iii. c. 3).   The latter again
appears as practised by drawing lots by arrows before the idol (Ezek. xxi. 21,
"he shook the arrows"), which was also a familiar form of divination among
the heathen Arabs (Journal of Phil., as cited above, xiii. 277 sqq.).   Under
the Levitical law the priestly lot exists in theory in a very modified form,
confined to the high priest, but in reality it was obsolete (Neh. vii. 65).

been connected with the priesthood and the sanctuary until
the close of the kingdom (Isa. xxviii. 7; Jer. xxiii. 11, xxvi.
11; comp. Hosea iv. 5). They were, in fact, part of the
establishment of the Temple, and subject to priestly discipline
(Jer. xxix. 26, xx. 1 *sq.*). They played into the priests' hands
(Jer. v. 31), had a special interest in the affairs of worship (Jer.
xxvii. 16), and appear in all their conflicts with Jeremiah as
the partisans of the theory that Jehovah's help is absolutely
secured by the Temple and its services.

But the prophecy which thus co-operates with the priests
is not spiritual prophecy. It is a kind of prophecy which the
Old Testament calls divination, which traffics in dreams in
place of Jehovah's word (Jer. xxiii. 28), and which, like
heathen divination, presents features akin to insanity that
require to be repressed by physical constraint (Jer. xxix. 26).
Spiritual prophecy, in the hands of Amos, Isaiah, and their
successors, has no such alliance with the sanctuary and its
ritual. It develops and enforces its own doctrine of the
intercourse of Jehovah with Israel, and the conditions of His
grace, without assigning the slightest value to priests and
sacrifices. The sum of religion, according to the prophets, is
to know Jehovah, and obey His precepts. Under the system
of the law enforced from the days of Ezra onwards an important part of these precepts was ritual. Malachi, a contemporary, or perhaps rather an immediate precursor of Ezra,
accepts this position as the basis of his prophetic exhortations.
The first proof of Israel's sin is to him neglect of the sacrificial
ritual. The language of the older prophets up to Jeremiah is
quite different. "What are your many sacrifices to me? saith
Jehovah : I delight not in the blood of bullocks, and lambs,
and he-goats. When ye come to see my face, who hath asked
this at your hands, to tread my courts? Bring no more vain
oblations . . . my soul hateth your new moons and your
feasts; they are a burden upon me; I am weary to bear

them" (Isa. i. 11 *sq.*). "I hate, I despise your feast days, and I will not take pleasure in your solemn assemblies. Take away from me the noise of thy songs, and let me not hear the melody of thy viols. But let justice flow as waters, and righteousness like a perennial stream" (Amos v. 21 *sq.*). It is sometimes argued that such passages mean only that Jehovah will not accept the sacrifice of the wicked, and that they are quite consistent with a belief that sacrifice and ritual are a necessary accompaniment of true religion. But there are other texts which absolutely exclude such a view. Sacrifice is not necessary to acceptable religion. Amos proves God's indifference to ritual by reminding the people that they offered no sacrifice and offerings to Him in the wilderness during those forty years of wandering which he elsewhere cites as a special proof of Jehovah's covenant grace (Amos ii. 10, v. 25).[1] Micah declares that Jehovah does not require sacrifice ; He asks nothing of His people, but "to do justly, and love mercy, and walk humbly with their God" (Micah vi. 8). And Jeremiah vii. 21 *sq.* says in express words, "Put your burnt offerings to your sacrifices and eat flesh. For I spake not to your fathers and gave them no command in the day that I brought them out of Egypt concerning burnt offerings or sacrifices. But this thing commanded I them, saying, Obey my voice, and I will be your God, and ye shall be my people," etc. (Comp. Isa. xliii. 23 *sq.*) The

---

[1] The argument of Amos v. 25 is obscured in the English translation by the rendering of the following verse. The verbs in that verse are not perfects, and the idea is not that in the wilderness Israel sacrificed to false gods in place of Jehovah. Verse 26 commences the prophecy of judgment, "Ye shall take up your idols, and " (not as E. V. "therefore") "I will send you into captivity." The words כוכב אלהיכם are a gloss, as is indicated by the fact that the Septuagint read them before Ραφαν = כין. The gloss arose from the idea that Chiun is equivalent to the Syriac Kêwân, a Persian name of the planet Saturn. But the date of Amos forbids this interpretation. Both סכות and כין must be common nouns in the construct state, probably "the *shrine* of your (idol) king and the *stand* of your images," *i.e.* the portable shrine and platform on which the idols were exhibited and borne in processions.

position here laid down is perfectly clear. When the prophets positively condemn the worship of their contemporaries, they do so because it is associated with immorality, because by it Israel hopes to gain God's favour without moral obedience. This does not prove that they have any objection to sacrifice and ritual in the abstract. But they deny that these things are of positive divine institution, or have any part in the scheme on which Jehovah's grace is administered in Israel. Jehovah, they say, has not enjoined sacrifice. This does not imply that He has never accepted sacrifice, or that ritual service is absolutely wrong. But it is at best mere form, which does not purchase any favour from Jehovah, and might be given up without offence. It is impossible to give a flatter contradiction to the traditional theory that the Levitical system was enacted in the wilderness. The theology of the prophets before Ezekiel has no place for the system of priestly sacrifice and ritual.

All this is so clear that it seems impossible to misunderstand it. Yet the position of the prophets is not only habitually explained away by those who are determined at any cost to maintain the traditional view of the Pentateuch, but is still more seriously misunderstood by a current rationalism not altogether confined to those who, on principle, deny the reality of positive revelation. It is a widespread opinion that the prophets are the advocates of natural religion, and that this is the reason of their indifference to a religion of ordinances and ritual. On the naturalistic theory of religion, *ethical monotheism* is the natural belief of mankind, not, indeed, attained at once in all races, but worked out for themselves by the great thinkers of humanity, continually reflecting on the ordinary phenomena of life and history. It is held that natural religion is the only true religion, that the proof of its truth lay open to all men in all countries, and that Christianity itself, so far as it is true, is merely the historical development, in one part of the world, of those ideas of ethical monotheism which other nations than Israel might have worked out equally well on the basis of their own experience and reflection.   From this point of view the prophets are regarded as advanced thinkers, who had not yet thrown aside all superstition, who were hampered by a belief in miracle and special revelation, but whose teaching has abiding value only in proportion as it reduced these elements to a subordinate place and struck out new ideas essentially independent of them.   The prophets, we are told, believed themselves to be inspired.   But their true inspiration was only profound thinking.   They were inspired as all great poetic and religious minds are inspired ; and when they say that God has told them certain things as to His nature and attributes, this only means that they have reached a profound conviction of spiritual truths concealed from their less intelligent contemporaries.   The permanent truths of religion are those which spring up in the breast without external revelation or traditional teaching.   The prophets had grasped these truths with great force, and so they were indifferent to the positive forms which made up the religion of the mass of their nation.   This theory has had an influence extending far beyond the circle of those who deliberately accept it in its whole compass. Even popular theology is not indisposed to solve the apparent contradiction between the Prophets and the Pentateuch, by saying that the former could afford to overlook the positive elements of Israel's religion, because their hearts were filled with spiritual truths belonging to another sphere.

But the prophets themselves put the case in a very different light.   According to them it is their religion which is positive, and the popular worship which is largely traditional and of human growth.   That Jehovah is the Judge, the Lawgiver, the King of Israel, is a proposition which they accept in the most literal sense.   Jehovah's word and thoughts

are as distinct from their own words and thoughts as those
of another human person.   The mark of a false prophet is
that he speaks " the vision of his own heart, not from Jehovah's
mouth " (Jer. xxiii. 16).   The word of Jehovah, the commandments and revelations of Jehovah, are given to them inter-
nally, but are not therefore identical with their own reflections.
They have an external authority, the authority of Him who
is the King and Master of Israel.   This is not the place for a
theory of revelation.   But it is well to observe, as a matter of
plain fact, that the inspiration of the prophets presents
phenomena quite distinct from those of any other religion.
In the crasser forms of religion the supernatural character of
an oracle is held to be proved by the absence of self-conscious
thought.   The dream, the ecstatic vision, the frenzy of the
Pythoness, seem divine because they are not intelligent.   But
these things are divination, not prophecy.   Jeremiah draws
an express contrast between dreams and the word of Jehovah
(Jer. xxiii. 25-28).   And the visions of the prophets, which
were certainly rare, and by no means the standard form of
revelation, are distinguished by the fact that the seer retains
his consciousness, his moral judgment, his power of thinking
(Isa. vi.).   On the other hand, the assertion so often made
that the prophets identify the word of Jehovah with their
own highest thoughts, just as the Vedic poets do, ignores an
essential difference between the two cases.   The prophets
drew a sharp distinction between their own word and God's
word, which these poets never do.   Nor is spiritual prophecy,
as other scholars hold, a natural product of Semitic religion.
Semitic religion, like other religions, naturally produces
diviners; but even Mohammed had no criterion apart from
his hysterical fits to distinguish his own thoughts from the
revelations of Allah.[1]

[1] The Greek doctrine of the inspiration of the poet never led to the
recognition of certain poems as sacred Scriptures.   But the Indian Vedas
were regarded in later times as infallible, eternal, divine.   In the priestly

According to the prophets, all true knowledge of God is reached, not by human reflection, but by the instruction of Jehovah Himself. Religion is to know Jehovah, to fear Him and obey His commandments, as one knows, fears, and obeys a father and a king. The relations of Jehovah to Israel are of a perfectly matter-of-fact kind. They rest on the historical fact that He chose the people of Israel, brought them up from Egypt, settled them in Canaan, and has ever since been present in the nation, issuing commands for its behaviour in every concern of national life. In every point of conduct Israel is referred, not to its own moral reflections and political wisdom, but to the Word of Jehovah.

According to the traditional view, the Word of Jehovah is embodied in a book-revelation. The Torah, "instruction," or, as we should say, revelation of God, is a written volume deposited with the priests, which gives rules for all national

bards, therefore (the *Rishis*), the first authors of the Vedic hymns, we may expect to find, if anywhere, a consciousness analogous to that of the prophets. Their accounts of themselves have been collected by Dr. John Muir in his *Sanscrit Texts*, vol. iii., and some recent writers have laid great stress on this supposed parallel to prophetic inspiration. But what are the facts? The Rishis frequently speak of their hymns as their own works, but also sometimes entertain the idea that their prayers, praises, and ceremonies generally were supernaturally inspired. The gods are said to "generate" prayer; the prayer is god-given. The poet, like a Grecian singer, calls on the gods to help his prayer. "May prayer, brilliant and divine, proceed from us." But in all this there is no stricter conception of inspiration than in the Greek poets. It is not the word of God that we hear, but the poet's word aided by the gods (compare Muir, p. 275). How different is this from the language of the prophets! "Where do the prophets," asks Merx (*Jenaer Lit. Zeit.*, 1876, p. 19), "pray for illumination of spirit, force of poetic expression, glowing power of composition?" The prophetic consciousness of inspiration is clearly separated both from the inspiration of the heathen μάντις and from the afflatus of the Indian or Grecian bard.

On Mohammed's inspiration see Nöldeke, *Geschichte des Qorâns*, p. 4. "He not only gave out his later revelations, composed with conscious deliberation and the use of foreign materials, as being, equally with the first glowing productions of his enthusiasm, angelic messages and proofs of the prophetic spirit, but made direct use of pious fraud to gain adherents, and employed the authority of the Koran to decide and adjust things that had nothing to do with religion."

and personal conduct, and also provides the proper means for regaining God's favour when it has been lost through sin. But to the prophets the Torah has a very different meaning.

The prophets did not invent the word Torah. It is a technical term of the current traditional religion. A Torah is any decision or instruction on matters of law and conduct given by a sacred authority. Thus *môreh*, or giver of Torah, may mean a soothsayer. The oak of the Torah-giver (Gen. xii. 6) is identical with the soothsayer's oak (Jud. ix. 37). You remember, in illustration of this name, that Deborah gave her prophetic judgments under "the palm-tree of Deborah" between Ramah and Bethel. More frequent are allusions to the Torah of the priests, which in like manner denotes, not a book which they had in their hands, but the sacred decisions given, by the priestly oracle or otherwise, in the sanctuary, which in early Israel was the seat of divine judgment (Exod. xviii. 19, xxi. 6, where for *the judges* read *God*; 1 Sam. ii. 25). Thus in Deut. xxxiii. 10 the business of the Levites is to give Torah to Israel and to offer sacrifice to God. In Jer. xviii. 18 the people give as a ground of their security against the evils predicted by Jeremiah that Torah shall not perish from the priest, nor counsel from the wise, nor the word from the prophet. The priests are "they that handle the Torah" (Jer. ii. 8). Micah complains that the priests give Torahs or legal decisions for hire (Micah iii. 11). In these passages the Torah is not a book but an oral decision ; and the grammatical form of the word, as an infinitive of the verb "to give a decision or instruction," shows this to be the primitive sense.

We have seen how spiritual prophecy branched off and separated itself from the popular prophecy which remained connected with the sanctuary and the priests. In doing so it carried its own spiritual Torah with it. When God bids Isaiah "bind up the testimony, seal the Torah among my

disciples," the reference is to the revelation just given to the
prophet himself (Isa. viii. 16).　To this Torah and testimony,
and not to wizards and consulters of the dead, Israel's appeal
for Divine guidance lies (ver. 20).　The Torah is the living
prophetic word.　"Hear the word of Jehovah," and "Give ear
to the Torah of our God," are parallel injunctions by which
the prophet demands attention to his divine message (Isa. i.
10).　The Torah is not yet a finished and complete system,
booked and reduced to a code, but a living word in the mouth
of the prophets.　In the latter days the proof that Jehovah is
King in Zion, exalting His chosen hill above all the mountains
of the earth, will still be that Torah proceeds from Zion and
the word of Jehovah from Jerusalem, so that all nations come
thither for judgment, and Jehovah's word establishes peace
among hostile peoples (Isa. ii. 2 *sq.* ; Micah v. 1 *sq.*).　It is
this continual living instruction of Jehovah present with His
people which the prophets, as we have already seen, regard as
essential to the welfare of Israel.　No written book would
satisfy the thirst for God's Word of which Amos speaks.　The
only thing that can supersede the Torah of the prophets is the
Torah written in every heart and spoken by every lip.　"This is
my covenant with them, saith Jehovah : my spirit that is upon
thee, and my words which I have put in thy mouth, shall not
depart out of thy mouth, nor out of the mouth of thy seed, nor
out of the mouth of thy seed's seed, saith Jehovah, from henceforth and for ever" (Isa. lix. 21).　God's Word, not in a book
but in the heart and mouth of His servants, is the ultimate
ideal as well as the first postulate of prophetic theology.

How then did this revelation, which is essentially living
speech, pass into the form of a written word such as we still
possess in the books of the Old Testament ?　To answer this
question as the prophets themselves would do, we must
remember that among primitive nations, and indeed among
Eastern nations to this day, books are not the foundation of

sound knowledge. The ideal of instruction is oral teaching,
and the worthiest shrine of truths that must not die is the
memory and heart of a faithful disciple. The ideal state of
things is that in which the Torah is written in Israel's heart,
and all his children are disciples of Jehovah (Isa. liv. 13).
But this ideal was far from the actual reality, and so in
religion, as in other branches of knowledge, the written roll
to which truth is committed supplies the lack of faithful
disciples. This comes out quite clearly in the case of the
prophetic books. The prophets write the words which their
contemporaries refuse to hear. So Isaiah seals his revelation
among the disciples of Jehovah; that is, he takes them as
witnesses to a document which is, as it were, a formal testimony against Israel (Isa. viii. 1 *sq.*, 16). So Jeremiah, after
three-and-twenty years spent in speaking to a rebellious
people, writes down his prophecies that they may have
another opportunity to hear and repent (Jer. xxxvi.). Jehovah's
Word has a scope that reaches beyond the immediate occasion,
and a living force which prevents it from returning to Him
without effect; and if it is not at once taken up into the
hearts of the people, it must be set in writing for future use
and for a testimony in time to come. Thus the prophets
become authors, and they and their disciples are students of
written revelation. The prophets give many signs of acquaintance with the writings of their predecessors, and sometimes
even quote them verbally. Thus Jer. xlix. 7-22 and the
Book of Obadiah seem both to make use of an earlier oracle
against Edom;[1] and the prophecy against Moab in Isa. xv. xvi.
is followed by the note of a later prophet : "This is the word
which Jehovah spake against Moab long ago. But now
Jehovah speaks, saying, Within three short years the glory of
Moab shall be abased" (Isa. xvi. 13, 14). Thus we see why

---

[1] See the article OBADIAH in *Enc. Brit.*, 9th ed., and Driver, *Introduction*, p. 298 *sq.*

the beginnings of prophetic literature in the eighth century coincide with the great breach between spiritual prophecy and the popular religion. Elisha had no need to write, for his word bore immediate fruit in the overthrow of the house of Omri and the destruction of the worshippers of Baal. The old prophecy left its record in social and political successes. The new prophecy that begins with Amos spoke to a people that would not hear, and looked to no immediate success, but only to a renovation of the remnant of Israel to follow on a completed work of judgment. When the people forbid the prophets to preach, they begin perforce to write (Amos ii. 12, vii. 12, 13 ; Micah ii. 6 ; Jer. xxxvi. 5 sq.).

But, though the properly prophetic literature begins in the eighth century B.C., do not the prophets, it may be asked, base their teaching on an earlier written revelation of another kind ? They certainly hold that the religion of Israel is as old as the Exodus. They speak of Moses. " By a prophet," says Hosea, " Jehovah brought Israel out of Egypt." " I brought thee up out of the land of Egypt, and redeemed thee out of the house of bondage," says Micah ; " and I sent before thee Moses, Aaron, and Miriam." Do not these references presuppose the written law of Moses ? This question requires careful consideration.

There is no doubt that the prophets regard themselves as successors of Moses. He is, as we see from Hosea, the first prophet of Israel. But the prophets of the eighth century never speak of a written law of Moses. The only passage which has been taken to do so is Hosea viii. 12. And here the grammatical translation is, " Though I wrote to him my Torah in ten thousand precepts, they would be esteemed as a strange thing." It is simple matter of fact that the prophets do not refer to a written Torah as the basis of their teaching, and we have seen that they absolutely deny the existence of a binding ritual law. But, on the other hand, it is clear that the Torah is not a new thing in the eighth century. The false religion of the mass of the nation is always described as a corruption of truths which Israel ought to know. "Thou hast forgotten the Torah of thy God," says Hosea to the priests (Hos. iv. 6). It cannot fairly be doubted that the Torah which the priests have forgotten is Mosaic Torah. For the prophets do not acknowledge the priests as organs of revelation. Their knowledge was essentially traditional. Such traditions are based on old-established law, and they themselves undoubtedly referred their wisdom to Moses, who, either directly or through Aaron,—for our argument it matters not which,—is the father of the priests as well as the father of the prophets (Deut. xxxiii. 4, 8 *sq.*; 1 Sam. ii. 27 *sq.*). That this should be so lies in the nature of the case. Jehovah as King of Israel must from the first have given permanent laws as well as precepts for immediate use. What is quite certain is that, according to the prophets, the Torah of Moses did not embrace a law of ritual. Worship by sacrifice, and all that belongs to it, is no part of the divine Torah to Israel. It forms, if you will, part of natural religion, which other nations share with Israel, and which is no feature in the distinctive precepts given at the Exodus. There is no doubt that this view is in accordance with the Bible history, and with what we know from other sources. Jacob is represented as paying tithes; all the patriarchs build altars and do sacrifice; the law of blood is as old as Noah; the consecration of firstlings is known to the Arabs; the autumn feast of the vintage is Canaanite as well as Hebrew; and these are but examples which might be largely multiplied.

The true distinction of Israel's religion lies in the character of the Deity who has made Himself personally known to His people, and demands of them a life conformed to His spiritual character as a righteous and forgiving God. The difference between Jehovah and the gods of the nations is that He does not require sacrifice, but only to do justly, and love mercy, and walk humbly with God. This standpoint is not confined to the prophetic books; it is the standpoint of the Ten Commandments, which contain no precept of positive worship. But according to many testimonies of the pre-exilic books, it is the Ten Commandments, the laws written on the two tables of stone, that are Jehovah's covenant with Israel. In 1 Kings viii. 9, 21 these tables are identified with the covenant deposited in the sanctuary. And with this the Book of Deuteronomy agrees (Deut. v. 2, 22). Whatever is more than the words spoken at Horeb is not strictly covenant, but prophetic teaching, continual divine guidance addressed to those needs which in heathen nations are met by divination, but which in Israel are supplied by the personal word of the revealing God ministered through a succession of prophets (Deut. xviii. 9 *sq.*). Even Ezra (ix. 11) still speaks of the law which forbids intermarriage with the people of Canaan as an ordinance of the prophets (plural). Yet this is now read as a Pentateuchal law (Deut. vii.).

To understand this view, we must remember that among the pure Semites even at the present day the sphere of legislation is far narrower than in our more complicated society. Ordinary affairs of life are always regulated by consuetudinary law, preserved without writing or the need for trained judges, in the memory and practice of the family and the tribe. It is only in cases of difficulty that an appeal is taken to the judge—the " Cadi of the Arabs." It was not otherwise in the days of Moses. It was only hard matters that were brought to him, and referred by him, not to a fixed code of law, but to Divine decision (Exod. xviii. 19-26), which formed a precedent for future use. Of this state of things the condition of affairs under the Judges is the natural sequel. But Moses did more than any " Cadi of the Arabs," who owes his authority to superior knowledge of legal tradition. He was

a prophet as well as a judge. As such he founded in Israel
the great principles of the moral religion of the righteous
Jehovah. All else was but a development of the fundamental
revelation, and from the standpoint of prophetic religion it is
not of importance whether these developments were given
directly by Moses, or only by the prophets his successors.
But all true Torah must move in the lines of the original
covenant. The standard of the prophets is the moral law,
and because the priests had forgotten this they declare them
to have forgotten the law, however copious their Torah, and
however great their interest in details of ritual. Forgotten
or perverted by the priests (Hos. iv. 6 ; Zeph. iii. 4), the true
Torah of Jehovah is preserved by the prophets. But the
prophets before Ezekiel have no concern in the law of ritual.
They make no effort to recall the priests to their duty in this
respect, except in the negative sense of condemning such
elements in the popular worship as are inconsistent with the
spiritual attributes of Jehovah.

From the ordinary presuppositions with which we are
accustomed to approach the Old Testament, there is one
point in this position of the prophets which still creates a
difficulty. If it is true that they exclude the sacrificial
worship from the positive elements of Israel's religion, what
becomes of the doctrine of the forgiveness of sins, which we
are accustomed to regard as mainly expressed in the typical
ordinances of atonement? It is necessary, in conclusion, to
say a word on this head. The point, I think, may be put
thus. When Micah, for example, says that Jehovah requires
nothing of man but to do justly, to love mercy, and to walk
humbly with God, we are apt to take this utterance as an
expression of Old Testament legalism. According to the law
of works, these things are of course sufficient. But sinful
man, sinful Israel, cannot perform them perfectly. Is it not
therefore necessary for the law to come in, with its atone-

ment, to supply the imperfection of Israel's obedience? I ask you to observe that such a view of the prophetic teaching is the purest rationalism, necessarily allied with the false idea that the prophets are advocates of natural morality. The prophetic theory of religion has nothing to do with the law of works. Religion, they teach, is the personal fellowship of Jehovah with Israel, in which He shapes His people to His own ends, impresses His own likeness upon them by a continual moral guidance. Such a religion cannot exist under a bare law of works. Jehovah did not find Israel a holy and righteous people; He has to make it so by wise discipline and loving guidance, which refuses to be frustrated by the people's shortcomings and sins. The continuance of Jehovah's love in spite of Israel's transgressions, which is set forth with so much force in the opening chapters of Hosea, is the forgiveness of sins.

Under the Old Testament the forgiveness of sins is not an abstract doctrine but a thing of actual experience. The proof, nay, the substance, of forgiveness is the continued enjoyment of those practical marks of Jehovah's favour which are experienced in peaceful occupation of Canaan and deliverance from all trouble. This practical way of estimating forgiveness is common to the prophets with their contemporaries. Jehovah's anger is felt in national calamity, forgiveness is realised in the removal of chastisement. The proof that Jehovah is a forgiving God is that He does not retain His anger for ever, but turns and has compassion on His people (Micah vii. 18 *sq.*; Isa. xii. 1). There is no metaphysic in this conception, it simply accepts the analogy of anger and forgiveness in human life.

In the popular religion the people hoped to influence Jehovah's disposition towards them by gifts and sacrifices (Micah vi. 4 *sq.*), by outward tokens of penitence. It is against this view that the prophets set forth the true doctrine of forgiveness. Jehovah's anger is not caprice but a just indignation, a necessary side of His moral kingship in Israel. He chastises to work penitence, and it is only to the penitent that He can extend forgiveness. By returning to obedience the people regain the marks of Jehovah's love, and again experience His goodness in deliverance from calamity and happy possession of a fruitful land. According to the prophets, this law of chastisement and forgiveness works directly, without the intervention of any ritual sacrament. Jehovah's love is never withdrawn from His people, even in their deepest sin and in His sternest chastisements. "How can I give thee up, Ephraim? How can I cast thee away, Israel? My heart burns within me, my compassion is all kindled. I will not execute the fierceness of my wrath; I will not turn to destroy thee: for I am God and not man, the Holy One in the midst of thee" (Hos. xi. 8). This inalienable Divine love, the sovereignty of God's own redeeming purpose, is the ground of forgiveness. "I, even I, am he that blotteth out thine iniquity for mine own sake" (Isa. xliii. 25). And so the prophets know, with a certainty that rests in the unchangeable heart of God, that through all chastisement, nay, through the ruin of the state, the true remnant of Israel shall return to Jehovah, not with sacrifices, but with lips instead of bullocks, as Hosea puts it, saying, Take away all iniquity and receive us graciously (Hos. xiv. 2). All prophetic prediction is but the development in many forms, and in answer to the needs of Israel in various times, of this supreme certainty, that God's love works triumphantly in all His judgments; that Israel once redeemed from Egypt shall again be redeemed not only from bondage but from sin; that Jehovah will perform the truth to Jacob, the mercy to Abraham, which He sware to Israel's fathers from the days of old (Micah vii. 20). Accordingly, the texts which call for obedience and not sacrifice (Micah vi.; Jer. vii. etc.), for humanity instead of outward tokens of contrition (Isa. lviii.), come in at the very same point with the atoning ordinances of the ritual law. They do not set forth the legal conditions of acceptance without forgiveness, but the requisites of forgiveness itself. According to the prophets, Jehovah asks only a penitent heart and desires no sacrifice; according to the ritual law, He desires a penitent heart approaching Him in certain sacrificial sacraments. The law adds something to the prophetic teaching, something which the prophets do not know, and which, if both are parts of one system of true revelation, was either superseded before the prophets rose, or began only after they had spoken. But the ritual law was not superseded by prophecy. It comes into full force only at the close of the prophetic period in the reformation of Ezra. And so the conclusion is inevitable that the ritual element which the law adds to the prophetic doctrine of forgiveness became part of the system of Old Testament religion only after the prophets had spoken.[1]

---

[1] Properly to understand the prophetic doctrine of forgiveness, we must remember that the problem of the acceptance of the individual with God was never fully solved in the Old Testament. The prophets always deal with the nation in its unity as the object of wrath and forgiveness. The religious life of the individual is still included in that of the nation. When we, by analogy, apply what the prophets say of the nation to the forgiveness of the individual, we must remember that Israel's history starts with a work of redemption—deliverance from Egypt. To this objective proof of Jehovah's love the prophets look back, just as we look to the finished work of Christ. In it is contained the pledge of Divine love, giving confidence to approach God and seek His forgiveness. But while the Old Testament believer had no difficulty in assuring himself of Jehovah's love to Israel, it was not so easy to find a pledge of His grace to the individual, and especially not easy to apprehend God as a forgiving God under personal affliction. Here especially the defect of the dispensation came out, and the problem of individual acceptance with God, which was acutely realised in and after the fall of the nation, when the righteous so often suffered with the wicked, is that most closely bound up with the interpretation of the atoning sacrifices of the Levitical ritual.

LECTURE XI

THE PENTATEUCH: THE FIRST LEGISLATION

THE results of our investigation up to this point are not critical but historical, and, if you will, theological. The Hebrews before the Exile knew a twofold Torah, the Torah of the priests and that of the prophets. Neither Torah corresponds with the present Pentateuch. The prophets altogether deny to the law of sacrifice the character of positive revelation; their attitude to questions of ritual is the negative attitude of the Ten Commandments, content to forbid what is inconsistent with the true nature of Jehovah, and for the rest to leave matters to their own course. The priests, on the contrary, have a ritual and legal Torah which has a recognised place in the state; but neither in the old priestly family of Eli nor in the Jerusalem priesthood of the sons of Zadok did the rules and practice of the priests correspond with the finished system of the Pentateuch.

These results have a much larger interest than the question of the date of the Pentateuch. It is more important to understand the method of God's grace in Israel than to settle when a particular book was written; and we now see that, whatever the age of the Pentateuch as a written code, the Levitical system of communion with God, the Levitical sacraments of atonement, were not the forms under which God's grace worked, and to which His revelation accommodated itself, in Israel before the Exile.

The Levitical ordinances, whether they existed before the Exile or not, were not yet God's word to Israel at that time. For God's word is the expression of His practical will. And the history and the prophets alike make it clear that God's will for Israel's salvation took quite another course.

The current view of the Pentateuch is mainly concerned to do literal justice to the phrase "The Lord spake unto Moses, saying" thus and thus. But to save the literal "unto Moses" is to sacrifice the far more important words "The Lord spake." The time when these ritual ordinances became God's word—that is, became a divinely sanctioned means for checking the rebellion of the Israelites and keeping them as close to spiritual religion as their imperfect understanding and hard hearts permitted—was subsequent to the work of the prophets. As a matter of historical fact, the Law continues the work of the prophets, and great part of the Law was not yet known to the prophets as God's word.

The ritual law is, strictly speaking, a fusion of prophetic and priestly Torah. Its object is to provide a scheme of worship, in the pre-Christian sense of that word, consistent with the unique holiness of Jehovah, and yet not beyond the possibility of practical realisation in a nation that was not ripe to enter into present fruition of the evangelical predictions of the prophets. From the time of Ezra downwards this object was practically realised. But before the Captivity it not only was not realised, but was not even contemplated. Ezekiel, himself an exile, is the first prophet who proposes a reconstruction of ritual in conformity with the spiritual truths of prophecy. And he does so, not like Ezra by recalling the nation to the law of Moses, but by sketching an independent scheme of ritual, which unquestionably had a great influence on the subsequent development. Jeremiah,

like Ezekiel, was a priest as well as a prophet, but there is
nothing in Jeremiah which recognises the necessity for such
a scheme of ritual as Ezekiel maps out.

When the Levitical law first comes on the stage of actual
history at the time of Ezra, it presents itself as the Law of
Moses. People who have not understood the Old Testament
are accustomed to say that this is either literally true or a
lie; that the Pentateuch is either the literary work of Moses,
or else a barefaced imposture. The reverent and thoughtful
student, who knows the complicated difficulties of the problem, will not willingly accept this statement of the question. If we are tied up to make a choice between these two
alternatives, it is impossible to deny that all the historical
evidence that has come before us points in the direction of
the second. If our present Pentateuch was written by Moses,
it was lost as completely as any book could be. The prophets know the history of Moses and the patriarchs, they
know that Moses is the founder of the Torah, but they do
not know that complete system which we have been accustomed to suppose his work. And the priests of Shiloh and
the Temple do not know the very parts of the Torah which
would have done most to raise their authority and influence.
At the time of Josiah a book of the Law is found, but it is
still not the whole Pentateuch, for it does not contain the
full Levitical system. From the death of Joshua to Ezra is,
on the usual chronology, just one thousand years. Where
was the Pentateuch all this time, if it was unknown to
every one of those who ought to have had most interest
in it?[1]

---

[1] I may here notice one passage which has been cited (*e.g.* by Keil, *Introduction*, vol. i. p. 170 of the Eng. tr.) as containing a reference to the written
law in the time of King Jehoash of Judah. In 2 Kings xi. 12 we read that
Jehoiadah " brought forth the king's son, and put the crown upon him and
gave him the testimony." But here everything turns on the words "gave
him," and these are not in the Hebrew, which must, according to grammar,
be rendered "put upon him the crown and the testimony." The "testimony,"

It is plain that no thinking man can be asked to accept
the Pentateuch as the composition of Moses without some
evidence to that effect.   But evidence a thousand years after
date is no evidence at all, when the intervening period bears
unanimous witness in a different sense.   By insisting that
the whole Pentateuch is one work of Moses and all of equal
date, the traditional view cuts off all possibility of proof that
its kernel is Mosaic.   For it is certain that Israel, before the
Exile, did not know all the Pentateuch.   Therefore, if the
Pentateuch is all one, they did not know any part of it.   If
we are shut up to choose between a Mosaic authorship of the
whole five books and the opinion that the Pentateuch is a
mere forgery, the sceptics must gain their case.

It is useless to appeal to the doctrine of inspiration for
help in such a strait; for all sound apologetic admits that the
proof that a book is credible must precede belief that it is
inspired.

But are we really shut up to choose between these
extreme alternatives?   The Pentateuch is known as the Law
of Moses in the age that begins with Ezra.   What is the
sense which the Jews themselves, from the age of Ezra downwards, attach to this expression?   In one way they certainly
take a false and unhistorical sense out of the words.   They
assume that the law of ordinances, or rather the law of works,
moral and ceremonial, was the principle of all Israel's religion.
They identify Mosaism with Pharisaism.   That is certainly an
error, as the History and the Prophets prove.   But, on the
other hand, the Jews are accustomed to use the word Mosaic
quite indifferently of the direct teaching of Moses, and of the
precepts drawn from Mosaic principles and adapted to later
needs.   According to a well-known passage in the Talmud,

therefore, is part of the royal insignia, which is absurd.   But the addition of
a single letter, הצעדות for העדרות, gives the excellent sense, "put on him the
crown and the bracelets."   The crown and the bracelet appear together as the
royal insignia in 2 Sam. i. 10,   This certain correction is due to Wellhausen.

even the Prophets and the Hagiographa were implicitly given
to Moses at Sinai. So far is this idea carried that the Torah
is often identified with the Decalogue, in which all other
parts of the Law are involved. Thus the words of Deut. v.
22, which refer to the Decalogue, are used as a proof that the
five books of Moses can never pass away.[1] The beginnings
of this way of thought are clearly seen in Ezra ix. 11, where
a law of the Pentateuch is cited as an ordinance of the
prophets. Mosaic law is not held to exclude post-Mosaic
developments. That the whole law is the Law of Moses does
not necessarily imply that every precept was developed in
detail in his days, but only that the distinctive law of Israel
owes to him the origin and principles in which all detailed
precepts are implicitly contained. The development into
explicitness of what Moses gave in principle is the work of
continuous divine teaching in connection with new historical
situations.

This way of looking at the law of Moses is not an invention of modern critics; it actually existed among the Jews. I
do not say that they made good use of it; on the contrary,
in the period of the Scribes, it led to a great overgrowth of
traditions, which almost buried the written word. But the
principle is older than its abuse, and it seems to offer a key
for the solution of the serious difficulties in which we are
involved by the apparent contradictions between the Pentateuch on the one hand and the historical books and the
Prophets on the other.

If the word Mosaic was sometimes understood as meaning
no more than Mosaic in principle, it is easy to see how the
fusion of priestly and prophetic Torah in our present Pentateuch may be called Mosaic, though many things in its

[1] *Berachoth Bab.* 5, *a* (p. 234 in Schwab's French translation, Paris, 1871).
Megilla Jer., cited in Lecture VI. p. 187. Compare Weber, *Syst. des altsynagog.
Theol.* (Leipzig, 1880), p. 89 *sq.*, and Dr. M. Wise in the *Hebrew Review,*
vol. i. p. 12 *sq.* (Cincinnati, 1880).

system were unknown to the History and the Prophets before
the Exile.   For Moses was priest as well as prophet, and both
priests and prophets referred the origin of their Torah to him.
In the age of the prophetic writings the two Torahs had fallen
apart.   The prophets do not acknowledge the priestly ordinances of their day as a part of Jehovah's commandments to
Israel.   The priests, they say, have forgotten or perverted the
Torah.   To reconcile the prophets and the priesthood, to
re-establish conformity between the practice of Israel's worship and the spiritual teachings of the prophets, was to return
to the standpoint of Moses, and bring back the Torah to its
original oneness.   Whether this was done by bringing to
light a forgotten Mosaic book, or by recasting the traditional
and consuetudinary law in accordance with Mosaic principles, is a question purely historical, which does not at all
affect the legitimacy of the work.

It is always for the interest of truth to discuss historical
questions by purely historical methods, without allowing
theological questions to come in till the historical analysis is
complete.   This, indeed, is the chief reason why scholars
indifferent to the religious value of the Bible have often done
good service by their philological and historical studies.   For
though no one can thoroughly understand the Bible without
spiritual sympathy, our spiritual sympathies are commonly
bound up with theological prejudices which have no real
basis in Scripture; and it is a wholesome exercise to see how
the Bible history presents itself to men who approach the
Bible from an altogether different point of view.   It is easier
to correct the errors of a rationalism with which we have no
sympathy, than to lay aside prejudices deeply interwoven
with our most cherished and truest convictions.

In strict method, then, we ought now to prosecute the
question of the origin of the Pentateuch by the ordinary
rules of historical inquiry; and only when a result has been

reached should we pause to consider the theological bearings
of what we have learned. But we have all been so much
accustomed to look at the subject from a dogmatical point
of view, that a few remarks at this stage on the theological
aspect of the problem may be useful in clearing the path of
critical investigation.

Christian theology is interested in the Law as a stage in
the dispensation of God's purpose of grace. As such it is
acknowledged by our Lord, who, though He came to supersede the Law, did so only by fulfilling it, or, more accurately,
by filling it up, and supplying in actual substance the good
things of which the Law presented only a shadow and
unsubstantial form. The Law, according to the Epistle to
the Hebrews, was weak and unprofitable ; it carried nothing
to its goal, and must give way to a better hope, by which we
draw near to God (Heb. vii. 18, 19). The Law on this view
never actually supplied the religious needs of Israel ; it served
only to direct the religious attitude of the people, to prevent
them from turning aside into devious paths and looking for
God's help in ways that might tempt them to forget His
spiritual nature and fall back into heathenism. For this
purpose the Law presents an artificial system of sanctity,
radiating from the sanctuary and extending to all parts of
Israel's life. The type of religion maintained by such a
system is certainly inferior to the religion of the prophets,
which is a thing not of form but of spirit. But the religion
of the prophets could not become the type of national religion
until Jehovah's spirit rested on all His people, and the knowledge of Him dwelt in every heart. This was not the case
under the old dispensation. The time to which Jeremiah
and Isaiah xl.-lxvi., look forward, when the prophetic word
shall be as it were incarnate in a regenerate nation, did not
succeed the restoration from Babylon. On the contrary, the
old prophetic converse of Jehovah with His people flagged

and soon died out, and the word of Jehovah, which in old
days had been a present reality, became a memory of the past
and a hope for the future. It was under these circumstances
that the dispensation of the Law became a practical power in
Israel. It did not bring Israel into such direct converse with
Jehovah as prophecy had done. But for the mass of the
people it nevertheless formed a distinct step in advance ; for
it put an end to the anomalous state of things in which
practical heathenism had filled the state, and the prophets
preached to deaf ears. The legal ritual did not satisfy the
highest spiritual needs, but it practically extinguished idolatry.
It gave palpable expression to the spiritual nature of Jehovah,
and, around and within the ritual, prophetic truths gained a
hold of Israel such as they had never had before. The Book
of Psalms is the proof how much of the highest religious
truth, derived not from the Law but from the Prophets, dwelt
in the heart of the nation, and gave spiritual substance to the
barren forms of the ritual.

These facts, quite apart from any theory as to the age and
authorship of the Pentateuch, vindicate for the Law the position which it holds in the teaching of Jesus and in Christian
theology. That the Law was a divine institution, that it
formed an actual part in the gracious scheme of guidance
which preserved the religion of Jehovah as a living power in
Israel till shadow became substance in the manifestation of
Christ, is no theory but an historical fact, which no criticism
as to the origin of the books of Moses can in the least degree
invalidate. On the other hand, the work of the Law, as we
have now viewed it, was essentially subsidiary. As S. Paul
puts it in Rom. v. 20, the Law came in from the side (νόμος
δὲ παρεισῆλθεν). It did not lie in the right line of direct
development, which, as the Epistle to the Hebrews points out,
leads straight from Jeremiah's conception of the New Covenant
to the fulfilment in Christ. Once more we are thrown back

on S. Paul's explanation. The Law was but a pedagogue, a servant to accompany a schoolboy in the streets, and lead him to the appointed meeting with his true teacher.

This explanation of the function of the Law is that of the New Testament, and it fits in with all the historical facts that we have had before us. But current theology, instead of recognising the historical proof of the divine purpose of the Law, is inclined to stake everything on the Mosaic authorship of the whole system. If the Law is not written by Moses, it cannot be part of the record of revelation. But if it could be proved that Moses wrote the Law, what would that add to the proof that its origin is from God? It is not true as a matter of history that Pentateuch criticism is the source of doubts as to the right of the Law to be regarded as a divine dispensation. The older sceptics, who believed that Moses wrote the Pentateuch, attacked the divine legation of Moses with many arguments which criticism has deprived of all force. You cannot prove a book to be God's word by showing that it is of a certain age. The proof of God's word is that it does His work in the world, and carries on His truth towards the final revelation in Christ Jesus. This proof the Pentateuch can adduce, but only for the time subsequent to Ezra. In reality, to insist that the whole Law is the work of Moses is to interpose a most serious difficulty in the way of its recognition as a divine dispensation. Before the Exile the law of ceremonies was not an effectual means to prevent defection in Israel, and Jehovah Himself never dispensed His grace according to its provisions. Is it possible that He laid down in the wilderness, with sanctions the most solemn, and with a precision which admitted no exception, an order of worship and ritual which has no further part in Israel's history for well-nigh a thousand years?

But I do not urge this point. I do not desire to raise difficulties against the common view, but to show that the

valid and sufficient proof that the Law has a legitimate place
in the record of Old Testament revelation, and that history
assigns to it the same place as it claims in Christian theology,
is derived from a quarter altogether independent of the
critical question as to the authorship and composition of the
Pentateuch. This being premised, we can turn with more
composure to inquire what the Pentateuch itself teaches as to
its composition and date.

The Pentateuch, as we have it, is not a formal law-book,
but a history beginning with the Creation and running on
continuously into the Book of Joshua. The Law, or rather
several distinct legal collections, are inserted in the historical
context. Confining our attention to the main elements, we
can readily distinguish three principal groups of laws or
ritual ordinances in addition to the Ten Commandments.

I. The collection Exod. xxi.-xxiii. This is an independent
body of laws, with a title, "These are the judgments which
thou shalt set before them," and contains a very simple system
of civil and religious polity, adequate to the wants of a
primitive agricultural people. I shall call this the First
Legislation. In its religious precepts it presents a close
parallel to the short collection of ordinances in Exod. xxxiv.
11-26, but the latter contains no social or civil statutes.

II. The Law of Deuteronomy. The Book of Deuteronomy
contains a good deal of matter rather hortatory than legislative. The Deuteronomic code proper begins at chap. xii.,
with the title, "These are the statutes and judgments which
ye shall observe to do," etc. ; and closes with the subscription
(Deut. xxvi. 16 *sq.*), "This day Jehovah thy God hath commanded thee to do these statutes and judgments," etc. The
Deuteronomic Code, as we may call Deut. xii.-xxvi., is not a
mere supplement to the First Legislation. It is an independent reproduction of its substance, sometimes merely
repeating the older laws, but at other times extending or

modifying them.   It covers the whole ground of the old law,
except one verse of ritual precept (Exod. xxiii. 18), the law
of treason (Exod. xxii. 28), and the details as to compensations to be paid for various injuries.   The Deuteronomic Code
presupposes a regular establishment of civil judges (Deut. xvi.
18), and the details of compensation in civil suits might
naturally be left in their hands.[1]

III.   Quite distinct from both these codes is the Levitical
Legislation, or, as it is often called, the Priests' Code.   (The

---

[1] It is of some importance to realise how completely Deuteronomy covers
the same ground with the First Legislation.   The following table exhibits
the facts of the case :—

Exod. xxi.   1-11 (Hebrew slaves)—Deut. xv. 12-18.
   „   „   12-14 (Murder and asylum)—Deut. xix. 1-13.
   „   „   15, 17 (Offences against parents)—Deut. xxi. 18-21.
   „   „   16 (Manstealing)—Deut. xxiv. 7.
   „   „   18-xxii. 15.   Compensations to be paid for various injuries.   This section is
               not repeated in Deuteronomy, except as regards the law of retaliation,
               Exod. xxi. 23-25, which in Deut. xix. 16-21 is applied to false witnesses.
Exod. xxii.   16, 17 (Seduction)—Deut. xxii. 28, 29.
   „   „   18 (Witch)—Deut. xviii. 10-12.
   „   „   19—Deut. xxvii. 21.
   „   „   20 (Worship of other gods)—Deut. xvii. 2-7.
   „   „   21-24 (Humanity to stranger, widow, and orphan)—Deut. xxiv. 17-22.
   „   „   25 (Usury)—Deut. xxiii. 19.
   „   „   26, 27 (Pledge of raiment)—Deut. xxiv. 10-13.
   „   „   28 (Treason)—Not in Deuteronomy.
   „   „   29, 30 (First fruits and firstlings)—Deut. xxvi. 1-11, xv. 19-23.
   „   „   31 (Unclean food)—Deut. xiv. 2-21.   The particular precept of Exodus occupies
               only ver. 21 ; but the principle of avoiding food inconsistent with holiness
               is expanded.
Exod. xxiii.   1 (False witness)—Deut. xix. 16-21.
   „   „   2, 3,   } (Just judgment)—Deut. xvi. 18-20.
   „   „   6, 7, 8,
   „   „   4, 5 (Animals strayed or fallen)—Deut. xxii. 1-4.
   „   „   9 (repetition of xxii. 21)—Deut. xxiv. 17-18.
   „   „   10-11—(Sabbatical year)—Deut. xv. 1-11.
   „   „   12 (Sabbath as a provision of humanity)—Deut. v. 14, 15.   [Not in the Code
               proper.]
   „   „   13 (Names of other gods)—Deut. vi. 13.
   „   „   14-17 (Annual feasts)—Deut. xvi. 1-17.
   „   „   18 (Leaven in sacrifice)—Not in Deuteronomy.
   „   „   19 (First fruits)—Deut. xxvi. 2-10.
   „   „   19 b (Kid in mother's milk)—Deut. xiv. 21.

The parallel becomes still more complete when we observe that to the
Code of Deuteronomy is prefixed an introduction, iv. 44-xi. 32, containing
the Ten Commandments, and so answering to Exod. xx.   A good table, following the order of Deuteronomy, and giving also the parallels from Exod. xxxiv.
and from the priestly Code or Levitical Legislation, will be found in Driver,
Introduction, p. 68 *sqq.*

latter term, however, as generally used, includes those parts
of the Pentateuchal history to which a common origin with
the Levitical Legislation is ascribed by critics.) The Levitical
ordinances, including directions for the equipment of the
sanctuary and priesthood, sacrificial laws, and the whole
system of threefold sanctity in priests, Levites, and people,
are scattered through several parts of Exodus and the Books
of Leviticus and Numbers. They do not form a compact
code ; but, as a whole, they are clearly marked off from both
the other legislations, and might be removed from the Pentateuch without making the rest unintelligible. The First
Legislation and the Code of Deuteronomy take the land of
Canaan as their basis. They give directions for the life of
Jehovah's people in the land He gives them. The Levitical
Legislation starts from the sanctuary and the priesthood. Its
object is to develop the theory of a religious life which has
its centre in the sanctuary, and is ruled by principles of
holiness radiating forth from Jehovah's dwelling-place. The
first two Legislations deal with Israel as a nation; in the
third Israel is a church, and as such is habitually addressed
as a "congregation" (*'ēdah*), a word characteristic of the
Priests' Code.

These three bodies of law are, in a certain sense, independent of the historical narrative of the Pentateuch in
which they now occur. For the first two Legislations this
is quite plain. They are formal codes which may very well
have existed as separate law-books before they were taken up
into the extant history. The Levitical Legislation seems at
first sight to stand on a different footing. Individual portions
of it, such as the chapters at the beginning and end of Leviticus, have a purely legal form; but a great part of the
ordinances of law or ritual takes the shape of narrative.
Thus, the law for the consecration of priests is given in a
narrative of the consecration of Aaron and his sons. The

form is historical, but the essential object is legal, the
ceremonies observed at Aaron's consecration constituting
an authoritative precedent for future ages.   There is nothing
surprising in this.   Among the Arabs, to this day, traditional
precedents are the essence of law, and the Cadi of the Arabs
is he who has inherited a knowledge of them.   Among early
nations precedent is particularly regarded in matters of ritual ;
and the oral Torah of the priests doubtless consisted, in great
measure, of case law.   But law of this kind is still essentially
law, not history.   It is preserved, not as a record of the past,
but as a guide for the present and the future.   The Pentateuch itself shows clearly that this law in historical form
is not an integral part of the continuous history of Israel's
movements in the wilderness, but a separate thing.   For in
Exodus xxxiii. 7, which is non-Levitical, we read that Moses
took the tabernacle and pitched it outside the camp, and
called it the tent of meeting.   But the Levitical account of
the setting up of the tabernacle, which is accompanied with
precise details as to the arrangements of the sanctuary, so as
to furnish a complete pattern for the ordering of the sacred
furniture in future ages, does not occur till chap. xl. (comp.
Num. ix. 15).   Again, in Numbers x. we have first the Levitical account of the fixed order of march of the Israelites from
Sinai with the ark in the midst of the host (verses 11-28), and
immediately afterwards the historical statement that when
the Israelites left Sinai the ark was not in their midst but
went before them a distance of three days' journey (verses 33-
36).[1]   It is plain that though the formal order of march with

---

[1] According to Exod. xxxiii. 7, Num. x. 33, the sanctuary is outside the
camp and at some considerable distance from it, both when the people are at
rest and when they are on the march.   That the ark precedes the host is
implied in Exod. xxiii. 20, xxxii. 34 ; Deut. i. 33.   The same order of march
is found in Joshua iii. 3, 4, where the distance between the ark and the host
is 2000 cubits, and the reason of this arrangement, as in Num. *l. c.*, is that
the ark is Israel's guide.   (Comp. Isa. lxiii. 11 *sq.*)   That the sanctuary
stood outside the camp is implied also in Num. xi. 24 *sq.*, xii. 4.   This

the ark in the centre, which the author sets forth as a standing
pattern, is here described in the historical guise of a record of
the departure of Israel from Sinai, the actual order of march
on that occasion was different. The same author cannot have
written both accounts. One is a law in narrative form ; the
other is actual history. These examples are forcible enough,
but they form only a fragment of a great chain of evidence
which critics have collected. By many marks, and particularly
by extremely well-defined peculiarities of language, a Levitical
document can be separated out from the Pentateuch, containing
the whole mass of priestly legislation and precedents, and leaving untouched the essentially historical part of the Pentateuch,
all that has for its direct aim to tell us what befell the Israelites
in the wilderness, and not what precedents the wilderness
offered for subsequent ritual observances. The hand that
penned the Levitical legislation can be traced even in the Book
of Genesis, for the plan of exhibiting the laws of Israel as far
as possible in the form of precedents made it necessary to go
back to Abraham for the institution of circumcision (Gen.
xvii.), to Noah for the so-called Noachic ordinances (Gen. ix.
1-17), and to the Creation itself for the law of the Sabbath
(Gen. ii. 1-3). Accordingly the Priests' Code takes formally
the shape of a continuous history of divine institution from
the Creation downwards. Of course this continuity could only
be attained by introducing a good deal of matter that has no
direct legal bearing; but the legal interest always predomi-

corresponds with the usage of the early sanctuaries in Canaan, which stood on
high points outside the cities (1 Sam. ix. 14, 25). So the Temple at Jerusalem
originally stood outside the city of David, which occupied the lower slope of
the Temple hill (comp. *Enc. Brit.*, 9th ed., articles JERUSALEM and TEMPLE).
But, as the city grew, ordinary buildings encroached on the Temple plateau
(Ezek. xliii. 8). This appears to Ezekiel to be derogatory to the sanctity of
the house (comp. Deut. xxiii. 14), and is the reason for the ordinance set forth
in symbolic form in Ezek. xlv. 1 *sq.*, xlviii., where the sanctuary stands in
the middle of Israel, but isolated, the priests and the Levites lodging between
it and the laity, as in the Levitical law, Num. i.-iii. Here, as in other cases,
the Levitical law appears as the latest stage of the historical development.

nates, and those parts of the history which throw no light on the ordinances of the Law are cut as short as possible and often are reduced to mere chronological and genealogical tables. As the Pentateuch now stands, this quasi-history, in which the narrative of events is strictly subordinate to a legal purpose, and the real history, written for its own sake, are intermingled, not only in the same book, but often in the same chapter. But originally they were quite distinct.[1]

The Pentateuch, then, is a history incorporating at least three bodies of law. The history does not profess to be written by Moses, but only notes from time to time that he wrote down certain special things (Exod. xvii. 14, xxiv. 4, xxxiv. 27; Num. xxxiii. 2; Deut. xxxi. 9, 22, 24). These notices of what Moses himself wrote are so far from proving him the author of the whole Pentateuch that they rather point in the opposite direction. What he wrote is dis-

---

[1] Of the immense literature dealing with the linguistic and other marks by which the Levitical document, or Priests' Code, may be separated out, it is enough to refer particularly to Nöldeke, *Untersuchungen zur Kritik des A. T.*, Kiel, 1869; Wellhausen, *Composition des Hexateuchs*, in the *Jahrb. f. D. T.*, 1876, p. 392 *sq.*, p. 531 *sq.*; 1877, p. 407 *sq.* (reprinted in his *Skizzen*, etc., Hft. ii., 1885, and again in *Comp. des Hex. und der histor. Bücher*, 1889), and many important articles by Kuenen in the *Theologisch Tijdschrift*. Kuenen's results are summed up in the second edition of his *Onderzoek*, vol. i. 1 (of which there is an English translation). The best account of the matter by an English scholar is that in Driver's *Introduction*. For the Book of Genesis the contents of the Priestly Code (generally referred to as P) are most conveniently exhibited (in a German translation) in Kautzsch and Socin's *Genesis* (2d ed., 1891), where the ancient narratives incorporated in the Pentateuch are all printed in different types. In Genesis the separation of P can be effected with great precision, and there are very few verses about which critics of every school are not agreed. For P's contributions to the other parts of the Pentateuch the reader may consult the tables in Driver's *Introduction*. The chief passages of legal importance are Exod. xii. 1-20, 43-51; xiii. 1, 2; xxv. 1-xxxi. 17; xxxv.-xl.; the Book of Leviticus as a whole (but here chapters xvii.-xxvi., the so-called Law of Holiness, form a separate section, akin to the mass of the Priests' Code, but with certain peculiarities); Num. i. 1-x. 28; xv.; part of xvi.; xvii.-xix.; xxv. 6-xxxi. 54; xxxiv.-xxxvi. For the narrative sections of P see Lecture XIII.

It ought, however, to be observed that the Levitical laws, though all of one general type in substance, and even in language, do not appear to be all

tinguished from the mass of the text, and he himself is
habitually spoken of in the third person. It is common to
explain this as a literary artifice analogous to that adopted
by Cæsar in his *Commentaries*. But it is a strong thing to
suppose that so artificial a way of writing is as old as Moses,
and belongs to the earliest age of Hebrew authorship. One
asks for proof that any Hebrew ever wrote of himself in the
third person, and particularly that Moses would write such
a verse as Numbers xii. 3, "The man Moses was very meek
above all men living."

The idea that Moses is author of the whole Pentateuch,
except the last chapter of Deuteronomy, is derived from the
old Jewish theory, which we found in Josephus (*supra*, p.
164), that every leader of Israel wrote down by Divine
authority the events of his own time, so that the sacred
history is like a day-book constantly written up to date. No
part of the Bible corresponds to this description, and the
Pentateuch as little as any. For example, the last chapter

of one date and by one hand. A good deal of valuable work has been done in
the way of separating the older and younger elements of the Levitical legislation ; but here, as will readily be conceived, the temptation to push conjecture
beyond the limits of possible verification is very great. On the other hand,
the broad lines of separation between this legislation and the other codes are
very clearly marked by the diversity of standpoint, style, and language.

A good example of the fundamental difference in legal style between the
Levitical laws and the Deuteronomic Code is found in Num. xxxv. compared
with Deut. xix. In Numbers, the technical expression city of refuge is
repeated at every turn. In Deuteronomy the word *refuge* does not occur,
and the cities are always described by a periphrasis. In Numbers the phrase
for "accidentally" is *bish'gaga*, in Deut. *bib'li da'at*. The judges in the one
are "the congregation," in the other "the elders of his city." The verb for
hate is different. The one account says again and again "to kill any person,"
the other "to kill his neighbour." The detailed description of the difference
between murder and accidental homicide is entirely diverse in language and
detail. The structure of the sentences is distinct, and in addition to all this
there is a substantial difference in the laws themselves, inasmuch as Deuteronomy says nothing about remaining in the city of refuge till the death of
the high priest. On a rough calculation, omitting auxiliary verbs, particles,
etc., Num. xxxv. 11-34 contains 19 nouns and verbs which also occur in
Deut. xix. 2-13, and 45 which do not occur in the parallel passage ; while the
law, as given in Deuteronomy, has 50 such words not in the law of Numbers.

of Deuteronomy, which on the common theory is a note
added by Joshua to the work in which Moses had carried
down the history till just before his death, cannot really have
been written till after Joshua was dead and gone. For it
speaks of the city Dan. Now Dan is the new name of Laish,
which that town received after the conquest of the Danites
in the age of the Judges, when Moses's grandson became
priest of their idolatrous sanctuary. But if the last chapter
of Deuteronomy is not contemporary history, what is the
evidence that the rest of that book is so? There is not an
atom of proof that the hand which wrote the last chapter had
no share in the rest of the Pentateuch.

As a matter of fact, the Pentateuchal history was written
in the land of Canaan, and if it is all by one hand it was not
composed before the period of the kings. Genesis xxxvi. 31
sq. gives a list of kings who reigned in Edom "before there
reigned a king of the children of Israel." This carries us
down at least to the time of Saul; but the probable meaning
of the passage is that these kings ruled before Edom was
subject to an Israelite monarch, which brings us to David at
any rate. Of course this conclusion may be evaded by saying
that certain verses or chapters are late additions, that the list
of Edomite kings, and such references to the conquest of
Canaan as are found in Deut. ii. 12, iv. 38, are insertions of
Ezra or another editor. This might be a fair enough thing
to say if any positive proof were forthcoming that Moses
wrote the mass of the Pentateuch; but in the absence of
such proof no one has a right to call a passage the insertion
of an editor without internal evidence that it is in a different
style or breaks the context. And as soon as we come to this
point we must apply the method consistently, and let internal
evidence tell its whole story. That, as we shall soon see, is
a good deal more than those who raise this potent spirit are
willing to hear.

The proof that the Pentateuch was written in Canaan does not turn on mere isolated texts which can be separated from the context. It lies equally in usages of language that cannot be due to an editor. There has been a great controversy about Deut. i. 1 and other similar passages, where the land east of the Jordan is said to be across Jordan, proving that the writer lived in Western Palestine. That this is the natural sense of the Hebrew word no one can doubt, but we have elaborate arguments that Hebrew was such an elastic language that the phrase can equally mean "on this side Jordan," as the English Version has it. The point is practically of no consequence, for there are other phrases which prove quite unambiguously that the Pentateuch was written in Canaan. In Hebrew the common phrase for "westward" is "seaward," and for southward "towards the Négeb." The word Négeb, which primarily means "parched land," is in Hebrew the proper name of the dry steppe district in the south of Judah. These expressions for west and south could only be formed within Palestine. Yet they are used in the Pentateuch, not only in the narrative but in the Sinaitic ordinance for the tabernacle in the wilderness (Exod. xxvii.). But at Mount Sinai the sea did not lie to the west, and the Négeb was to the north. Moses could no more call the south side the Négeb side of the tabernacle than a Glasgow man could say that the sun set over Edinburgh. The answer attempted to this is that the Hebrews might have adopted these phrases in patriarchal times, and never given them up in the ensuing four hundred and thirty years ; but that is nonsense. When a man says "towards the sea" he means it. The Egyptian Arabs say seaward for northward, and so the Israelites must have done when they were in Egypt. To an Arab in Western Arabia, on the contrary, seaward means towards the Red Sea. Again, the Pentateuch displays an exact topographical knowledge of Palestine, but by no means so exact a knowledge of the wilderness of the wandering. The narrative has the names of the places famous in the forty years' wandering ; but for Canaan it gives local details, and describes them with exactitude as they were in later times (*e.g.* Gen. xii. 8, xxxiii. 18, xxxv. 19, 20). Accordingly, the patriarchal sites can still be set down on the map with definiteness ; but geographers are unable to assign with certainty the site of Mount Sinai, because the narrative has none of that topographical colour which the story of an eye-witness is sure to possess. Once more, the Pentateuch cites as authorities poetical records which are not earlier than the time of Moses. One of these records is a book, the Book of the Wars of Jehovah (Num. xxi. 14); did Moses, writing contemporary history, find and cite a book already current, containing poetry on the wars of Jehovah and His people, which began in his own times ? Another poetical authority cited is a poem circulating among the *Môshelîm* or reciters of sarcastic verses (Num. xxi. 27 *sq.*). It refers to the victory over Sihon, which took place at the very end of the forty years' wandering. If Moses wrote the Pentateuch, what oc- casion could he have to authenticate his narrative by reference to these traditional depositaries of ancient poetry ?

The Pentateuch, then, was not written in the wilderness ; but moreover it is not, even in its narrative parts, a single continuous work, but a combination of several narratives originally independent. The first key to the complex struc- ture of the history was found in the use of the names of God in Genesis. Some parts of Genesis habitually speak of Jehovah, others as regularly use the word Elohim ; and as early as 1753 the French physician Astruc showed that if the text of Genesis be divided into two columns, all the Elohim passages standing on one side, and the Jehovah passages on the other, we get two parallel narratives which are still practically independent. This of course was no

more than a hint for further investigation. In reality there
are two independent documents in Genesis which use Elohim,
the second and younger of these being in fact the historical
introduction to the Levitical Legislation, or Priests' Code. A
third document uses Jehovah, and the process by which the
three were finally interwoven into one book is somewhat
difficult to follow. Astruc supposed that these documents
were all older than Moses, and that he was the final editor.
But later critics have shown that the same documents can be
traced through the whole Pentateuch, and even to the end of
the Book of Joshua. To prove this in detail would occupy
several lectures. I can only give one or two illustrations to
prove that these results are not imaginary.

A modern writer, making a history with the aid of older
records, masters their contents and then writes a wholly new
book. That is not the way of Eastern historians. If we take
up the great Arabic historians we often find passages occurring almost word for word in each. All use directly or in-
directly the same sources, and copy these sources verbally as
far as is consistent with the scope and scale of their several
works. Thus a comparatively modern book has often the
freshness and full colour of a contemporary narrative, and
we can still separate out the old sources from their modern
setting. So it is in the Bible, as we have already seen in the
case of the Books of Kings. It is this way of writing that
makes the Bible history so vivid and interesting, in spite of
its extraordinary brevity in comparison with the vast periods
of time that it covers. Think only what a mass of veracious
detail we were able to gather in Lecture IX. for the state of
ritual in ancient Israel. No compend on the same scale
written on modern principles could have preserved so much
of the genuine life of antique times. It stands to reason that
the Pentateuch should exhibit the same features ; and the
superciliousness with which traditionalists declare the labours

of the critics to be visionary is merely the contempt of ignorance, which has never handled old Eastern histories, and judges everything from a Western and modern standpoint.

Every one can see that, when we have this general key to the method of ancient Eastern historians, it is quite a practical undertaking to try to separate the sources from which a Hebrew author worked. It will not always be possible to carry the analysis out fully; but it is no hopeless task to distribute the main masses of the story between the several authors whose books he used. Marked peculiarities of language, of which the use of the names of God is the most celebrated but not the most conclusive, are a great help ; and along with these a multitude of other indications come in, as the analysis proceeds.

A very clear case is the account of the Flood. As it now stands the narrative has the most singular repetitions, and things come in in the strangest order. But as soon as we separate the Jehovah and Elohim documents all is clear. The first narrative tells that Jehovah saw the wickedness of men and determined to destroy them. But Noah found grace in His eyes, and was called to enter the ark with a pair of all unclean beasts, and clean beasts and fowls by sevens ; for, he is told, after seven days a forty days' rain will ensue and destroy all life. Noah obeys the command, the seven days elapse, and the rain follows as predicted, floating the ark but destroying all outside of it. Then the rain ceases and the waters sink. Noah opens the window of the ark and sends out the raven, which flies to and fro till the earth dries. The dove is also sent forth, but soon returns to the ark. Seven days later the same messenger is sent forth, and returns in the evening with a fresh twig of olive. Another week passes, and then the dove, sent out for the third time, does not return. Thereupon Noah removes the covering of the ark, finds the ground dry, builds an altar and does sacrifice, receiving the promise that the flood shall not again recur and disturb the course of the seasons. The parallel Elohistic narrative (which in this case belongs to the younger Elohistic document, *i.e.* to the narrative framework of the Priests' Code) is equally complete. It also relates God's anger with mankind. Noah receives orders to build the ark and take in the animals in pairs (there is no mention of the sevens of clean beasts). The flood begins when Noah is six hundred years old. The fountains of the great deep are broken up, and the windows of heaven opened; but on the same day Noah, his family, and the pairs of animals enter the ark. The waters rise till they cover the hills, and swell for a hundred and fifty days, when they are assuaged by a great wind, and the fountains of the deep and the windows of heaven are closed. The waters now begin to fall, and just five months after the flood commenced the ark rests on a point in the mountains of Ararat. The waters still continue to decrease for two months and a half, till the tops of the mountains are seen. In other three months the face of the earth was freed of water, but it was not till the lapse of a full solar year that Noah was permitted to leave the ark, when he received God's blessing, the so-called Noachic ordinances, and the sign of the bow. These two accounts are plainly independent. It is impossible that the work of one author could so divide itself into two complete narratives, and have for each a different name of God.[1]

---

[1] The following table will make the analysis more clear :—

Jehovist,	vi. 5-8	vii. 1-5	vii. 7-10	vii. 12
Priestly Elohist,	vi. 9-22	vii. 6	vii. 11	

J.		vii. 16 (last clause), 17		vii. 22, 23
P.	vii. 13-16 except the last clause.		vii. 18-21	

J.		viii. 2 *b*, 3 *a*		viii. 6-12
P.	vii. 24, viii. 1, 2 *a*		viii. 3 *b*-5	

J.		viii. 13 *b*	viii. 20-22	
P.	viii. 13 *a*	viii. 14-19	ix. 1-17	

The proof that the same variety of hands runs through to the end of the Book of Joshua would carry us too far, and is the less necessary because the fact will hardly be denied by those who admit the existence of separate sources in the Pentateuch at all. For those who cannot follow the details of the original text it is more profitable to concentrate attention on the legal parts of the Pentateuch. What has been said is enough to show that the Pentateuch is a much more complex book than appears at first sight, and that in its present form it was written after the time of Moses, nay, after that of Joshua. It is now no longer permissible to insist that the reference to the kingship of Israel over Edom and similar things are necessarily isolated phenomena. We cannot venture to assert that the composition of the Pentateuch out of older sources of various date took place before the time of the kings. How much of it is early, how much comparatively late, must be determined by a wider inquiry, and for this the laws give the best starting-point.

The post-Mosaic date of the narrative does not in itself prove that the laws were not all written by Moses. Two of our three legislative *Corpora* are independent of the history. The third is at least independent of the main thread of the narrative, and deals with history only for legal and ritual purposes. But does the Pentateuch represent Moses as having written the legal codes which it embodies ? So far as the ritual of the Levitical legislation is concerned, we can answer this question at once with a decisive negative. It is nowhere said that Moses wrote down the description of the tabernacle and its ordinances, or the law of sacrifice. And in many

In one or two places some slight modifications seem to have been made on the narrative of J. when the two accounts were combined. Thus in vii. 9 the distinction proper to J. between the sevens of clean beasts and the pairs of beasts not clean has disappeared. In the same verse the Hebrew text has God (Elohim) where we expect Jehovah, but Jehovah was certainly the original reading, and has been preserved in the Samaritan text, in the Targum and Vulgate, and in some MSS. of the Septuagint.

places the laws of this legislation are expressly set forth as
oral. Moses is commanded to speak to Aaron or to the
Israelites, as the case may be, and communicate to them
God's will. This fact is significant when we remember that
the Torah of the priests referred to by the prophets is plainly
oral instruction. There is nothing in the Pentateuch that
does not confirm the prior probability that ritual law was
long an affair of practice and tradition, resting on knowledge
that belonged to the priestly guild. But the priests, according to Hosea, forgot the Torah, and we have seen that neither
at Shiloh nor in Jerusalem did the ritual law exist in its
present form, or even its present theory. Thus we are reduced to this alternative:—either the ritual law was written
down by the priests immediately after Moses gave it to them,
or at least in the first years of residence in Canaan, and then
completely forgotten by them; or else it was not written till
long after, when the priests who forgot the law were chastised
by exile, and a new race arose which accepted the rebukes of
the prophets. The former hypothesis implies that a book
specially meant for the priests, and kept in their custody,
survived many centuries of total neglect and frequent re-
movals of the sanctuary, and that too at a time when books
were written in such a way that damp soon made them
illegible. Yet the text of this book, which the priests had
forgotten, is much more perfect than that of the Psalms or
the Books of Samuel. These are grave difficulties; and they
must become decisive when we show that an earlier code,
contradicting the Levitical legislation in important points, was
actually current in ancient times as the divine law of Israel.

With regard to the other two bodies of law the case is
different. In Exod. xxiv. 4-7 we are told that Moses "wrote
all the words of Jehovah" which had been communicated to
him on Mount Sinai, and pledged the people to obey them in
a formal covenant. The writing to which the people were

thus pledged is called in verse 7 the Book of the Covenant.
There has been some dispute as to what this Book of the
Covenant contained, and it has been argued that a distinction
must be drawn between "the words of Jehovah" in verse 4
and "the judgments" in verse 3, and that the former alone
were written in the Book of the Covenant. And since "the
judgments" appear, on comparison of xxi. 1, to be identical
with the code of Exod. xxi.-xxiii., it has been inferred that the
Book of the Covenant consisted only of the Ten Commandments (Exod. xx. 2-17). This view certainly appears somewhat
strained, for the distinction between "words" and "judgments" is rather imported into the passage than naturally
conveyed by it. But on the other hand, the identification of
the Book of the Covenant with the Decalogue is in accordance
with Exod. xxxiv. 27, 28, where the words of Jehovah's
covenant with Israel, which Moses was ordered to write on
the tables of stone, are expressly called the Ten Words. So
also in Deut. v. 2-22 the Ten Commandments are evidently
set forth as forming the whole compass of the covenant at
Horeb (comp. Deut. ix. 9, 15 ; 1 Kings viii. 9). These arguments appear to be cogent, *if we may take it for granted that
all the accounts of the covenant at Sinai are in perfect accord.*
It will then appear that at Sinai no other laws were committed to writing than the Ten Commandments. Nor is the
lawgiver recorded to have written down any further ordinances during the wilderness wanderings. But in Deut. xxxi.
9, 24 the account of Moses's last address to the people in the
plains of Moab is followed by the statement that he wrote
"the words of this law" in a book, which he deposited with
the Levites to be preserved beside the ark. In the context,
the expression "this law" can only mean the law of Deuteronomy, which is often so called in the earlier chapters of the
book ; it cannot possibly mean the whole Pentateuch. Thus,
on the assumption that there is no discrepancy or uncertainty

in the various notices contained in different parts of the
Pentateuch, we may conclude that, in addition to the Ten
Commandments written at Sinai, a larger body of laws,
corresponding to the Deuteronomic code, was committed to
writing by Moses just before his death.   Even so it would
not be safe to assume that the whole law of Deuteronomy, as
it is contained in chaps. xii.-xxvi., has reached us in the
precise words that Moses wrote, without modification or
addition.   We have learned in earlier parts of these Lectures
that additions were made in the course of ages to many
portions of the Bible.   But of all books a code of laws,
which is useless if it is not kept up to date, is most likely
to receive additions, or even to be entirely recast to meet a
change in social conditions ; nor would the consideration
that the ordinances of Moses had divine authority prevent
this from taking place in a nation that was continually
guided by the priestly oracle and the prophetic word, and
in which every decision of the judges of the sacred court was
accepted as a decision of God (*supra*, p. 299).   The testimony
of Deut. xxxi. cannot therefore dispense us from inquiry
whether the Deuteronomic code is the very writing of Moses,
or a more modern expansion and development of the law
given on the plains of Moab, which retains the name of
Moses, not because he completed the legislative system, but
because he laid its foundations.

All this may be fairly urged even on the assumption that
the narrative parts of the Pentateuch bear a single unambiguous testimony to the nature and extent of Moses's written
laws.   But a candid examination compels us to admit that,
while all parts of the Pentateuch are unanimous in their
witness to Moses as the founder of the Law, the details of
the law-giving are involved in great obscurity, and were
evidently represented in different ways by the various
narrators from whose accounts the Pentateuch is made up.

In short, we here find on a larger scale the same phenomenon
that we have already met with in the story of the Flood. The
extant narrative is a twisted strand combined out of several
narratives diverse the one from the other not only in form
but in substance.

First of all let us note that the assumption, on which we
have hitherto proceeded, that Exod. xxiv. 3-7, Exod. xxxiv.
27, 28, and Deut. v. 2-22, present a consistent account of the
Covenant at Sinai will not bear closer examination. The
account in Deuteronomy is unambiguous; the covenant
consisted only of the Ten Commandments (in Hebrew the
Ten Words), and nothing more was written down till Moses
was about to die. It is true that Deuteronomy iv. 14, v. 31
give us to understand that Moses received a further body of
laws at Horeb ; but these, as we are expressly told, were for
use in Canaan (iv. 14), and therefore they were not published
till the people stood on the borders of the promised land
(iv. 1 *sqq.*). Exodus xxxiv. agrees with this in so far as it
identifies the words of the Covenant with the Ten Words
written on the two tables of stone ; but, while Deuteronomy
(v. 22, x. 4) is quite explicit in saying that the tables contained the Ten Commandments of Exod. xx. 2-17, Deut. v.
6-21, the Ten Words of Exod. xxxiv. 27, 28 are necessarily
the words found in verses 10-26 of the same chapter, *i.e.* a
series of laws of religious observance closely corresponding
to the religious and ritual precepts of the First Legislation
(Exod. xxi.-xxiii.). We are so accustomed to look on the
Ten Words written on the tables of stone as the very
foundation-stone of the Mosaic law that it is hard for us
to realise that in ancient Israel there were two opinions as
to what these Words were; and, for my own part, I confess
that I have struggled as long as I could to explain the
discrepancy away. But the thing is too plain to be denied,
and the hypothesis which I once ventured to advance that

Exod. xxxiv. 10-26 may have got out of its true place at
some stage in the redaction of the Pentateuch does not help
matters.   For in any case it would still have to be admitted
that the editor to whom we owe the present form of the
chapter identified this little code of religious observances
with the Ten Words.   The difficulty, therefore, would still
remain the same.[1]

Now, if we can no longer regard Deuteronomy and Exodus
xxxiv. as giving a single sound on the matter of the Sinaitic
Covenant, the chief reason for thinking that the Book of the
Covenant in Exod. xxiv. is identical with the Decalogue
falls to the ground.   We are no longer entitled to draw a
strained distinction between "the words" and "the judgments" in order to maintain the harmony between all the
accounts; and on the other hand we observe that the words
which Moses received and wrote (ver. 4) can hardly be the
same as the Decalogue which was proclaimed from Sinai in
the ears of all.   The Decalogue was not given to Moses to
be written from memory, but was written on the Mount
itself, and that, too, according to the present order of the
narrative, *after* the Covenant had been written and ratified
(xxiv. 12).   Thus we are led, after all, to identify the Book
of the Covenant with the First Legislation (Exod. xxi.-xxiv.),
and to admit that the Pentateuch presents three divergent
views of the contents of the Sinaitic Covenant.[2]

---

[1] The hypothesis of a displacement in Exod. xxxiv., which I put forward
in the *Encyclopædia Britannica*, 9th ed., article DECALOGUE (1877), was independently worked out by Kuenen in an article in *Theol. Tijdschrift*, xv. (1881),
p. 164 *sqq.*   He regards Exod. xxxiv. 1, 4, and the last words of verse 28,
as belonging to a different document from xxxiv. 2, 3, 5, 10-27, and so is able
to maintain that the Ten Words of xxxiv. 28 are the same as the Decalogue
of chap. xx.   Wellhausen has criticised this view in the latest edition of
his *Composition* (1889), p. 327 *sqq.*, justly remarking that in that case the
editor who gave the text its present form "has introduced the most serious
internal contradiction found in the Old Testament."

[2] Any one who carefully reads through the narrative of the transactions of
Sinai must recognise that the story has reached us in a very confused state.
"After the proclamation of the Decalogue Moses pays a first, a second, and a

Such being the state of the extant history of Moses's work, it is not only legitimate but absolutely necessary to undertake a critical examination of the several bodies of laws, in the hope that internal evidence may do something to help us through the uncertainties in which the narrative of the law-giving is involved, and throw light on the question when and by what stages the divine Torah, of which Moses was the originator, assumed the form it has in the extant written codes.

Now it is a very remarkable fact, to begin with, that all the sacred law of Israel is comprised in the Pentateuch, and that, apart from the Levitical legislation, it is presented in codified form. On the traditional view, three successive bodies of law were given to Israel within forty years. Within that short time many ordinances were modified, and the

third visit to Sinai, always with the same object of receiving laws. It is clear that when, after the first visit (Exod. xx. 21, xxiv. 3), all the words and judgments of Jehovah are written down and the people are solemnly pledged to them, this must have originally indicated that the legislation is formally brought to a close (xxiv. 3-8) ; but as the story now stands the conclusion of the Covenant is a mere interlude. For scarcely is the solemnity over when Moses (with Joshua) again goes up to God in the Mount, and remains there a long time, receiving further divine communications, doubtless of a legal character. Finally, in chap. xxxiv. there is another long visit to Mount Sinai, and there for a third time he receives words and writes them on two tables of stone. The third visit, indeed, is explained by the breaking of the first tables, which have to be renewed ; but what is dictated to him is not a repetition of the old matter but a series of new precepts." Wellhausen, *Composition* (1889), p. 84 *sq.* (The whole passage should be read.)

The perplexities of Exod. xix.-xxxiv. have made these chapters the *locus desperatus* of criticism. It is easy to remove the priestly additions (chaps. xxv.-xxxi. and a few verses elsewhere), and to point out in what remains clear indications that at least two parallel and independent narratives have been worked into a single tissue. Thus in xix. 20 Jehovah descends upon Sinai, but in the previous verses he is already there ; hence xix. 3-19 and xix. 20-25 seem originally to have belonged to distinct narratives, though the points of difference have been softened by the hand of the redactor (*e.g.* by the insertion of verses 23, 24). Again xxiv. 1, 2 is continued in verses 9-11, while the intervening verses belong to a different context. But the whole section has been so often worked over by editorial hands, touching and retouching, making omissions, additions, and transpositions, that it is impossible to separate the original sources with the certainty and precision

whole law of Sinai recast on the plains of Moab. But from
the days of Moses there was no change. With his death
the Israelites entered on a new career, which transformed
the nomads of Goshen into the civilised inhabitants of vineyard land and cities in Canaan. But the Divine laws given
them beyond Jordan were to remain unmodified through all
the long centuries of development in Canaan, an absolute
and immutable code. I say, with all reverence, that this is
impossible. God no doubt could have given, by Moses's
mouth, a law fit for the age of Solomon or Hezekiah, but
such a law could not be fit for immediate application in the
days of Moses and Joshua. Every historical lawyer knows
that in the nature of things the law of the wilderness is
different from the law of a land of high agriculture and
populous cities. God can do all things, but He cannot
contradict Himself, and He who shaped the eventful development of Israel's history must have framed His law to
correspond with it.

It is no conjecture, but plain historical fact stated in

which belong to the analysis of the story of the Deluge. Broadly speaking,
it appears that the oldest narrator (J), whose account is very imperfectly
preserved, and whose hand is to be recognised mainly in xix. 20-22, 25, and
in chap. xxxiv., did not mention the present Decalogue at all, but told how
Moses was called up to the mountain and received there the Ten Words of
chap. xxxiv. The second narrator (E), like the Book of Deuteronomy, confined the law proclaimed at Sinai to the Decalogue of Exod. xx., but also
related how Moses was called up to the Mount to receive further revelations
(not for immediate publication). In his absence the incident of the golden
calf took place, and as a punishment the people were at once dismissed from
the seat of Jehovah's holy presence. Finally, the First Legislation or Book
of the Covenant, for which no place can be found in either of these narratives,
may perhaps be best accounted for by the very ingenious conjecture of
Kuenen, that chaps. xxi.-xxiii., with verses 3-8 of chap. xxiv., are part of the
narrative of E, but originally stood in quite another place, that, in fact, they
are the old account of the legislation in the plains of Moab, of which the
Deuteronomic code is a new and enlarged edition. When both editions came
to be brought together in one book the old code was thrown back among the
transactions at Mount Sinai. On the view the original narrative of E was
in full harmony with the Deuteronomic account of the successive stages of the
legislation.

Exod. xviii., that Moses judged his contemporaries by bringing individual hard cases before Jehovah for decision.   This
was the actual method of his Torah, a method strictly
practical, and in precise conformity with the genius and
requirements of primitive nations.   The events of Sinai, and
the establishment of the covenant on the basis of the Ten
Words, did not cut short this kind of Torah.   On the
contrary, there is clear proof that direct appeal to a Divine
judgment continued to be practised in Israel.   The First
Legislation (Exod. xxi. 6, xxii. 8) speaks of bringing a case
to God, and receiving the sentence of God, where our version
has "the judges."   The sanctuary was the seat of judgment,
and the decisions were Jehovah's Torah.   So still, in the
time of Eli, we read that, if man offend against man, God
gives judgment as daysman between them (1 Sam. ii. 25).
Jehovah is in Israel a living judge, a living and present lawgiver.   He has all the functions of an actual king present
among his people (Isa. xxxiii. 22).   So the prophets still view
Jehovah's law as a living and growing thing, communicated
to Israel as to weanlings, "precept upon precept, line upon
line, here a little and there a little" (Isa. xxviii. 9 *sq.*); and
their religion, drawn direct from Jehovah, is contrasted with
the traditional religion, which is "a command of men learned
and taught" (Isa. xxix. 13).   A code is of necessity the final
result and crystallised form of such a living divine Torah,
just as in all nations consuetudinary and judge-made law
precedes codification and statute law.   The difference between
Israel and other nations lay essentially in this, that Jehovah
was Israel's Judge, and therefore Israel's Lawgiver.   This
divine Torah begins with Moses.   As all goes back to his
initiative, the Israelites were not concerned to remember the
precise history of each new precept ; and, when the whole
system developed under continuous divine guidance is summed
up in a code, that code is simply set down as Mosaic Torah.

We still call the steam-engine by the name of Watt, though the steam-engine of to-day has many parts that his had not.

The Bible has not so narrow a conception of revelation as we sometimes cling to. According to Isaiah xxviii. 23 *sq.* the rules of good husbandry are a "judgment" taught to the ploughman by Jehovah, part of Jehovah's Torah (ver. 26). The piety of Israel recognised every sound and wholesome ordinance of daily and social life as a direct gift of Jehovah's wisdom. "This also cometh forth from Jehovah of hosts, whose counsel is miraculous, and His wisdom great." Accordingly Jehovah's law contains, not only institutes of direct revelation in our limited sense of that word, but old consuetudinary usages, laws identical with those of other early peoples, which had become sacred by being taken up into the God-given polity of Israel, and worked into harmony with the very present reality of His redeeming sovereignty. We shall best picture to ourselves what the ancient Hebrews understood by divine statutes, by a brief survey of the manner of life prescribed in the First Legislation.

The society contemplated in this legislation is of very simple structure. The basis of life is agricultural. Cattle and agricultural produce are the elements of wealth, and the laws of property deal almost exclusively with them. The principles of civil and criminal justice are those still current among the Arabs of the desert. They are two in number, retaliation and pecuniary compensation. Murder is dealt with by the law of blood-revenge, but the innocent manslayer may seek asylum at God's altar. With murder are ranked manstealing, offences against parents, and witchcraft. Other injuries are occasions of self-help or of private suits to be adjusted at the sanctuary. Personal injuries fall under the law of retaliation, just as murder does. Blow for blow is still the law of the Arabs, and in Canaan no doubt, as in the

desert, the retaliation was usually sought in the way of
self-help. The principle of retaliation is conceived as
legitimate vengeance, xxi. 20, 21, *margin*. Except in this
form there is no punishment, but only compensation, which
in some cases is at the will of the injured party (who has
the alternative of direct revenge), but in general is defined
by law.

Degrading punishments, as imprisonment or the bastinado,
are unknown, and loss of liberty is inflicted only on the thief
who cannot pay a fine. The slave retains definite rights.
He recovers his freedom after seven years, unless he prefers
to remain a bondman, and to seal this determination by a
symbolical act at the door of the sanctuary. His right of
blood-revenge against his master is limited, and, instead of
the *lex talionis*, for minor injuries he can claim his liberty.
Women do not enjoy full social equality with men. Women
slaves were slaves for life, but were usually married to
members of the family or servants of the household. The
daughter was her father's property, who received a price for
surrendering her to a husband ; and so a daughter's dis-
honour is compensated by law as a pecuniary loss to her
father. The Israelites directly contemplated in these laws
are evidently men of independent bearing and personal
dignity, such as are still found in secluded parts of the
Semitic world under a half-patriarchal constitution of society
where every freeman is a small landholder. But there is no
strong central authority. The tribunal of the sanctuary is
arbiter, not executive. No man is secure without his own
aid, and the widow or orphan looks for help, not to man, but
to Jehovah Himself. But if the executive is weak, a strict
regard for justice is inculcated. Jehovah is behind the law,
and He will vindicate the right. He requires of Israel
humanity as well as justice. The Gêr, or stranger living
under the protection of a family or community, has no legal

status, but he must not be oppressed.[1] The Sabbath is enforced as an ordinance of humanity, and to the same end the
produce of every field or vineyard must be left to the poor
one year in seven. The precepts of religious worship are
simple. He who sacrifices to any God but Jehovah falls
under the ban. The only ordinance of ceremonial sanctity is
to abstain from the flesh of animals torn by wild beasts.
The sacred dues are the firstlings and first fruits : the former
must be presented at the sanctuary on the eighth day. This,
of course, presupposes a plurality of sanctuaries, and in fact
Exodus xx. 24, 25, explains that an altar of stone may be
built, and Jehovah acceptably approached, in every place
where He sets a memorial of His name. The stated occasions
of sacrifice are the feast of unleavened bread, in commemoration of the exodus, the feast of harvest, and that of ingathering. These feasts mark the cycle of the agricultural year,
and at them every male must present his homage before
Jehovah. The essential points of sacrificial ritual are abstin-
ence from leaven in connection with the blood of the sacrifice,
and the rule that the fat must be burnt the same night.

You see at once that this is no abstract divine legislation.
It is a social system adapted to a very definite type of
national life. On the common view, many of its precepts
were immediately superseded by the Levitical or Deutero-

---

[1] The Hebrew Gêr exactly corresponds to the Arabian Jâr, on whose
position see *Kinship and Marriage*, p. 41 *sqq.* The protected stranger is still
known in Arabia. Among the Hodheil at Zeimeh I found in 1880 an Indian
boy, the son of a Suleimâny or wandering smith, who was under the protection of the community, every member of which would have made the lad's
quarrel his own. In old Arabia such strangers often came at last to be merged
in the tribe of their protectors, and this must have happened on a large scale
in old Israel, and accounts for the absorption of the Canaanite population
between the time of the Judges and the Exile. But in Deuteronomy the
distinctive position of an Israelite is more sharply defined. In Deut. xiv. 21
unclean food, which the First Legislation commands to be thrown to the dogs,
may be given to the Gêr. In the Levitical legislation the word Gêr is already
on the way to assume the later technical sense of proselyte.

nomic code, before they ever had a chance of being put in operation in Canaan. But this hypothesis, so dishonouring to the Divine Legislator, who can do nothing in vain, is refuted by the whole tenor of the code, which undoubtedly is as living and real a system of law as was ever written. The details of the system are almost all such as are found among other nations. The law of Israel does not yet aim at singularity; it is enough that it is pervaded by a constant sense that the righteous and gracious Jehovah is behind the law and wields it in conformity with His own holy nature. The law, therefore, makes no pretence at ideality. It contains precepts adapted, as our Lord puts it, to the hardness of the people's heart. The ordinances are not abstractly perfect, and fit to be a rule of life in every state of society, but they are fit to make Israel a righteous, humane, and God-fearing people, and to facilitate a healthy growth towards better things.

The important point that reference to Jehovah and His character determines the spirit rather than the details of the legislation cannot be too strongly accentuated. The civil laws are exactly such as the comparative lawyer is familiar with in other nations. Even the religious ordinances are far from unique in their formal elements. The feast of unleavened bread has a special reference to the deliverance from Egypt, which is the historical basis of Israel's distinctive religion. But even this feast has also a more general reference, for it is clearly connected in Exod. xiii. 3-6, xxxiv. 18-20, with the sacrifice of the firstlings of the flocks and herds, which is a form of worship known also to the ancient Arabs; and the two other feasts, which are purely agricultural, are quite analogous to what is found in other nations. The feast of harvest reappears in all parts of the ancient world, and the Canaanite vintage feast at Shechem offers a close parallel to the feast of ingathering (*supra*, p. 269).

The distinctive character of the religion appears in the laws directed against polytheism and witchcraft, in the prominence given to righteousness and humanity as the things which are most pleasing to Jehovah and constitute the true significance of such an ordinance as the Sabbath, and, above all, in the clearness with which the law holds forth the truth that Jehovah's goodness to Israel is no mere natural relation such as binds Moab to Chemosh, that His favour to His people is directed by moral principles and is forfeited by moral iniquity. In this code we already read the foundation of the thesis of Amos, that just because Jehovah knows Israel He observes and punishes the nation's sins (Amos iii. 2 ; Exod. xxii. 23, 27, xxiii. 7).

Now, we have seen that before the Exile the most characteristic features of the Levitical legislation, and so the most prominent things in our present Pentateuch, had no influence on Israel, either on the righteous or the wicked. This result involved us in great perplexity. For, if the traditional view of the age of the Pentateuch is correct, there was through all these centuries an absolute divorce between God's written law and the practical workings of His grace. And the perplexity was only increased when we found that, nevertheless, there was a Torah in Israel before the prophetic books, to which the prophets appeal as the indisputable standard of Jehovah's will. But the puzzle is solved when we compare the history with this First Legislation. This law did not remain without fruit in Israel, and as we have just seen in the case of Amos, its conception of Jehovah's government affords a firm footing for the prophetic word. There is abundant proof that the principles of this legislation were acknowledged in Israel. The appeal to God as judge appears in 1 Sam. ii. 25 ; the law of blood-revenge, administered, not by a central authority, but by the family of the deceased, occurs in 2 Sam. iii. 30, xiv. 7, etc.;

the altar is the asylum in 1 Kings i. 50, and elsewhere ; the thief taken in the breach (Exod. xxii. 2) is alluded to by Jer. ii. 34 ; and so forth. The sacred ordinances agree with those in the history, or, if exceptions are noted, they are stigmatised as irregular. The plurality of altars accords with this law. The annual feasts—at least that of the autumn, which seems to have been best observed—are often alluded to ; and the night service of commemoration for the exodus appears in Isa. xxx. 29. The rule that the pilgrim must bring an offering was recognised at Shiloh (1 Sam. i. 21). So, too, the complaint against Eli's sons for their delay in burning the fat is based on the same principle as Exod. xxiii. 18 ; and the use of leavened bread on the altar, which is forbidden in Exod. xxiii. 18, was indeed admitted in the northern shrines at the time of Amos, but is referred to by that prophet in sarcastic terms, as if it were a departure from the ancient ritual of Jehovah's sanctuaries (Amos iv. 5). The prohibition to eat blood, which is essentially one with the prohibition of torn flesh, is sedulously observed by Saul (1 Sam. xiv. 33 *sq.*), and Saul also distinguishes himself by suppressing witchcraft. The proof that this law was known and acknowledged in all its leading provisions is as complete as the proof that the Levitical law was still unheard of. This result confirms, and at the same time supplements, our previous argument. We have now brought the history into positive relation to one part of the Pentateuch, and the critical analysis of the books of Moses has already filled up one of those breaches between law and history which the traditional view can do nothing to heal.

LECTURE XII

THE DEUTERONOMIC CODE AND THE LEVITICAL LAW

In the First Legislation the question of correct ritual has little prominence. The simple rules laid down are little more than the necessary and natural expression of that principle which we saw in Lecture VIII. to be the presupposition of the popular worship of Israel, even when it diverged most widely from the Levitical forms. Jehovah alone is Israel's God. It is a crime, analogous to treason, to depart from Him and sacrifice to other gods. As the Lord of Israel and Israel's land, the giver of all good gifts to His people, He has a manifest claim on Israel's homage, and receives at their hands such dues as their neighbours paid to their gods, such dues as a king receives from his people (comp. 1 Sam. viii. 15, 17). The occasions of homage are those seasons of natural gladness which an agricultural life suggests. The joy of harvest and vintage is a rejoicing before Jehovah, when the worshipper brings a gift in his hand, as he would do in approaching an earthly sovereign, and presents the choicest first fruits at the altar, just as his Canaanite neighbour does in the house of Baal (Jud. ix. 27). The whole worship is spontaneous and natural. It has hardly the character of a positive legislation, and its distinction from heathen rites lies less in the outward form than in the different conception of Jehovah which the true worshipper should bear in his heart. To a people which "knows Jehovah," this unambitious service, in which the expression of grateful homage to Him runs through all the simple joys of a placid agricultural life, was sufficient to form the visible basis of a pure and earnest piety. But its forms gave no protection against deflection into heathenism and immorality when Jehovah's spiritual nature and moral precepts were forgotten. The feasts and sacrifices might still run their accustomed round when Jehovah was practically confounded with the Baalim, and there was no more truth or mercy or knowledge of God in the land (Hosea iv. 1).

Such, in fact, was the state of things in the eighth century, the age of the earliest prophetic books. The declensions of Israel had not checked the outward zeal with which Jehovah was worshipped. Never had the national sanctuaries been more sedulously frequented, never had the feasts been more splendid or the offerings more copious. But the foundations of the old life were breaking up. The external prosperity of the state covered an abyss of social disorder. Profusion and luxury among the higher classes stood in startling contrast to the misery of the poor. Lawlessness and open crime were on the increase. The rulers of the nation grew fat upon oppression, but there was none who was grieved for the wound of Joseph. These evils were earliest and most acutely felt in the kingdom of Ephraim, where Amos declares them to be already incurable under the outwardly prosperous reign of Jeroboam II. With the downfall of Jehu's dynasty the last bonds of social order were dissolved, and the Assyrian found an easy prey in a land already reduced to practical anarchy. The smaller realm of Judah seemed at first to show more hopeful symptoms (Hosea iv. 15). But the separation of the kingdoms had not broken the subtle links that connected Judah with the greater Israel of the North. At all periods, the fortunes and internal movements of Ephraim had powerfully reacted on the Southern Kingdom. Isaiah and Micah describe a corruption within the house of David altogether similar to the sin of Samaria. "The statutes of Omri were kept, and all the works of the house of Ahab" (Micah vi. 16).

The prominence which the prophets assign to social grievances and civil disorders has often led to their being described as politicians, a democratic Opposition in the aristocratic state. This is a total misconception. The prophets of the eighth century have no new theories of government, and propose no practical scheme of political readjustment. They are the friends of the poor because they hate oppression, and they attack the governing classes for their selfishness and injustice; but their cry is not for better institutions but for better men, not for the abolition of aristocratic privileges but for an honest and godly use of them. The work of the prophets is purely religious; they censure what is inconsistent with the knowledge and fear of Jehovah, but see no way of remedy save in the repentance and return to Him of all classes of society, after a sifting work of judgment has destroyed the sinners of Jehovah's people without suffering one grain of true wheat to fall to the ground (Amos ix. 9 *sq.*; Isa. vi., etc.). But to the prophets the observance of justice and mercy in the state are the first elements of religion. The religious subject, the worshipping individual, Jehovah's son, was not the individual Israelite, but the nation *qua* nation, and the Old Testament analogue to the peace of conscience which marks a healthy condition of spiritual life in the Christian was that inner peace and harmony of the estates of the realm which can only be secured where justice is done and mercy loved. The ideal of the prophets in the eighth century is not different from that of the First Legislation. In the old law the worship of feasts and sacrifices is the natural consecration, in act, of a simple, happy society,

nourished by Jehovah's good gifts in answer to the labour
of the husbandman, and cemented by a regard for justice and
habits of social kindliness. When the old healthy harmony
of classes was dissolved, when the rich and the poor were no
longer knit together by a kindly sympathy and patriarchal
bond of dependence, but confronted one another as oppressor
and oppressed, when the strain thus put on all social relations
burst the weak bonds of outer order and filled the land with
unexpiated bloodshed, the pretence of homage to Jehovah at
His sanctuary was but the crowning proof that Israel knew
not his God. "When ye spread forth your hands, I will hide
mine eyes from you ; yea, when ye make many prayers I will
not hear : your hands are full of blood" (Isa. i. 15).

The causes of the inner disintegration of Israel were
manifold, and we cannot pause to examine them fully. But
in this, as in many similar cases which history exhibits, the
strain which snapped the old bands of social unity proceeded
mainly from the effects of warlike invasion reacting on a one-
sided progress in material prosperity, to which the order of
the state had not been able to readjust itself. The luxury of
the higher classes, described by Amos and Isaiah, shows that
the nobles of Israel were no longer great farmers, as Saul and
Nabal had been, living among the peasantry and sharing their
toil. The connection with Tyre, which commenced in the
days of David, opened a profitable foreign market for the
agricultural produce of Palestine (Ezek. xxvii. 17), and introduced foreign luxuries in return. The landowners became
merchants and forestallers of grain (Amos viii. 5 ; Hosea xii.
7). The introduction of such a commerce, throwing the
Hebrews into immediate relations with the great emporium
of international traffic, necessarily led to accumulation of
wealth in a few hands, and to the corresponding impoverish-
ment of the landless class, as exportation raised the price of
the necessaries of life. In times of famine, or under the

distress wrought by prolonged and ferocious warfare with Syria, the once independent peasantry fell into the condition now so universal in the East. They were loaded with debt, cheated on all hands, and often had to relinquish their personal liberty (Amos ii. 6, 7; Micah iii. 2 *sq.*, vi. 10 *sq.*, etc.). The order of the state, entirely based on the old pre-commercial state of things when trade was the affair of the Canaanites — Canaanite, in old Hebrew, is the word for a trader—was not able to adjust itself to the new circumstances. How entirely commercial avocations were unknown to the old law appears from the circumstance that the idea of capital is unknown. It is assumed in Exod. xxii. 25 that no one borrows money except for personal distress, and all interest is conceived as usury (comp. Psalm xv. 5). In proportion, therefore, as the nation began to share the wealth and luxury of the Canaanite trading cities of the coast, it divorced itself from the old social forms of the religion of Jehovah. The Canaanite influence affected religion in affecting the national life, and it was inevitable that the worship of the sanctuary, which had always been in the closest *rapport* with the daily habits of the people, should itself assume the colour of Canaanite luxury and Canaanite immorality. This tendency was not checked by the extirpation of professed worship of the Tyrian Baal. Jehovah Himself in His many shrines assumed the features of the local Baalim of the Canaanite sanctuaries, and horrible orgies of unrestrained sensuality, of which we no longer dare to speak in unveiled words, polluted the temples where Jehovah still reigned in name, and where His help was confidently expected to save Israel from Damascus and Assyria.

The prophets, as I have already said, never profess to devise a scheme of political and social reformation to meet these evils. Their business is not to govern, but to teach the nation to know Jehovah, and to lay bare the guilt of every

departure from Him. It is for the righteous ruler to determine how the principles of justice, mercy, and God-fearing
can be made practically operative in society. Thus the
criticism of the prophets on established usages is mainly
negative. The healing of Israel must come from Jehovah.
It is useless to seek help from political combinations, and
it is a mistake to fancy that international commerce and
foreign culture are additions to true happiness. This judgment proceeds from no theories of political economy. It
would be a fallacy to cite the prophets as witness that
commerce and material civilisation are bad in themselves.
All that they say is that these things, as they found them
in their own time, have undone Israel, and that the first step
towards deliverance must be a judgment which sweeps away
all the spurious show of prosperity that has come between
Jehovah's people and the true knowledge of their God (Isa.
ii. ; Micah v.). Israel must again pass through the wilderness. All the good gifts of fertile Canaan must be taken
away by a desolating calamity. Then the valley of trouble
shall again become a gate of hope, and Jehovah's covenant
shall renew its course on its old principles, but with far
more perfect realisation (Hos. ii.). The prophetic pictures of
Israel's final felicity are at this time all framed on the pattern
of the past. The days of David shall return under a righteous
king (Micah v. 2 *sq.* ; Hos. iii. 5 ; Isa. xi. 1 *sq.*), and Israel
shall realise, as it had never done in the past, the old ideal of
simple agricultural life, in which every good gift is received
directly from Jehovah's hand, and is supplied by Him in a
plenty that testifies to His perfect reconciliation with His
people (Hos. ii. 21 *sq.*; Amos ix. 11 *sq.* ; Micah iv. 4, vii. 14 ;
Isa. iv. 2).

This picture is ideal. It was never literally fulfilled to
Israel in Canaan, and now that the people of God has become
a spiritual society, dissociated from national limitations and

relation to the land of Canaan, it never can be fulfilled save
in a spiritual sense. The restoration of Israel to Palestine
would be no fulfilment of prophecy now, for the good things
of the land never had any other value to the prophets than
that they were the expression of Jehovah's love to the people
of His choice, which is now more clearly declared in Christ
Jesus, and brought nigh to the heart by His spirit. But the
ideal supplied a practical impulse. It did not provide the
sketch of a new legislation which could cure the deeper
ills of the state without the divine judgment which the
prophets foretold, but it indicated evils that must be cleared
away, and with which the old divine laws were unable to
grapple.

One point, in particular, became thoroughly plain. The
sacrificial worship was corrupt to the core, and could never
again be purified by the mere removal of foreign elements
from the local high places. The first step towards reformation must lie in the abolition of these polluted shrines, and
to this task the adherents of the prophets addressed themselves.

At this point in the history the centre of interest is
transferred from Ephraim to Judah. In Ephraim the
sanctuaries perished with the fall of the old kingdom, or
sank, if possible, to a lower depth in the worship of the
mixed populations introduced by the conqueror. In Judah
there was still some hope of better things. The party of
reform was for a space in the ascendant under King
Hezekiah, when the miraculous overthrow of the Assyrian
vindicated the authority of the prophet Isaiah and justified
his confident prediction that Jehovah would protect His
sacred hearth on Mount Zion. But the victory was not
gained in a moment. Under Manasseh a terrible reaction
set in, and the corrupt popular religion crushed the prophetic party, not without bloodshed. The truth was cast

down, but not overthrown. In Josiah's reign the tide of
battle turned, and then it was that "the book of the Torah"
was found in the Temple. Its words smote the hearts of
the king and the people, for though the book had no external
credentials it bore its evidence within itself, and it was
stamped with the approval of the prophetess Huldah. The
Torah was adopted in formal covenant, and on its lines,
—the lines of the Deuteronomic Code, as we have already
seen (*supra*, p. 258),—the reformation of Josiah was carried
out.

The details of the process of reformation which cul-
minated in the eighteenth year of Josiah are far from
clear, but a few leading points can be established with
precision. The central difference between the Deuteronomic
Code, on which Josiah acted, and the old code of the First
Legislation, lies in the principle that the Temple at Jerusalem is the only legitimate sanctuary. The legislator in
Deuteronomy expressly puts forth this ordinance as an
innovation: "Ye shall not do, as we do here this day,
every man whatsoever is right in his own eyes" (Deut.
xii. 8). Moreover, it is explained that the law which
confines sacrifice to one altar involves modifications of
ancient usage. If the land of Israel becomes so large
that the sanctuary is not easily accessible, bullocks and
sheep may be eaten at home, as game is eaten, without
being sacrificed, the blood only being poured on the
ground. We have already seen that the earlier custom
here presupposed, on which every feast of beef or mutton
was sacrificial, obtained long after the settlement of Israel
in Canaan, on the basis of the principle of many altars
laid down in Exod. xx. 24, and presupposed in the First
Legislation. But further, the Book of Deuteronomy, which
reproduces almost every precept of the older code, with
or without modification, remodels the ordinances which

23

presuppose a plurality of sanctuaries. According to Exod.
xxii. 30, the firstlings are to be offered on the eighth day.
This is impracticable under the law of one altar; and so
in Deut. xv. 19 *sq.* it is appointed that they shall be eaten
year by year at the sanctuary, and that meantime no work
shall be done with the firstling bullock, and that a firstling
sheep shall not be shorn. Again, the asylum for the manslayer in Exod. xxi. 12-14 is Jehovah's altar, and so, in fact,
the altar was used in the time of David and Solomon. But
under the law of Deuteronomy there are to be three fixed
cities of refuge (Deut. xix. 1 *sq.*).

The law, then, is quite distinctly a law for the abolition of
the local sanctuaries, which are recognised by the First Legislation, and had been frequented under it without offence during
many generations. The reason for the change comes out in
Deut. xii. 2 *sq.* The one sanctuary is ordained to prevent
assimilation between Jehovah-worship and the Canaanite service. The Israelites in the eighth century did service on the
hill-tops and under the green trees (Hos. iv. 13; Isa. i. 29),
and in these local sanctuaries they practically merged their
Jehovah-worship in the abominations of the heathen. The
Deuteronomic law designs to make such syncretism henceforth
impossible by separating the sanctuary of Jehovah from all
heathen shrines. And so, in particular, the old marks of a
sanctuary, the *maççēba* and *ashēra* (*supra*, p. 241), which had
been used by the patriarchs, and continued to exist in sanctuaries of Jehovah down to the eighth century, are declared
illegitimate (Deut. xvi. 21; Josh. xxiv. 26; 1 Sam. vi. 14, vii.
12; 2 Sam. xx. 8; 1 Kings i. 9; Hosea iii. 4; 1 Kings vii. 21).
This detail is one of the clearest proofs that Deuteronomy
was unknown till long after the days of Moses. How could
Joshua, if he had known such a law, have erected a *maççēba*
or sacred pillar of unhewn stone under the sacred tree by the
sanctuary at Shechem ? Nay, this law was still unknown to

Isaiah, who attacks idolatry, but recognises *maççēba* and altar
as the marks of the sanctuary of Jehovah. "In that day," he
says, prophesying the conversion of Egypt, "there shall be an
altar to Jehovah within the land of Egypt, and a *maççēba* at
the border thereof to Jehovah" (Isa. xix. 19). Isaiah could
not refer to a forbidden symbol as a *maççēba* to Jehovah. He
takes it for granted that Egypt, when converted, will serve
Jehovah by sacrifice (ver. 21), and do so under the familiar
forms which Jehovah has not yet abrogated.

This passage gives us a superior limit for the date of the
Deuteronomic Code. It was not known to Isaiah, and therefore the reforms of Hezekiah cannot have been based upon it.
Indeed the prophets of the eighth century, approaching the
problem of true worship, not from the legal and practical side,
but from the religious principles involved, never get so far as
to indicate a detailed plan for the reorganisation of the
sanctuaries. Micah proclaims God's wrath against the
maççēbas and *ashēras*; but they perish in the general fall of
the cities of Judah with all their corrupt civilisation (Micah
v. 10 *sq.*). Even Jerusalem and the Temple of Zion must
share the general fate (chap. iii. 12). Such a prediction offers
little assistance for a plan of reformed worship. In the
prophecies of Isaiah again, where the *maççēba* is still recognised as legitimate, the idols of the Judæan sanctuaries are
viewed as the chief element in the nation's rebellion, and the
mark of repentance is to cast them away (Isa. xxx. 22, xxxi.
6 *sq.*, ii. 7, 20). It does not seem impossible that Isaiah
would have been content with this reform, for he never
proclaims war against the local sanctuaries as he does against
their idols. He perceives, indeed, that not only the idols but
the altars come between Israel and Jehovah, and lead the
people to look to the work of their own hands instead of to
their Maker (Isa. xvii. 7 *sq.*). Yet even here the contrast is
not between one altar and many, but between the material

and man-made sanctuary and the Holy One of Israel. The
prophetic thought seems to hesitate on the verge of transition
to the spiritual worship of the New Covenant. But the time
was not yet ripe for so decisive a change.

To Isaiah, Jehovah's presence with His people is still a
local thing. It could not, indeed, be otherwise, for the people
of Jehovah was itself a conception geographically defined,
bound up with the land of Canaan, and having its centre in
Jerusalem. In the crisis of the Assyrian wars, the fundamental religious thought that Jehovah's gracious purpose, and
therefore Jehovah's people, are indestructible, took in Isaiah's
mind the definite form of an assurance that Jerusalem could
not fall before the enemy. " Jehovah hath founded Zion,
and the poor of his people shall trust in it " (Isa. xiv. 32).
Jehovah, who hath his fire in Zion, and his furnace in
Jerusalem, will protect his holy mountain, hovering over it
as birds over their nest (Isa. xxxi. 5, 9). Zion is the inviolable seat of Jehovah's sovereignty, where he dwells as a
devouring fire, purging the sin of His people by consuming
judgment, but also asserting His majesty against all invaders
(Isa. xxxiii. 13 *sq.*, iv. 4 *sq.*). This conception is nowhere
specially connected with the Temple. Rather is it the whole
plateau of Zion (chap. iv. 5) which is the seat of Jehovah's
presence with His people. But, according to the whole
manner of thought in the Old Testament, the seat of
Jehovah's presence to Israel, the centre from which his
Torah goes forth (Isa. ii. 3 ; Micah iv. 1 ; cf. Amos i. 2), the
mountain of Jehovah and Jehovah's house (Isa. xxx. 29,
ii. 2), the hearth of God (*Ariel*, Isa. xxix. 1), the place of
solemn and festal assembly (Isa. iv. 5, xxxiii. 20), must be
the place of acceptable sacrifice, if sacrifice is to continue at
all. Isaiah, perhaps, was not concerned to draw this inference. His thoughts were rather full of the spiritual side of
Jehovah's presence to His people, the word of revelation

guiding their path (xxx. 20, 21), the privilege of dwelling un-
harmed in the fire of Jehovah's presence, and seeing the King
in His glory, which belongs to the man that walketh in
righteousness, and speaketh upright words; who despiseth
the gain of oppression, shaking his hands from the holding
of bribes, stopping his ears from the hearing of blood, and
shutting his eyes from looking on evil (xxxiii. 14 *sq.*).   But
a practical scheme of reformation, resting on these premisses,
and deriving courage from the fulfilment of Isaiah's promise
of deliverance, could hardly fail to aim at the unification of
worship in Jerusalem.   Hezekiah may at first have sought
only to purge the sanctuaries of idols.   But the whole
worship of these shrines was bound up with their idolatrous
practices, while the Temple on Zion, the sanctuary of the ark,
might well be purged of heathenish corruptions, and still
retain in this ancient Mosaic symbol a mark of Jehovah's
presence palpable enough to draw the homage even of the
masses who had no ears for the lofty teaching of Isaiah.   The
history informs us that Hezekiah actually worked in this
direction.   We cannot tell the measure of his success, for
what he effected was presently undone by Manasseh ; but, at
least, it was under him that the problem first took practical
shape.

It is very noteworthy, and, on the traditional view, quite
inexplicable, that the Mosaic sanctuary of the ark is never
mentioned in the Deuteronomic Code.   The author of this
law occupies the standpoint of Isaiah, to whom the whole
plateau of Zion is holy ; or of Jeremiah, who forbids men to
search for the ark or remake it, because Jerusalem is the
throne of Jehovah (Jer. iii. 16, 17).   But he formulates
Isaiah's doctrine in the line of Hezekiah's practical essay to
suppress the high places, and he develops a scheme for fuller
and effective execution of this object with a precision of
detail that shows a clear sense of the practical difficulties of

the undertaking. It was no light thing to overturn the whole popular worship of Judah. It is highly probable that Hezekiah failed to produce a permanent result because he had not duly provided for the practical difficulties to which his scheme would give rise. The Deuteronomic Code has realised these difficulties, and meets the most serious of them by the modifications of the old law already discussed, and by making special provision for the priests of the suppressed shrines.

The First Legislation has no law of priesthood, no provision as to priestly dues. The permission of many altars, which it presupposes, is given in Exodus xx. 24-26 in a form that assumes the right of laymen to offer sacrifice,[1] as we actually find them doing in so many parts of the history (*supra*, p. 274). Yet a closer observation shows that the old law presupposes a priesthood, whose business lies less with sacrifice than with the divine Torah which they administer

---

[1] Exod. xx. 26 is addressed not to the priests but to Israel at large, and implies that any Israelite may approach the altar. Comp. Exod. xxi. 14, and contrast Num. iv. 15, xviii. 3. That the old law allows any Israelite to approach the altar appears most clearly from the prohibition of an altar with steps, lest the worshipper should expose his person to the holy structure. In the case of the Levitical priests this danger was provided against in another way, by the use of linen breeches (Exod. xxviii. 43). In the case of the brazen altar, which was five feet high, or of Solomon's huge altar, ten cubits in height, there must have been steps of some kind (Lev. ix. 22), and for Ezekiel's altar (xliii. 17) this is expressly stated. The important distinction between the altars of Exod. xx., which are approached by laymen in their ordinary dress, and the brazen altar approached by priests protected against exposure by their special costume, was not understood by the later Jews, and consequently it was held that the prohibition of steps (*ma'alôth*) did not prevent the use of an ascent of some other kind—as, for example, a sloping bridge or mound (see the Targum of Jonathan on our passage, and also Rashi's Commentary). In Herod's Temple the altar was a vast platform of unhewn stone, fifteen cubits high and fifty in length and breadth, and the ascent to it formed a gentle incline (Joseph. *B. J.* Lib. v. cap. 5, § 6 ; Mishna, *Zebachim* v., *Tamid* i. 4). But the expression *ma'alôth* seems to cover all kinds of ascent, and the risk of exposing the person *to the altar* would be unaffected by the nature of the ascent. In fact, with a large altar the priest could not put the blood of a victim on the four horns without standing and walking on the altar (*Zebachim*, l. c.), which is clearly against the spirit of Exod. xx., except on the understanding that that law does not apply to priests appropriately clad for the office.

in the sanctuary as successors of Moses. For the sanctuary is the seat of judgment (*supra*, p. 339), and this implies a qualified *personnel* through whom judgment is given. According to the unanimous testimony of all the older records of the Old Testament, this priesthood, charged with the Torah administered at the sanctuary, is none other than the house of Levi, the kinsmen or descendants of Moses. (See especially Deuteronomy xxxiii. 8 ; 1 Samuel ii. 27 *sq*.) The history of the Levites after the Conquest is veiled in much obscurity. The principal branch of the family, which remained with the ark, and is known to us as the house of Eli, lost its supremacy when Solomon deposed Abiathar and set Zadok in his place (1 Kings ii. 26, 27). In this event the author of Kings sees the fulfilment of the prophecy in 1 Sam. ii., which declares that Eli's clan, the priestly house originally chosen by Jehovah, shall be dispossessed in favour of a faithful priest. Hence it would appear that Zadok had no connection with the ancient priesthood of the ark ; but he was the head of a body of Levites (2 Samuel xv. 24). Another Levitical family which claimed direct descent from Moses held the priesthood of the sanctuary of Dan, and in the later times of the kingdom all the priests of local sanctuaries were viewed as Levites. Whether this implies that they were all lineal descendants of the old house of Levi may well be doubted. But in early times guilds are hereditary bodies, modified by a right of adoption, and it was understood that the priesthood ran in the family to which Moses belonged. In the time of Ezekiel the Jerusalem priesthood consisted of the Levites of the guild of Zadok. The subordinate ministers of the Temple were not Levites, but, as we have already seen, the foreign janissaries, and presumably other foreign slaves, the progenitors of the *Nethinim*, who appear in the list of returning exiles in Ezra ii. with names for the most part not Israelite. The Levites who are not Zadokites are by Ezekiel expressly identified with the priests of the high places (Ezek. xliv. 9 *sq.; supra,* p. 260 and *note*). These historical facts—for they are no conjecture, but the express testimony of the sacred record—are presupposed in the Code of Deuteronomy. The priests, according to Deuteronomy xxi. 5, are the sons of Levi ; "for them hath Jehovah thy God chosen to minister to him and to bless in his name, and according to their decision is every controversy and every stroke." Deuteronomy knows no Levites who cannot be priests, and no priests who are not Levites. The two ideas are absolutely identical. But these Levites, who are priests of Jehovah's own appointment, were, in the period when the code was composed, scattered through the land as priests of the local sanctuaries. They had no territorial possessions (Deut. xviii. 1), and were viewed as Gêrîm, or strangers under the protection of the community in the places where they sojourned (ver. 6). Apart from the revenues of the sanctuary, their position was altogether dependent (xiv. 27, 29, etc.).[1]

[1] I give here some fuller details of the evidence on this important topic.

1°. Except in the Levitical legislation and in Chronicles, Ezra, and Nehemiah, where the *usus loquendi* is conformed to the final form of the Pentateuchal ordinance, Levite never means a sacred minister who is not a priest, and has not the right to offer sacrifice. On the contrary, Levite is regularly used as a priestly title. See the list of texts in Wellhausen, *Prolegomena,* 3d ed., p. 147. The only passage to the contrary is 1 Kings viii. 4, where "the priests and the Levites" appear instead of "the Levite priests." But here the particle "and"—a single letter in Hebrew—appears to be an insertion in accordance with the later law. The Chronicler still reads the verse without the "and" (2 Chron. v. 5). The older books know a distinction between the chief priest and lower priests (*e.g.* 1 Sam. ii. 35, 36), but all alike are priests, that is, do sacrifice, wear the ephod, etc. The priesthood is God's gift to Levi (Deut. x. 8, xviii. 1, xxi. 5, xxxiii. 8 *sq.*), and Jeroboam's fault, according to 1 Kings xii. 31, was that he chose priests who were not Levites. From the first, no doubt, there must have been a difference between the chief priest of the ark (Aaron, Eli, Abiathar, Zadok) and his subordinate brethren, but there is no trace of such a distinction as is made in the Levitical law.

2°. Ezekiel knows nothing of Levites who were not priests in time past ; he knows only the Zadokite Levites, the priests of the Temple, and other Levites who had formerly been priests, but are to be degraded under the new Temple, because they had ministered in the idolatrous shrines of the local high places. The usual explanation that these Levites were the sons of

In the abolition of the local sanctuaries it was necessary
to make provision for these Levites. And this the new code
does in two ways : it provides, in the first place, that any
Levite from the provinces who chooses to come up to Jerusalem shall be admitted to equal privileges with his brethren
the Levites who stand there before Jehovah—not to the
privilege of a servant in the sanctuary, but to the full priesthood, as is expressly conveyed by the terms used. Thus

Ithamar is impossible. For the guild of Ithamar appears only after the Exile
as the name of a subordinate family of priests who were never degraded as
the prophet prescribes. Moreover, Ezek. xlviii. 11-13 clearly declares that
all Levites but the Zadokites shall be degraded. Ezekiel's Levites are the
priests of the local high places whom Josiah brought to Jerusalem, and who
were supported there on offerings which the non-priestly Levites under the
Levitical law had no right to eat.

3°. In Deuteronomy all Levitical functions are priestly, and to these
functions the whole tribe was chosen (x. 8, xxi. 5). The summary of
Levitical functions in x. 8 is (1) *to carry the ark*, which in old Israel was a
priestly function (*supra*, p. 276) ; (2) *to stand before Jehovah and minister to
Him*, an expression that invariably denotes priesthood proper ; see especially
Ezek. xliv. 13, 15 ; Jer. xxxiii. 18, 21, 22 : the Levites of the later law
minister not to God but to Aaron, Num. iii. 6 ; (3) *to bless in Jehovah's name.*
In the Levitical law this is the office of Aaron and his sons (Num. vi.). Accordingly in Deut. xviii. 1 *sq.*, the whole tribe of Levi has a claim on the
altar gifts, the first fruits and other priestly offerings, and any Levite can
actually gain a share in these by going to Jerusalem and doing priestly
service. In the Levitical law common Levites have no share in these
revenues, but are nourished by the tithes and live in Levitical cities. There
were no Levitical cities in this sense in the time of the Deuteronomist, for all
those mentioned in Joshua—in passages which are really part of the Priests'
Code—lay outside the kingdom of Judah. And Deuteronomy knows
nothing of a Levitical tithe, though it allows the poor Levites a share in the
charity tithe. The Levite who is not in service at the sanctuary is always
represented as a needy sojourner, without visible means of support ; and this
agrees with Judges xvii. 7, 8 ; 1 Sam. ii. 36.

That the priesthood of Dan was a Levitical priesthood descended from
Moses is generally admitted. In Judges xviii. 30, the N which changes

Moses to Manasseh is inserted above the line thus : משה, Moses ; מ‎ֹשה,
Manasseh. The reading of our English Bible was therefore a correction in
the archetype (*supra*, p. 57). On the whole subject of the Levites before the
Exile, see especially Graf in Merx's *Archiv*, i.; Kuenen, *Theol. Tijdschr.*,
1872 ; and Wellhausen, *Prolegomena*, Kap. iv. Baudissin's book, *Gesch. des
A Tlichen Priesterthums* (Leipzig, 1889), which seeks to find an intermediate
position between the old view and the new, does not give much help.

ministering, he receives for his support an equal share of the priestly dues paid in kind (Deut. xviii. 6 *sq.*).   Those Levites, on the other hand, who remain dispersed through the provinces receive no emolument from the sanctuary, and having no property in land (xviii. 1), have a far from enviable lot, which the legislator seeks to mitigate by recommending them in a special manner, along with the widow and the orphan, to the charity of the landed classes under whose protection they dwell (xii. 12, 18 ; xiv. 27, 29 ; xvi. 11, 14 ; xxvi. 11 *sq.*).   The method of such charity is to some extent defined. Once in three years every farmer is called upon to store up a tithe of the produce of his land, which he retains in his own hands, but must dispense to the dependents or Levites who come and ask a meal.   The legislator, it is plain, aims at something like a voluntary poor-rate.   The condition of the landless class, with whose sufferings the prophets are so often exercised, had become a social problem, owing to the increase of large estates and other causes (Isa. v. 8 ; Micah ii.), and demanded a remedy ; but it is not proposed to enforce the assessment through the executive.   The matter is left to every man's conscience as a religious duty, of which he is called to give account before Jehovah in the sanctuary (xxvi. 12 *sq.*).   And the bond between charity and religion is drawn still closer by the provision that the well-to-do landholder, when he comes up to the sanctuary to make merry before God, feasting on the firstlings, tithes, etc., must bring with him his dependents and the Levite who is within his gates, that they too may have their part in the occasions of religious joy.   This law of charity appears to supersede the old rule of leaving the produce of every field to the poor one year in seven, which is obviously a more primitive and less practical arrangement.   In place of this, the Deuteronomic Code requires that, at the close of every seven years, there shall be a release of Hebrew debtors by their creditors (xv. 1 *sq.*).

I return to the Levites, in order to point out that the comparison of Deut. xviii. with 2 Kings xxiii. 8 *sq.* effectually disproves the idea of some critics that the Deuteronomic Code was a forgery of the Temple priests, or of their head, the high priest Hilkiah. The proposal to give the Levites of the provinces—that is, the priests of the local sanctuaries—equal priestly rights at Jerusalem could not commend itself to the Temple hierarchy. And in this point Josiah was not able to carry out the ordinances of the book. The priests who were brought up to Jerusalem received support from the Temple dues, but were not permitted to minister at the altar. This proves that the code did not emanate from Hilkiah and the Zadokite priests, whose class interests were strong enough to frustrate the law which, on the theory of a forgery, was their own work.

Whence, then, did the book derive the authority which made its discovery the signal for so great a reformation? How did it approve itself as an expression of the Divine will, first to Hilkiah and Josiah, and then to the whole nation? To this question there can be but one answer. The authority that lay behind Deuteronomy was the power of the prophetic teaching which half a century of persecution had not been able to suppress. After the work of Isaiah and his fellows, it was impossible for any earnest movement of reformation to adopt other principles than those of the prophetic word on which Jehovah Himself had set His seal by the deliverance from Assyria. What the Deuteronomic Code supplied was a clear and practical scheme of reformation on the prophetic lines. It showed that it was possible to adjust the old religious constitution in conformity with present needs, and this was enough to kindle into new flame the slumbering fire of the word of the prophets. The book became the programme of Josiah's reformation, because it gathered up in practical form the results of the great movement under

Hezekiah and Isaiah, and the new divine teaching then given to Israel. It was of no consequence to Josiah—it is of equally little consequence to us—to know the exact date and authorship of the book. Its prophetic doctrine, and the practical character of the scheme which it set forth—in which the new teaching and the old Torah were fused into an intelligible unity—were enough to commend it.

The law of the one sanctuary, which is aimed against assimilation of Jehovah-worship to the religion of Canaan, and seeks entirely to separate the people from the worship of Canaanite shrines, is only one expression of a thought common to the prophets, that the unique religion of Jehovah was in constant danger from intercourse between Israel and the nations. Isaiah complains that the people were always ready to "strike hands with the children of strangers," and recognises a chief danger to faith in the policy of the nobles, who were dazzled with the splendour and courted the alliance of the great empires on the Nile and the Tigris (Isa. ii. 6, xxx. 1 *sq.*; comp. Hosea vii. 8, viii. 9, xiv. 3). The vocation of Israel as Jehovah's people has no points of contact with the aims and political combinations of the surrounding nations, and Micah vii. 14 looks forward to a time when Israel shall be like a flock feeding in solitude in the woods of Bashan or Carmel. Isaiah expresses this unique destiny of Israel in the word *holiness*. Jehovah is the Holy One of Israel, and conversely His true people are a holy seed. The notion of holiness is primarily connected with the sanctuary and all things pertaining to intercourse with the deity. The old Israelite consecrated himself before a sacrifice. In the First Legislation the notion of Israel's holiness appears only in the law against eating flesh torn in the field, of which the blood had not been duly offered to God on His altar. But Isaiah raises the notion beyond the sphere of ritual, and places Israel's holiness in direct relation to the personal presence of Jehovah on Zion, in the centre of His people, as their living Sanctuary, whose glory fills all the earth (Isa. vi. 3, iv. 3 *sq.*). The Code of Deuteronomy appropriates this principle; but in its character of a law, seeking definite practical expression for religious principles, it develops the idea of unique holiness and separation from the profane nations in prohibitive ordinances. The essential object of the short law of the kingdom (xvii. 14 *sq.*) is to guard against admixture with foreigners and participation in foreign policy. Other precepts regulate contact with the adjoining nations (xxiii. 3 *sq.*), and a vast number of statutes are directed against the immoralities of Canaanite nature-worship, which, as we know from the prophets and the Books of Kings, had deeply tainted the service of Jehovah. Not a few details, which to the modern eye seem trivial or irrational, disclose to the student of Semitic antiquity an energetic protest against the moral grossness of Canaanite heathenism. These precepts give the law a certain air of ritual formalism, but the formalism lies only on the surface, and there is a moral idea below. The ceremonial observances of Deuteronomy are directed against heathen usages. Thus in Deut. xxii. 5 women are forbidden to wear men's garments and men women's garments. This is not a mere rule of conventional propriety, but is directed against those simulated changes of sex which occur in Canaanite and Syrian heathenism. We learn from Servius that sacrifice was done to the bearded Astarte of Cyprus by men dressed as women and women dressed as men; and the Galli, with their female dress and ornaments, are one of the most disgusting features of the Syrian and Phœnician sanctuaries.[1] So again the

[1] See Servius on *Æn.* ii. 632; Macrob. *Saturn.* iii. 8; Lucian, *De Syria Dea*, § 51; Euseb. *Vit. Const.* iii. 55. The Galli of later times seem to be identical with the vile class named in Deut. xxiii. 17 and the "dogs" of the following verse. The same figurative use of the word dog is found in the painted inscription of Citium; *C. I. S.* No. 86

forms of mourning prohibited in Deut. xiv. 1 are ancient practices which among the other Semites have a religious significance. They occur not only in mourning but in the worship of the gods, and belong to the sphere of heathen superstition.[1] Another example of rules that have a deeper significance than appears on the surface is found in Deut. xiv. 3-21, in the list of forbidden foods. We know as a fact that some of the unclean animals were sacrament-ally eaten in certain heathen rituals (Isa. lxvi. 17, lxv. 4, lxvi. 3), and in general the rules as to eating and not eating certain kinds of flesh among the heathen Semites, as in other early nations, were directly connected with ancient superstitions, which in the last resort must have arisen out of ideas closely analogous to the totemism of modern savages. All primitive people have rules for-bidding the use of certain kinds of food, out of religious scruple, or on the other hand they never eat certain kinds of flesh except as a solemn act of worship. An animal that may not be eaten, or that may be eaten only in solemn sacraments, is primarily a holy animal, and is often an object of worship ; for in primitive religion the ideas holy and un-clean meet. Now we learn from Ezekiel viii. 10, 11 that one of the forms of low superstition practised at Jerusalem in the last days of the old kingdom was the worship of unclean creatures. This must be a relic of very ancient heathenism, which had lingered for centuries in the obscure depths of society, and came to the surface again in the general despair of Jehovah's help which drove Ezekiel's contemporaries into all manner of degrading superstitions. Some parts of the law of forbidden food in Deuteronomy probably do no more than formulate antique prejudices, which to the mass of the people had long lost all religious significance, but had come to be regarded as points of

---

[1] See *Religion of the Semites*, i. 304 *sqq.*

propriety and self-respect ; but it can hardly be doubted that other parts are directly aimed at heathen sacraments, such as the eating of swine's flesh spoken of in the Book of Isaiah, and similar rites that might well occur in connection with the superstitions described by Ezekiel. Similar prohibitions have been enforced in Christian times on converts from heathen-ism, in order to cut them off from participation in idolatrous feasts. Thus Simeon Stylites forbade his Saracen converts to eat the flesh of the camel, which was the chief element in the sacrificial meals of the Arabs, and our own prejudice against the use of horse flesh is a relic of an old ecclesi-astical prohibition framed at the time when the eating of such food was an act of worship to Odin.[1]

This constant polemical reference to Canaanite worship and Canaanite morality gives to the element of ritual and forms of worship a much larger place in Deuteronomy than these things hold in the First Legislation. In points of civil order the new law still moves on the old lines. Its object is not legislative innovation, but to bring the old consuetudinary law into relation to the fundamental principle that Jehovah is Israel's Lawgiver, and that all social order exists under His sanction.

[1] This subject is fully treated in my *Religion of the Semites*, vol. i. (1889), to which I refer for details as to ancient laws of forbidden meats. Two of the prohibitions in Deuteronomy (xiv. 21) rest on the older legislation ; but these have a character of their own. The first of them is the law against eating carrion (Exod. xxii. 31), which evidently rests on the old rule that all lawful slaughter must be sacrificial, but is equally consistent with the Deuteronomic modification of that rule (Deut. xii. 15). The other is the very curious law against seething a kid in its mother's milk, *i.e.* in goats' milk, on which see *op. cit.* p. 204 note. From the occurrence in Deut. xiv. 12-19 of some charac-teristic priestly expressions Kuenen infers that this law was derived by the Deuteronomist from the oral Torah of the priests (comp. xxiv. 8) ; but it is also possible that these details were added later, and that the original law confined itself to allowing all clean birds to be eaten (ver. 11), thus glancing obliquely at the rule of the Astarte-worshippers of Canaan, who would not eat the dove (*op. cit.* p. 202 note). The permission to eat all fish having scales and fins also stands in contrast to a widespread superstition of the Syrian Astarte-worshippers (*op. cit.* p. 430).

Thus we still find some details which bear the stamp of primeval Semitic culture. In chap. xxi. 10 *sq.* we have marriage by capture as it was practised by the Arabs before Mohammed, and even the detail as to the paring of the nails of the captive before marriage is identical with one of the old Arabic methods of terminating the widow's period of seclusion and setting her free to marry again.

But in general we see that the civil laws of Deuteronomy belong to a later stage of society than the First Legislation. For example, the law of retaliation, which has so large a range in the First Legislation, is prescribed in Deut. xix. 16 *sq.* only for the case of false witness.[1] And with this goes the introduction of a new punishment, which, in the old law, was confined to slaves. A man who injures another may be brought before the judge and sentenced to the bastinado (xxv. 1 *sq.*). The introduction of this degrading punishment in the case of freemen indicates a change in social feeling. Among the Bedouins no sheikh would dare to flog a man, for he would thereby bring himself under the law of retaliation; and so it was in Israel in the old time. But Eastern kingship breaks down this sense of personal independence, while, at the same time, it modifies the strict law of revenge. In general, the executive system of Deuteronomy is more advanced. The sanctuary is still the highest seat of law, but the priest is now associated with a supreme civil judge (xvii. 9, 12), who seems to be identical with the king; and even the subordinate judges are not merely the natural sheikhs, or elders of the local communities, but include officers appointed with national authority (xvi. 18). Again, the law of manumission undergoes an important modification. On the old law a father could sell his daughter as a slave, and the bond-woman was absolute property; the master could wed her to

---

[1] It may indeed be inferred from this passage that the *talio* existed in theory in other cases also, but was not commonly enforced in practice.

one of his servants, and retain her when the servant left. In Deuteronomy all this has disappeared, and a Hebrew woman has a right to manumission after seven years, like a man (xv. 12, 17). A similar advance appears in the change on the law of seduction. By the old law this case was treated as one of pecuniary loss to the father, who must be compensated by the seducer purchasing the damsel as wife for the full price (*môhar*) of a virgin. In Deuteronomy the law is removed from among the laws of property to laws of moral purity, and the payment of full *môhar* is changed to a fixed fine (Exod. xxii. 16, 17; Deut. xxii. 28 *sq.*).

In other cases the new code softens the rudeness of ancient custom. In Arabic warfare the destruction of an enemy's palm-groves is a favourite exploit, and fertile lands are thus often reduced to desert. In 2 Kings iii. 19 we find that the same practice was enjoined on Israel by the prophet Elisha in war with Moab; every good tree was to be cut down. But Deut. xx. 19 *sq.* forbids this barbarous destruction of fruit-trees. Still more remarkable is the law of Deut. xxii. 30. It was a custom among many of the ancient Arabs that a man took possession of his father's wives along with the property (his own mother, of course, excepted). The only law of forbidden degrees in the Deuteronomic Code is directed against this practice, which Ezekiel xxii. 10 mentions as still current in Jerusalem. But in early times such marriages were made without offence. The Israelites understood Absalom's appropriation of David's secondary wives as a formal way of declaring that his father was dead to him, and that he served himself his heir (2 Sam. xvi.); and when Adonijah asked the hand of Abishag, Solomon understood him as claiming the inheritance (1 Kings ii. 22). The same custom explains the anger of Ishbosheth at Abner (2 Sam. iii. 7). The new code, you perceive, marks a growth in morality and refinement. It is still no ideal law fit for all time, but a practical code largely incorporating elements of actual custom. But the growth of custom and usage is on the whole upward, and ancient social usages which survived for many centuries after the age of Josiah among the heathen of Arabia and Syria already lie behind the Deuteronomic Code. With all the hardness of Israel's heart, the religion of Jehovah had proved itself in its influence on the nation a better religion than that of the Baalim.[1]

From Josiah's covenant to the fall of the Jewish state the Code of Deuteronomy had but a generation to run. Even in this short time it appeared that the reformation had not accomplished its task, and that the introduction of the written law was not enough to avert the judgment which the prophets had declared inevitable for the purification of the nation. The crusade against the high places was most permanent in its results. In the time of Jeremiah popular superstition clung to the Temple as it had formerly clung to the high places, and in the Temple the populace and the false prophets found the pledge that Jehovah could never forsake His nation. This fact is easily understood. The prophetic ideas of Isaiah, which were the real spring of the Deuteronomic reformation, had never been spiritually grasped by the mass

---

[1] See on marriage with a stepmother my *Kinship*, p. 86 *sqq.* It is not, of course, to be supposed that no other rule of forbidden degrees was recognised, but only that no other case required to be provided against. Yet marriage with a half-sister not uterine was allowed in old Israel, and not unknown in the days of Ezekiel (*supra*, p. 280), though it is condemned by him and in the "Framework" of Deuteronomy (chap. xxvii. 22). Why does the code not mention this case, which was certainly not to be passed over in silence? In such a case silence seems to imply consent; and this may supply an additional argument for assigning to Deut. xxvii. a later date than the code of chaps. xii.-xxvi. The advance in the laws of forbidden degrees from the Deuteronomic Code through the "Framework" (Deut. xxvii.) and Ezekiel (xxii. 10, 11) to the full Levitical law is one of the clearest proofs of the true order of succession in the Pentateuchal laws. Marriage with a half-sister was known among the Phœnicians in the time of Achilles Tatius, and indeed forbidden marriages, including that with a father's wife, seem to have been practised pretty openly in Roman Syria down to the fifth Christian century. See Bruns and Sachau, *Syrisch-Römisches Rechtsbuch*, p. 30 (Leipzig, 1880).

of the people, though the *éclat* attending the overthrow of Sennacherib had given them a certain currency. The conception of Jehovah's throne on Zion was materialised in the Temple, and the moral conditions of acceptance with the King of Zion, on which Isaiah laid so much weight, were forgotten. Jehovah received ritual homage in lieu of moral obedience; and Jeremiah has again occasion to declare that the latter alone is the positive content of the divine Torah, and that a law of sacrifice is no part of the original covenant with Israel. In speaking thus the prophet does not separate himself from the Deuteronomic law; for the moral precepts of that code—as, for example, the Deuteronomic form of the law of manumission (Jer. xxxiv. 13-16)—he accepts as part of the covenant of the Exodus. To Jeremiah, therefore, the Code of Deuteronomy does not appear in the light of a positive law of sacrifice; and this judgment is undoubtedly correct. The ritual details of Deuteronomy are directed against heathen worship; they are negative, not positive. In the matter of sacrifice and festal observances the new code simply diverts the old homage of Israel from the local sanctuaries to the central shrine, and all material offerings are summed up under the principles of gladness before Jehovah at the great agricultural feasts, and of homage paid to Him in acknowledgment that the good things of the land of Canaan are His gift (xxvi. 10). The firstlings, first fruits, and so forth remain on their old footing as natural expressions of devotion, which did not begin with the Exodus and are not peculiar to Israel. Even the festal sacrifices retain the character of "a voluntary tribute" (Deut. xvi. 10), and the paschal victim itself may be chosen indifferently from the flock or the herd (xvi. 2), and is still, according to the Hebrew of xvi. 7, presumed to be boiled, not roasted, as is the case in all old sacrifices of which the history speaks. Deuteronomy knows nothing of a sacrificial priestly Torah, though it refers the

people to the Torah of the priests on the subject of leprosy
(xxiv. 8), and acknowledges their authority as judges in law-
suits.   In the Deuteronomic Code the idea of sin is never
connected with matters of ritual.   A sin means a crime, an
offence to law and justice (xix. 15, xxi. 22, xxii. 26, xxiv. 16),
an act of heathenism (xx. 18), a breach of faith towards
Jehovah (xxiii. 21, 22), or a lack of kindliness to the poor
(xxiv. 15).   And such offences are expiated, not by sacrifice,
but by punishment at the hand of man or God.   This moral
side of the law, which exactly corresponds to prophetic teaching, continued to be neglected in Judah.   Oppression, bloodshed, impurity, idolatry, filled the land ; and for these things
Jeremiah threatens a judgment, which the Temple and its
ritual can do nothing to avert (Jer. vii.).

In all this Deuteronomy and Jeremiah alike still stand
outside the priestly Torah.   As far as Deuteronomy goes, this
is usually explained by saying that it is a law for the people,
and does not take up points of ritual which specially belonged
to the priests.   But the code, which refers to the priestly law
of leprosy, says nothing of ordinances of ritual atonement and
stated sacrifice, and Jeremiah denies in express terms that a
law of sacrifice forms any part of the divine commands to
Israel.   The priestly and prophetic Torahs are not yet absorbed
into one system.

Nevertheless there can be no doubt that there was at this
time a ritual Torah in the hands of the priests, containing
elements which the prophets and the old codes pass by.   In
the time of Ahaz there was a daily burnt offering in the
morning, a stated cereal offering in the evening (2 Kings xvi.
15).   There was also an atoning ritual.   In the time of
Jehoash the atonements paid to the priests were pecuniary—
a common enough thing in ancient times.   But atoning
sacrifice was also of ancient standing.   It occurs in 1 Sam. iii.
14,—" The guilt of the house of Eli shall not be wiped out by

sacrifice or oblation for ever." The idea of atonement in the
sacrificial blood must be very ancient, and a trace of it is found
in the Book of Deuteronomy (xxi. 4) in the curious ordinance
which provides for the atonement of the blood of untraced
homicide by the slaughter of a heifer.[1] Along with these
things we find ancient ordinances of ceremonial holiness in
the sanctuary at Nob (1 Sam. xxi. 4), and all this necessarily
supposes a ritual law, the property of the priests. Only, we
have already seen that the details still preserved to us of the
Temple ritual are not identical with the full Levitical system.
They contained many germs of that system, but they also
contained much that was radically different. And in particular the Temple worship itself was not stringently differentiated from everything heathenish, as appears with the
utmost clearness in the admission of uncircumcised foreigners
to certain ministerial functions, in the easy way in which
Isaiah's friend Urijah accepted the foreign innovations of
King Ahaz, and in the fact that prophets whom Jeremiah
regards as heathen diviners still continued to be attached to
the Temple up to the last days of the state, while worshippers
from Samaria made pilgrimages to Jerusalem with heathenish
ceremonies expressly forbidden in Deuteronomy as well as in
Leviticus (Jer. xli. 5; Lev. xix. 27, 28; Deut. xiv. 1; Isa.
xv. 2). We see, then, that even Josiah's reformation left
many things in the Temple which savoured of heathenism,
and the presence of the priests of the high places was little
calculated to improve the spirituality of the observances of
Jehovah's house. In all this there was a manifest danger to
true religion. If ritual and sacrifice were to continue at all,
it was highly desirable that some order should be taken with
the priestly ritual, and an attempt made to reorganise it in
conformity with the prophetic conception of Jehovah's moral

[1] Analogies to this peculiar form of atonement are given in *Religion of the
Semites*, p. 351.

holiness. But no effort to complete Josiah's work in this direction seems to have been made in the last troublous years of Jerusalem. On the contrary, Ezekiel describes the grossest heathenism as practised at the Temple, and hardly without the countenance of the priests (Ezek. viii.).

The Temple and its worship fell with the destruction of the city. Fourteen years later, Ezekiel, dwelling in captivity, had a vision of a new Temple, a place of worship for repentant Israel, and heard a voice commanding him to lay before the people a pattern of remodelled worship. "If they be ashamed of all that they have done, shew them the form of the house . . . and all its ordinances, and all the Torahs thereof: and write them before them that they may keep all the form thereof, and all the ordinances thereof, and do them" (Ezek. xliii. 10, 11).

A great mystery has been made of this law of Ezekiel, but the prophet himself makes none. He says in the clearest words that the revelation is a sketch of ritual for the period of restoration, and again and again he places his new ordinances in contrast with the actual corrupt usage of the first Temple (xliii. 7, xliv. 5 *sq.*, xlv. 8, 9). He makes no appeal to a previous law of ritual. The whole scheme of a written law of the house is new, and so Ezekiel only confirms Jeremiah, who knew no divine law of sacrifice under the First Temple. It is needless to rehearse more than the chief points of Ezekiel's legislation. The first that strikes us is the degradation of the Levites. The ministers of the old Temple, he tells us, were uncircumcised foreigners, whose presence was an insult to Jehovah's sanctuary. Such men shall no more enter the house, but in their place shall come the Levites not of the house of Zadok, who are to be degraded from the priesthood because they officiated in old Israel before the idolatrous shrines (xliv. 5 *sq.*). This one point is sufficient to fix the date of the Levitical law as later than Ezekiel. In all the

earlier history, and in the Code of Deuteronomy, a Levite is
a priest, or at least qualified to assume priestly functions ;
and even in Josiah's reformation the Levite priests of the
high places received a modified priestly status at Jerusalem.
Ezekiel knows that it has been so in the past ; but he
declares that it shall be otherwise in the future, as a punishment for the offence of ministering at the idolatrous altars.
He knows nothing of an earlier law, in which priests and
Levites are already distinguished, in which the office of Levite
is itself a high privilege (Num. xvi. 9).

A second point in Ezekiel's law is a provision for stated
and regular sacrifices. These sacrifices are to be provided by
the prince, who in turn is to receive from the people no
arbitrary tax, but a fixed tribute in kind upon all agricultural
produce and flocks. Here again we see a reference to pre-
exilic practice, when the Temple was essentially the king's
sanctuary, and the stated offerings were his gift. In the old
codes the people at large are under no obligation to do stated
sacrifice. That was the king's voluntary offering, and so it
was at first after the Exile, at least in theory. The early
decrees of Persian monarchs in favour of the Jews provide
for regular sacrifice at the king's expense (Ezra vi. 9, vii.
17) ;[1] and only at the convocation of Nehemiah do the people
agree to defray the stated offering by a voluntary poll-tax of
a third of a shekel (Neh. x. 32). It is disputed whether, in
Exod. xxx. 16, "the service of the tabernacle," defrayed by
the fixed tribute of half a shekel, refers to the continual sacrifices. If it does so, this law was still unknown to Nehemiah,
and must be a late addition to the Pentateuch. If it does not,
it is still impossible that the costly Levitical ordinance of stated

---

[1] The history in Ezra-Nehemiah makes it clear that these decrees had
little practical result ; and it has been questioned whether in their present
form they are perfectly authentic. But they show at least that the theory
of the Jews was that public sacrifices should be defrayed by the supreme civil
authority.

offerings could have preceded the existence of a provision for
supplying them. Again we are brought back to Jeremiah's
words. The stated sacrifices were not prescribed in the
wilderness.

A third point in Ezekiel's law is the prominence given to
the sin offering and atoning ritual. The altar must be purged
with sin offerings for seven consecutive days before burnt
sacrifices are acceptably offered on it (xliii. 18 *sq.*). The
Levitical law (Exod. xxix. 36, 37) prescribes a similar ceremony, but with more costly victims. At the dedication of
Solomon's Temple, on the contrary (1 Kings viii. 62), the
altar is at once assumed to be fit for use, in accordance with
Exod. xx. 24, and with all the early cases of altar-building
outside the Pentateuch. But, besides this first expiatory
ceremonial, Ezekiel appoints two atoning services yearly, at
the beginning of the first and the seventh month (xlv. 18, 20,
LXX.), to purge the house. This is the first appearance, outside of the Levitical code, of anything corresponding to the
great day of atonement in the seventh month, and it is plain
that the simple service in Ezekiel is still far short of that
solemn ceremony. The day of atonement was also a fast day.
But in Zech. vii. 5, viii. 19, the fast of the seventh month is
alluded to as one of the four fasts commemorating the destruction of Jerusalem, which had been practised for the last
seventy years. The fast of the seventh month was not yet
united with the "purging of the house" ordained by Ezekiel.
Even in the great convocation of Neh. viii.-x., where we have
a record of proceedings from the first day of the seventh
month onwards to the twenty-fourth, there is no mention of
the day of expiation on the tenth, which thus appears as the
very last stone in the ritual edifice.

I pass over other features of Ezekiel's legislation. The
detailed proof that in every point Ezekiel's Torah prepares
the way for the Levitical law, but represents a more ele-

mentary ritual, may be read in the text itself with the aid of
Smend's Commentary. The whole scheme presents itself
with absolute clearness as a first sketch of a written priestly
Torah, resting not on the law of Moses but on old priestly
usage, and reshaped so as to bring the ordinances of the house
into due conformity with the holiness of Jehovah in the sense
of the prophets and the Deuteronomic Code. The thought
that underlies Ezekiel's code is clearly brought out in xliii. 7,
xliv. 6 *sqq*. To Ezekiel, who is himself a priest, the whore-
dom of Israel, their foul departure from Jehovah after filthy
idols, appears in a peculiarly painful light in connection with
the service of the sanctuary, the throne of Jehovah, the place
of the soles of His feet, where He dwells in the midst of
Israel for ever. In time past the people of Israel have defiled
Jehovah's name by their abominations, and for this they have
suffered His wrath. The new law is a gift to the people on
their repentance—a scheme to protect them from again falling
into like sins. The unregulated character of the old service
gave room for the introduction of heathen abominations.
The new service shall be reduced to a divine rule, leaving no
door for what is unholy. But so long as worship takes place
with material ceremonies in an earthly sanctuary, the idea of
holiness cannot be divested of a material element. From the
earliest times the sanctity of God's worship had regard to
provisions of physical holiness, especially to lustrations and
rules of cleanness and uncleanness, which, in their origin,
were not different in principle from the similar rules found
among all ancient nations, but which nevertheless could be
used, as we find them used in Deuteronomy, to furnish a
barrier against certain forms of foreign heathenism. From the
priestly point of view, material and moral observances of
sanctity run into one. Ezekiel finds equal fault with
idolatry in the Temple and with the profanation of its
plateau by the sepulchres of the kings (xliii. 7). And so his

ritual, though its fundamental idea is moral, branches out
into a variety of ordinances which from our modern point of
view seem merely formal, but which were yet inevitable
unless the principle of sacrifice and an earthly sanctuary
was to be altogether superseded. If the material sanctuary
was to be preserved at all, the symbolic observances of its
holiness must be made stringent, and to this end the new
ordinance of the Levites and Ezekiel's other provisions were
altogether suitable.

In proportion, now, as the whole theory of worship is
remodelled and reduced to rule on the scheme of an exclusive
sanctity, which presents, so to speak, an armed front to
every abomination of impure heathenism, the ritual becomes
abstract, and the services remote from ordinary life. In the
old worship all was spontaneous. It was as natural for an
Israelite to worship Jehovah as for a Moabite to worship
Chemosh. To worship God was a holiday, an occasion of
feasting. Religion, in its sacrificial form, was a part of
common life, which had its well-known and established
forms, but which no one deemed it necessary to reduce to
written rules. Even in Deuteronomy this view predomi-
nates. The sacrificial feasts are still the consecration of
natural occasions of joy; men eat, drink, and make merry
before God. The sense of God's favour, not the sense of sin,
is what rules at the sanctuary. But the unification of the
sanctuary already tended to break up this old type of religion.
Worship ceased to be an everyday thing, and so it ceased to
be the expression of everyday religion. In Ezekiel this
change has produced its natural result in a change of the
whole standpoint from which he views the service of the
Temple. The offerings of individuals are no longer the chief
reason for which the Temple exists. All weight lies on the
stated service, which the prince provides out of national
funds, and which is, as it were, the representative service of

Israel. The individual Israelite who, in the old law, stood at the altar himself and brought his own victim, is now separated from it, not only by the double cordon of priests and Levites, but by the fact that his personal offering is thrown into the background by the stated national sacrifice.

The whole tendency of this is to make personal religion more and more independent of offerings. The emotion with which the worshipper approaches the second Temple, as recorded in the Psalter, has little to do with sacrifice, but rests rather on the fact that the whole wondrous history of Jehovah's grace to Israel is vividly and personally realised as he stands amidst the festal crowd at the ancient seat of God's throne, and adds his voice to the swelling song of praise. The daily religion of the Restoration found new forms. The devotional study of the Scriptures, the synagogue, the practice of prayer elsewhere than before the altar, were all independent of the old idea of worship, and naturally prepared the way for the New Testament. The narrowing of the privilege of access to God at the altar would have been a retrograde step if altar-worship had still remained the form of all religion. But this was not so, and therefore the new ritual was a practical means of separating personal religion from forms destined soon to pass away. The very features of the Levitical ordinances which seem most inconsistent with spirituality, if we place them in the days of Moses, when all religion took shape before the altar, appear in a very different light in the age after the Exile, when the non-ritual religion of the prophets went side by side with the Law, and supplied daily nourishment to the spiritual life of those who were far from the sanctuary.

With all this there went another change not less important. In the old ritual, sacrifice and offering were essentially an expression of homage (in the presentation of

the altar gift), and an act of communion (in the sacrificial
feast that followed), while the element of atonement for sin
held a very subsidiary place in ordinary acts of worship.
But the ideas of sacrificial homage and communion lost great
part of their force when the sacrifices of the sanctuary were
so much divorced from individual life, and became a sort of
abstract representative service. In Ezekiel, and still more
in the Levitical legislation, the element of atonement takes a
foremost place. The sense of sin had grown deeper under
the teaching of the prophets, and amidst the proofs of
Jehovah's anger that darkened the last days of the Jewish
state. Sin and forgiveness were the main themes of prophetic discourse. The problem of acceptance with God
exercised every thoughtful mind, as we see not only from
the Psalms and the prophets of the Exile and Restoration,
but above all from the Book of Job, which is certainly later
than the time of Jeremiah. The acceptance of the worship
of the sanctuary had always been regarded as the visible
sacrament of Jehovah's acceptance of the worshipper, "when
He came to him and blessed him." And now, more than in
any former time, the first point in acceptance was felt to be
the forgiveness of sin, and the weightiest element in the
ritual was that which symbolised the atonement or "wiping
out" of iniquity. The details of this symbolism cannot
occupy us here. In point of form the atoning ordinances of
the Levitical law are not essentially different from the expiatory rites of other ancient nations, and they must therefore be
taken, not as innovations but as a reshaping of ancient ritual
to fit the conditions of the second Temple. As regards their
meaning the law is generally silent, and it was left to the
worshipper to interpret the symbolism as he could. In some
cases the meaning was transparent enough, in others the
original significance of the acts prescribed was probably
forgotten at the time when the old ritual traditions were

codified.[1] They were conventions to which God had attached
the promise of forgiveness; and their real significance as a
factor in the religious life of Judaism lay not in the details
of the ritual but in that they constantly impressed on the
people the sense of abiding sin, the need of forgiveness, and
above all the assurance that the religion of Israel was
grounded on a promise of forgiveness to those who sought
God in the way that He prescribed. For the promise of
forgiveness is the only foundation on which a God-fearing
life can be built. "With thee is forgiveness that thou
mayest be feared" (Ps. cxxx. 4).

The Levitical legislation in our present Pentateuch is the
practical adaptation of these principles to the circumstances
of the second Temple, when Jerusalem was no longer the
seat of a free state, but only the centre of a religious
community possessing certain municipal privileges of self-
government. Its distinctive features are all found in
Ezekiel's Torah—the care with which the Temple and its
vicinity are preserved from the approach of unclean things
and persons, the corresponding institution of a class of

---

[1] I have attempted an historical and comparative investigation into the
meaning of the atoning ceremonies of the Hebrews in my *Religion of the
Semites*, to which the curious reader may refer. The question as to the
etymological meaning of the Hebrew root כפר, from the second stem of which
the technical terms connected with atonement are derived, is obscure. The
root idea is commonly taken to be "to cover" (after the Arabic); but in
Syriac the sense of the simple stem is "to wipe off" or "wipe clean." This
sense appears in Hebrew (in the second stem) if the text of Isa. xxviii. 18 is
sound, which, however, is very doubtful. The sequence of the various Hebrew
usages is very ingeniously worked out by Wellhausen (*Geschichte*, i. 66 *sqq.*;
Composition, p. 335), starting from the sense "cover"; but it seems to me
that his argument might be easily accommodated to the other possible
etymology. There are Semitic analogies for regarding the forgiveness of sin
either as "covering" or as "wiping out," and the phrase חלה פנים=כפר פנים
is not decisive, though on the whole it seems easiest to take this to mean
"to wipe clean the face" blackened by displeasure, as the Arabs say "whiten
the face." The most important point is that except in the Priests' Code it is
God, not the priest, who (on the one etymology) wipes out sin or (on the other)
regards it as covered.

holy ministers in the person of the Levites, the greater
distance thus interposed between the people and the altar,
the concentration of sacrifice in the two forms of stated
representative offerings (the *tamîd*) and atoning sacrifices.
In all these points, as we have seen, the usage of the
Law is in distinct contrast to that of the first Temple,
where the Temple plateau was polluted by the royal
sepulchres, where the servants of the sanctuary were uncircumcised foreigners, the stated service the affair of the
king, regulated at will by him (2 Kings xvi.), and the
atoning offerings commonly took the shape of fines paid to
the priests of the sanctuary (2 Kings xii. 16).   That
Ezekiel in these matters speaks, not merely as a priest
recording old usage, but as a prophet ordaining new Torah
with Divine authority, is his own express claim, and
therefore the Pentateuchal ordinances that go with Ezekiel
against the praxis of the first Temple must have been
written after Ezekiel and under his influence.

The development of the details of the system falls therefore between the time of Ezekiel and the work of Ezra,
or to speak exactly, between 572 and 444 B.C. ; and the
circumstance already referred to, that the culminating and
most solemn ceremony of the great day of expiation was
not observed in the year of Ezra's covenant, shows that the
last touches were not added to the ritual until, through Ezra's
agency, it was put into practical operation.[1]   But, while the
historical student is thus compelled to speak of the ritual
code as the law of the second Temple, it would be a great
mistake to think of it as altogether new.   Ezekiel's ordinances are nothing else than a reshaping of the old priestly
Torah ; and a close study of the Levitical laws, especially in
Lev. xvii.-xxvi., shows that many ancient Torahs were worked

---

[1] See additional Note F, *The development of the ritual system between
Ezekiel and Ezra.*

up, by successive processes, into the complete system as we now possess it. In Lev. xxiv. 19 *sq.*, for example, we find the old law of retaliation for injuries not mortal, which is already obsolescent in the Deuteronomic Code. The preservation of such a Torah shows that the priests did not give up all their old traditional law for the written Code of Deuteronomy. They doubtless continued till the time of Ezra to give oral Torahs, as we see from Haggai i. 11. The analogy of all early law makes this procedure quite intelligible to us. Nothing is more common than to find an antique legislation handed down, in the mouth of a priestly or legal guild, in certain set forms of words.

To trace out in detail how much of the Levitical legislation consists of such old Torahs handed down from time immemorial in the priestly families, and how much is new, is a task which we cannot now attempt, and which indeed has not yet been finally accomplished by scholars.[1] The chief

---

[1] One of the chief innovations of the ritual law is the increased provision for the priesthood. This occurs in two ways. In the first place they receive a larger share in the gifts which on the old usage were the material of feasts at the sanctuary. In Deuteronomy the firstlings are eaten by the worshipper at the annual feasts, the priest of course receiving the usual share of each victim. But in Num. xviii. 18 they belong entirely and absolutely to the priest. This difference cannot be explained away ; for according to Deut. xiv. 24 the firstlings might be turned into money, and materials of a feast bought with them, while in Num. xviii. 17 it is forbidden to redeem any firstling fit for sacrifice. Again, in Deuteronomy the annual produce of the soil, but not of the herd, was tithed for the religious use of the owner, who ate the tithes at the feasts. But in the Levitical law the tithe includes the herd and the flock (Lev. xxvii. 32), and is a tribute paid to the Levites, who in turn pay a tithe to the priests (Num. xviii.). This is quite another thing from the Deuteronomic annual tithe, which is not a tribute, but a provision for the popular religious festivals ; and the only ordinance of Deuteronomy at all analogous to it is the charity tithe of the third year, in which the Levites had a share along with the other poor of the township. But here also the points of difference are greater than the points of likeness. The charity tithe was stored in each township and eaten by dependents where it was stored (Deut. xxvi. 12, 13, where for *brought away* read *consumed* : the tithe was consumed where it lay ; see verse 14 Heb.). The Levitical tithe might be eaten by the Levites where they pleased, and in later times was stored in the Temple. Once more, the priest's share of a sacrifice in Deuteronomy consists of inferior parts, the head and maw, which

interest of this inquiry lies in its bearing on the early history
of Israel.　It is for the historian to determine how far the
Priests' Code (*i.e.* the Levitical law and the narrative sections
of the Pentateuch that go with it, and are mainly directed to
enforce law by rehearsing precedents) is mere law, of which
we can say no more than that it was law for the second
Temple, and how far it is also history which can be used in
describing the original sanctuary of the ark in the days of
Moses.　But in following out this inquiry we cannot assume
that every law which is called a law of Moses was meant to
be understood as literally given in the wilderness.　For it is
a familiar fact that in the early law of all nations necessary
modifications on old law are habitually carried out by means
of what lawyers call *legal fictions*.　This name is somewhat
misleading ; for a legal fiction is no deceit, but a convention
which all parties understand.　In short, it is found more convenient to present the new law in a form which enables it to
be treated as an integral part of the old legislation.　Thus in
Roman jurisprudence all law was supposed to be derived from
the Laws of the Twelve Tables (Maine, *Ancient Law*, p. 33

in Arabia are still the butcher's fee, and the shoulder, which is not the
choicest joint (Pseudo-Wâkidy, p. 15, and Hamaker's note), though not the
worst (Ezek. xxiv. 4 ; Freytag, *Ar. Prov.* ii. 320).　In fact Exod. xii. 9
requires to make special provision that the head and inwards be not left
uneaten in the paschal lamb, which proves that they were not esteemed.
But in the Levitical law the priests' part is the breast and the leg (not as
E. V. the shoulder), which is the best part (1 Sam. ix. 24).

In the second place, the Levitical law, following a hint of Ezekiel (xlv. 4,
5), assigns towns and pasture grounds to the priests and Levites.　The list of
such towns in Josh. xxi. is part of the Priests' Code and not of the old history.
In ancient times many of these towns certainly did not belong either to
priests or Levites.　Gezer was not conquered till the time of Solomon (1 Kings
ix. 16).　Shechem, Gibeon, and Hebron had quite a different population in the
time of the Judges.　Anathoth was a priestly city, but its priests held the land
on terms quite different from those of the later law.　As a matter of fact, the
assignation of cities and suburbs to the priests and Levites was never carried
out, as Jewish tradition itself admits for the period of the second Temple.

On the Levitical modifications of the festivals, see Hupfeld, *De primitiva
et vera festorum ratione*, Halle, 1852-65 ; Wellhausen, *Prolegomena*, Kap. iii.
On this topic the last word has not yet been spoken.

sq.), just as in Israel all law was held to be derived from the teaching of Moses. The whole object of this way of treating the law was to maintain the continuity of the legal system. But *legal fiction* has much more curious developments. In old English law many writs give a quite imaginary history of the case, alleging, for example, that the plaintiff is the king's debtor, and cannot pay his debts by reason of the default of the defendant. This instance is not directly parallel to anything in the Old Testament; but it shows how impossible it would be to explain any system of ancient law on the assumption that every statement which seems to be plain narrative of fact is actually meant to be so taken. It would be the highest presumption to affirm that what is found in all other ancient laws cannot occur in the Old Testament. The very universality of these conventions shows that in certain stages of society they form the easiest and most intelligible way of introducing necessary modifications of law; and the Israelites had the same habits of thought with other primitive nations, and doubtless required to be taught and to think things out on the same lines. In our state of society legal fictions are out of date; in English law they have long been mere antiquarian lumber. But Israel's law was given for the practical use of an ancient people, and required to take the forms which we know, as a matter of fact, to be those which primitive nations best understand.

If we find, then, by actual comparison of different parts of Scripture, that some points of law and ceremony are related in historical form, as if based on Mosaic precedent, but that there is other evidence, as in the case of the march from Sinai (*supra*, p. 321), that the thing did not happen so in Moses's own time, we have to consider the probability that the form of the narrative which aims at setting forth law in the shape of precedent is nothing more than a case of legal convention; for one well-known type of this is to relate a

25

new law in the form of an ancient precedent. Let me illustrate this by an example from Sir H. Maine's *Village Communities*, p. 110. In India, when the Government brings a new water supply into a village, the village authorities make rules for its use and distribution; but "these rules do not purport to emanate from the personal authority of their author or authors; there is always a sort of fiction under which some customs as to the distribution of water are supposed to have existed from all antiquity, although, in fact, no artificial supply had been even so much as thought of." In the same way the new laws of the Levitical code might be presented as ordinances of Moses, though, when they were first promulgated, every one knew that they were not so, and though Ezra himself speaks of some of them as ordinances of the prophets.

A good illustration occurs in the law of war. According to 1 Sam. xxx. 24, 25, the standing law of Israel as to the distribution of booty was enacted by David, and goes back only to a precedent in his war with the Amalekites who burned Ziklag. In the priestly legislation the same law is given as a Mosaic precedent from the war with Midian (Num. xxxi. 27). Here one can hardly avoid the conclusion that the Pentateuchal narrator has no other object than to set forth a certain rule of war as the ancient and sacred law of Israel. The older historian is content to refer this statute and ordinance of Israel to David. But the Priestly Code had to exhibit the whole system of Israel's law as a unity, and if the conventional methods of his time led him (as they did) to cast his exposition into historical form, he could only attain the unity requisite in a law-book by throwing David's ordinance back into the Mosaic age. Whether in this or any other particular case he was consciously applying the method of legal fiction, or whether long before his time younger laws had been largely referred to Moses by common consent, as the traditional way of acknowledging that they had co-ordinate authority with the earliest sacred legislation, is a matter of detail. The important point for us as historical students is to realise the necessity of distinguishing between quasi-historical precedents, which are to be taken only as laws, and the actual history, which is to be taken literally. To indolent theologians this necessity is naturally unwelcome; but to the diligent and reverent student it affords the key for the solution of many difficulties, and enables us to gain a much more consistent and instructive view of the early history of Israel than is possible on the traditional assumption that the whole law which regulated the life of the Jews in the age of Pericles was already extant and in force long before the Trojan war, in a nation that was only just emerging from the primitive conditions of pastoral life in the desert. The conclusion to which modern critics have been led is that the whole Priests' Code, alike in those parts which are formally legislative and in those which a superficial reading might regard as purely historical, is to be taken as essentially a law-book, and must not be used as an independent source for the actual history of the Mosaic time. For history, as distinct from law, the priestly author appears to have had no other authorities than those older books of which the greater part is still preserved to us in the non-priestly sections of the Pentateuch. Some account of the manner in which the Priests' Code deals with these older sources, of the way in which it strings its legal precepts on an historical thread, and of the way in which it allows itself to reshape the narrative in order to set forth later laws under the conventional form of Mosaic precedent, is necessary to complete the most summary view of the origin of the Pentateuch. The first edition of this book stopped at the point which we have now reached; I shall now attempt to supply the defect by a supplementary Lecture.

LECTURE XIII

THE NARRATIVE OF THE HEXATEUCH

IN the last Lecture the critical argument about the dates of the three Pentateuchal Codes was carried to its conclusion. The proof that the three great strata of laws embodied in the so-called books of Moses are not all of one age but correspond to three stages in the development of Israel's institutions, which can still be clearly recognised in the narrative of the historical books, is the most important achievement of Old Testament criticism. When the codes are set in their right places the main source of confusion in the study of the Old Testament is removed, the central problem of criticism is solved, and the controversy between modern criticism and conservative tradition is really decided.

Behind this central problem there lie of course a multitude of other questions that must be answered before the task of the critic is completed. The Pentateuch is a composite book, in which several bodies of law belonging to different periods occur embedded in a narrative. The narrative in its present form cannot be older than the youngest body of laws,[1] and therefore must have been completed some time between the age of Ezekiel and that of Ezra. On the other hand, the final narrator certainly used older written documents, from which he made copious extracts *verbatim*. It is manifestly

---

[1] It is of course quite possible that single laws, such as that about the poll-tax (*supra*, p. 51), may have been added later.

of great importance to determine all that can be determined as to the nature and age of these documents, and the process by which they and the several bodies of laws were ultimately fused together in a single volume.

In the course of twelve Lectures, which made up the first edition of this book, I had no room to give more than a few general hints on this branch of the critical problem. Nor can I now attempt a complete exposition of all that critics have made out as to the structure of the Pentateuchal narrative, and of the arguments by which their results have been attained. For such an exposition it would be necessary to go through the whole Hebrew text, book by book, and chapter by chapter—a task unsuitable to the plan of the present volume. Those who wish to follow out the critical analysis in detail will find the necessary help in the first volume of Kuenen's *Onderzoek*, which is the standard work on the subject, and accessible in an English translation, or, in a more compendious and easier form, in Prof. Driver's *Introduction*. I have no desire to say again what is so well said in these books; but those who have followed my argument thus far may naturally desire to have, in conclusion, at least a general sketch of the whole results of Pentateuch criticism. I have met with many persons who admit that they can detect no flaw in the critical arguments by which the dates of the codes are established, but who yet suspend their judgment, and are tempted to regard the whole Pentateuch question as a hopeless puzzle, because they cannot understand how the Mosaic history is to be read in the light of the new critical discoveries; and it is certainly true that if the dates assigned to the codes are correct they ought to find their most important verification in the analysis of the Pentateuchal narrative. And so in point of fact they do.

The method by which the codes are assigned to their proper place in Hebrew history, and the method by which the narratives of the Pentateuch can be analysed into their component parts, and shown to be made up of extracts from several documents, are to a great extent independent ; and, in point of fact, very considerable progress had been made in the second branch of analysis before anything important was settled on the question of the laws. The strength of the present position of Pentateuch criticism is in good measure due to the fact that two lines of inquiry have converged to a common result.

These two lines of inquiry may be called respectively the historical and the literary. The historical method compares the institutions set forth in the several codes with the actual working institutions of Israel, as we see them in the historical books ; the literary method compares the several parts of the Pentateuch with one another, taking note of diversities of style and manner, of internal contradictions or incongruities, and of all other points that forbid us to regard the whole Torah as the homogeneous composition of a single writer. In the first period of Pentateuch criticism, of which Nöldeke's *Untersuchungen* (Kiel, 1869) may be taken as the last important utterance, most scholars threw their whole strength into the literary line of inquiry. It was already settled that the Code of Deuteronomy was Josiah's Law-book, and that the Book of the Covenant must be older, but there was no agreement about the Priestly Code. On the other hand, it had been clearly seen that the priestly laws form an integral part of a great document, running through the whole Pentateuch from Genesis onwards and extending into Joshua. And it had also been shown that this document displays so many marked peculiarities of language, mannerisms of style, and characteristic ways of looking at things, that it is possible to separate it out with much precision from the other sources with which it is now interwoven.

Thus when the new school of criticism came forward with

its historical argument to prove that the priestly laws, as a whole, are later than Ezekiel, the means were at hand for subjecting this conclusion to a severe test of an independent kind. If the new criticism was right, the document embodying the priestly laws was the latest element in the Pentateuch and Joshua, and when it was separated out the parts of the Hexateuch that remained could not contain any reference, direct or indirect, to the priestly document. It was found on careful examination that this was actually the case. Some apparent instances to the contrary were indeed brought forward; but the list of places where the non-priestly sources seemed to be dependent on the priestly document was from the first extraordinarily meagre and little fitted to produce conviction; and on closer examination it shrank to nothing. For example, the introductory chapters of the Book of Deuteronomy contain a summary of the story of the forty years' wandering. By far the greater part of the history of this period, as it stands in our present Pentateuch, belongs to the priestly document; but everything peculiar to that document is remarkable by its absence from the historical retrospect in Deuteronomy. At first the opponents of the new views were not prepared to concede this; they could not deny that the retrospect was silent about the priestly tabernacle and its ordinances, that it ignored the whole series of revelations to Moses and Aaron on which the priestly system of Israel's sanctity rests; but they thought that they could point out some few minor details in which the Deuteronomic writer betrayed acquaintance with the priestly document. If this had been correct it could only have led to the startling result that the Deuteronomist deliberately ignored the main teaching of the priestly document, and aimed at suppressing an essential part of the sacred law. But it was soon shown that there was no occasion to adopt any such sensational theory; the supposed points of contact between Deuteronomy and the priestly document were found either to be illusory or to admit of an explanation consistent with the priority of the former work.[1]

This coincidence between the results of historical and literary criticism is the more striking because the literary determination of the limits of the priestly document or group was carried out almost entirely by scholars who took it for granted that this document was certainly older than Deuteronomy, and probably the oldest thing in the Hexateuch. There can therefore be no suspicion that their analysis was influenced by arguments drawn from the historico-legal line of inquiry.

[1] In justification of these statements it may suffice to refer to the latest important publication on the other side. Prof. Dillmann, of Berlin, is now the only scholar of eminence who dissents from the new critical construction of the Pentateuch, and has given his reasons for doing so after a full consideration of the researches of Kuenen and Wellhausen. One is not bound to take note in this connection of views set forth before the two scholars last named had put the whole matter in a fresh light, or of newer utterances, like those of Renan, which simply ignore the more modern criticism. Between Dillmann and the school of Kuenen and Wellhausen there is no controversy as to the broad lines of division that mark out the Hexateuch as consisting of four essential parts, viz. the priestly document, or group of documents (for it is not affirmed and not essential to the argument that all the priestly pieces are by one hand : it is enough that they belong to one school) ; the Deuteronomic document (or group) ; and two earlier documents commonly known as the Jahvistic and the Elohistic. Dillmann admits that the two documents last named are older than Deuteronomy and the priestly document or group, but he does not admit that the last is younger than Deuteronomy. And he thinks that the Jahvistic, Elohistic, and priestly parts of the Hexateuch were united into a single book before Deuteronomy was added. But when it comes to the question whether the Deuteronomic writings presuppose the existence of the priestly group, he admits that this cannot be proved with absolute certainty. On the other hand, he feels sure that R^d (i.e. the writer who incorporated Deuteronomy for the first time with the other parts of the Pentateuch) knew the priestly writings. In other words, the proof that the priestly group is not the youngest part of the Pentateuch cannot be effected by comparison with the other great masses of Pentateuchal writing, but turns on a particular theory of the steps by which the original documents were fused together. I venture to say that this argument proves nothing. Suppose it true that Deuteronomy was still a separate book after the other three documents or groups were fused together, this does not in the slightest degree affect the force of the historical argument for putting the Deuteronomic Code

I have already explained that I cannot undertake to carry you through the details of the analysis on which the delimitation of the priestly group of writings rests. But I think I can give such a sketch of the methods of analysis, with illustrations from particular cases, as will satisfy reasonable persons that the critics have been working on sound lines. And when this is taken along with the fact that the results of the literary analysis agree with what can be proved from history as to the date of the codes, you will, I think, have as much evidence before you as persons who are not specialists can ever expect to have in a complicated problem of ancient history. Speaking broadly, the critics divide the Hexateuch into three groups of literature ; the oldest history, represented by two documents that are cited as the Jahvistic and Elohistic stories, or more briefly as J and E ; the Deuteronomic Code with its appendages (cited as D) ; and the group of priestly writings (cited as P). For our purposes it will be most convenient to begin with the Deuteronomic group. We start with the facts already established, that the code of Deut. xii.-xxvi. is a reshaping of the old law under the influence of the teaching of the prophets of the eighth century, and that it is the law on which Josiah's Reformation proceeded (621 B.C.). In our present Book of Deuteronomy the code is preceded and followed by a series of discourses, Deut. i.-xi. on the one side and Deut. xxvii.-xxx. on the

and its appendages before the Priests' Code and the rest of the priestly writings. And the very significant fact that the Deuteronomic sketch of the history ignores all that is characteristic in the priestly history also remains untouched. On this point, indeed, Dillmann replies with a *tu quoque*. If Deuteronomy ignores the Priests' Code and history, he says, it must equally be admitted on the other side that the latter ignores Deuteronomy. Really ? Is it not plain that the whole system of the Priests' Code rests on the cardinal Deuteronomic doctrine of the one sanctuary, which is so completely taken for granted by the later writer that it does not even receive formal expression and justification ? See Dillmann, *Die Bücher Num., Deut., and Jos.* (Leipzig, 1886), p. 668, and comp. on the whole matter Driver, *Introduction*, p. 77 *sq.*, p. 130, p. 137 *sq.*

other.[1] That in substance and style these chapters are
closely akin to the code of Deut. xii.-xxvi., and stand apart
from the rest of the Pentateuch, must be plain to every
attentive reader, but we shall hardly be justified in conclud-
ing that Deut. i.-xxx. is all by one hand, and that all these
chapters were contained in the book laid before King Josiah.
Note in particular that chap. xxvii. breaks the connection
between xxvi. and xxviii., and further that the occurrence of a
series of titles and subscriptions at different points (chap. i. 1,
v. 1, xii. 1, xxix. 1 [Heb. xxviii. 69]) suggests rather that the
code may have appeared in successive editions with fresh
exhortations added by way of preface and conclusion. This,
however, is a matter of detail that need not concern us at
present.

The date of the whole Deuteronomic group is of course
dependent on the date of the code, *i.e.* no part of Deut.
i.-xxx. can be older than the seventh century B.C.; while if
the theory of successive editions is correct, some parts may be
a good deal later than Josiah's Reformation in 621 B.C. But
the whole group is manifestly older than the Priestly Code;
for there is not the slightest trace of the distinction between
Priests and Levites (see Deut. x. 8), and the sketch of the
events of the wilderness journey contained in the opening
chapters of Deuteronomy passes in silence over all those
histories in the middle books of the Pentateuch which imply
that the Priestly Code was already in force in the days of
Moses.[2]

If the Deuteronomic Code was not in existence before the
seventh century B.C., we cannot regard the speeches and
exhortations of Moses contained in the Deuteronomic group
as anything else than free compositions. We have in them
not what Moses actually said in the plains of Moab, but

---

[1] Deut. xxxi. belongs only in part to this group, and in its present form
must be regarded as the link uniting D to the rest of the Pentateuch.

[2] Some apparent exceptions will come up for consideration later.

admonitions conceived in the spirit of Moses and first
addressed to the men of Josiah's time, or in part, perhaps, to
the next generation. As a matter of literary form this way
of enforcing the lessons of past history has evidently much to
recommend it, and it was not introduced for the first time in
the age of Josiah. In Joshua xxiv., which all critics assign
to one of the pre-Deuteronomic sources of the Pentateuch (E),
Joshua is introduced in the same way, recapitulating how
God had led Israel in the past, and drawing a practical
conclusion. The Deuteronomic writers, therefore, were
employing a recognised literary form which was not likely to
be misunderstood in a society that had reached so high a
pitch of literary culture as Judah in the reign of Josiah. To
suppose that the speeches were forged in Moses's name to
support the halting authority of the code is simply absurd.
In all probability the code had already been accepted as the
law of the land before the speeches were added ; or, if some
of the speeches were already included in the book that was
brought to Josiah, it is puerile to think that the heads of a
nation in which letters had flourished for centuries, and which
possessed such masterpieces of literary workmanship as the
older histories and the prophetical books of the eighth century,
could have failed to observe that a speech written in the name
of Moses was not necessarily genuine. It was the intrinsic
merits of Deuteronomy that gained it acceptance ; and if the
book had not set forth such a combination of the old law of
the realm with the principles of the prophets as commended
itself to the national conscience and indicated a practical
course of Reformation, the mere name of Moses would not
have prevented it from being tossed aside.

While the speeches of Deuteronomy were not absolutely a
new departure in literary art, we can see that they made a
profound impression on the literary aims and methods of the
period immediately subsequent to Josiah's Reformation.

Thus the Book of Joshua contains considerable passages, *e.g.*
the greater part of chap. i. and the whole of chap. xxiii.,
which are obviously imitations of the parenetic manner of
Deuteronomy; and additions of the same kind can be
detected in Judges, Samuel, and Kings. These insertions
hardly touch the substance of the history, which, as we have
already seen, makes it quite plain that the law of Deuteronomy
was not known before the time of Josiah; they consist mainly
of a series of reflections on the meaning and lessons of the
story, sometimes in the shape of speeches, and sometimes in
the writer's own name, but all framed in the Deuteronomic
manner and on the assumption that the law of Deuteronomy
is the standard by which national conduct must be judged.
In the language of critics, it appears that the historical books
from Judges to Kings have passed through the hands of at
least one Deuteronomic redactor.

The group Deut. i.-xxx. offers little difficulty to the critical analyst, because it has been transferred to the present
Hexateuch entire, and in continuous form. In like manner
it is probable that Lev. xvii.-xxvi. once existed as a separate
book, very nearly in the shape in which we now read it.
This section belongs in general character to the priestly
group, and probably represents the earliest attempt to codify
the priestly ordinances. But the mass of the Hexateuch,
after Deut. i.-xxx. has been set on one side, is made up of
extracts from several sources pieced together in a complicated way. And here the difficulties of critical analysis
begin.

How complex the structure of the narrative sometimes is
has already been shown in Lecture XI. by the example of the
story of the Deluge. But fortunately for the critics this close
interweaving of single sentences from two sources is not the
general rule; there are long continuous tracts in the Hexateuch where a single source is followed and nothing more

serious than an occasional editorial touch comes in to break
the unity of the exposition.   Thus in the middle books of the
Pentateuch we can at once mark off a series of sections, comprising the mass of the priestly laws and a certain amount of
narrative intimately connected with these laws.   Such are
Exod. xxv.-xxxi., and then again, after a break of three
chapters, Exod. xxxv.-xl.; further the whole Book of Leviticus (save that xvii.-xxvi. were mainly taken over into
the priestly document from an older book); Num. i. 1-x. 28.
In the last verses of Num. x. we pass to another and discrepant source, as was shown in Lecture XI. (*supra*, p. 321),
and from this point the phenomena become more complex.
But the priestly source reappears without anything suggestive
of admixture in Num. xv. xvii.-xix. xxvi.-xxxi., and finally in
Num. xxxiii.-xxxvi.

I do not think it is necessary to argue in detail that all
these passages are closely connected and must be drawn from
a single source; it will be more instructive to look at some of
the reasons why I have passed over certain chapters as being
either of mixed origin or wholly derived from a different
source.   And first then, as regards Exodus xxxii.-xxxiv., or
more exactly xxxii. xxxiii. xxxiv. 1-28.[1]

The analysis of these chapters presents several points of
difficulty on which critics are not yet fully agreed.   That
the whole is not derived from a single source is pretty clear;
thus xxxii. 7-14, where Moses is informed about the sin of the
golden calf, and obtains God's forgiveness for the people before
leaving the mount for the first time, is hardly of one piece
with xxxii. 30-34, where the same forgiveness is obtained at
a second visit to Sinai, nor indeed with the angry surprise of

---

[1] Exod. xxxiv. 29-35 is really the close of chap. xxxi., containing several
expressions highly characteristic of P.   It does not run quite smoothly with
what follows (comp. xxxiv. 32 with xxxv. 1); but there are reasons for
thinking that chaps. xxxv. *sqq.* have at any rate been largely retouched by a
late hand.

Moses as he approaches the camp, xxxii. 17-19. There are
other signs that the narrative is not homogeneous throughout,
but on these and the various analyses to which they have
given rise I need not dwell. The point to be noticed is
that these chapters as a whole interrupt the sequence of the
priestly narrative, and present a different view of the course
of events. In Exod. xxv.-xxxi. Moses is on the mount receiving instructions for the construction of the ark and
tabernacle, and for the institution of the Aaronic priesthood,
that Jehovah may take up his dwelling in the midst of Israel.
In chapters xxxv. *sqq.* Moses communicates his instructions
to the people, and the tabernacle is made and set up. Further
ordinances follow in the Book of Leviticus and the early
chapters of Numbers. These things take up much time, and
it is almost a year after the first arrival at Sinai before the
people break up to pursue their journey towards Canaan
(Num. x. 11, compared with Exod. xix. 1). All this is
simple and self-consistent, and leaves us with a clear conception that the main purpose of the visit to Sinai was to
furnish the people with the pattern of ritual and priesthood
necessary to a holy nation, in whose midst Jehovah dwells.
But now observe how chaps. xxxii.-xxxiv. break the tenor
of the narrative. While Moses is on the mount the people
fall to worship the golden calf, and for this sin they are
chastised. There would be no difficulty in this if we could
treat the affair of the calf as a mere episode which produced
no permanent effect on Israel's relations to Jehovah. And
we must treat it so if we take chap. xxxv. as the natural
sequel to chap. xxxiv.; for in it Moses, after revisiting Sinai
to replace the broken tables, quietly passes over all the recent
events and begins to rehearse the ordinances about the tabernacle, exactly as if the calf had never been made and the
vocation of the holy nation had never been in jeopardy. But
this is not the view of chaps. xxxii.-xxxiv. There the people's

sin is indeed pardoned, but the pardon is accompanied by a
sentence of banishment from the Mount of God (xxxiii. 1).
Moreover, though Jehovah promises to guide the people,
sending His angel before them (xxxii. 34, xxxiii. 2), He
warns them that He cannot go in the midst of them (xxxiii.
3); and the practical application of this is seen in xxxiii. 7
sq., where the tabernacle, the seat of revelation, is pitched
outside the camp and remote from it. Both these points are
entirely ignored in the priestly narrative. The order to depart is never withdrawn, yet the people remain at Sinai as if
nothing had happened. And in xxxv. *sqq.* the construction
of the priestly tabernacle, within which God is to dwell in
the centre of the camp, proceeds without any reference to
the existence of the tabernacle of chap. xxxiii., standing outside the camp. But can we suppose at least that Jehovah's
refusal to go in the midst of the people was tacitly withdrawn,
and the first tabernacle replaced by the priestly tent? No;
for the sanctuary outside the camp reappears long after, in
Num. xi. 24, 26, in Num. xii. 4, and by implication also in
Num. x. 33, where the ark goes before the host, not in the
midst of it.[1]

Still more inexplicable is the relation of the priestly ordinances to the covenant between Jehovah and Israel, of which
the terms are set forth in Exod. xxxiv. 10-27. This covenant
is announced in express terms as the foundation of Israel's
relations to Jehovah. But it has nothing in common with
the elaborate priestly ordinances already revealed in chaps.
xxv.-xxxi. Did Jehovah give all the details of priesthood
and tabernacle before he fixed the fundamental lines of
Israel's religion? Or are we rather to assume that the
rebellion and the breaking of the first tables rendered it
necessary to make an entirely new beginning and a new

---

[1] Note also that in Deut. x. 1 *sqq.* the ark is made at the same time as the
renewed tables of stone.

fundamental covenant? And if so how comes it that, according to chap. xxxv., Moses, when he descends from the mount, is silent as to the covenant of chap. xxxiv., and goes back to take up the thread of chap. xxxi.? From all this the conclusion is inevitable that chap. xxxv. attaches itself directly to chap. xxxi., and has nothing in common with Exod. xxxii.-xxxiv.[1]

We may now pass on to the break in the priestly narrative at Num. x. 28. Upon x. 29 *sqq.* enough has been said at p. 321. In chaps. xi. xii. the position of the tabernacle outside the camp is sufficient proof that the narrative is not priestly; and we also observe that in chap. xii. Aaron is not priest but prophet. In chaps. xiii. xiv. again, which contain the history of the spies that were sent to search the land of Canaan, and of the rebellion that followed on their report, we have plainly to deal with a compound narrative, the elements of which may be exhibited as follows in parallel columns :—

Num. xiii. 1-17 *a.*—Moses, by the commandment of the LORD, sends forth twelve men from the wilderness of Paran to spy out the land of Canaan. . . . (21.) So they went up and spied out the land from the wilderness of Zin as far as Rehob and the frontier of Hamath. . . . (25.) And they returned from spying out the land after forty days, (26) and went and came to Moses and Aaron and to all the congregation of the children of Israel in the wilderness of Paran, . . . and made their report to them and to the whole congregation. . . . (32.) And they brought up an evil report of the land which they had spied out

17 *b*-20. . . . and said to them, Go up through the Negeb, and go up into the mountain-land, and see the land what it is, and the people that dwell in it, whether they be strong or weak, few or many, etc. And take ye of the fruit of the land. Now the time was the time of the first ripe grapes. . . . (22.) So they went up through the Negeb, and came as far as Hebron, etc. . . . (23, 24.) From Eshcol [near Hebron] they took a huge bunch of grapes with pomegranates and figs. . . . (26.) [Then they returned] to Kadesh . . . and showed them the fruit of the land. (27-29.) And they told him [Moses] that the land flowed with

---

[1] It is probable that Exod. xxxv.-xl. have been expanded by later hands from a much shorter account of the carrying out of the directions in chaps. xxv.-xxxi. ; see *supra*, p. 125. But this does not affect the argument, since chaps. xxxii.-xxxiv. are ignored by the whole priestly legislation.

unto the children of Israel, saying, The land, through which we have gone to spy it out, is a land that eateth up the inhabitants thereof. . . . (xiv. 1.) And all the congregation lifted up their voice, and cried. . . . (2, 3.) And all the children of Israel murmured against Moses and Aaron : and the whole congregation said unto them, Would that we had died in the land of Egypt, etc. . . . (5.) And Moses and Aaron fell on their faces before all the congregation of the children of Israel. (6.) And Joshua and Caleb, two of the spies, rent their clothes, (7) and spake unto the whole congregation of the children of Israel, saying, The land is an exceeding good land. . . (10.) But the whole congregation bade stone them with stones. And the glory of the LORD appeared in the tabernacle before all the children of Israel. . . (26-35.) And the Lord spake unto Moses and Aaron announcing that the whole generation of rebels should die in the wilderness, only Caleb and Joshua surviving to enter the promised land. (36-38.) The other ten spies die of plague before the LORD.

milk and honey, but that the people were strong, with great walled cities. (30.) And Caleb stilled the people before Moses, saying, Let us go up at once and possess it ; for we are well able to overcome it. (31.) But the men who went up with him said, We be not able to go up against the people, for they are stronger than we, . . (32) and all the people that we saw in it are men of great stature, (33) and there we saw the giants, etc. . . (xiv. 1.) And the people wept that night. . . . (4.) And they said one to another, Let us make a captain and return to Egypt. *Here there is a lacuna which seems to have contained a remonstrance by Moses or Caleb, of which verses 8, 9 are a fragment. The thread is resumed in verse 11.* (11-25.) And the Lord said unto Moses, How long will this people provoke me ? etc. I will smite them with pestilence, and disinherit them, and make of thee a greater nation and mightier than they. Moses intercedes for the people, and obtains forgiveness for them. But the rebellious generation must die in the wilderness, and shall not see the land of promise, with the sole exception of Caleb. " To-morrow turn ye, and get ye into the wilderness." . . . (39-45.) When this sentence is conveyed to the people they mourn greatly, and insist on repairing their error by an attack on the Canaanite frontier, in which they undergo defeat.

These accounts are plainly independent, and each of them is nearly complete in itself, though that in the right hand column has lost its beginning and a few links at other points. In it the spies start from Kadesh, go no farther than Hebron,

and report very favourably of the land, were it not that the
inhabitants are too strong to be conquered. The only one
who dissents from this judgment is Caleb, and he alone is exempted from the sentence of death in the wilderness. In the
other account the spies start from the wilderness of Paran,
reach the extreme north of Palestine, and report that the land
is one in which it is hardly possible to live (xiii. 32 ; comp.
Ezek. xxxvi. 13). Caleb and Joshua, on the other hand, say
that the land is good, and they two are exempted from
the judgment of God against the rebels. Of these two
accounts the first is followed in every point in Deut. i. 22-36,
39, 40,[1] and also in Josh. xiv. 6-14, save that in this passage
some glossator has added in verse 6 the words "and concerning thee," thus including Joshua among the spies, against the
plain sense of verse 8. Thus we see that the narrative which
includes Joshua among the spies is later than Deuteronomy ;
and in fact it is assigned to the priestly group by its style
and characteristic expressions. Note, for example, that in it
God speaks to Moses and Aaron, as is common in the priestly
laws, and that the people are spoken of as "the congregation"
('ēdah), a term that never occurs in the non-priestly parts
of the Hexateuch, and is very rare in the other historical
books.

When we pass on to chap. xvi. we again find signs of
mixture in the narrative. Taken as a whole, as we now read
it, Num. xvi. is priestly, i.e. the events it details and the way
of telling them read smoothly enough with the chapters that
follow and with the general tenor of the priestly legislation.
But Dathan and Abiram, the Reubenites, who object to the

---

[1] Verses 37, 38 do not make against this ; for they do not imply that
Joshua was one of the spies. But they disturb the context, and probably are an
addition to the original text of Deuteronomy ; for God's anger with Moses and
the appointment of Joshua as his successor belong to a different place, and have
no connection with the matter of the spies. Further, the first words of verse
39 as far as "a prey" are wanting in LXX., and have been inserted from
Num. xiv. 31 (priestly) by a late hand. Comp. Dillmann on the passage.

civil authority exercised by Moses, have nothing in common with Korah, who objects to the special claims of priestly sanctity put forth by Moses and Aaron.   This, of course, proves nothing by itself; for modern as well as ancient history is full of examples of the union of distinct political parties against a common antagonist.   But the curious thing is that Korah on the one hand, Dathan and Abiram on the other, are separate not only in their aims but in their action and in their doom.   In verse 1, and again in verses 24, 27, all three are mentioned together in a formal way (which may very well be due to an editor), but in substance the revolt of Korah and that of Dathan and Abiram are quite distinct. The former and his adherents are challenged by Moses to appear before the tabernacle in an act of priestly service, and, accepting the challenge, are consumed by fire from the LORD ; the latter refuse to meet Moses, and are swallowed up by earthquake in their tents.   Now in Deut. xi. 6 the revolt and catastrophe of Dathan and Abiram are referred to without one word of reference to Korah : can we doubt, then, that the old history, prior to Deuteronomy, which we have recognised in one of the constituent elements of Num. 13, 14, reappears also in chap. xvi. in the verses which speak of Dathan and Abiram and are silent about Korah ?   It is Korah's part of the story that has to do with the privileges of Levi and Aaron, *i.e.* with the theory of the priestly law and narrative ; and so we have another proof that the priestly system is later than Deuteronomy.[1]

---

[1] The beginning of the pre-Deuteronomic narrative of the revolt of Dathan and Abiram is lost, save a fragment giving the names of the rebels in verse 1. But from verse 12 onwards the story is complete as follows :—(12-14.) Moses summons Dathan and Abiram, who refuse to obey or to acknowledge his right to play the prince.   (15.) And Moses was very wroth, and said, I have not taken one ass from them, neither have I hurt one of them [which implies that his judicial impartiality in civil matters was the thing impugned].   (25, 26.) Moses, followed by the elders, goes to Dathan and Abiram, and warns the people to withdraw from the rebels and their tents.   (27 *b.*) And Dathan and Abiram came out and stood in the door of their tents, etc.   (28-31.) Moses

From Exodus xxv. down to Numbers xix., I have been able to treat the priestly document as the main stock of the narrative, accepting the burden of proof when I undertake to show that it is interrupted from time to time by extracts from other sources. And the same way of approaching the question may also be applied to Num. xxv. 6 - xxxvi. 13, where, except in chap. xxxii., there is nothing to suggest plurality of authorship.[1]

This whole section may safely be assigned to the priestly group; for it consists partly of laws, conceived and set forth in the priestly manner, partly of histories, in which Eleazar, the son and successor of Aaron, has all the precedence proper to him under the priestly code, and partly of statistics and lists, for which the priestly narrator has a special predilection. The list of stations in the wilderness journey is very useful as a check on the analysis of the preceding history. For example, we have seen that in the older narrative the spies went forth from Kadesh, but in the priestly narrative from the wilderness of Paran. And accordingly in Num. xxxiii.

announces that the rebels will be swallowed up alive; and straightway the ground clave asunder, (32 a) and the earth opened her mouth and swallowed up them and their tents; (33) and they and all that appertained to them went down alive into the pit, etc.; (34) and all Israel seeing it fled in terror.

The full explanation of the remainder of the chapter cannot be effected without distinguishing two strata in the priestly narrative; see Kuenen in *Theol. Tijdschrift*, xii. (1878), p. 139 *sqq.*, whose analysis has commanded general assent.

[1] This section of the priestly document begins abruptly, and something has been lost. For the presupposition of xxv. 6 *sqq.* is that the Israelites were seduced into filthy idolatry by the Midianites, and were smitten with a plague which was stayed by Phinehas's act of judgment. Verses 1-5 do not correspond with this. The seducers are not the Midianites (who in fact are quite out of place in the plains of Moab), but the women of Moab. Further, though a plague seems to be implied in verses 3, 4, it is stayed in quite a different way by Moses (ver. 4) or by the judges of the people (ver. 5). Note also that verses 3, 5 (and Deut. iv. 3) speak of Baal-Peor, *i.e.* the local deity of Mount Peor (xxiii. 28), whereas in verse 18, and again in xxxi. 16, as also in the priestly part of Joshua (xxii. 17), Peor is the name of the god.

For the compound chap. xxxii. see Driver, p. 64; but especially two papers by Kuenen in *Theol. Tijdschrift*, xi. (1877).

36 the Hebrews do not reach Kadesh till near the close of their wanderings.

In Numbers xx.-xxiv., on the other hand, the phenomena are complicated, and one can see that a great part of the narrative belongs to the non-priestly and pre-Deuteronomic sources. To these we must reckon, first of all, the whole episode of Balaam (chaps. xxii.-xxiv.). For, apart from considerations of language and style, which it is impossible to set forth in this place, we note an absolute inconsistency between these chapters and the reference to Balaam in the priestly chapter xxxi. In the former, Balaam, who, though no friend to Israel, is careful to avoid Jehovah's anger, returns to his home on the Euphrates, *i.e.* to Mesopotamia,[1] as soon as God has turned his curse into a blessing. But in Num. xxxi. 8, 16 Balaam is found among the Midianites, *i.e.* in the country between Edom and the Red Sea, where he has been engaged in devising the seduction of Israel through the worship of Peor. And once more we observe that it is the non-priestly conception of Balaam that appears in Deut. xxiii. 4, 5 [Heb. 5, 6] and in the eighth-century prophet Micah.

There remain chaps. xx. xxi. In chap. xx. the death of Aaron and consecration of Eleazar are evidently priestly.[2] And this carries with it a part at least of xx. 2-13, where Moses and Aaron are sentenced to die in the wilderness. But in what remains of chaps. xx. xxi. there is nothing

---

[1] In Num. xxii. 5 read with R. V. "to Pethor, which is by the River, to the land," *etc.* The River is the Euphrates ; comp. Deut. xxiii. 4 (Heb. 5).

[2] This is one of the few priestly passages to which the Deuteronomist has been supposed to make reference. But according to Deut. x. 6 Aaron dies at Mosera (the same as Moseroth of Num. xxxiii. 30), a place separated from Mount Hor by six marches. Thus, if the text of Deuteronomy is in order, the author had a different account of Aaron's death, and did not draw from P. It is, however, very plain that the words of Deut. x. 6 following "Mosera" are a late and unauthorised gloss, since according to verse 8 the first institution of the Levitical priesthood did not take place till a later stage of the wanderings.

priestly except one or two notes of stations which correspond
with chap. xxxiii. (xx. 1 *a*, xxi. 4 *a* to the word "Hor," xxi.
10, 11, and also xxii. 1). This appears from the following
considerations. In xx. 1 *b* the people are still encamped at
Kadesh, on the southern border of Canaan, whence the spies
were sent out. From Kadesh (ver. 14) they send messengers
to the Edomites, who occupied the whole region between
Moab and the Gulf of Akaba, asking passage through their
country. This was refused, and accordingly there was no
way to reach Eastern Palestine without another desert
journey all round Edom by the head of the gulf. And so
we read (xx. 21): "And Israel turned aside from him [Edom]
(xxi. 4) in the direction of the Red Sea to compass the land
of Edom."[1] Then follow the details of the journey, with a
number of stations that do not reappear in chap. xxxiii.
The Hebrews emerge from the desert in the district of the
Arnon, and the conquest of Eastern Canaan follows. This
great circuit through the wilderness from Kadesh to the
Arnon was inevitable when the people's faithlessness caused
the direct attack on Southern Canaan to be given up ; and
the sufferings it involved were the natural punishment of
their want of faith. But there was no arbitrary marching
up and down the wilderness. According to Deut. i. 46, ii. 1,
a passage which quite agrees with all that has survived of
the older narrative, the Israelites spent a long time at
Kadesh, and only left it to "compass Mount Seir." The
priestly account, as appears by comparison of Num. xiv.
33 *sqq.* with the lists of Num. xxxiii., is quite different.
Here the greater part of the forty years is spent on purpose-
less wandering as far as Ezion-gaber, on the Gulf of Akaba
(xxxiii. 35), and thence to Kadesh, which, according to chap.
xxxiii., appears to be reached for the first time in the last

---

[1] xxi. 1-3 is a little separate narrative, which is hardly in place where it
stands ; comp. Judges i. 16, 17.

year of the wilderness journey. In the fifth month of the
fortieth year the Hebrews are still at Mount Hor, but one
stage from Kadesh; a view of the course of Israel's wanderings plainly inconsistent with chap. xxi. Indeed, one is led
to think that the priestly narrator did not realise how wide
a circuit lay between Kadesh and the plains of Moab, and
how much time the entire conquest of the kingdoms of
Sihon and Og must have occupied, else he could hardly
have left no more than a brief seven months for all the
events between the death of Aaron and the passage of the
Jordan (Num. xxxiii. 38 compared with Deut. i. 3, Josh.
iv. 19).

    We have now run in a cursory way through the whole nar-
rative of Israel's adventures between Sinai and the plains of
Moab. The results of such a first survey ought not to be
taken as more than provisional, but they bear out, so far as
they go, two important conclusions at which we had already
arrived by another path. (1) They show us that we must
distinguish in the middle books of the Pentateuch between a
priestly series of laws, accompanied by narratives in harmony
with the priestly laws, and another series of narratives that
do not presuppose the Aaronic priesthood and its sanctuary.
(2) They show us, too, that only the latter series of narratives
is presupposed in the Book of Deuteronomy. Taking note of
these conclusions, our next task is to subject them to a further
test by an inductive method. We have provisionally marked
out the text of the middle books of the Pentateuch into two
main groups. Let us carefully collect all characteristics of
language, all mannerisms of style, in each provisional group,
and see whether they bear out our classification, or point to
a cross division. In the latter case we shall have cause to
amend our analysis: otherwise it will be powerfully confirmed. This is a part of the argument that I cannot
profitably go into without citing a mass of Hebrew phrases;

but surely in such a matter the English reader may safely trust to Oriental scholars. Those who are too sceptical to do this may consult Driver, who gives the main results of the linguistic analysis with great care : they will find that the results of the linguistic test have been tabulated, and that they confirm all that we have hitherto learned in a provisional way on a broader line of inquiry. It is shown by tables and figures which cannot be gainsaid that the priestly document or group has a distinct style and vocabulary of its own, and further that its peculiarities, whether of grammar or of lexicon, forbid us to assign the priestly writings to an early date, and allow, if they do not compel, us to place it after Ezekiel, as the historic-legal argument requires.

Though the English reader cannot hope to make himself master of these linguistic arguments, he may learn to appreciate their force by a careful attention to points of style and manner that do not disappear in translation. Thus among phrases characteristic of the priestly group he may note such as these : "throughout your generations," "after their families," the technical term "father's house" for a clan or family, the habitual designation of Israel as a "congregation" (*ēdah*), and of the princes as "chief of the congregation," or the like ; also standing formulas like "this is the thing that the Lord hath commanded," and "according to the word [*lit.* mouth] of the Lord." And in general he can observe that the priestly style is formal and mannered, deficient, as compared with the older narratives, in freedom and variety of expression. With this goes a love for formal headings and subscriptions, and a monotonous way of piling up particulars which reaches its climax in Num. vii. No one with the smallest knowledge of literature will believe that this chapter comes from the same pen that wrote the exquisite history of Joseph and the other masterpieces of Pentateuchal narrative.

But beneath all these points of phrase and style there lies something deeper and more fundamentally characteristic ; to wit, no small tincture of the abstract and unreal way of constructing the sacred history, that we saw in Lecture V. to be characteristic of Rabbinical Judaism, and of some later parts of the Old Testament. The Moses of Exodus xxxii.-xxxiv., or Numbers xi. xii., with his swift and hot anger on the one hand, his tender and passionate intercession on the other, is a living man ; the Moses of the priestly narrative is a lay-figure only fit to convey to the people rules about sacred upholstery and millinery. When the people rebel in the priestly story, Moses and Aaron at once get the better of them by a simple and uniform process. They have only to fall down on their faces in supplication (Num. xiv. 5, xvi. 4, xx. 6) to obtain an immediate supernatural interposition. The older narratives are not less full of the supernatural, but they do not reduce it in this way to a mechanical uniformity, and they allow us to see a natural harmony between the divine action and the historical circumstances, which is quite lost in the later account. Thus in the old story the wilderness wanderings from Kadesh to Arnon have a purpose as well as a penal effect ; they bring the people to another and easier point for the attack of Canaan. But in the priestly story they are mere wanderings for the sake of wandering. Or again in the priestly story the camping-places of the people are absolutely determined by the miraculous cloud (Num. ix. 15 *sqq.*). In the other narrative the cloud accompanies the march, but the local knowledge of Hobab is called into requisition in the choice of places to camp (Num. x. 29 *sqq.*). Even to the old history the wilderness journey is a continued portent, in which the play of human causes falls into the background, and is obscured by the ever-present splendour of the divine guidance, but in the priestly history the human and even the physical background disappears altogether. Consider, for example, the gorgeousness of the priestly tabernacle and its service, the gold and silver, the rich hangings of rare purple, the incense and unguents of costly spices. How came these things to be found in the wilderness ? It is absurd to say, as is commonly said, that the tabernacle was furnished from the spoil of the Egyptians (Exod. xi. 2, xii. 35), and that the serfs who left Egypt carrying on their shoulders a wretched provision of dough tied up in their cloaks (Exod. xii. 34), were at the same time laden with all the wealth of Asia and Africa, including such strange furniture for a long journey on foot as stores of purple yarn, and the like. But it is not worth while to spend time over these details. The decisive point is that the Mosaic tabernacle is not the tabernacle of the old pre-Deuteronomic history of Moses, and that it is equally unknown to the history of the Former Prophets. It is, in short, not a fact but an idea, an imaginary picture of such a tabernacle as might serve as a pattern for the service of the second Temple.[1] By much the greater part of the variations of the priestly narrative from the older story flow directly from the author's design to exhibit the whole ritual system as complete and at work in the wilderness ; in short, we have here to do not with a fresh source for ancient history, but with a body of legal Haggada, borrowing its outlines from the older narratives, but treating them with absolute freedom, so as to produce a picture of the ideal institutions of Israel's worship projected back into the Mosaic age. Such divergences of the priestly narrative from the older history of the wilderness wanderings as are not directly explicable on this principle are yet connected with it in an indirect way ; the most characteristic parts of the old story being omitted, or reduced to a bare and not very exact summary, if they do not fall in with the main purpose of the priestly document. Throughout the

---

[1] The arrangements agree with those of the second Temple in various particulars where Solomon's Temple was different, *e.g.* there is one golden candlestick and not ten (*supra*, p. 143).

priestly narrative Israel is not so much a nation as a church, and when it is not engaged in some act of rebellion against Moses and Aaron, it is employed in receiving legal instruction or discharging ritual duties. Even the rebellions have interest for this narrator only in so far as they elucidate some point of ecclesiastical discipline (Korah), or have a particular importance for the history of the priesthood, as when the sedition at Meribah leads to the exclusion of Aaron from the promised land, or the affair of Baal-Peor earns for Phinehas and his descendants a promise of everlasting priesthood. On the other hand, the golden calf and a whole series of later rebellions, which had no significance for the ecclesiastical polity of Israel, are passed by in silence : it is true that the affair of the spies is mentioned, but as this was the cause of the prolonged sojourn in the wilderness it evidently could not be omitted. Finally, one whole side of the history, the relations of the Hebrews with the Kenites, with Edom, with Moab, is ignored ; for this was not ecclesiastical but civil history. Even the conquest of Eastern Palestine seems to have been passed over in a word ; to compensate for this we have a war with Midian ; but the actual campaign is disposed of in a couple of verses, without the loss of a single man, and is merely a text on which to hang a long law of booty, in which the claims of the sanctuary are duly attended to.[1]

The middle books offer the best field on which to begin the analysis of the priestly element in the Pentateuch; for here we have a great mass of priestly writing, and are soon able to form a clear idea of the character of the narrative, and to collect a list of distinctive words and phrases that may serve as our guides in dissecting complicated chapters. It is much easier to commence one's critical studies in the wilderness than to start with the Book of Genesis and work onwards.

---

[1] Comp. what has been said above, p. 386, where we have seen that the main point in the law of booty only goes back to David.

But if you have followed my argument thus far you will have
no difficulty in pursuing the thread of the priestly writing
through the rest of the Hexateuch with the aid of a good
manual of Biblical Introduction. In what remains, therefore,
I will be very brief, and indicate results without dwelling on
processes.

First, then, as regards the priestly elements subsequent to
the Book of Numbers. In Deuteronomy these are limited to
a few verses about the death of Moses, chap. xxxii. 48-52,
the first words of xxxiv. 1, and xxxiv. 8, 9. So, too, the first
twelve chapters of Joshua contain only occasional traces of
the priestly style and manner, in one or two precise dates
answering to the priestly chronology (iv. 9, v. 10-12), and
especially in the story of the Gibeonites (ix. 15 *b*, 17-21;
" congregation," " princes of the congregation "), and how they
were made slaves of the sanctuary. In the second, or statistical, part of the Book of Joshua it is easy to prove that the
lists of tribal settlements and boundaries are not all from one
source, but the nature of the matter does not give us much
opportunity of using linguistic criteria to determine which of
the Pentateuchal sources are used. There are, however, a
sufficient number of verses containing characteristic priestly
matter or phrases (*e.g.* xiii. 15-32, xiv. 1-5, xv. 1, 20, " by their
families," xvi. 8, etc.) to make it clear that the priestly narrative
gave a statistical account of the settlement of Canaan. To this
account belongs chap. xxi. (the Levitical and priestly cities),
and also chap. xx. (in the text of the LXX.). In the priestly
narrative the allotment of territory is made by Eleazar the
priest, with Joshua and the heads of " fathers' houses " (xiv.
1), and applies to all the tribes alike; but there is another
account in chap. xviii., according to which Judah and Joseph
are first settled, apparently without the use of the lot (comp.
xiv. 6 *sqq.*, xvii. 14 *sqq.*), while the lots for the remaining
seven western tribes are cast at Shiloh by Joshua alone.

The mass of the narrative of Joshua is clearly not priestly, and does not presuppose the priestly institutions. Chap. xxii. 9-34 is a very peculiar piece, which has its closest parallel in Judges xx. Both chapters are for the most part post-priestly and certainly not historical.

It is probable that the priestly document proper, *i.e.* the main priestly story, as distinct from such late additions as chap. xxii., treated the conquest of Canaan very briefly. The story of the Gibeonites was important in connection with the sanctuary, and here alone have we any sign that the narrative was more than the barest epitome. In like manner the conquest of Eastern Canaan is not described in the priestly part of Numbers. There was no legal application to be made of a war of extermination such as could not occur again, and so, in order to bring in a law about ordinary war and captives, the priestly writer passes over Sihon and spends his strength on a war with Midian, of which the old sources know nothing. On the other hand, an account of the settlement in Canaan, according to law, made the natural completion of his work, rounding out the delineation of Israel's sacred institutions. It should be observed that Ezekiel's legislation also ends with a chapter of sacred topography.

I now go back to consider the priestly element in Genesis and the early chapters of Exodus. Here the analysis is more dependent, in the first instance, on linguistic arguments, since, before the Sinaitic revelation, there can be no direct reference to the characteristic priestly institutions. But an important general clue to the treatment of the patriarchal period by the priestly source is obtained by considering the following series of passages :—

Gen. xvii. Jehovah makes a covenant with Abraham under the name of El-Shaddai (A. V. "the Almighty God"), and gives him the seal of circumcision.

   ,,   xxviii. 1-5. Isaac blesses Jacob in the name of El-Shaddai, and with reference to the divine promises in chap. xvii.

Gen. xxxv. 9-15. God (Elohim) appears to Jacob, changes His name
　　　to Israel, reveals Himself as El-Shaddai, and renews
　　　the same promises.

,, 　xlviii. 3-6. Jacob rehearses to Joseph the revelation of El-
　　　Shaddai last cited, and adopts his grandchildren
　　　Ephraim and Manasseh as his own sons [*i.e.* as two
　　　full tribes, in which character they always appear in
　　　the priestly document].

Exod. vi. 2-8. God (Elohim) speaks to Moses, saying, "I am Jeho-
　　　vah. And I appeared to Abraham, Isaac, and Jacob
　　　as El-Shaddai, but by my name Jehovah I was not
　　　known to them." Then follows a promise of deliver-
　　　ance in terms based on the earlier passages already cited.

These passages are in substance and form a connected series.
They must all be from one pen, and the pen is that of the
priestly narrator, whose characteristic phrases and mannerisms are not to be mistaken, especially in Gen. xvii. The
priestly narrator, then, regards the name of Jehovah as characteristic of Mosaism, and accordingly we observe that he
avoids the use of that word in the patriarchal period, employing Elohim in its place. But he views the Mosaic revelation
as based on a previous covenant with Abraham, and carries
back to his day the ordinance of circumcision, which in the
priestly laws is taken as the necessary mark of admission
into the community of true religion (Lev. xii. 3 ; Exod. xii.
44, 48).

It was long ago observed that in the Book of Genesis the
names Jehovah and Elohim do not occur at random but in
two distinct series of narratives, which generally can be
separated from each other without trouble. And when we
find Jehovah and Elohim alternating in the same narrative, as
in the story of the Flood, we find also, on closer examination,
that the story is composite and can still be resolved into two
threads, one Jahvistic and the other Elohistic (*supra*, p. 327 *sq.*).
We now see that in seeking to determine the priestly elements
in Genesis and the early chapters of Exodus we may begin by
setting the whole Jahvistic narrative on one side.

In the earlier chapters of Genesis all that remains is priestly; to wit, the first (and more abstract) of the two stories of the Creation (Gen. i. 1-ii. 4 *a*); then a line of genealogy from Adam to Noah (Gen. v.; but not verse 29, which uses the name Jehovah and refers to the Jahvistic story of the Fall); then one form of the Flood-story (*supra*, p. 329 *sq.*), which was necessary to the writer's legal purpose because the Flood was followed by a covenant with Noah (ix. 1-17) the conditions of which passed over into Mosaism; then another series of genealogies (parts of x., xi. 10-26), and a very brief sketch of Abraham's life, containing little more than a sequence of names and dates, and carrying us on to the covenant of chap. xvii.[1] Here the author has reached a topic of legal importance, and again expands into copious and somewhat redundant detail.

About this point it becomes plain that the Jahvist and the priestly writer are not the only contributors to the

---

[1] It may be instructive to give the priestly story of the first ninety-nine years of Abraham's life in full :—

"Now these are the generations of Terah : Terah begat Abram and Nahor and Haran ; and Haran begat Lot. And Terah took Abram his son, and Lot the son of Haran his son's son, and Sarai his daughter-in-law, his son Abram's wife ; and they went forth with them from Ur of the Chaldees, to go into the land of Canaan ; and they came unto Haran, and dwelt there. And the days of Terah were two hundred and five years : and Terah died in Haran. And Abram was seventy-five years old when he departed out of Haran. And Abram took Sarai his wife, and Lot his brother's son, and all their substance that they had gathered, and the souls that they had gotten in Haran ; and they went forth to go into the land of Canaan ; and into the land of Canaan they came. And the land was not able to bear them to dwell together : for their substance was great, so that they could not dwell together. So they separated themselves the one from the other. Abram dwelt in the land of Canaan, and Lot dwelt in the cities of the plain. And Sarai Abram's wife bare him no children. And Sarai Abram's wife took Hagar her Egyptian handmaid, after Abram had dwelt ten years in the land of Canaan, and gave her to her husband Abram to be his wife. And Hagar bare Abram a son : and Abram called his son's name, which Hagar bare, Ishmael. And Abram was eighty-six years old, when Hagar bare Ishmael to Abram" (xi. 27, 31, 32 ; xii. 4 *b*, 5 ; xiii. 6, 11 *b*, 12 *a* ; xvi. 1 *a*, 3, 15, 16). The monotonous wordiness is as characteristic of the priestly style as the individual expressions.

story of Genesis. In chap. xiv. we meet with a narrative
that stands quite by itself, and is probably distinct in origin
from all other parts of the Pentateuch; while chap. xv.,
though it contains nothing suggestive of the priestly hand,
can hardly be taken as an integral part of the Jahvistic document.[1]   In the latter chapter we have at least the suspicion
that a third source has begun to show itself, and the suspicion
is raised to certainty in chap. xx. 1-17 (Abraham and Abimelech at Gerar), the first of a long series of narratives in
which the use of Elohim is associated with no other mark of
the priestly hand.   The Elohist (as the new narrator is
usually called) has a style and characteristic features of his
own ; but in language, standpoint, and choice of matter he
stands much nearer to the Jahvist than to P ; and his
narratives, taken as a whole, form a parallel series to those
of the Jahvist, giving the same or similar stories, with such
variations as are commonly found in the primitive traditions
of ancient races.   Thus the Elohistic story of Abraham and
Abimelech at Gerar (xx. 1-17) is a traditional variant of the
Jahvistic stories of Abraham and Pharaoh (chap. xii.), and
Isaac and Abimelech (xxvi. 7-11).   Or again the Jahvistic
account of Jacob's vision in Bethel is contained in xxviii.
13-16, 19 ; the Elohistic parallel in verses 11, 12, 17, 18,
20-22.   The ladder with the angels, the anointed stone, and
the vow are only in the Elohistic verses, and this is the
version referred to in the subsequent Elohistic passages
xxxi. 13, xxxv. 1-8.   The revelations at Bethel form one of
the best tests for the threefold critical division of Genesis ;
for here we have a third account (Gen. xxxv. 9-15), which
we have already assigned to the priestly document.   These
verses are not the continuation of the Elohistic story immediately preceding (verses 1-8), but a separate narrative,
as appears especially in verse 15.

---

[1] The analysis of this chapter is still uncertain.

I may add one more illustration of the relations of the Elohist to the priestly narrator on the one hand and the Jahvist on the other. In the Jahvistic story the destiny of Ishmael is revealed to Hagar before his birth, at the well Lahai-roi, whither she has fled from her mistress's hard treatment (Gen. xvi. 4-14). In the Elohistic version a similar revelation, at a well, is given after she and her son are banished (xxi. 8-21). In this story Ishmael is a little child ("playing," ver. 9, not "mocking," as A. V.), and is carried on his mother's shoulder (ver. 14, where read with LXX. "and he put the child on her shoulder and sent her away"; ver. 15). But according to the priestly chronology Ishmael was thirteen years old a year before Isaac's birth, and so at this date would have been a lad of fifteen at least.

The Jahvist and Elohist together are responsible for the great mass of the patriarchal history, and for all those stories that make Genesis one of the most delightful of books. What remains for the priestly writer is meagre enough; the continuous thread of his narrative is no more than a string of names, dates, and other dry bones of history, mainly in systematic form under the standing heading, "These are the generations of . . ."[1] Apart from the El-Shaddai passages already noted, perhaps[2] the only place where he expands into fulness is chap. xxiii., which details at length how Abraham became legal possessor of an inalienable family grave.[3]

---

[1] The successive recurrences of this phrase are the clue to the formal arrangement of the priestly narrative in Genesis, as the El-Shaddai passages are the clue to its purpose and meaning; comp. Driver, p. 5.

[2] I say "perhaps," that I may not seem to speak positively on the difficult chapter, Gen. xxxiv. But there is a high measure of probability that everything in this chapter which is not pre-Deuteronomic belongs to a very late redaction, subsequent to the union of the older sources in our present Pentateuch (so Kuenen and now also Wellhausen).

[3] The importance which P attaches to this subject (to which he returns in xxv. 9 *sq.*, xlix. 29 *sqq.*) is in accordance with the general feelings of the Semites; see for the Arabs Wellhausen, *Reste Ar. Heid.* p. 160. The best

The same abstract brevity prevails in the opening chapters
of Exodus (i. 1-5, 7, 13, 14; ii. 23 b, 25) up to the call of
Moses, who appears suddenly in vi. 2, without any account
of his previous life. The opening of his mission is told fully
enough in chaps. vi. vii. 1-13, with this difference from the
older story that from the first he demands the complete
emancipation of his people and not merely (as in v. vii. 14-18,
etc.; comp. iii. 18) leave for them to celebrate a feast in
the wilderness. Then follow brief notices of the plagues of
blood, frogs, mosquitoes (A. V. "lice"), and plague-boils on
man and beast,[1] while the final judgment, the death of the
firstborn (xii. 12), gives occasion for a full legal discussion of
the Passover (xii. 1-20, 28, 37 a, 40-51; xiii. 1, 2). The
account of the flight and the deliverance at the Red Sea is
again meagre (xiii. 20, xiv. 1-4, 8, 9, 15-18, 21 first and last
clause, 22, 23, 26, 27 a, 28, 29), but characteristic, inasmuch
as the east wind that drives back the sea in the old story

illustrations of Gen. xxiii. are, however, to be found in the inscriptions on
the tombs of the Nabataeans of Al-Hejr (Euting, *Nabatäische Inschrr. aus
Arabien*, 1885, *passim*) and the Syrians of Palmyra, where the inalienable
character of the family grave is guarded with special solicitude. From these
parallels we may perhaps infer that Abraham's care to secure such a grave is
set forth as a pattern for his descendants. In the Jahvistic narrative Jacob
desires to be buried with his fathers, and not in Egypt; but the place where
his wake was held (and where, therefore, in all probability, his grave was,
according to this tradition) is not the cave of Machpelah, but the Floor of
Atad or Abel-Mizraim (Gen. xlvii. 29-31, l. 10, where Dillmann's reference to
Jerome should be supplemented by the more interesting passage in Epiph.
De Pond. et Mens. § 62 [Syriac text]). The Elohistic variant of this is the
conveyance of the bones of Joseph to Canaan at the Exodus (Gen. l. 25;
Exod. xiii. 19; Josh. xxiv. 32), to which there is a striking Arabic parallel
in Wetzstein, *Reisebericht uber Hauran* (Berlin, 1860), p. 27 : "Take my bones
and carry them whithersoever ye journey," etc.

[1] Exod. vii. 19, 20 a, 21 b, 22; viii. 5-7, 15 b [Heb. 1-3, 11 b]; 16-19 [Heb.
12-15]; ix. 8-12. In the older sources the plagues are: blood (in the Nile
only; not also, as in P, in pools and vessels; see vii. 24); frogs; swarms
of insects (under a different name from the mosquitoes of P); murrain; hail;
locusts; darkness; then the death of the firstborn. The darkness appears
as a separate plague only in the Elohist (x. 21-23); and the Jahvistic account,
in which it is merely an incident in the plague of locusts (ver. 15), seems to
give a more primitive form of the tradition.

disappears, and the outstretched hand of Moses takes its place. The share of the priestly narrator in Exod. xvi. is disputed, and between this chapter and the ordinances of the tabernacle we have nothing but a bare notice of the arrival at Sinai (xix. 1, 2), and of Moses's ascent to the mountain of the law to receive the ritual ordinances (xxiv. 15 *sqq.*).

Except in one or two hard cases (Exod. xvi., and perhaps Gen. xxxiv.), the compass of the priestly document in the early history is determined by such a concurrence of internal evidences that there is no dispute about it among those who admit criticism at all. And when we look at the priestly passages as a whole there can be no serious doubt as to their essential unity or their essential character. For the most part the group is so homogeneous that the main mass of it must have come from a single pen; though when we carry out the analysis with the utmost nicety we find signs that the main narrator had predecessors and successors in the priestly school. Thus Kuenen, whose sagacity and patience in this kind of research are unrivalled, would teach us to speak of P^1, *i.e.* the oldest priestly collection of laws in Lev. xvii.-xxvi.; P^2, the main priestly narrator and legist; and, finally, a series of later priestly writers (P^3, P^4, etc.) who added their touches to the narrative of Korah's rebellion and certain other passages, in which an absolutely homogeneous story is not left even when all non-priestly elements are removed. But these niceties of analysis do not affect the main result; the whole priestly literature belongs to one school; and that school builds upon Ezekiel (who already lies behind Lev. xvii.-xxvi.), and had practically completed its work at the date of Ezra's Reformation.

The general character of the main priestly document has already been sketched from the materials presented in the middle books, and our analysis of Genesis and Joshua only confirms what those books teach. The priestly writing

is only in form an historical document; in substance it is a
body of laws and precedents having the value of law, strung
on a thread of history so meagre that it often consists of
nothing more than a chronological scheme and a sequence of
bare names.   If we read the document as literal history, all
that it teaches and that the older parts of the Hexateuch do
not teach may be summed up in one comprehensive sentence:
*The ordinances of Judaism, as we know them from the time of
Ezra downwards, already existed and were enforced in the days
of Moses.*   That this is not historical fact can be proved, and
has been proved in the previous pages, by a succession of
arguments.   The supposed Mosaic ordinances, and the narratives that go with them, are unknown to the history and
the prophets before Ezra; they are unknown to the
Deuteronomic writers, and they are unknown to the non-
priestly parts of the Pentateuch, which Deuteronomy presupposes.   And from this it follows with certainty that the
priestly recasting of the origins of Israel is not history (save
in so far as it merely summarises and reproduces the old
traditions in the other parts of the Hexateuch) but Haggada,
i.e. that it uses old names and old stories, not for the purpose
of conveying historical facts, but solely for purposes of legal
and ethical instruction.   A book must be read in the spirit
wherein it was written if the reader desires to profit; and
therefore we must not go to the priestly literature for
historical information, but only to understand the nature
of the institutions which were devised some little time before
Ezra's Reformation, and actually put in force at that Reformation, as the necessary and efficient means of preserving the
little community of Judaism from being swallowed up in the
surrounding heathenism.   It is useless to argue that if this
be so the Priests' Code has no right to stand in our Bible; for
under Providence the Code of Ezra and the Reformation of
Ezra were the means, amidst the general dissolution of the

Persian and Hellenic East, of preserving and maturing among
the Jews those elements of true spiritual religion out of
which Christianity sprang.   In the nineteenth century of
Christendom it is too late to make an *Index Expurgatorius* of
the books on which our Christian religion does, as a matter of
history, rest; but it is not too late to seek to understand them
by the best lights that God in His providence gives us to use.

I know of no attempt, on the part of apologists for
tradition, to meet directly the historical arguments that
establish the fundamental doctrine of modern criticism, the
late date of the Priests' Code.   The position always taken up
by traditionalists is that there are sufficient reasons of some
other kind for holding all the Pentateuchal laws (with the
conjoined histories) to be Mosaic, and that therefore everything in the Bible that appears to be inconsistent with that
opinion must be explained away at any cost.   But explaining
things away is a process that has no place in fair historical
inquiry, though unfortunately it has long played a great part
in Biblical interpretation.   The reason why unnatural interpretations, which would not be tolerated in any other field,
are accepted without difficulty in the case of the Bible is not
far to seek.   Till a very recent date it was assumed on all
hands that the authority of Scripture, as a rule of faith and
life, involves the inerrancy of all parts of the sacred record.
The Bible could not contradict itself, and therefore, if two
passages appeared to be at variance, one of them must be
explained away.   This is not the place for a discussion of
theological principles ; it is enough to observe that there is a
very long step between the doctrine that the Bible is a sure
rule of faith and life, and the inference that every historical
statement of a Biblical book is necessarily free from error.
To make such an inference cogent, one must adopt a definition
of faith which is neither that of the Reformers nor of the Old
Catholic and Mediæval Church (*supra*, Lecture I.).   And

when we turn from theological assumptions to deal with actual facts, we find clear evidence, as has been shown in more than one part of these Lectures, that the Biblical writers were not all equally well informed in matters of history, that their statements are not always in strict accordance with one another, and that we can no more dispense with the task of sifting and comparing sources in the study of Israel's history than in any other branch of historical research. When this is admitted, all that part of the apologetical argument which consists in the explaining away of plain texts at once falls to the ground. To explain away the concurrent evidence of the older histories and prophets where it does not agree with tradition is really nothing else than to reject that evidence ; a proceeding manifestly inconsistent with every rule of historical research.

While the traditionalists thus fail altogether in their attempt to meet the historical arguments of the critics, their own positive argument for believing that all the Pentateuchal laws date from Moses is admittedly theological rather than historical. They appeal to the authority of the New Testament, or, putting the argument more broadly, urge that it is incredible that God in His providence should have allowed His Church to hold and teach for so many centuries an opinion concerning the origin of Israel's sacred institutions which is not historically correct. I do not propose to go into these arguments, because I do not know any way of deciding whether they are sound or not except by bringing them to the test of history. God has given us intellects to judge of historical evidence, and He has preserved to us in the Bible ample materials for deciding the date of the Pentateuchal laws and narratives by strict historical methods. And as He has thus put it in our power to learn what the actual course of Providence has been, I decline to be led into an *a priori* argument as to what it ought to have been.

With all this, it is still true that the priestly writings,
or rather such part of them as once formed an independent
work, make a very strange book, and it is an object of
legitimate inquiry how such a book ever came to be written.
It is doubtful whether we can hope to answer this question
fully from the materials that remain to us; but there are
some things to be said on the subject which at least go far to
diminish the sense of strangeness that the critical account of
the book awakens in the modern reader. It is possible to give
an intelligible account both of the motives by which the
author was guided and of the models that influenced the form
of his work; but to understand this, we must go back to the
other and older elements of the Hexateuch.

We have seen that, for the Book of Genesis, what remains
of the ancient historical traditions of the Hebrews consists of
two parallel streams, which received literary form in the works
of the Jahvist and Elohist respectively.[1] The same two sources
still flow, and can be distinguished with some degree of
certainty, in the early chapters of Exodus; but as we proceed
through the middle books the analysis becomes more difficult,
though from time to time the same thing is told twice
over, with more or less variation in expression and detail.
These "doublets" are sufficiently numerous and characteristic
to satisfy us that we are still dependent, throughout the
pre-Deuteronomic narrative, on the Jahvistic and Elohistic
sources, though the two have been so interwoven by an
editorial hand that in many places it is now impossible to
separate them. Even in Genesis there are some passages
where it seems hopeless to attempt to resolve the complex
narrative JE into its primitive elements; and the patriarchal
history, from its very nature, and especially because it is
largely made up of traditions associated with the many

---

[1] This statement is at least broadly true; and for the present purpose it
is not necessary to consider whether some fragments of genuine tradition have
come to us from other sources, e.g. Gen. xiv.

local sanctuaries of ancient Israel (Hebron, Beersheba,
Shechem, Bethel, etc.), may be presumed to have offered a
more varied series of traditions than the wilderness journeys;
so that the editor would find less occasion in the latter case to
preserve great part of both the old histories intact.   And to
this it must be added that in the middle books the criterion
of origin derived from the Divine Names generally fails us;
whether it be that the Elohist took no pains to avoid the use
of the name Jehovah, after he had recorded the revelation
made in that name to Moses at the Bush (Exod. iii.); or
whether, as some suppose, the original prevalence of Elohim
in his narrative has disappeared at some stage of the subsequent redaction.   Be this as it may, there remain sufficient
indications of dual authorship to satisfy us that all through
the Hexateuch the old history consists of a twofold thread,
and that the Deuteronomic writers are not exclusively
dependent either on the Jahvist alone or on the Elohist
alone.   Now, it is very clear that the Deuteronomic retrospects are not based on mere oral tradition; their verbal
coincidences with the non-priestly parts of Exodus and
Numbers are unmistakable; and as these coincidences are
with the non-priestly narrative as a whole, and not with one
element in it, the presumption is that the two old histories
were already fused into a single narrative before the close of
the seventh century B.C., and that this compound story was
the written source that lay before the Deuteronomic authors.[1]

---

[1] The argument that the Jahvistic and Elohistic books did not lie before
the Deuteronomistic writers in separate form, but that these writers (or at
least, as Kuenen would limit the contention [*Onderzoek*, i. § 13, note 27], the
author of Deut. i.-iv. xxix. *sq.*, and the Deuteronomic hand in Joshua) had
before them the compound book JE (consisting of parts of J + parts of E
+ some editorial matter) is commonly made to turn on Deuteronomic
references to passages which the critical analysis assigns to the redactor of
JE.   But a simpler and more generally intelligible argument may serve to
make the same thing very probable.   For the parenetic purpose of Deuteronomy
there was no need to use two histories, and work their statements into a continuous whole; and therefore, if it can be shown that the Deuteronomic

On this and other grounds it is generally recognised that the first step towards the formation of our present compound Pentateuch was the fusion of the Jahvistic and Elohistic documents in a single book (JE). The next step was a very obvious one. We have already seen that the influence of Deuteronomy on the literary labours of the period of the Exile is exhibited in a Deuteronomic redaction of all the historical books (*supra*, p. 396). The process by which the whole history of Israel down to the Captivity was worked into a continuous narrative (for as such we now read it), interspersed with comments and other additions, enforcing the lessons of the history in the Deuteronomic manner, cannot now be followed in detail; and probably the work was not all done at once or by one hand. That the Deuteronomistic redaction extended to the history of JE is manifest in the case of Joshua, and with this redaction must have gone the union of JE with the Book of Deuteronomy. Every one can see for himself that the first chapter of Joshua as we now read it is meant to be continuous with Deuteronomy. Thus all the non-priestly parts of the Hexateuch were united into one book, to which Judges, Samuel, and Kings, in the Deuteronomistic redaction, formed the continuation.

During the first ninety years of the new Jerusalem, from Cyrus to Ezra, the Law of Moses meant the law as embodied in this great history, and especially in the Book of Deuteronomy, which might fairly be taken as the whole law, since its fuller and more modern precepts covered the ground of the smaller codes in Exod. xxi.-xxiii., Exod. xxxiv. When Malachi says, "Remember the Torah of Moses my servant, which I commanded him in Horeb for all Israel, *even* statutes and judgments" (Mal. iv. 4), it is the Code of Deuteronomy

retrospects of the old history sometimes give a compound story, the inference that they read it in compound form (*i.e.* read JE not J and E) is almost irresistible. This is apparently the case in several places, *e.g.* in the account of the events at Sinai.

that he has in view. For his words are made up of the
expressions characteristic of Deuteronomy and the Deuteronomistic redactor of Joshua ; and the statement that the
" statutes and judgments," *i.e.* the contents of the Deuteronomic Code (Deut. xii. 1, xxvi. 16), were given to Moses in
Horeb (though they were not published till forty years later),
is in accordance with Deut v. 31.[1] Malachi, therefore, had in
his hands the Deuteronomic Code, with the historical introduction ; and apparently he read this book as part of the
Deuteronomistic edition of the whole pre-priestly Hexateuch.
But his Torah of Moses did not yet embrace the Priests'
Code, as appears not only from Mal. iv. 4, but from the other
references he makes to the laws and institutions of Israel.
In particular he still views the covenant of priesthood as
given to Levi generally (Mal. ii. 1-8 ; comp. Deut. xxxiii. 8
sqq.), and assigns to the oral Torah of the priests an importance
hardly consistent with a date subsequent to Ezra's Reformation (ii. 6), but suitable to what we know of the early
practice of the second Temple from the prophets Haggai and
Zechariah (Hag. ii. 11 ; Zech. vii. 3).[2]

---

[1] The phrases "Torah of Moses," "Moses my servant," are proper to the
Deuteronomic redaction of Joshua and the historical books ; the former is found
in Josh. viii. 31, 32, xxiii. 6 ; 2 Kings xiv. 6, xxiii. 25, and never again before
Malachi ; the latter in Num. xii. 7 ; Deut. xxxiv. 5, and then frequently in
the Deuteronomistic parts of Joshua. "Horeb" is Elohistic and Deuteronomistic ; in P the mountain of the law is "Sinai." "Statutes and judgments" is a standing Deuteronomic phrase, and occurs but once in the rest
of the Pentateuch, viz. Lev. xxvi. 46 (with "Sinai," not "Horeb").

[2] Note further Mal. i. 8 (Deut. xv. 21) ; Mal. i. 14 (where it is assumed
that a votive sacrifice ought to be a male, against Lev. iii. 1, 6, but apparently
in accordance with old Semitic usage ; comp. *Religion of the Semites*, p. 280) ;
iii. 5 (based on the Decalogue and on Deut. xviii. 10, Deut. xxiv. 17 *sqq.*,
and following the expressions of these passages, not those of the equivalent
priestly laws, Lev. xix. 31, 33 *sqq.*, xx. 6) ; the blessing on obedience, iv. 10
(which follows the expressions of Deut. xxviii. 12, not of the priestly parallel,
Lev. xxvi.).   There are other points of verbal coincidence with the pre-
priestly Torah, *e.g.* the rare word *s'gullah* (iii. 17 ; comp. Exod. xix. 5 ; Deut.
vii. 6, xiv. 2, xxvi. 18 ; nowhere else in a similar application save Ps. cxxxv.
4).   Objections to this view of Malachi's date are dealt with in the next
footnote but one, and *infra*, p. 446.

Malachi represents his contemporaries as weary of serving
God and ready to fall altogether away from His worship, and
this coldness he rebukes from the standpoint of the pre-
priestly Hexateuch, which was therefore the acknowledged
fountain of sacred instruction.   In like manner Nehemiah's
prayer in Neh. i. is wholly based on Deuteronomy; and
when Ezra first came up to Jerusalem (458 B.C.) and began
those efforts at reformation which were not crowned with
success till they were backed, fourteen years later, by the
civil authority of the Tirshatha, it was to the Deuteronomic
law that he appealed.[1] The first aim that Ezra set before
himself was the abolition of mixed marriages, and this
measure he recommended on the ground of Deut. vii. 1-3
(Ezra ix. 11 *sqq.*).[2]

Thus during the first ninety years after the return, and
the first seventy of the second Temple (which was completed
in 516 B.C.), there was a written sacred law for the general
use of the community, but no authoritative written code for
the direction of priestly ritual. The latter was still left to
the oral tradition and oral Torah of the priests.

For the priests themselves there was doubtless a certain
convenience in this. Oral tradition is more elastic than a
written code; and the conditions of the second Temple were

---

[1] On the history of Ezra see especially Kuenen in the *Versl. en. Meded.*
of the Amsterdam Academy (Afd. *Letterkunde,* 1890, p. 273 *sqq.*), where it
is shown that the events recorded in Ezra ix. x. must have been followed by
a reaction and a long struggle of parties.

[2] See also Neh. xiii. 1-3, where the separation of the Israelites from the
mixed multitude (*'ereb,* synon. with the *'ammê haáreç* of Ezra x. 11) is based
on Deut. xxiii. 3-5. Neh. xiii. 1-3 is a fragment torn from its original context, as appears from the opening words of verse 1, and I strongly suspect
that verses 1, 2 originally belonged to the same context with Ezra ix. x. They
would come in well between Ezra x. 9, 10. In any case the whole movement
for separation from the heathen was based on Deuteronomy, and began
fourteen years before the publication of the priestly edition of the Pentateuch,
so that Malachi's polemic against marriage with "the daughters of a strange
god," in no way weakens the proof that his Torah did not include the Priests'
Code. He may have written after 458, but he certainly wrote before 444.

so different from those of the first that a considerable re-modelling of points of ritual necessarily took place after the return.[1] On the other hand, there were several considerations that made a codification of the priestly Torah desirable. There were many ritual rules, particularly those of ceremonial purity, which could be observed in exile as readily as at Jerusalem. It is probable that in the first instance such rules had reference mainly to formal acts of worship, and defined the conditions of participation in sacrificial meals and similar holy actions. They were therefore part of the priestly Torah; and the priests were still their only inter-preters. But in the actual praxis of the exiles, when sacrifice was impossible, all ceremonial rules that could be detached from the altar ritual acquired an independent importance. And in the scattered state of the nation it was impossible to maintain unity in this branch of ceremonial tradition with-out reducing it to writing. It is to be presumed that the first written collections of priestly Torahs would address themselves to this need; and in fact the earlier chapters of Lev. xvii.-xxvi. are mainly occupied with laws equally applicable in Canaan and in the Dispersion, which may once have formed several small independent books, as the titles and subscriptions of chaps. xviii. and xix. appear to indicate.

A codification of the Temple ritual was not so immedi-ately necessary. Yet this, too, must in process of time have appeared to be desirable alike from a practical and a theo-retical point of view; from the former because the written Torah of Moses, contained in Deuteronomy, did at various points touch on ritual matters, so that there was a constant danger of conflict between the oral and the written law; from the latter because a systematical exposition of the whole doctrine of Israel's holiness on the lines first sketched

---

[1] See *infra*, p. 443 *sqq.*

by Ezekiel was necessary to complete the theory of Israel's religion in its post-exile form.

The early draft of a law of holiness which is preserved in Lev. xvii.-xxvi. has probably not reached us entire, and to some extent its original form is obscured by later additions.[1] But in it we already see a distinct effort to systematise the ceremonial law on the principle of Israel's holiness; and we can also see that in seeking a literary form proper to this systematic exposition the writer was largely guided by the Book of Deuteronomy. The closing exhortation in Lev. xxvi. is based on Deut. xxviii., and the laws are set forth as laws of Moses, or even (xxv. 1, xxvi. 46) as laws given to Moses on Sinai. In considering how the writer felt himself at liberty to use these forms we must remember, *first*, that the priests had always referred their traditional Torah to Moses as the father of their guild, and *second*, that the principle of an implicit Mosaic law had long before received its expression in the parabolic form that God gave to Moses at Sinai, laws that were meant for future use and so not published at the time (Deut. iv. 14, v. 31 with vi. 1 : the same thing, perhaps, appeared already in the Elohist's book, Exod. xxiv. 12). The Hebrews had no abstract philosophical forms of language or of thought, and when they had to express conceptions involving "the ideal" or "the implicit" they could only do so in figurative speech. Every one is familiar with the Jewish use of "heavenly" in the sense of "ideal," as we find it in the Epistle to the Hebrews; the ark, for example, which was only an idea under the second Temple, was represented as still existing in heaven (comp. Rev. xi. 19). In matters of law "Sinaitic" had a similar figurative sense. To express the whole priestly ordinances of holiness in the terms of this old figure involved a much more elaborate machinery than

---

[1] See Driver, p. 43 *sqq.*, for the linguistic and other marks of distinction between earlier and later hands in these chapters, and for traces of the earlier hand in other parts of the Pentateuch.

that of the Book of Deuteronomy, and the task was not carried out all at once. But we note that even the laws of Lev. xvii. *sqq.* already make use of the Tabernacle as the Sinaitic model of the true sanctuary.

The finished Priestly Code takes up the task that had been left incomplete in the first law of holiness, and carries it out with a systematic completeness that cannot but compel our admiration if we place ourselves on the author's standpoint. His object is not to supersede the older law and the history that was read with it, but to set over against it a counterpart and necessary companion-piece. He chooses a canvas as large as that of the pre-priestly Torah, and throws the exposition of the system of Israel's sacred ordinances into the form of a history from the Creation to the complete settlement in Canaan. This whole history his plan compels him to idealise or allegorise, and he does so boldly. But we have no right to say that he meant his idealisation to be read in a literal sense and to supersede the old law and the old history. So long as the two expositions, JE + D on the one hand (the prophetical and Deuteronomic Torah), and P on the other (the systematised Priestly Torah), stood separate and side by side, no one who cared for the distinction between history and Haggada could possibly have been at a loss as to the true nature of the second book. But it seems probable that in the age of Ezra no one did care much for this distinction; for presently the two books were fused together in one; a step which had much to recommend it from an immediate practical point of view, inasmuch as it reduced the whole law to a single code, but which at the same time made all true historical study of the origins of Israel's history and religion impossible without that work of criticism which only these latter days have begun to realise as possible and necessary.

ADDITIONAL NOTES

ADDITIONAL NOTE A (p. 122).—THE TEXT OF 1 SAM. XVII.

THE view that the Greek text of 1 Sam. xvii. 1-xviii. 5 is to be preferred to the Hebrew is by no means universally accepted. Wellhausen, who argued in favour of the Greek text in his *Text der Bücher Samuelis* (1871), is now of opinion that even the shorter text of chap. xvii. is inconsistent with chap. xvi. 14-23, and therefore deems it probable that the omissions of the Septuagint are due to an attempt to remove difficulties which has not quite attained its end. (See his remarks in the 4th ed. of Bleek's *Einleitung*, reprinted in *Comp. des Hexateuchs*, etc., 1889, p. 249 *sq.*). Kuenen, *Onderzoek* (2d ed., 1887), i. 391 *sq.*, accepts this argument, and fortifies it by the observation that the covenant between David and Jonathan (xviii. 3) is alluded to in 1 Sam. xx. 8. Budde, *Bücher Richter und Samuel* (Giessen, 1890), takes a like view, and also argues (quite consistently as it appears to me) that if xvii. 25 is not to be rejected, the omissions of the LXX. with regard to David and Merab must also be condemned, although in the latter case the superiority of the Greek text has approved itself to almost all critics.

The main point with all these critics is that in xvi. 18 David is already described to Saul as a valiant man and a man of war, whereas in chap. xvii., in the short text as well as in the long, he is a mere lad unused to other arms than the shepherd's staff and sling. This argument is striking, but I cannot accept it as conclusive. If we take xvi. 14-23 as a whole, and do not confine our attention to the expressions in verse 18 (where, in putting words into the mouth of one of Saul's servants, the author may have allowed himself some proleptic freedom of description), we must necessarily conclude that David came to Saul's court as a mere stripling. An armour-bearer was not a full warrior, but a sort of page or apprentice in arms (comp. Ibn Hishâm, p. 119, l. 1), whose most warlike

function is to kill outright those whom his master has struck down
(1 Sam. xiv. 13; 2 Sam. xviii. 15)—an office which among the
Arabs was often performed by women. Further, the way in which
David's movements are represented as entirely dependent on his
father's consent is hardly consistent with the idea that he was
already a full-grown warrior. On the contrary, he is still a lad
tending sheep (ver. 19), which was not a grown man's occupation.
To delete the words אשר בצאן is perfectly arbitrary, unless we
are prepared to go much farther and regard the whole passage as
composite. Now it is quite reasonable that a stripling and apprentice
at arms should prefer to meet Goliath with the boyish weapon of
which he knew himself to be a master. This indeed will not
account for the shepherd's bag in xvii. 40, but that, as Wellhausen
has seen, is a mere gloss on בילקוט, and no proper part of the text.

That the story of xvii. 12-31 is self-contained, and not only
independent of verses 1-11, but built on different lines, has been
shown in the text of the Lecture. I should here say expressly, what
I have there only hinted, that verses 15, 16 are no proper part
of the narrative but a harmonistic interpolation. And further, the
words of the Philistine have been omitted in verse 23, and a
reference back to verse 8 substituted for them. Let me also direct
attention to the awkwardness of the junctions between verses 11 and
12, verses 31 and 32. As regards the latter, it requires some courage
to translate ויקחהו, " and he sent for him " [= וישלח ויקחהו, Gen. xx.
2; 1 Sam. xvi. 11]. Apparently the word should be read as a
plural, " and they took him," which requires some addition to make
complete sense (comp. Lucian, καὶ παρέλαβον αὐτὸν καὶ εἰσήγαγον
πρὸς Σαούλ). In any case we expect the unknown lad to answer
a question of the king's, not to speak first; so that here we have an
external mark of discontinuity in the narrative. Again, verse 12
begins awkwardly, but is obviously a new beginning, breaking off
from verse 11 altogether. It is to be observed that the later Greek
version of ver. 12 sqq., as we have it in the Cod. Al., begins καὶ
εἶπεν Δαυείδ. These are the first words of verse 32, and seem to
mark that what follows was originally a gloss on that verse. I
conjecture that the source from which the gloss was taken began
(like 1 Sam. i. 1, ix. 1), "And there was a man, an Ephrathite
of Bethlehem Judah, whose name was Jesse."

If now we accept xii. 12-31 as an independent fragment, breaking off abruptly with the words, " and they took him," it is to be
asked how the story went on. The fight itself must have been told

nearly as in the other version, and therefore nothing is preserved of
it but the fragments xvii. 41, 50. But even these show a difference. For in verse 51 (where the words "and drew it out of the
sheath thereof" are absent from the LXX.) the sword which David
takes to kill the giant outright is his own sword (comp. verse 39),
the weapon proper to armour-bearers, and used by them for de-
spatching the wounded. (See the passages already quoted, and also
Judg. ix. 54 ; 1 Sam. xxxi. 4.) But in verse 50 David has no
sword, and the blow with the sling-stone is itself fatal. Again, I
think it is plain that in the story of verses 12-31, etc., Saul had no
interview with David, though (unless verse 31 has been retouched)
he must have given permission to him to try his fortune. For at
verse 55 Saul sees David for the first time as he goes forth against
the Philistine, and does not even know his name.[1] Thus the independence of the narrative is fully maintained to the close of chap.
xvii., and this carries xviii. 1-2 with it. As regards xviii. 3-5 the
case is not so clear, both on account of the point raised by Kuenen,
and because verse 3, if it belongs to the same source as verse 1,
ought not to have been separated from it by verse 2.

A word in conclusion on the bearing of this analysis on the
larger questions of criticism in the Book of Samuel. All that I
suppose myself to have proved is that in chap. xvii. we must start
from the text of LXX., and that this text is the continuation of the
present form of xvi. 14-23. That the latter verses are themselves
of composite structure, and contain (especially in ver. 18) traces of
an older narrative, which made David first come to Saul as a full-
grown warrior, is not inconceivable, especially in view of 2 Sam.
xxi. 19. But such a theory must not be based on the longer text
of 1 Sam. xvii., and for my own part I do not see that there are in
xvi. 14 *sqq.* plain enough marks of dual origin to justify it.

ADDITIONAL NOTE B (p. 124).—HEBREW FRAGMENTS PRESERVED
IN THE SEPTUAGINT

The insertion of the Septuagint in 1 Kings viii. 53 deserves

---

[1] I think also (though here I speak with diffidence) that there is a difference
between verse 7 and verse 41. For if we translate the latter verse in accordance with
the invariable idiomatic use of וְהָאִישׁ (as a stronger equivalent of וְהוּא, especially
in resumption, after another person has been named or referred to by a pronoun),
the sense is, "and the man (*i.e.* the Philistine) bore his shield in front of him (as
he advanced)," so that only his forehead was vulnerable. This, I admit, raises the
question whether verse 7 has not been retouched, after the interpolation, by some
one who misunderstood verse 41. But have we any copy of LXX. so free from
Hexaplar additions as to make this incredible without confirmation from the Greek?

special notice for its intrinsic interest. In 1 Kings viii. 12, 13, the Hebrew text reads, "Jehovah hath determined (said) to dwell in darkness. I have built a house of habitation for thee, a place for thee to dwell in eternally." These verses are omitted in LXX., but at verse 53 we find instead a fuller form of the same words of Solomon. In the common editions of the LXX. the words run thus :— " The sun he made known in heaven : the Lord hath said that he will dwell in darkness. Build my house, a comely house for thyself to dwell in newness. Behold, is it not written in the book of song ? " The variations from the Hebrew text are partly mistakes. The word " comely " is a rendering elsewhere used in the LXX. for the Hebrew word *naweh*, which in this connection must rather be rendered " house of habitation," giving the same sense as the Hebrew of verse 13, with a variation in the expression. Then the phrase " in newness " at once exhibits itself to the Hebrew scholar as a mistaken reading of the Hebrew word " eternally." Again, " build my house " differs in the Hebrew from " I have built " only by the omission of a single letter. We may correct the LXX. accordingly, getting exactly the sense of the Massoretic text of verse 12 ; or conversely, we may correct the Hebrew by the aid of the Septuagint, in which case one other letter must be changed, so that the verse runs, " Build my house, an house of habitation for me ; a place to dwell eternally." We now come to the additions of the LXX. " The sun he made known in heaven " gives no good sense. But many MSS. read, "The sun he set in heaven." These two readings, ἐγνώρισεν and ἔστησεν, have no resemblance in Greek. But the corresponding Hebrew words are הבין and הכין respectively, which are so like that they could easily be mistaken. There can be no doubt that the latter is right ; and the error in the common Septuagint text shows that the addition really was found by the translators in Hebrew, not inserted out of their own head. We can now restore the whole original, divide it into lines as poetry, and render—

> " Jehovah set the sun in the heavens,
> But He hath determined to dwell in darkness.
> Build my house, an house of habitation for me,
> A place to dwell in eternally."

Or on the other reading—

> " I have built an house of habitation for thee,
> A place to dwell in eternally."

The character of the expression in these lines, taken with the circumstance of their transposition to another place in the LXX., would of itself prove that this is a fragment from an ancient source, not part of the context of the narrative of the chapter. But the LXX. expressly says that the words are taken from "The Book of Song." There might perhaps be an ancient book of that name, as we have in Arabic the great historical and poetical collection of El Isfahâny, called "The Book of Songs." But the transposition of a single letter in the Hebrew converts the unknown Book of Song into the well-known Book of Jashar. This correction seems certain. The slip of the Septuagint translator was not unnatural; indeed, the same change is made by the Syriac in Josh. x. 13.

Another example of an ancient and valuable notice preserved in the Greek but not in the Hebrew is found in 2 Kings xiii. 22, where (in Lucian's recension) we read, "And Hazael took the Philistine out of his hand from the Western Sea unto Aphek." This note, as Wellhausen has brought out, enables us to assign the true position of Aphek, on the northern border of the Philistines, and throws light on the whole history of the invasions of Central Israel by the Philistines and by the Syrians, for which Aphek habitually served as base. The Syrians, we see, did not attack Samaria in front, from the north, but made a lodgment in the northern part of the Philistine plain, to which there was an easy road by way of Megiddo, and thus took their enemy on the flank. See Wellhausen, *Composition*, p. 254. The text of Lucian's recension of LXX. for Genesis to Esther has been determined and published by Lagarde (Göttingen, 1883). For the historical books this recension is very important.

ADDITIONAL NOTE C (p. 197).—SOURCES OF PSALM LXXXVI

1. Incline, O Lord, thine ear, answer me : for I am poor and needy.

1. *a.* Usual invocation ; Isa. xxxvii. 17 ; Ps. xvii. 6, etc.

    b. Ps. xl. 17.—"I am poor and needy ;" Ps. xxv. 16.

2. Preserve my soul for I am holy : O thou, my God, save thy servant that trusteth in thee.

2. Ps. xxv. 20.—"Preserve my soul and deliver me : let me not be ashamed, for I take refuge with thee."

3. Be gracious to me, O Lord : for unto thee I cry continually.

3. Current phrases ; *e.g.* Ps. xxx. 8.— "To thee, O Jehovah, I cry ;" verse 10.— "Hear, O Jehovah, and be gracious to me."

4. Make glad the soul of thy servant : for to thee, O Lord, do I lift up my soul.

4. *a.* Ps. xc. 15.—"Make us glad ;' li. 8.—"Make me hear joy and gladness," etc.

    b. Ps. xxv. 1.—"Unto thee, Jehovah, I lift up my soul."

5. For thou, Lord, art good and forgiving: and abundant in mercy unto all that call upon thee.

5. Modification of Exod. xxxiv. 6, 7.—"Abundant in mercy . . . forgiving iniquity."

6. Give ear, O Lord, unto my prayer: and hearken to the voice of my supplications.

6. Ps. v. 1, 2.—"Give ear to my words, Jehovah . . . hearken to the voice of my cry."

7. In the day of my distress I call on thee: for thou wilt answer me.

7. Ps. cxx. 1.—"I called to Jehovah in my distress, and he answered me; lxxvii. 2.—"In the day of my distress I sought the Lord."

8. There is none like thee among the gods, O Lord: and there is nought like thy works.

8. Ex. xv. 11.—"Who is like thee among the gods, O Jehovah?" Deut. iii. 24.—"Who is a God that can do like thy works?"

9. All nations whom thou hast made shall come and worship before thee, O Lord: and shall glorify thy name.

9. Ps. xxii. 27.—"All ends of the earth shall . . . return unto Jehovah, and before thee shall all families of the nations worship."

10. For thou art great and doest wonders: thou, O God, alone.

10. Ex. xv. 11.—"Doing wonders."

11. Teach me thy way, O Jehovah; let me walk in thy truth: unite my heart to fear thy name.

11. a. Ps. xxvii. 11.—"Teach me thy way, O Jehovah;" xxv. 5.—"Guide me in thy truth."

b. Jer. xxxii. 39.—"I will give them one heart, and one way to fear me continually."

12. I will praise thee, O Lord my God, with all my heart: and I will glorify thy name for ever.

12. Ps. ix. 1.—"I will praise thee, Jehovah, with all my heart," etc.

13. For great is thy mercy towards me: and thou hast delivered my soul from deep Sheol (the place of the dead).

13. a. Ps. lvii. 10.—"For thy mercy is great unto the heavens."

b. Ps. lvi. 13.—"For thou hast delivered my soul from death."

14. O God, proud men are risen against me, and an assembly of tyrants seek my life: and have not set thee before them.

14. Ps. liv. 3.—"For strangers are risen against me, and tyrants seek my life who have not set God before them." [In Hebrew, "proud men" ZēDIM and "strangers" ZāRIM, differ by a single letter, and D and R in the old character are often not to be distinguished.]

15. But thou, Lord, art a God merciful and gracious, long-suffering, and plenteous in mercy and truth.

15. Quotation from Ex. xxxiv. 6, word for word.

16. Turn unto me and be gracious to me: give thy strength unto thy servant, and save the son of thy handmaid.

16. a. Ps. xxv. 16.—"Turn unto me, and be gracious to me."

b. God the strength (protection) of his people, as Ps. xxviii. 8, and often; Ps. cxvi. 16.—"I am thy servant, the son of thy handmaid."

17. Work with me a token (miracle) for good : that they which hate me may see it and be ashamed : because thou, O Lord, hast holpen me and comforted me.	17. Ps. xl. 3.—"Many shall see it and fear;" Ps. vi. 10.—"Let all mine enemies be ashamed and sore vexed," etc. etc.

ADDITIONAL NOTE D (p. 208).—MACCABEE PSALMS IN BOOKS I.-III.
OF THE PSALTER

In discussing the question of Maccabee Psalms in the first part of the Psalter most recent critics ignore the difficulties that arise from the history of the redaction ; so, for example, Cornill, the author of the latest German *Einleitung* (Freiburg, 1891), and Prof. Driver, from whom I had hoped for some help in revising the conclusions set forth by me five years ago in the *Enc. Brit.* (art. PSALMS). Even Prof. Cheyne, in his *Origin of the Psalter* (1891), does not seem to me to give quite enough weight to the only sound principle for the historical study of the Psalter, viz. that the discussion of the age of individual psalms must be preceded by an inquiry into the date of the several collections. My friend Cheyne, however, recognises that the Elohistic Psalter was completed, and the designation "sons of Korah" obsolete, before the Maccabee period, and he accounts for the presence of a certain number of Maccabee Psalms in Books I.-III. by supposing that they were inserted in the older collections by the Maccabean editor. This is not impossible in the abstract, but to make Pss. xliv. lxxiv. lxxix. Maccabee hymns it is further necessary to suppose that the editor "threw himself into the spirit of the original collector" of the Elohistic Psalm - book, "and made his additions Elohistic to correspond to the earlier psalms" (Cheyne, p. 100). And we must also suppose that he furnished his additions with titles which (at least in the case of xliv.) had no longer any meaning. This is a complicated hypothesis and not to be accepted without further examination. If the last editor incorporated contemporary hymns in the old parts of the Psalter instead of placing them in the new collection at the end of the book, his motive must have been *liturgical, i.e.* he must have designed them to be sung in sequence with other pieces. That insertions of this kind were actually made in the older collections is highly probable from the presence of four anonymous psalms in the Davidic collections, for here anonymity is in itself a mark of later addition. Moreover, Pss. xxxiii. lxvi. lxvii. have an obviously liturgical character; Ps. xxxiii. is linked to the previous psalm by the way in which its first verse takes up xxxii. 11, and Pss. lxvi. lxvii. form an admirable sequence to lxv. if we take the whole group as songs for the presentation of first fruits at the passover. Ps. xxxiii. may have been added by the final collector; but in lxvi. lxvii. there is nothing to imply so late a date or to lead us to doubt that these Elohistic pieces were set in their place by the Elohistic collector. They do not therefore diminish the improbability of Maccabee additions in Elohistic form and furnished with titles of obsolete type. The Elohistic Psalms which Prof. Cheyne assigns to the Maccabee period are xliv. lx. lxi. lxiii. lxxiv. lxxix. lxxxiii. In the case of Ps. lx., verses 5-12 (Heb. 7-14) are repeated in Ps. cviii. (retaining their Elohistic peculiarity) which is hardly conceivable if the former psalm is of Maccabee date. Pss. lxi. and lxiii. are assigned to the Hasmonean period because they speak of a human king (not prophetically) and yet are manifestly post-exilic. But I think that a careful observation of these psalms leads to the conclusion that in both of them the closing reference to the king comes in somewhat unnaturally, and that the better hypothesis is that lxi. 6-8 (Heb. 7-9), and at least the last verse of lxiii., are liturgical additions. Thus the strength of the case for Maccabee Psalms in the Elohistic Psalter lies in xliv. lxxiv. lxxix. and lxxxiii., especially in the first three. (Psalm lxxx., which is frequently associated with these, Prof. Cheyne prefers to assign to the Persian period). It seems to me that the objection to placing these psalms in the reign of Ochus comes mainly from laying too much weight on what Josephus relates about Bagoses (*Ant.* xi. 7. 1). That Bagoses forced his way into the Temple, and that he laid a tax on the daily sacrifices, is certainly not enough to justify the language of the Psalms. But for this whole period Josephus is very ill informed; he is quite silent about the revolt and the Hyrcanian captivity, and the whole Bagoses story looks like a pragmatical invention designed partly to soften the catastrophe of the Jews and partly to explain it by the sin of the High Priest. The important fact of the captivity to Hyrcania stands on quite independent evidence (Euseb. *Chron.*, *Anno* 1658 *Abr.*), but comes to us without any details. The captivity implies a revolt, and the long account given by Diodorus (xvi. 40 *sqq.*) of Ochus's doings in Phœnicia and Egypt shows how that ruthless king treated rebels. In Egypt the temples were pillaged and the sacred books carried away (*ibid.* c. 51). Why should we suppose that the Temple at Jerusalem and the synagogues fared better? Such sacrilege was the rule in Persian warfare; it was practised by Xerxes in Greece and also at Babylon (Herod. i. 183 ; comp. Nöldeke in *Enc. Brit.* xviii. 572).   I have observed in the text that a rising of the Jews at this period could not fail to take a theocratic character, and that the war would necessarily appear as a religious war.   Certainly the later Jews looked on the Persians as persecutors ; the citation from Pseudo-Hecataeus in Jos. *c. Ap.* i. 22, though worthless as history, is good evidence for this ; and it is also probable that the wars under Ochus form the historical background of the Book of Judith, and that the name Holophernes is taken from that of a general of Ochus (Diod. xxxi. 19) who took a prominent part in the Egyptian campaign (Gutschmid, Nöldeke).

In Psalm lxxxiii. Judah appears as threatened by the neighbouring peoples, who are supported (but apparently not led) by Asshur (the satrap of Syria ?).   This situation is much more easily understood under the loose rule of the Persians than under the Greeks, and the association of Tyre with Philistia (which appears also in lxxxvii. 4) agrees with the notice of Pseudo-Scylax (written under Artaxerxes Ochus), which makes Ascalon a Tyrian possession. If this psalm has a definite historical background, which many interpreters doubt, it must be later than the destruction of Sidon by Ochus, which restored to Tyre its old pre-eminence in Phœnicia. That it is not of the Assyrian age is obvious from the mention of Arab tribes.

Prof. Cheyne thinks that there are also in the Elohistic Psalmbook a few pieces of the pre-Maccabean Greek period, viz. xlii. and xliii. xlv. lxviii. lxxii. and perhaps lxxiii.   To me the situation assigned (after Hitzig) to xlii. and xliii. seems entirely fanciful, and that xlv. and lxxii. speak of foreign monarchs is very hard to believe.   I am not sure that the ideal picture of Psalm lxxii. requires any historical background : "Entrust thy judgments to a king and thy righteousness to a king's son " may very well be a prayer for the re-establishment of the Davidic dynasty under a Messianic king according to prophecy.   Psalm xlv. is a great crux, but I still think that it is easiest to take it as a poem of the old kingdom.   As regards lxviii., the arguments in favour of a Greek date during the wars of Syria and Egypt for the possession of Palestine turn entirely on verse 30 (Heb. 31), the "wild beast of the reeds" (R.V.) being taken to mean the Egyptians, and the "multitude of bulls" the Syrians. But the psalm, which combines an historical retrospect of Jehovah's mighty deeds of old with the hope that He will speedily arise once more to confound the nations, redeem His people, and raise Israel to the estate of glory predicted by Isa. lx. and similar passages, really contains no definite historical reference ; though one may guess that the hopes it expresses on the ground of ancient prophecy had been kindled into fresh ardour by signs of dissolution in the world-kingdoms. It *may* date from the catastrophe of the Persian empire ; and I doubt whether any date later than this, and yet prior to the Maccabee period, was calculated to revive theocratic hopes and ideals that had slept through the long period of slavery to Persia. Psalms lxviii. lxxii. ought, I think, to be considered along with the Book of Joel and chaps. xxiv.-xxvii. of Isaiah.

ADDITIONAL NOTE E (p. 221).—THE FIFTY-FIRST PSALM

Recent supporters of the Davidic authorship of Ps. li. take the two last verses as a later addition (Perowne, Delitzsch). But every one can see that the omission of these verses makes the Psalm end abruptly, and a closer examination reveals a connection of thought between verses 16, 17 (Heb. 18, 19) and verses 18, 19 (Heb. 20, 21). At present, says the Psalmist, God desires no material sacrifice, but will not despise a contrite heart. How does the Psalmist know that God takes no pleasure in sacrifice ? Not on the principle that the sacrifice of the wicked is sin, for the sacrifice of the contrite whose person God accepts must be acceptable if any sacrifice is so. But does the Psalmist then mean to say, absolutely and in general, that sacrifice is a superseded thing ? No ; for he adds that when Jerusalem is rebuilt the sacrifice of Israel (not merely his own sacrifice) will be pleasing to God. He lives, therefore, in a time when the fall of Jerusalem has temporarily suspended the sacrificial ordinances, but—and this is the great lesson of the Psalm—has not closed the door of forgiveness to the penitent heart.

Let us now turn to the main thought of the Psalm, and see whether it does not suit this situation as well as the supposed reference to the life of David. The two special points in the Psalm on which the historical reference may be held to turn are verse 14, "Deliver me from blood-guiltiness," and verse 11, "Take not thy Holy Spirit from me." Under the Old Testament the Holy Spirit is not given to every believer, but to Israel as a nation (Isa. lxiii. 10, 11), residing in chosen organs, especially in the prophets, who are *par excellence* "men of the Spirit" (Hos. ix. 7). But the Spirit of Jehovah was also given to David (1 Sam. xvi. 13 ; 2 Sam. xxiii.

2). The Psalm then, so far as this phrase goes, may be a Psalm of Israel collectively, of a prophet, or of David. Again, the phrase "Deliver me from blood-guiltiness" is to be understood after Psalm xxxix. 8, "Deliver me from all my transgressions, make me not the reproach of the foolish." In the Old Testament the experience of forgiveness is no mere subjective feeling; it rests on facts. In the New Testament the assurance of forgiveness lays hold of the work and victory of Christ, it lies in the actual realisation of victory over the world in Him. In the Old Testament, in like manner, some saving act of God is the evidence of forgiveness. The sense of forgiveness is the joy of God's salvation (ver. 12), and the word "salvation" (ישע) is, I believe, always used of some visible delivery and enlargement from distress. God's wrath is felt in His chastisement, His forgiveness in the removal of affliction, when His people cease to be the reproach of the foolish. Hence the expression "deliver me." But blood-guiltiness (דמים) does not necessarily mean the guilt of murder. It means mortal sin (Ezek. xviii. 13), such sin as, if it remains unatoned, withdraws God's favour from His land and people (Deut. xxi. 8 *sq.*; Isa. i. 15). Bloodshed is the typical offence among those which under the ancient law of the First Legislation are not to be atoned for by a pecuniary compensation, but demand the death of the sinner. The situation of the Psalm, therefore, does not necessarily presuppose such a case as David's. It is equally applicable to the prophet, labouring under a deep sense that he has discharged his calling inadequately and may have the guilt of lost lives on his head (Ezek. xxxiii.), or to collective Israel in the Captivity, when, according to the prophets, it was the guilt of blood equally with the guilt of idolatry that removed God's favour from His land (Jer. vii. 6; Hosea iv. 2, vi. 8; Isa. iv. 4). Nay, from the Old Testament point of view, in which the experience of wrath and forgiveness stands generally in such immediate relation to Jehovah's actual dealings with the nation, the whole thought of the Psalm is most simply understood as a prayer for the restoration and sanctification of Israel in the mouth of a prophet of the Exile. For the immediate fruit of forgiveness is that the singer will resume the prophetic function of teaching sinners Jehovah's ways (ver. 13). This is little appropriate to David, whose natural and right feeling in connection with his great sin must rather have been that of silent humiliation than of an instant desire to preach his forgiveness to other sinners. The whole experience of David with Nathan moves in another plane. The Psalmist writes out of the midst of present judgments of God (the Captivity).   To David, the pain of death, remitted on his repentance, lay in the future (2 Sam. xii. 13) as an anticipated judgment of God, the remission of which would hardly produce the exultant joy of verse 12.   On the other hand, the whole thought of the Psalm, as Hitzig points out and Delitzsch acknowledges, moves in exact parallel with the spiritual experience of Israel in the Exile as conceived in connection with the personal experience of a prophet in Isa. xl.-lxvi.   The Psalm is a psalm of the true Israel of the Exile in the mouth of a prophet, perhaps of the very prophet who wrote the last chapters of the Book of Isaiah.

ADDITIONAL NOTE F (p. 382).—THE DEVELOPMENT OF THE RITUAL SYSTEM BETWEEN EZEKIEL AND EZRA

Ezekiel's ideal sketch of institutions for the restored theocracy was written in 572, the return from exile followed in 538, the rebuilding of the Temple was completed in 516, Ezra's covenant and the first introduction of the present Pentateuch fall in 444 B.C.   In the text of Lecture XII. I have limited myself to the broad and indisputable statement that the development of the priestly system falls between 572 and 444.   Is it possible to throw any further light on the details of the process?   Not much, perhaps, since our sources for the history of Jerusalem in this period are very meagre, and our knowledge of the Jews in Babylonia and Susiana, from whom Ezra and Nehemiah came, is still more defective ; but there are one or two things to be said on the subject which may be worth bearing in mind.

(1.) It is plain that Ezekiel's sketch could not have been taken by the returning exiles as a practical code of ritual.   It is an ideal picture, presupposing a complete restoration of all the tribes and their resettlement under a native prince in a land prepared for their reception by physical changes of a miraculous kind.   In giving this imaginative form to his picture of what restored Israel ought to be, Ezekiel uses the literary freedom appropriate to the prophetic style ; but for that very reason his sketch could only supply general principles and suggestive hints on points of detail for the actual constitution of the community of the second Temple.

(2.) That the Book of Ezekiel was known to the leaders of the returning exiles, and influenced their conduct, is inferred from the fact that the distinction between priests and Levites is recognised in the list of those who came up with Zerubbabel (Neh. vii.).   The

foundation of this distinction is indeed older than Ezekiel, for it is
at bottom merely the distinction between the Temple priests and
the priests of the high places.   And up to the time of Nehemiah
one family seems to have held an ambiguous position, claiming the
rights of priesthood, but unable to prove it by showing their genealogy (Neh. vii. 63 *sqq.*).   Yet it is difficult to believe that, apart
from Ezekiel, the distinction would have been drawn so sharply at
the first moment of the return ; especially when we consider that
the written law of the age of the Restoration was the Deuteronomic
Code, and that the theory of that code, in which there is no contrast
between the priesthood and the house of Levi, still dominates in the
prophecy of Malachi, which no one will place earlier than 450-460
B.C.   That the incongruity between the Deuteronomic theory and
the actual organisation of the Temple ministry was not felt in
Malachi's time appears to receive a sufficient explanation from the
relatively inconsiderable number of Levites who were not recognised
as priests ; [1] the list of Neh. vii. gives 4289 priests to 74 Levites,
and this disproportion was not corrected by the admission into the
ranks of the Levites of singers, porters, and other subordinate
ministers, till after the Reformation of Ezra (*supra*, p. 204).

Another trace of the influence of Ezekiel may perhaps be seen
in the stone platform that served as an altar in the second Temple.
But it is more likely that both Ezekiel and the returning exiles
followed the model of the altar of Ahaz.

A less ambiguous sign of Ezekiel's influence appears in Zech.
iii. 7, where a principal function of the high priest is to keep God's
courts.   Here we have an unmistakable indication that Ezekiel's
conception of holiness, and his jealousy of profane contact with holy
things, had been taken up by the spiritual leaders of the new Jerusalem.   There is, therefore, a strong presumption that from the first
the arrangements and ritual of the second Temple were more closely
conformed to the principle of concentric circles of holiness than those
of the first Temple had been.

Once more—and this is the most important point of all—it will
hardly be questioned that, from the first days of the return, the
spontaneous service of the people fell into the background behind
the stated representative ritual.   This is one of the most characteristic points of Ezekiel's Torah ; and it was the less likely to be
without practical influence, because all the conditions of the time

---

[1] Compare the older priestly account of the rebellion of Korah, according to
Kuenen's analysis.

co-operated in its favour. To prove that the stated public sacrifices were regularly maintained before Ezra's Reformation, we cannot appeal with confidence to Ezra iii. 2 *sqq.*, vi. 17 *sqq.*, for these verses are due to the compiler of Ezra-Nehemiah-Chronicles, with whose indifference to historical perspective we are now familiar. And it is certain that before Ezra's covenant the Levitical ritual was not maintained in all its parts. But it is equally certain that the compiler is right in affirming that the altar was built before the Temple (comp. Hag. ii. 14), and that he must have learned this fact from good historical sources. Now the altar of the second Temple is essentially an altar of burnt-offering, *i.e.* destined for public and atoning functions, not for the reception of the blood of private sacrifices. That the stated services of the first ninety years of the new Jerusalem were much less elaborate and costly than the Priestly Code prescribes seems to follow from Ezra ix. 5, where we learn that in 458 B.C. the evening oblation was still only a *minha*, or cereal offering. The same thing follows still more clearly from Neh. x. 32, where we see that a new voluntary tax became necessary when the full Pentateuchal ritual was introduced. Before that time the stated service appears to have been maintained, with much grumbling and in an imperfect way, at the expense of the priests (Mal. i. 6-13) ;[1] for it will readily be understood that in an empire so loosely organised as that of Persia, the royal grants in favour of the Temple mentioned in the Book of Ezra would receive little attention from the local authorities, who viewed the Jews with no favour. That in spite of all this the stated service was in some measure kept up, proves that great importance was attached to it. In fact, we see from Malachi that Jehovah's blessing on the land was held to be conditional on a proper discharge of the representative priestly service of the house of Levi (Mal. ii. 2, iii. 3, 4) ; so that

---

[1] The whole of this passage refers to the imperfect maintenance by the priests of the stated service, and especially of the stated burnt-offering. The recognition of this fact has been impeded by a graphical error in the text of verse 12, where for וניבו נבזה we must read ונבזה ; by accident נב was written twice over. The sense, therefore, is not that the priests grumbled at the food they derived from the altar, but that they thought Jehovah's altar a vile thing for which any oblation was good enough. The phrase אכלו is exactly equivalent to the ritual term לחם יהוה, and the whole passage shows that Malachi, whose law-book is Deuteronomy, and who does not know the Priestly Code (comp. *supra*, p. 425 *sq.*), entirely agrees with the importance attached by that code to the *tamîd*. The emendation here proposed for Mal. i. 12 has already appeared in the Cambridge Bible for Schools ; having been communicated by me to the Editor of that Series. I mention this because it appears there (doubtless by inadvertence) without acknowledgment.

in this respect the actual praxis of the second Temple moved on the lines of Ezekiel, and in the direction of the Priestly Code.

(3.) A movement beyond Ezekiel and in the direction of the finished Priestly Code can be most clearly observed with regard to the position of the high priest. The second Temple never had a high priest corresponding to the full priestly ideal—a high priest with Urim and Thummim (Neh. vii. 65). But from the time of Ezra downwards, a certain princely character attached to the office, and the very insignia of the high priest described in the Code, his crown and his purple robes, correspond with this. For that these insignia are not priestly but princely, is practically acknowledged in the ritual of the Great Day of Atonement. This also is a change in the line of natural historical development, as appears from the fact that princely high priests are found all over the East at great sanctuaries, after the fall of the old nationalities (comp. *Enc. Brit.*, 9th ed., art. PRIEST). Under the kings the chief priest had no monarchical character, even in sacred things, and Ezekiel, who looks for the restoration of a modified kingship, does not speak of a high priest. But the restored community had no civil independence, and it was only in exceptional cases that its civil head was a pious Jew (Zerubbabel, Nehemiah), in sympathy with the distinctive religious aims and principles which were the only surviving expression of Hebrew nationality. Hence the patriots in Israel necessarily came to look on the priesthood as their natural heads, and the chief priest as the leader of the community; and there were obvious reasons of convenience which would lead the civil authorities to accept him, for many purposes, as the representative of the people, in much the same way as the heads of Christian churches in the East are now accepted by Moslem governments. We do not see much of this in the Books of Ezra and Nehemiah, for special reasons. At this time there was a great slackness in religious things, which Malachi ascribes mainly to want of loyalty to Jehovah on the part of the priesthood. Before Nehemiah's arrival Ezra's chief opponents in the matter of mixed marriages were found among the priests, while his supporters were the lay aristocracy (Ezra ix. x. ; comp. Mal. ii. 12, 13); and Nehemiah came in with a high hand superseding all local authority. But the practical failure of Ezra's first attempt at reformation, in 458, was doubtless due to the opposition of the priests, and is the best evidence of their power; and indeed the reason why the priests were not hearty in the cause of reformation was that they, and especially the high priestly family, had formed matrimonial alliances with the heads of foreign communities (Neh. xiii. 4, 28). That such alliances were made and sought, shows that by those outside the house of Eliashib the high priest was regarded as the highest aristocracy of Jerusalem. But indeed the pre-eminence of the high priest is already clearly marked, in the first generation after the return, in the Book of Zechariah. I agree with Ewald, and others after him, that Zechariah vi. 9-15 has been retouched, and that the crowns (or crown) of verse 11 must in the original text have been set on the head of *Zerubbabel and* Joshua (or perhaps of Zerubbabel alone : so Wellhausen) ; for in verse 13 the high priest's throne is still clearly distinguished from that of the civil prince. But even so the place of the high priest is much higher than it had ever been under the first Temple ; and even the unction of the high priest, which is a notable point in the Priests' Code, is prefigured in Zech. iv. 14, while the tiara is conferred upon him in Zech. iii. 5.[1]

(4.) I now come to a matter on which there is more dispute. One of the most notable points in the Priests' Code is the greatly-increased provision for the clergy. Does the law in this point also follow lines of development that had already been marked out in the praxis of the second Temple ? I think that it does.

It is self-evident that the provision for the priesthood contained in the Deuteronomic Code could not (in a small and poor community) have sufficed for the maintenance of the Temple ministry and ritual even on the most meagre scale. It was supplemented, no doubt, by gifts, especially from pious Jews of the Diaspora ; but the need for an increased stated provision must have been felt very soon. One departure from the Deuteronomic law was certainly made—the priests and Levites were allowed to hold land (Neh. iii. 22, xiii. 10). But this did not provide for the maintenance of the ministers in actual attendance at the Temple ; and from Mal. iii. 8, 9, it appears that the food of Jehovah's household was derived from the tithe and the *t'rûma* (A. V. tithes and offerings). It is commonly assumed that Malachi wrote after 444 B.C., and is here referring to the Levitical tithe of the Priestly Code ; but this view is, I think, inadmissible, when we consider the unambiguous proofs afforded by all other parts of the book that the written Torah of Malachi is the pre-priestly Pentateuch, especially Deuteronomy (*supra*, p. 426). Even in the verse before us the

---

[1] A. V. "mitre," Hebrew צָנִיף. Zechariah had not the Priestly Code before him, else he would have used the word מִצְנֶפֶת ; but the two words mean the same thing, viz. the princely tiara.

expressions used are those of Deuteronomy,[1] and the "whole tithe" is the technical Deuteronomic name for the charity-tithe of the third year, in which the poor Levites had a part (Deut. xiv. 28, xxvi. 12). That under the circumstances of the second Temple the sacred ministers absorbed the whole charity-tithe, and that, instead of being stored and consumed in the country towns, it was brought up to the Temple treasury for the use of the ministers on duty, are changes perfectly natural, or even inevitable, which required no new written law to justify them.

(5.) There is direct evidence that the elaborate festal ordinances of the Priests' Code contained things that had never been practised under the second Temple. And with this it agrees that the oldest priestly calendar of festal ordinances (contained in Lev. xxiii.) is simpler than the calendar of Num. xxviii. xxix., which belongs to the main body of the code, though even this simpler rule contains things that were not practised before Ezra (verses 40 *sqq.* compared with Neh. viii. 17). But the type of the priestly feasts was already given in practice; for in Mal. ii. 3 the festal sacrifices (A. V. feasts) are the sacrifices of the priests, *i.e.* a representative service, not the free-will offerings of the pre-exile festivities. And the crowning stone of the priestly edifice, the Day of Atonement, was indeed an innovation, but one for which the way had been prepared by the annual fasts mentioned in Zech. vii. 3, 5.

(6.) The stricter observance of the Sabbath, and of other ceremonies that could be practised in the Dispersion as easily as at Jerusalem, seems to have begun in the Diaspora, where these means of realising Israel's holiness in the midst of the Gentiles would naturally have a special value for the pious ; cp. Isa. lvi., lviii. 13. On the other hand, Malachi, writing at Jerusalem, does not touch on the observance of the Sabbath, though this was one of the points of discipline which Nehemiah found particular difficulty in enforcing (Neh. xiii. 15 *sqq.*). In this matter, as in that of mixed marriages, the Diaspora took the lead, and Jerusalem followed reluctantly. And in other matters also it is to be presumed that the Jews who remained in exile had a substantial part in the development of all points of ceremonial not directly connected with the Temple, *e.g.* the domestic rites of the passover.[2]

---

[1] Tithe and *t'rûma* are associated as in Deut. xii. 6, 11. In the Priestly Code *t'rûma* always means a due paid to the priests as distinct from the Levites, so that tithe and *t'rûma* would be disparate ideas, not a closely connected pair as in Deuteronomy and Malachi.

[2] The paschal lamb is unknown to Deuteronomy and to Ezekiel. Its ritual

(7.) There are some things in the Priests' Code, such as the ordinance for Levitical cities and the law of Jubilee, which were never put in practice, and which, at the time when they were written, must have been regarded as purely ideal. They were necessary to round off the system of ordinances from a theoretical point of view, but their presence in the Code has no other practical significance than to indicate that under the existing political conditions a perfect theocracy was unattainable. But these features must not prevent us from recognising the skill with which the priestly writer combines in systematic form a vast complex of ordinances old and new, making up a complete theory of individual and national holiness, and yet keeping so close to existing practice or existing tendencies that his work served as the permanent basis of all Jewish life since Ezra.

It may be observed in conclusion that while the code is written throughout from a priestly standpoint, it cannot possibly be regarded as the programme of the priestly aristocracy in Jerusalem. It is true that, among other results of greater importance, Ezra's Reformation, like that of Josiah before it, did in the long run give a great increase of importance to the higher priesthood. But to infer that it was the work of the chief priests of Jerusalem would be as absurd and unhistorical as to make Abû Sofyân the author of Islam, because the Meccan aristocracy, and his family in particular, reaped the material fruits of Mohammed's work. All the historical indications point to the priestly aristocracy as being the chief opponents of Ezra; their opposition, no doubt, was short-sighted; but the heads of a hereditary aristocracy are not generally gifted with the kind of insight which comes of broad sympathies and a large comprehension of the spiritual and political movements of their time. The Priests' Code has far too many points of contact with the actual situation at Jerusalem, and the actual usage of the second Temple, to lend plausibility to the view that it was an abstract system evolved in Babylonia, by some one who was remote from the contemporary movement at Jerusalem; but on the other hand its author must have stood (whether by his

presents some very antique features, but cannot in its final form be older than the Exile. In the Priestly Code this domestic sacrifice is still quite distinct from the public ritual, as is indicated by the fact that its institution (like that of the Sabbath, the Noachic ordinances, and circumcision) is placed before the Sinaitic revelation. It was ultimately incorporated in the rites of the sanctuary by the traditional rule that the paschal lamb must be killed at the Temple. This was already the practice in the time of the Chronicler (2 Chron. xxx. 17, xxxv. 6, 11; Ezra vi. 20).

circumstances, or by his strength of mind and firm faith in the principles on which his work is based) outside the petty local entanglements that hampered the Judæan priests. So much it is safe to say; to go farther and conjecture that Ezra himself was the author of the Priests' Code is to step into a region of purely arbitrary guesswork. And such a conjecture is at least not favoured by the consideration that the Torah of 444 B.C. was not the Priests' Code by itself but (essentially) our present complex Pentateuch. It is hardly probable that the same man first wrote the Priestly Code, then combined it with the pre-priestly book to form a Hexateuch, and finally obtained canonical authority, not for his whole book, but for five-sixths of it. The Canon of 444 must surely have been the Pentateuch alone; for how else could the Book of Joshua have fallen into the lower position of a prophetical book? And if this be so the presumption is strong that Ezra, the man of action, had no personal share in the shaping of the Pentateuch, unless perhaps it was he who cut off the Book of Joshua, so as to limit the compass of the Law to matters directly practical.

INDEX OF SOME PASSAGES DISCUSSED
OR ILLUSTRATED

Gen. vi. 5-ix. 17, 330
    xxi. 8 *sq.*, 417
    xxiii., 417
Exod. xix.-xxxiv., 336 *note*
    xx. 26, 358 *note*
    xxi.-xxiii., 318 *sq.*, 340 *sq.*
    xxxii.-xxxiv., 397 *sq.*
    xxxiv., 335
    xxxv.-xl., 124 *sq.*
Lev. xvii.-xxvi., 396, 428 *sq.*
Num. x. 29 *sq.*, 321, 409
    xi. xii., 400
    xiii. xiv., 400 *sq.*
    xvi., 402 *sq.*
    xx.-xxiv., 405 *sq.*
    xxv. 1-5, 404 *note*
    xxxiii., 404, 406
Deut. i. 22-40, 402
    i.-xxx., 393 *sq.*
    x. 6, 405
    x. 8, 361 *note*
    xii.-xxvi., 258, 318, 356 *sq.*
    xiv. 3-21, 366 *sq.*
    xxi. 10 *sq.*, 368
    xxii. 5, 365
    xxii. 30, 369
    xxvii. 22, 370 *note*
Josh. viii., 133
    xiv. 6-14, 402
    xxiv., 395
Judg. i., 131
    v. 25, 132
    xviii. 30, 361 *note*
1 Sam. i. 20 *sq.*, 269
    ii. 27-36, 266 *note*
    ix.-xi., 135 *sq.*
    xiii. 7-15, 134
    xiv. 18, 81
    xvii. 120 *sq.*, 431
    xviii., 122
    xix. 24, 130

1 Sam. xx. 19, 41, 80 *sq.*
    xxx. 24, 25, 386
2 Sam. iv. 5-7, 82
    xvii. 3, 83
1 Kings viii. 53 (LXX.), 124, 433
    xi. 29-39, 118
    xii. 1 *sq.*, 117
    xiv., 119
2 Kings iii. 16 *sq.*, 147
    xi. 12, 311 *note*
    xiii. 22 (LXX.), 435
    xxii. xxiii., 257 *sq.*
1 Chron. iii. 19 *sq.*, 140 *note*
2 Chron. xxxiv. 3, 144 *note*
Neh. xiii. 1-3, 427 *note*
Ps. xlii. xliii., 193 *note*
    xliv. lxxiv. lxxix., 207 *sq.*, 438
    li., 221, 440
    lxi. lxiii., 438
    lxxviii., 213 *note*
    lxxxiii., 439
    lxxxvi., 197, 435
    cxxxiii., 212 *note*
Isa. xl.-lxvi., 98 *sq.*
    lxv. 8, 209
Jer. xxvii. 1, 97
    xxvii. 5-22, 104 *sq.*
    xxxiii. 14-26, 107
    l. li., 97
Ezek. xliv. 6-15, 260, 377
Hos. iii. 240 *note*
    ix. 3 *sq.*, 150
Am. v. 25 (emended), 294
Zech. iii. 7, 443
    vi. 9-15, 446
Mal. i. 12 (emended), 444
    iii. 8, 9, 446
    iv. 4, 425 *sq.*
2 Mac. ii. 13 *sq.*, 170
2 Esdr. xiv. 44 *sq.*, 168

GENERAL INDEX

AARON, death of, 405 ; sons of, 246, 257, 266 *note*

Abraham, Priestly story of, 415 *sq.*

Acrostic psalms, 193

Ahab, 116, 237

Ahaz, 265, 443

Ai, taking of, 133

Akiba, exegetic method of, 63 ; and the Canon, 184 *sq.*

Alphabet, Semitic, 70

Al-taschith, 209

Altar, holiness of, 229 ; consecration of, 376 ; as asylum, 340, 354 ; of Ahaz, 265, 443 ; brazen, 265, 276 ; with steps, 358 *note* ; of the second Temple, *ib.*, 443 ; altar-worship in old Israel, 239 ; law of the one altar, 245, 353

Amôra, 50 *note*

Amos, 283, 288, etc.

Anonymous books, 92 *sq.* ; psalms, to whom ascribed, 103

Antilegomena, 166 *sq.* ; in the Old Testament, 178-187

Antiochus Epiphanes, 72, 207

Aphek, 273, 435

Apocrypha, 29 *sq.*, 153 *sq.* ; suppressed by the Rabbins, 167, 184

Aquila, 30 *note*, 63 *note*, 64

Aramaic, 35, 208 ; versions of Scripture, *see* Targum

Archetype of the Massoretic text, 57 *sq.*, 69 *sq.*

Aristeas, 85

Ark in the wilderness, 321 ; at Shiloh, 268, 270 ; borne by priests, 144 ; in the Priests' Code, 246, 398 ; in Jeremiah, 107 ; not mentioned in Deuteronomic Code, 357 ; in heaven, 429

Artaxerxes Ochus, 207 *sq.*, 438

Asaph, Asaphites, 204 *sq.*

Ashēra, 241, 354

Astarte (Ashtoreth), 237, 243, 365

Astruc, 327

Asylum, 354

Atonement, 372, 380 *sq.* ; by blood, 229, 373 ; great Day of, 229, 376, 445

BAAL, 68, 285 ; Tyrian, 237 ; prophets of, 287 ; Baal-Peor, 404 *note*

Baalim, local, 243

Bagoses, 438

Balaam, 404

Bethel, revelations at, 416 ; sanctuary at, 242, 264

Bible, order of books in the Hebrew, 149 *sq.* ; Jerome's version of, 25 ; Protestant versions, 21 *sq.*

Blood not to be eaten, 249 *sq.*, 345 ; offered on altar, 229 ; *see* Atonement

Book of the Covenant, 333 *sq.* ; Josiah's, 258

Books, number of the Old Testament, 150 *sq.* ; sacred, destroyed by Antiochus, 72, 170

Booty, law of, 386

CADI OF THE ARABS, 304, 321

Caleb, 402 ; eponym of the Calibbites, 279 *note*

Canaan, conquest of, 130 *sq.*, 413

Canaanite = trader, 350

Canaanites absorbed among Israel, 280

Canon, ecclesiastical, 25 ; of Scripture, 149 *sq.*, ; history of the Jewish, 163 *sq.* ; Protestant Canon, 31 ; Tridentine Canon, 28 *sq.* ; Canon and tradition, 173 *sq.*

Canticles, canonicity of, 185 ; read in Synagogue, 173 *note* ; allegorical interpretation of, 164 *note* ; sung at banquets, 186

Cappellus, Ludovicus, 75

Captain of the guard, 262 *note*

Carites, 262 *note*

Charm, Ex. xv. 26 used as, 185 *note*

Chemarim, 259

Cherethites and Pelethites, 262 *note*

Cheyne, Prof., 189 *note*, 437 *sq.*

Chronicles, date of, 140 ; originally one book with Ezra-Neh., 182 *sq.*; historical character of, 140 *sq.*

Copyists, freedom used by, 91, 126 *sq.*

Covenant, Mosaic, 304, 333, 399 ; Josiah's, 257 *sq.*, 353 ; Ezra's, 43, 382

Criminal laws, in the First Legislation, 340 ; in Deut., 368

DAN, sanctuary of, 242 ; priesthood of, 359, 361 *note*

Daniel, Book of, 180, 183 ; Septuagint version of, 154

Dathan and Abiram, 402 *sq.*

David, and Goliath, 120 *sq.*, 431 *sq.*; and Saul, 123 ; as musician, 219 ; psalms of, 197, 213 *sq.*

Decadence of Israel, 347 ; causes of, 349

Decalogue, *see* Ten Commandments

Dedication of the House, *see* Encænia

Deluge, story of the, 329 *sq.*

Deuteronomic Code, 318 ; compared with Exod. xxi.-xxiii., 319 *note* ; the basis of Josiah's reforms, 258 ; relation of, to Exod. xxi.-xxiii., 319 *note*; to Isaiah, 355 *sq.*, 364 *sq.*; not forged by Hilkiah, 363 ; laws of sanctity in, 365 *sq.*; civil laws of, 368

Deuteronomistic redaction of the old history, 396, 425

Deuteronomy, historical matter in, 391 ; speeches in, 394 *sq.*; fused with JE, 425 ; authority of, after the Exile, 425 *sq.*; priestly elements in, 412

Dillmann, 392 *note*

Divination, 285 *sq.*; and prophecy, 288

"Dogs," 365 *note*

Doxologies in the Psalter, 194 *sq.*

Driver, Prof., 227 *note*, 245 *note*, 389

Ecclesiastes, canonicity of, 185 *sq.*; in the Synagogue, 173 *note*

Ecclesiasticus, standpoint of the author, 159 *sq.*; prologue to, 178

Egypt, plagues of, 418

Eli, house of, 266, 268

Elias Levita, 169

Elohim, in the Psalter, 198 ; in the Pentateuch, 327 *sq.*, 414, 416, 424

Elohist, Elohistic document, 393, 416 *sq.*, 423 *sq.*

Encænia, feast, 190, 211

Ephod, 241 ; linen, 270, 272

2 *Esdras*, 151, 157, 168

Esther, canonicity of, 183 *sq.*; twofold Greek recension of, 155 *note*

Ethical monotheism, 295

Exegesis, Catholic and Protestant, 22 *sq.*; of the mediæval Rabbins, 53

Exodus, laws of, 318 ; priestly elements in, 397 *sq.*, 418 *sq.*

Ezekiel, controversy as to his book, 176 *note*; his Torah, 310, 374 *sq.*, 442

Ezra, the Scribe, 42 *sq.*; and the Canon, 171, 449 ; Reformation of, 43, 226, 427, 445 ; legends about, 168, 277 ; his book, 182 *sq.*

FASTS, annual, 376

Feast of Tabernacles, 43, 257

Feasts, annual, at Shiloh, 268 *sq.*; in the First Legislation, 342 ; in Deut., 371 ; in the Priests' Code, 447

First Legislation, 318, 340 *sq.*; identical with the Book of the Covenant, 336

Flood, the, 329 *sq.*

Forbidden degrees, 370 *note*

Forbidden meats, 366

Forgeries of books, 17, 171

Forgiveness, doctrine of, 306 *sq.*; ritual machinery of, 229 *sq.*; *see* Atonement

GALLI, 365

Gemara, 50 *note*

Genesis, sources of, 323 *note*, 327 *sq.*, 413 *sq.*

Gêr, or protected stranger, 342 *note*

Gibeon, high place of, 276

Gibeonites, 412 *sq.*

Gittites, 262 *note*

Golden calves, 240, 242, 244

Great Synagogue, 169

HAGAR, story of, 417

Haggada, 44, 180

Hagiographa, 150, 178 *sq.* ; in the Synagogue, 173 ; translated into Greek, 201

Halacha, 44, 51, 77, 180

Hallel, the, 190 *sq.*, 211

Hallelujah psalms, 190, 211

Hands, the Scriptures defile the, 185

Hasmonean dynasty, 48

Hebrew, so-called, in the New Testament, 35 ; vowel points and accents, 58 *sq.*; scholarship of the Rabbins, 37, 53 ; of the Christian Fathers, 23 *sq.*; of the Reformers, 32

Hexapla of Origen, 30, 89

Hexateuch (Pentateuch and Joshua), 388 *sq.*

Hezekiah, 256, 352, 357
Higher criticism, 90 *sq.*
High places, 236, 239, 241, 243, 248, 275, 322 *note*; abolished by Josiah, 257; in Deut., 354 *sq.*; priests of the, 257, 360
High priest, 445
Hillel, 63, 184 *note*
Historians, method of Eastern, 113 *sq.*, 328
Historical books, anonymous, 92 *sq.*; composite character of the, in Old Testament, 129 *sq.*
Holiness, in Pentateuch, 228; in Deut., 365 *sq.*; in Ezekiel, 377; Isaiah's doctrine of, 364; Law of (Lev. xvii.-xxvi.), 323 *note*, 428 *sq.*
Hyrcania, Jews led captive to, 208, 438
Hyrcanus, John, 52, 159, 211

IAMNIA, discussion on the Canon at, 185; seat of the Scribes, 186 *note*
Idolatry, 240 *sq.*, 355
Ink, 71
Isaiah attacks the popular worship, 293; and the idols, 355; his doctrine of holiness, 364; of the sanctity of Zion, 356
Isaiah, Book of, 100 *sq.*
Ishbosheth or Eshbaal, 68
Israel, personified in the Psalter, 189, 220; the primary subject of Old Testament religion, 291, 308 *note,* 348
Ithamar, 360 *note*

JAEL AND SISERA, 132
Jashar, Book of, 124, 435
Jahvist, Jahvistic document, 393, 414 *sq.*, 423
Jehoiada, 259, 262
Jehoash, coronation of, 262, 311 *note*; deals with the Temple revenues, 264
Jehovah (Iahwè), 77, 245; popular worship of, 242 *sq.*, 282; not a Canaanite god, 245; dwells in Zion, 356; in the *mishkan,* 246; shows himself in the thunderstorm, 247; Lord of the whole earth, 282; prophetic doctrine of his relation to Israel, 283 *sq.*, 298; his word, 290, 298; moral precepts of, 304
Jeremiah, interpolations in his book, 97, 104; prophecies of, against the nations, 109
Jeroboam, history of, 117 *sq.*; his religious policy, 244
Jerome, his translation of the Bible,

25, 29 *sq.*; his account of the Apocrypha, 29; Hebrew text read by, 56; his enumeration of the Old Testament books, 151
Josephus and the Canon, 151, 163 *sq.*
Joshua, Book of, composite character of, 131, 133; Deuteronomistic elements in, 396; Priestly do., 412
Josiah, 144, 147, 256 *sq.*, 353
Jubilees, Book of, 62, 152 *note*
Judah, foreign elements in, 279
Judges, age of the, 235, 267
Judith, Book of, 439

KABBALA, 161, 173
Kadesh, 404 *sq.*
Kadhi, *see* Cadi
Kâhin, diviner, same word as Kôhen, priest, 292
Kemarim (Chemarim), 259
Kenizzites, 279 *note*
Kerî and Kethîb, 59 *sq.*
Kimhi, R. David, 32 *sq.*
Kings, Books of, their structure, 115 *sq.*
Korah, Korahites, 204 *sq.*, 402 *sq.*
Kuenen, 226, 245, 323 *note,* 389, 419, 427

Lamentations ascribed to Jeremiah, 181; importance of the book, 219
Law, function of the, 315 *sq.*
Law, oral, 45 *sq.*, 161, 173; consuetudinary, 304, 339; of Moses, 311 *sq.*
Law, Prophets and Psalms, 177 *sq.*
Leaven in sacrifice, 345
Legal fictions, 384 *sq.*
Leptogenesis, 152 *note*
Levites, 247; before Deuteronomy, 359; in Ezekiel, 359 *sq.*; in the second Temple, 443; as singers, 204
Levitical law, its system, 228, 245; unknown to Josiah, 256; in Solomon's Temple, 259; at Shiloh, 265; to Samuel, 272 *sq.*; to the prophets, 293
Levitical law-book, 319, 322; *see* Priests' Code
Levitical Psalm-book, 203 *sq.*
Lot, sacred, 292
Luther and the Bible, 7 *sq.*

MACCABEE PSALMS, 210 *sq.*, 437 *sq.*
Maççêba, 240 *sq.*, 260, 354 *sq.*
Machpelah, cave of, 418 *note*
Mahanaim, 248 *note*
Maine, Sir H., 384, 386

Malachi, 425 *sq.*, 443 *sq.*; date of, 427 *note*
Marriage with a half-sister, 280, 370 *note*; with a father's wife, 369 *sq.*; by capture, 368
Marriages, mixed, 260, 266, 427, 445
Massorets, 58
Mediation, priestly, 229, 247, 251
Megilloth, the five, 150 ; use in the Synagogue, 173
Melito's Canon, 184
Men in women's garments, 365
Mephibosheth or Meribaal, 68
Meturgeman, 36, 64 *note*, 154
Micah the prophet, 244, 287 *sq.*, 294, 305
Micah's sanctuary, 241 *sq.*, 292
Midrash, 154
Midrashic sources of Chronicles, 147, 205 *note*
Mikra, 161
Mishna, 50
Mohammed, 298 *note*
Morinus, J., 74 *sq.*
Moses as prophet, 302 ; as priest, 303 ; as judge, 304 ; founder of the law, 311 *sq.*; his writings, 323 ; in the Priests' Code, 409

NATURE-RELIGIONS, 285
Nehemiah, 43, 445 ; and the Canon, 170 ; his book reckoned with Ezra, 150 ; relation to Chronicles, 182 *sq.*
Nethînîm, 359
Nicanor, day of, 183
Noachic ordinances, 322
Nob, sanctuary of, 272
Nöldeke, 182 *note*, 390

OCHUS, 207 *sq.*, 438
Old Testament, standard text of, 62 *sq.*
Onkelos, 65 *note*
Oracles, 285
Oral law, *see* Law
Origen and his Hexapla, 30, 89

PASSOVER, 447
Paul of Tella, 30 *note*
Pentateuch, the, contains several distinct codes, 318 ; not written by Moses, 323 ; composite structure of, 327 ; steps in the redaction of, 425 *sq.*; narrative of, 388 *sq.*; use in the Synagogue, 83, 173 ; held more sacred than other Scriptures, 161 ; Samaritan, 61
Pharisees, 47 *sq.*
Philistine guards in the Temple, 261

Philo of Alexandria, does not quote Apocrypha, 155 ; nor all Hagiographa, 152 ; his theory of inspiration, 286 *note*
Pillars, brazen, of Solomon's Temple, 260
Pirkê Abôth, 42 *note*, 165
Poll tax, 51, 375, 444
Precedents, legal, 304, 321
Priests in old Israel, 358 ; at Shiloh, 268 *sq.*; at Nob, 272 ; of the high places, 257, 360 ; in Deuteronomy, 360 ; after the return, 443 ; in the Priests' Code, 229 ; revenues of the, 383 *note*
Priests' Code (Levitical Legislation), 319 *sq.*; relation to Ezekiel, 381 *sq.*; narrative of, 397 *sq.*, 409 *sq.*; in Genesis, 413 *sq.*; in Exodus, 397 *sq.*, 418 ; in Numbers, 397, 400 *sq.*; unknown to the Deuteronomic writers, 391 *sq.* ; relation to the Deuteronomic Torah, 428 *sq.*
Prophecy, anonymous, 101 ; cessation of, 158
Prophetic books, arrangement of, 100, 149 *sq.*; canonical collection of, 170, 174 *sq.*; read in the Synagogue, 36, 173
Prophets, their work, 279 ; mark of true prophets, 283 ; their consecration, 289 ; their inspiration, 297 ; their Torah, 299 *sq.*; their writings, 98 *sq.*, 301 ; doctrine of forgiveness, 305 *sq.*; not politicians, 348 ; their ideal, 290 *sq.*; Canaanite, 287 ; professional, 288 ; prophets and priests, 292
Proverbs, structure of the book, 111 *sq.*; canonicity of, 181
Psalmody in old Israel, 209, 218 *sq.*
Psalms, titles of, 96 *sq.*, 195, 202 *sq.*; musical do., 209 ; text of, 193 ; five books of, 194 ; Davidic, 197, 214 *sq.*; Elohistic, 198 ; Levitical, 203 *sq.*; of Persian period, 205 *sq.*, 438; Maccabee, 210 *sq.* ; in the Temple service, 190, 191 *note*, 211 ; anonymous, 103
Psalms of Solomon, 48 *note*, 211
Psalter, the, 188 *sq.*
Pseudo-Scylax, 439
Puncta extraordinaria, 57, 69
Purim, feast of, 183

RASHI (R. Solomon of Troyes), 33
Redaction, editorial, 103 *sq.*; of the Pentateuch, 425, 430
Reformation, the, and the Bible, 7 *sq.*

Reformers, scholarship of the, 32 *sq.*

Refuge, cities of, 324 *note*, 354

Religion, tribal or national, 237, 281 ; popular, of Israel, 237 *sq.* ; prophetic, 282, 291 *sq.*

Reuchlin, John, 32

Retaliation, law of, 340, 368

Revelation, Jewish theory of, 158 *sq.* ; prophetic, 297, 340

Rishis of India compared with the prophets, 297 *note*

Ritual in old Israel, 242, 268

Ruth, Book of, 182 ; read at Pentecost, 173

SABBATH, 319 *note*, 322, 447

Sacred dues, 247, 264, 383 *note*, 447 ; at Shiloh, 269

Sacrifice, all worship takes the form of, 239 ; Pentateuchal law of, unknown to Amos, 251, 294 ; to Jeremiah, *ib.*; atoning, 229, 263 *note*, 373 *sq.* ; by laymen, 260, 274 *sq.*, 358 ; and slaughter originally identical, 249 ; the king's sacrifices, 262 *note*, 375 ; stated sacrifices, 247, 372, 375, 444

Sacrificial feasts, 248, 250

Sadducees, or party of the chief priests, 48 *note*

Samaritan Pentateuch, 61, 70

Samuel, 270, 272 ; and Saul, 134 *sq.*

Sanctuary, Levitical theory of the, 229, 246 ; as seat of judgment, 299, 339 ; plurality of sanctuaries in the old law, 342 ; abolished in Deuteronomy, 353 *sq.*

Sanhedrin (Synedrion), 49

Saul, among the prophets, 130 ; election of, 135 *sq.*; rejection of, 134 ; builds altars, 250, 272 ; and David, 122 *sq.*; religious zeal of, 271

Scribes, 42 *sq.* ; and Pharisees, 47 ; work of the, 44 ; as critics, 65 *sq.*; guilds of, 44 ; modified Pentateuchal laws, 52

Septuagint, the, 72-184 ; in the ancient Church, 23, 25 ; characteristics of, 76 *sq.* ; importance of, for textual criticism, 74 *sq.*, 79 *sq.* ; origin of, 85 *sq.* ; its reputation in Palestine, 87 ; state of its text, 89 ; value for higher criticism, 90 *sq.* ; transpositions in, 109 *sq.*; variant narratives in, 117 *sq.*; ancient Hebrew fragments preserved in, 124, 433 *sq.* ; Canon of, 153 *sq.*

Sepulchre, inalienable, 417 *note*

Shiloh, Temple of, 268 *sq.*

Sin and trespass money, 263

Sinai, transactions at, 335 *sq.*, 397 *sq.*; called Horeb by the Elohist and in Deuteronomy, 426 *note*

Singers, Temple, 204

Sisera, death of, 132

Songs of Degrees, or pilgrim songs, 203, 212

Soothsayers, 286

Spies, narrative of the, 400

Stated service of the Temple, 378 ; *see* Sacrifice

Subscriptions, 101 ; in the Psalter, 195 *sq.*

Synagogue worship, 173, 207, 252, 379

Syncretism, 243, 277, 354

Syriac hymns, melodies of, 209

TABERNACLE, 246; of the Priests' Code, 321, 410 ; of the older history, 321, 399

Talmud, 50 *note*

Tamîd, 382

Tanna, 50 *note*

Tarshish ships, 146

Tehillîm, 191

Temple of Solomon, 260 *sq.*, 322 *note*; the second, 143, 410 ; MSS. preserved at the, 65, 66 *note*

Ten Commandments, 304, 313, 335

Tikkûnê Sôpherîm, 66 *sq.*

Tithes, 362, 383 *note*, 446

Titles of books, 92 *sq.* ; of Psalms, 96, 195, 202 *sq.*

Torah, meaning of, 299, 340 ; prophetic, 300 ; priestly, 299, 303, 372, 382, 426 *sq.*; Mosaic, 303, 313 ; Ezekiel's, 374 *sq.* ; Jewish estimate of the, 160

Traditional law, growth of, 46 *sq.* ; Rabbinical theory of, 165 ; *see* Law, oral

Traditional theory of the Old Testament history, 231 *sq.*

Trees, sacred, 241

Trent, Council of, 26 *sq.*

Typical interpretation of the law, 230 *sq.*

Tyre, 439

UNCIRCUMCISED IN THE TEMPLE, 260 *sq.*

Unclean animals, 366

Unclean land, 250

VEDAS, inspiration of the, 297

Vintage feast, 268

Vintage song, 209

Vowel points and accents, 37, 58 *sq.*
Vows, 239

WAR, law of, 369
Wellhausen, 226 *note*, 312 *note*, 323
　note, 435, 446
Worship, notion of, in Old Testament,
　238 ; popular, in Israel, 237 *sq.*,
　240 *sq.*; in Judah, 244 ; under the

second Temple, 252, 279, 443
sq.; representative, 251 *sq.*, 254,
382

ZADOK, 266, 359
Zadokites, 261 *note*, 266, 359 *sq.*
Zechariah, Book of, 102
Zerubbabel, 446
Zûgoth, 165

THE END

Printed by R. & R. CLARK, LIMITED, *Edinburgh.*

BOOKS BY CONTRIBUTORS
TO THE "ENCYCLOPÆDIA BIBLICA"
AND OTHERS

PUBLISHED BY A. & C. BLACK, SOHO SQUARE, LONDON.

ABBOTT, Edwin A., M.A., D.D.

St. Thomas of Canterbury : His Death and Miracles. In two volumes. Demy 8vo, Cloth. With a Photogravure Frontispiece. Price **24s.**

"It is clear that I cannot say much of these six hundred and sixty large pages in the same number of lines. But I would commend them to students of the New Testament, to critics and theologians, as furnishing, with admirable candour, no small addition to their means of following out certain long-debated problems, until they arrive at a solution which shall be true to the evidence."—*Bookman.*

Clue. A Guide through Greek to Hebrew Scripture. In one volume. Demy 8vo, Cloth. Price **7s. 6d.** net.

"The book is learned, acute, and ingenious."—*British Weekly.*
"Of extraordinary interest and suggestiveness."—*Manchester Guardian.*
"Candid and dispassionate, and should be heard without prejudice and judged on its merits."—*Dundee Advertiser.*

The Corrections of Mark adopted by Matthew and Luke. In one volume. Demy 8vo, Cloth. Price **15s.** net.

"The industry and ingenuity displayed through the work are marvellous. In this attempt to solve the Synoptic variations Dr. Abbott is as ploddingly persevering as he is dazzlingly original."—*Expository Times.*

CHARLES, Rev. Professor R. H., D.D.

The Book of Jubilees : Edited with Introduction, Notes, and Index. In one volume. Demy 8vo, Cloth. [*Ready June* 1902.

The Book of Jubilees is the oldest commentary in the world on Genesis and the early chapters of Exodus. It was written in Hebrew in the latter half of the second century B.C., and therefore forms an independent witness to the form of the Hebrew text of the Pentateuch at that date. From Hebrew it was translated into Greek, and from Greek into Ethiopic and Latin. The entire Ethiopic version has come down to us, but only fragments of the original and the other versions have been preserved. The book forms a manifesto of Early Pharisaism against Hellenism, which was undermining Judaism and the Law. Its author seeks to establish the eternal validity of the law, and for this purpose he re-edits Genesis from the standpoint of his own time. Thus the sabbath was observed in heaven before it was revealed on earth, and likewise circumcision, for the angels were created circumcised. The book is full of interest both to Christian and Jewish scholars. It was used by some of the writers of the New Testament, and it possesses older forms of the halacha than are found in the Mishna and older forms of haggada than appear in the Talmud.

I

CHARLES, Rev. Professor R. H., D.D.—*continued.*

The Apocalypse of Baruch. Translated from the Syriac. In one volume. Crown 8vo, Cloth. Price **7s. 6d.** net.

"Mr. Charles's work will have a hearty welcome from students of Syriac whose interest is linguistic, and from theological students who have learned the value of Jewish and Christian pseudepigraphy ; and the educated general reader will find much of high interest in it, regard being had to its date and its theological standpoint."—*Record.*

The Assumption of Moses. Translated from the Latin Sixth Century MS., the unemended Text of which is published herewith, together with the Text in its restored and critically emended form. Edited, with Introduction, Notes, and Indices. In one volume. Crown 8vo, Cloth. Price **7s. 6d.**

"In this admirable little book the Rev. R. H. Charles has added another to the excellent series of editions by which he has earned the gratitude of all students of early Christian literature."—*Times.*

A Critical History of the Doctrine of a Future Life in Israel, in Judaism, and in Christianity ; or, Hebrew, Jewish, and Christian Eschatology from Pre-Prophetic Times till the Close of the New Testament Canon (the Jowett Lectures for 1898-99). In one volume. Demy 8vo, Cloth. Price **15s.**

"If the Jowett Lectures rise always to this height, we shall receive a series of volumes which will rival in value any lectureship in existence. For this is a thoroughly capable treatment of perhaps the most difficult subject in theology."—*Expository Times.*

The Ascension of Isaiah : Texts, Translations, and Commentary. In one volume. Crown 8vo, Cloth. Price **7s. 6d.** net.

"By editing this and other apocrypha Mr. Charles is doing service which cannot be too warmly acknowledged, and by his learned and scholarly notes he succeeds in throwing a flood of light on the New Testament."—*British Weekly.*
"A solid contribution to the literature which scholars love."—*Dundee Advertiser.*

CHEYNE, Rev. Professor T. K., D.D.

Introduction to the Book of Isaiah. With an Appendix containing the Undoubted Portions of the Two Chief Prophetic Writers in a Translation. In one volume. Demy 8vo, Cloth. Price **24s.**

"This elaborate and scholarly work. . . . We must leave to professed scholars the detailed appreciation of Professor Cheyne's work. His own learning and reputation suffice to attest its importance. '—*Times.*

CONE, Orello, D.D.

Rich and Poor in the New Testament. A Study of the Primitive Christian Doctrine of Earthly Possessions. In one volume. Crown 8vo, Cloth. Price **6s.**

It has been the endeavour of the writer of this book to interpret the New Testament teachers historically and grammatically, and to find what there may be in the spirit of their teachings that is applicable to modern social conditions. He deems it no great loss if in this process the letter of their words is not in all cases found to be available.
It is believed that the chapter on "Conditions and Teachings before Christ," setting forth the humanity of the Old Testament, will be found to furnish an instructive introduction to the central theme of the book.

2

CONE, Orello, D.D.—*continued.*

Paul: The Man, the Missionary, and the Teacher. In one volume Post 8vo, Cloth. Price **10s. 6d.**

"One of the excellencies of Dr. Cone's work is that it is mainly exegetical. He denies himself the luxury of expanding Paul's positions either speculatively or experimentally. It may be presumed that no interpreter escapes from the influence of certain presuppositions, but in Dr. Cone there is, at any rate, an obvious attempt to be fair and unbiassed. His exposition of the teaching of St. Paul will stand comparison with any hitherto published, and will be found most instructive."—Dr. Marcus Dods in the *British Weekly.*

DEISSMAN, Professor ADOLPH.

The Epistle of Psenosiris: An Original Document from the Diocletian Persecution of the Christians. (Papyrus 713, British Museum). In one volume. Crown 8vo, Cloth. Containing Facsimile Plate of the Papyrus. Probable Price **2s. 6d.**

In this essay Professor Deissman (author of "Bible Studies," etc.) deals with a papyrus leaf discovered some years ago amongst other papyri. The leaf contains an ancient letter, as to the interpretation of which Professor Deissman claims to have made a new discovery. He had read the text when it was just published soon after the discovery of the papyri; but a new light dawned upon him only quite recently when he had occasion to read the letter carefully again. As a result of his new study he found that, by attaching a different value to one single letter of a word, the whole nature of the leaf is changed. In this essay, in which he gives (1) the text as it appears in the papyrus, (2) the text with accents and punctuation, (3) a translation, (4) his own explanation, etc., he endeavours to show that his new reading is justified. The letter seems to have been written in troublous times; Professor Deissman gives a vivid picture of the circumstances of persecution under which he supposes it to have been written, and of the characters mentioned. The book is in the form of an essay, not of a "Commentary." A facsimile of the papyrus is included.

GARDNER, Percy, Litt.D.

Exploratio Evangelica: a Brief Examination of the Basis and Origin of Christian Belief. In one volume. Demy 8vo, Cloth. Price **15s.**

"Professor Gardner sets forth clearly, almost coldly—though the glow of an intense spiritual emotion is not wholly concealed—the things which belong to all religious experience, and which give religion a place in human nature which is incomplete without it. This is the constructive side of the book. . . . The importance of Professor Gardner's work is that it insists upon free historical criticism being carried out fully, or else wholly and avowedly rejected."—*Guardian.*

An Historic View of the New Testament. The Jowett Lectures for 1901. Large Crown 8vo, Cloth. Price **6s.**

"Dr. Percy Gardner's earlier and larger work, *Exploratio Evangelica*, is now so generally reckoned by liberal theologians in this country as the most important English publication of its class that has appeared since *Ecce Homo* that a new work from the same hand is bound to attract attention. Nor will purchasers of this book be disappointed. . . . The lectures deserve to be widely read, as being thoughtful, scholarly, and illuminating."— *The Westminster Gazette.*

GRAY, G. Buchanan, M.A.

Studies in Hebrew Proper Names. In one volume. Crown 8vo, Cloth. Price **7s. 6d.** net.

"These 'Studies' may be warmly commended as a step in the right direction. They bring out into clear relief progress of religious ideas in Israel, and make an important contribution to the criticisms of Old Testament documents."—C. H. Toy, Harvard University.

3

GRAY, G. BUCHANAN, M.A.—*continued.*

The Divine Discipline of Israel : an Address and Three Lectures on the Growth of Ideas in the Old Testament. In one volume. Crown 8vo, Cloth. Price 2s. 6d. net.

"The address and lectures are alike scholarly and thoughtful, and furnish a good specimen of the constructive criticism of the Old Testament, which is steadily being developed by the Higher Critics."—*Guardian.*

HAECKEL, ERNST.

Monism, as Connecting Religion and Science : the Confession of Faith of a Man of Science. Translated from the German by J. D. F. GILCHRIST. In one volume. Crown 8vo, Cloth. Price 1s. 6d. net.

"We may readily admit that Professor Haeckel has stated his case with the clearness and courage which we should expect of him, and that his lecture may be regarded as a fair and authoritative statement of the views now held by a large number of scientifically educated people."—*Times.*

HARNACK, Professor ADOLF.

Christianity and History. Translated, with the Author's sanction, by THOMAS BAILEY SAUNDERS, with an Introductory Note. Second Edition. In one volume. Crown 8vo, Cloth. Price 1s. 6d. net.

"It is highly interesting and full of thought. The short introductory note with which Mr. Saunders prefaces it is valuable for its information and excellent in its tone."— *Athenæum.*

Thoughts on the Present Position of Protestantism. Translated by THOMAS BAILEY SAUNDERS. In one volume. Crown 8vo, Cloth. Price 1s. 6d. net.

This is a version of a recent utterance on the question at issue between the Catholic and the Protestant by the most distinguished German theologian now living. Professor Harnack treats of this question in a brief compass, but with a breadth of view and vigour of expression which must make what he says interesting to readers of every shade of opinion.

Sources of the Apostolic Canons ; with a Treatise on the Origin of the Readership and other Lower Orders. Translated by LEONARD A. WHEATLEY. With an Introductory Essay on the Organisation of the Early Church and the Evolution of the Reader by the Rev. JOHN OWEN, Author of "Evenings with the Skeptics." In one volume. Demy 8vo, Cloth. Price 7s. 6d. net.

"The wide circulation of this volume would be of the happiest augury for a more scientific and worthy conception of the organisation of the primitive Church."—Dr. MARCUS DODS in *The Bookman.*

The Apostles' Creed. Translated by THOMAS BAILEY SAUNDERS. In one volume. Crown 8vo, Cloth. Price 1s. 6d. net.

"It is a great advantage to have in so accessible a form the views of the greatest living German theologian on the vexed problem of the origins of this creed."—*The Examiner.*

MACDONALD, Rev. Duff, B.D.

The Revised Catechism : Being an Examination and Revision of the Westminster Assembly's Shorter Catechism. In one volume. Crown 8vo, Cloth. Probable Price **2s. 6d.** net.

The teaching of the Shorter Catechism has been revised again and again, but the man engrossed in commerce or industry cannot tell where to find all the commentaries or essays in some corner of which these revisions lie scattered about. Modern scholarship has done a great deal, but unfortunately its best results have not been systematically brought close to the great body of the people. Hence we might expect that an examination of a book so well known as the Shorter Catechism might be helpful in many ways, and in the short examination attempted in this book the great endeavour has been to make every statement easy to understand.

PFLEIDERER, Otto, D.D.

Evolution and Theology. Edited by Dr. Orello Cone, Lombard University. In one volume. Crown 8vo, Cloth. Price **5s.** net.

" No one will question Dr. Pfleiderer's learning and ability, especially in dealing with questions of religious philosophy. Even those who differ most from him will learn much from his graceful expositions."—*Methodist Times.*

SABATIER, A., D.D. (Dean of the Faculty of Protestant Theology, Paris).

The Vitality of Christian Dogmas, and their Power of Evolution : a Study in Religious Philosophy. Translated by Mrs. Emmanuel Christen. With a Preface by the Very Rev. the Hon. W. H. Fremantle, D.D., Dean of Ripon. In one volume. Crown 8vo, Cloth. Price **1s. 6d.** net.

" Dr. Sabatier has rendered a good and timely service, alike to theology and religion, by discussing, as he does here, the relation in which dogma stands to the reality of religious feeling and experience."—*Glasgow Herald.*

SCHECHTER, S., M.A.

Studies in Judaism. In one volume. Demy 8vo, Cloth. Price **7s. 6d.**

" He lifts the veil, and we get a glimpse of Jewish teachers and revivalists, of Jewish philosophy and mysticism, and above all of Jewish devotion to the Torah. Read the article on the Chassidim, and you will find a community the like of which we have never been taught to expect in Israel. The contrast of the fine spirit of Israel Baalshem and the extraordinary perversion of his teaching by his followers, is at once enlightening and pathetic. . . . The book is written throughout in a vigorous clear style, with constant flashes of sly humour, and it will, we have no doubt, find multitudes of readers who will endorse our verdict in thanking Mr. Schechter for a most interesting and delightful piece of work."—*Cambridge Review.*

SMITH, the late W. ROBERTSON, M.A., LL.D.

Lectures on the Religion of the Semites, the Fundamental Institutions. New Edition, revised throughout by the Author. In one volume. Demy 8vo, Cloth. Price **15s.** net.

The Old Testament in the Jewish Church: A Course of Lectures on Biblical Criticism. Second Edition, revised and much enlarged. In one volume. Demy 8vo, Cloth. Price **10s. 6d.**

The Prophets of Israel, and their Place in History to the Close of the Eighth Century, B.C. With Introduction and additional Notes, by the Rev. T. K. CHEYNE, M.A., D.D., Oriel Professor of the Interpretation of Holy Scripture at Oxford, Canon of Rochester. Second Edition. In one volume. Large Crown 8vo, Cloth. Price **10s. 6d.**

WARD, JAMES, Sc.D., Hon. LL.D. Edin.

Naturalism and Agnosticism: The Gifford Lectures of 1896-1898. In two volumes. Demy 8vo, Cloth. Price **18s.** net.

" It cannot be doubted that it will have a wide influence on the higher thought of the country, and may even do something to restore to Philosophy the pre-eminent place it once occupied in English thought."—*Athenæum.*

WELLHAUSEN, Professor J.

Sketch of the History of Israel and Judah. Third Edition. In one volume. Crown 8vo, Cloth. Price **5s.**

" A sketch which has created such widespread and profound interest as this could not be kept in the pages of a voluminous encyclopædia. Wellhausen's words necessarily have exceptional importance, even in the esteem of those who differ from him *toto cœlo.* '—*Baptist Magazine.*

WILLIAMS, Rev. T. RHONDDA.

Shall We Understand the Bible? Second Edition, revised and enlarged. Crown 8vo, Limp Cloth. Price **1s.** net.

Dr. CLIFFORD, M.A., says :—" A capital contribution to the subject, and will be of immense service to many minds."
Dr. R. F. HORTON, M.A., says :—" I want to express my admiration for its lucidity and interest and courage. I shall use it and recommend it."
Prof. W. F. ADENEY, M.A., says: " A clear and sound presentation of the true critical views of the Bible."

WRIGHT, the late WILLIAM, LL.D.

A Short History of Syriac Literature. In one volume. Crown 8vo, Cloth. Price **6s.** net.

" A masterly account of the literature written in that language. It may safely be said that there is no one in England—or even in Europe—at the present time capable of speaking with anything like his authority in matters appertaining to Syriac literature."—*Record.*

A. & C. BLACK, SOHO SQUARE, LONDON.